Digitising Enterprise

In an Information Age

Digitising Enterprise

In an Information Age

David L. Olson
College of Business Administration
University of Nebraska–Lincoln, USA

****

Subodh Kesharwani
School of Management Studies
Indira Gandhi National Open University
New Delhi-110068, India.

CRC Press
Taylor & Francis Group
Boca Raton London New York

CRC Press is an imprint of the
Taylor & Francis Group, an **informa** business

Manakin
PRESS

First published 2021
by CRC Press
2 Park Square, Milton Park, Abingdon, Oxon, OX14 4RN

and by CRC Press
6000 Broken Sound Parkway NW, Suite 300, Boca Raton, FL 33487-2742

British Library Cataloguing-in-Publication Data
A catalogue record for this book is available from the British Library

Library of Congress Cataloging-in-Publication Data
A catalog record has been requested

ISBN: 978-1-032-06630-1 (hbk)
ISBN: 978-1-003-20313-1 (ebk)

Manakin
PRESS

Brief Contents

Detailed Contents

Preface

In the new age of the Internet of Everything (IoE), enterprises need to rationalize their information systems and optimize their infrastructures. They will also need to convert operating models to foster innovation and positively influence transformation to these optimal systems. Digital makeovers will be needed to enable organizations to be competitive a factor that is crucial to survival in the new IoE age. Firms established before the digital age are being forced to adapt or die. Amazon/eBay/Alibaba and other businesses with new forms of customer interaction have revolutionized retail, forcing businesses to adapt (Barnes & Noble) or close (Borders Bookstores). Amazon continues their invasion into new forms of retail, including cloud technology as well as new product lines such as toys, clothing, and groceries. Information technology (IT) plays a key role in form adaptation to react to this new business environment. Thus future business survival will require business organizations to keep us with innovations in both IT as well as retail delivery to customers.

Digital enterprise transformation is not only adding a stratus of digital technology to traditional business. Successful transformation will require innovation across the spectrum, from reaching new sources, transporting material and transforming it into innovative products, as well as service, using a digitized work environment to enable employees to rapidly respond to threats as well as opportunities. Retail business will require closer interaction with customers, often through use of social media. This new environment allows firms to reach new customers from around the world, connecting all of us in a more fruitful manner.

Digitization of enterprises taxes IT in three ways. First, it requires development and use of advanced technology, to include enterprise resource planning and advances in focused systems. Second, better performance will be demanded of IT, calling for customized systems with more effective business process reengineering. Third, IT must more effectively support strategic managers by providing custom information tailored to make top-management capable of monitoring events and to detect problems in real-time. The digital transformation required for these things to happen will require improved technology architecture, improved customer service, and cultural change by making the Internet of Everything a part of daily life. Automated decision making can be incorporated with self-service, which leads to replacement of many traditional jobs by automation. This will require society to find new uses for displaced human resources. In turn, governments will be taxed to refocus systems by providing training and new opportunities for their peoples.

This book, "Digitizing Enterprise: In an Information Age: is a step in this direction. It provides many views of this new IT environment, giving a holistic view across the organizational hierarchy from top to bottom, describing the paradigm shift that gave birth to the term digitization. Technology enterprises will continue to develop opportunities affecting the market, perceiving ways in which organizations to transform virtually every sector in applying knowledge to smooth progress. This book also throws light on related concepts to include cloud computing and "anything-as-a-service."

We anticipate that this book will provide many promising ideas related to this emerging environment. You are welcome to e-mail us at dolson3@unl. edu or skesharwani@ignou.ac with your observations and opinions. We thank the many authors of this edited book for their many interesting and innovation ideas.

Editors

PART 1

Information System

Contemporary Research Issues in Business–IT Alignment

Himanshu Aggarwal[1]

The importance and the Strategic (Business and information technology (FI) alignment has been wed established For die past 20 years the researchers and practitioners are working hard for achieving alignment In this chapter an effort has been made to emphasize the need and importance of strategic alignment derive its definition from research literature and explore various contemporary research issues. Design/ Methodology/Approach: In this chapter an attempt has been made to conceptualize and present die various research issues with their meanings and notions adopted By various researchers in this field. These will help those researchers who want to pursue research in this field. Research limitations/Implications: The study is Based on few research articles only. It is possible to identify more research By more intensively reviewing the existing research literature. Originality/Value: This is important because the many research issues in this research area have contradictory and chaotic existence. Here the authors have a strong notion that presently there is a shortage of research articles in die existing literature presenting these research issues in a systematic and comprehensive manner.

KEYWORDS   Business | IT | SIM | Strategic | Research

1.1 INTRODUCTION

The existing research literature reveals that strategic alignment is imperative for the business organizations to survive and compete in the market. Yet achieving alignment continues to be a major concern for the business executives. Strategic alignment boosts the IT effectiveness (Porter, 1 987; Galliers, 1991; Ciborra, 1997), leading to business profitability (Luftman, 1996). Therefore, alignment has been a major concern for the academicians, practitioners, business consultants and research organizations since 1990's. Such an effort has been highlighted by a recent study conducted by Society for Information Management (SIM). The study has identified alignment as the first management concern among all groups surveyed for the Top 10

---

[1] Department of Computer Engineering, Punjabi University, Patiala

concerns that included 300 senior IT managers (Trainor, 2003). Galliers and Newell (2003) call it a central tenant of much of the theory and practice of Information System (IS) strategy. Further the importance of alignment has been reinforced by several industrial surveys that reveal executives' perceptions of alignment (Head, 2000; Kennedy, 2000; Weil, 2001). Therefore, the managers and practitioners have been continuously making efforts to identify and device new strategies for achieving alignment between Business and IT.

The research in the area is primarily conceptual and lacks practical considerations (Campbell, Kay and Avison, 2005). There is little agreement on 'how to achieve alignment' and 'how it should be researched' but there are many studies on 'how to practice alignment'. Luftman (1996), Hsaio and Omerod (1998) and Burn (1997) provide some practical aspects of implementation of alignment through enablers and inhibitors of alignment. However, the literature provides little guidance on how to achieve alignment between Business and IT strategies. Also, the judgment and the impact of misalignment on the organization have been difficult to diagnose (Luftman, 1996). Therefore, the prime focus here are achieving alignment and doing research on it.

This chapter reviews the definition and the common perception of alignment along with major research issues.

1.2 DEFINITION OF ALIGNMENT

Strategic alignment has many pseudonyms. It has been referred to as "Coordination" (Lederer and Mendelow,1986),"Harmony" (Woolfe, 1993; Luftman, 1996), "fit" (Porter, 1996), "Linkage" (Reich and Benbasat, 1996), "bridge" (Ciborra, 1997), "fusion" (Smaczny, 2001). However, the common theme of all these studies has been integration of strategies relating to Information Technology (IT) and Business. There is still indefiniteness in the definition of alignment such as Tallon et al. (1998) defined alignment as "the alignment of Information systems strategy to the business strategy" and Reich and Benbasat (2000, p.82) as "the degree to which the information technology mission, objectives and plans support and are supported by the business mission, objectives and plans". Therefore, in research literature it is difficult to find an unequivocal definition of alignment.

Strategic Alignment in present context is concerned with the correspondence and compatibility of IT and the business strategy within an organization (Chang 2006; Henderson & Venkatraman, 1999) persistently appears in practice (Mieritz 2004,Stepanek 2002) and academic media reports (Allnoch 1997; Ball & Adams 2003) and is a key concern of the Top and general management (Eid, Trueman & Ahmed 2002; Laosethakul & Boulton, 2007).

The next section discusses various contemporary research issues in the strategic Business and IT alignment.

1.3 RESEARCH ISSUES

The important research issues are:

Issue l: "Whether IT alignment is an issue in its own right?"

There is debate on the issue that whether alignment of Information System (IS/IT) is an issue in its own right. Some researchers such as Smaczny (2001) emphasize that the IS is so pervasive in business that it cannot be separated from the business strategy, and therefore the issue of alignment does not arise. However, the IT management is actually a problem of aligning the business and IT infrastructure (Reich and Benbasat, 1996) and identifying opportunities to utilize IT for competitive advantage (Ives and Learmonth, 1984, Wiseman, 1985) and/or analyzing internal processes and patterns of data dispersion throughout the organization (Brancheau and Wetherbe, 1 986; Godhue et al., 1992).

Having understood the IT alignment as an issue the next important issue is their role of IT and its alignment in providing the competitive advantage, which is the next research issue.

Issue 2: "Are IT and IT Alignment Sources of Sustainable Competitive Advantage?"

It is ridiculous to look for IT alignment when it is not clearly known whether IT is a source of competitive advantage or not. Traditionally there is a common notion that IT and IT alignment are sources of competitive advantage. IT can add to the economic value to a firm by either by reducing costs or differentiating its products and services (Bakos and Treacy, 1986; McFarlan, 1984; Wiseman, 1988). However, adding value to a firm either by reducing costs or increasing revenues is not the same as the IT being a source of sustainable competitive advantage. For example, Walmart adopted its purchase and distribution system and K-mart also developed similar system (Steven, 1992). Thus, the Walmart had a temporary and not sustainable competitive advantage (Barney, 1994). The same idea has been supported by a large number of researchers such as Cecil and Goldstein,1990;and Galliers, 1991.

On contrary several studies point toward falling productivity and rising IT expenditure referred to as "productivity paradox" in the research literatre. Loveman (1994) suggests that the IT investment produces negligible benefits. The same idea has been supported by Bakos (1998), Brynjolfsson (1993),Venkatraman (1997), Avison et al.(1999a), Papp (2001). However, the "productivity paradox" has been condemned by Dejager (1995) and Rayner(1995). According to them IT has been found to increase productivity by improving customer satisfaction, quality of product, service and convenience in many organizations.

Lederer and Mendelow(1989) suggest that alignment increases the likelihood of developing a system more critical to the organization and obtaining support of the Top management. As the IT assumes greater role in developing corporate strategy, alignment will facilitate a more competitive and profitable organization (Galliers, 1993). Economic performance is also enhanced by better fitting between external positioning and internal arrangements (Ciborra, 1997). Through greater alignment of strategy and infrastructure, organizations achieve more synergy, better plan development, increase profitability and efficiency (Avison, 2004). Therefore, alignment in the organizations allows application of IT as a means to leverage their core competencies, skills and technology scope, resulting in improved efficiency (Papp, 1999).

Further, many researchers argue that the insufficient payoffs are due to low level of strategic alignment while others suggest that alignment may not be the solution to the low IT returns in all cases. For example in case of the organizations competing globally strategic alignment can limit the flexibility and aligning IS and business strategy may force the organizations to follow a particular path from which it cannot escape. If a company values flexibility but is facing the environmental flexibility, the strategic alignment is not the best solution. While strategic alignment can contribute towards pay-offs but may limit organizational flexibility and responsiveness to the external conditions.

Hence, contribution of IT in providing competitive advantage has been noticed but do the existing models/frameworks sufficient in achieving alignment?

Issue 3: "Do the existing Models and Frameworks Sufficient for Achieving Alignment?"

A number of models and frameworks have been proposed to help the business managers to better understand alignment and in the continuous search for the significant opportunities for gaining benefits from IT. The application of these try to apply the concepts of strategic fit between resources and opportunities, external and internal environments within an organization, generic strategies of low cost versus differentiation versus focus; and strategic goals, strategies and tactics that make the strategic process rigid (Henderson and Venkatraman, 1993). The alignment will have a positive impact if specifically and meticulously planned, followed and implemented (Hamel and Prahalad, 1990). On the contrary strategic planning may create hindrance to the creative thinking and misguide organizations who adopt it unreservedly (Mintzburg, 1987). Therefore, none of the models provide a way to implement alignment in a practical manner and hence the alignment process is a serious exercise that must be carried out with great care and caution.

Hence, models and frameworks are not sufficient in providing alignment. Then next pertinent question is practicing alignment, which is te next research issue.

Issue 4: How to practice alignment?

The notion adopted by many of the researchers is strategizing IT and Business plan in an appropriate way (Henderson and Venkatraman, 1999; Avison et al., 2004). Therefore, there is dominantly an emphasis on structured, systematic and somewhat stable strategy in the research literature despite the fact that there is uncertainty, dynamism and articulation of the strategic intent is difficult (Ciborra, 1997). Real life strategizing is 'messy' and human thinking and actions rarely follow strict modular approach (Avison et al., 1 999a,b).

In practicing alignment the following sub-issues are quite important:

- "Whether the IT strategy can meet the challenge of dynamism of business strategy(if it exists)?"

  The business processes are often emergent, serendipitous and continuously changing. The IT strategy must also be dynamic accordingly. The IT tries to define the applications with strong element of stability, predictability, systematic and structured manner which is contradictory to the dynamic business strategy having dynamism, agility and ability to capture diverse, fluid and informal characteristic. On the other hand in the opinion of the IT professional strategy is functional, quantifiable and has an element of certainty. Therefore, not only business processes but the IT process engineering is quite important.

- "Are the Business processes in the organization are well structured as per the technology upgrades? Will only aligning of IT be important in future?"

  Business processes are seldom structured with the possibilities of new technologies in mind, and therefore the full potential of technology is actually not fully tapped (Giaglis, 1999). Even worse, some of the researchers argue that most of the organizations have actually never designed their business processes at all and rather they have evolved over time (Hansen, 1 994). Due to their ad- hoc evolution, they are not suitable for streamlining, cost-effectiveness and appropriately aligned to the business objectives, goals and strategy. Most of the studies in research literature focus on aligning IT. However, there is a need to make efforts in Business engineering that involves process based organization design, IS development and execution.

↯ "Is management in full control? Can the information infrastructure be aligned as per the management insights?"

The management is in full control is a hypothetical notion. Involvement of all the people in the strategic alignment planning and implementation, culture building are quite important (Aggarwal et al. 2005) for practicing alignment.

Practicing alignment is questionable if it is not possible to measure IT and its alignment which is the next research issue.

Issue 5: "Is it possible to measure IT and IT alignment?"

The measurement of alignment persists as a research issue whose solution is not very clear or obvious. Most of the benefits related to IT and IT alignment are so intangible and implicit that it is almost impossible to measure the impact of IT alignment through the conventional approach primarily based on financial measures. These measures study the firm performance on the basis of firm output, measured using value added by the organization, and total sales; business results, assessed using return-on- assets (ROA), and return-on-equity (ROE) measures of financial performance; and intermediate performance, assessed using labour productivity and administrative productivity (Rai et al., 1997). These measures do not address the benefits imparted through IT such as higher customer satisfaction, product innovation and providing business opportunities which would have been un-imaginable without IT.

According to Ciborra (1997) management through knowledge and understanding of alignment can classify their strategy in terms of linear boxes and strategies. But in real world it is practically not possible for them to measure these relationships and apply alignment maps.

In research literature there are two approaches have been predominantly followed with the first approach focusing on process of achieving alignment and other on how the firms have aligned there IS's with organizational strategy. For example, Atkins (1994) adopted three different models to measure strategy and assess alignment (McFarlan 1984; Ansoff, 1965 and Miles and Snow, 1978).

The most comprehensive attempt in this area has been given by Chan *et al.* (1997) via empirical investigation based on development of four survey instruments to measure each construct of business strategy, IS strategy, IS effectiveness and Business performance. Here, Venkatraman's (1989) STROBE instrument has been adopted together with STORIS instrument development by Chan to assess IS strategy. Both instruments were used to check the strategic fit.

Measures are required that align everyone every functionality within the organization with the key goals of the organization, to achieve strategic alignment, but there is no clear idea about what these measures might be (Labovitz and Rosanky, 1997).

Even if it is assumed that the measurement of alignment is possible, it is important to find if it is a final or continuous process which is the next research issue.

Issue 6: "Whether strategic alignment should be treated as an outcome or as a dynamic process?"

The former view had been dominant in the past (Weill and Broadbent, 1998, Earl, 1989) and the need to maintain alignment was rarely acknowledged. But, more recent studies support the dynamic alignment (Labovitz and Rosansky, 1 997; Venkatraman, 2000).

However Smaczny (2001) argue that there are no studies focusing on how organizations actually achieve alignment or alignment is the right way of looking at the issue. Most of the researchers have adopted a clinched approach of adopting alignment and developed theories based on it and overlooked the question that alignment is an outdated notion. Most of the models developed adopt mechanistic and planning oriented management approaches to the business objectives. Therefore, Smaczny recommends developing Business and IT strategies simultaneously and implementing them simultaneously.

If the processes are dynamic than they are applicable homogeneously or not is the next research issue.

Issue 7: "Are the firms homogeneous with respect to the strategic processes?"

The early work on strategic processes essentially viewed the firms as homogeneous. However, the recent research focuses on competencies and capabilities. This is particularly a more realistic thought as the resources are heterogeneously distributed in the firms and they are differently able to utilize them. Tallon et al. (2000) suggest that the strategic alignment is the most important issue in the opinion of the IT executives and they have very different goals for IT. The environment in which IT operates is the key factor in determining payoffs. They have examined the executive's perceptions of the Business value of IT. Based on the different corporate goals the firms can be classified into four focus types - unfocused, operations focus, market focus and dual focus. These differently focused firms use different techniques for analyzing the impacts of IT. The focused firms are better able to realize the Business value of IT and make greater use of IT investment evaluation. In unfocussed firms do not have clear goals for IT and executives are indifferent to it. Here, IT is viewed as an expanse, so management delays IT related purchase decisions and after its purchase mis-manages the IT investments. In the operations focused organizations, the aim is achieving operational effectiveness of IT. In market focused firms, IT is useful in enhancing the strategic positioning by creating or improving value propositions for the customers. The dual-focus firms use IT to improve operational effectiveness and market position by improving market reach and new market creation. In the research authors have assessed strategic alignment using a single dimension: extent to which Business strategy supports the IT strategy. The results of the study show that the dual focus firms are able to realize highest pay-offs from IT investments, followed by market-focus, operations-focus and finally unfocused firms. Executives with more focused goals for IT perceive higher extent of alignment resulting in realization of higher Business value of IT.

Although it has been established that the firms are heterogeneous with respect to the strategic processes but performance implications are still questionable, which is the next research issue.

Issue 8: "What are performance implications of alignment? Whether alignment affects performance for all or some of the business strategies?"

Shifting from firm focus, Sabherwal and Chan (2001) using Miles and Snow's (1978) typography showed that the alignment improves business performance. Prospectors should develop market information system and strategic decision support systems rather than the operational support system. Moreover, imitating competitor's systems is less advantageous to a business than expected, unless there are strong similarities in the firms' business strategies. There is a significant correlation between alignment and performance for Prospectors and Analyzers but not the Defenders. Hence, the managers within Defenders should not emphasize alignment.

Having categorized the firms into Prospectors, Analyzers and Defenders it is important to know the handling of the alignment by these types of firms, which is the next research issue.

Issue 9: "How Prospectors, Analyzers and Defenders differentially tackle the alignment problem?"

Hirschheim and Sabherwal (2001) identified three problems in tackling alignment namely paradoxical decisions, excessive transformations and uncertain turnaround. They are due to sequential attention to goals, knowledge gaps, and division of user responsibilities and underestimation of the extent of problem. Defenders have 'utility' profile for IS usage, achieved through low cost delivery though outsourcing. Analyzers will look for alliances, most likely through strategic sourcing. Prospectors will have infusion profile involving alignment through business leadership. Here, IS is in-sourced. The suggestion of the authors is employment of knowledge and process integration, process planning involving multiple perspectives and transitional figures or powerful external forces can aid the IS alignment endeavour.

The next research issue is to determine the Critical Success Factors in the form of enablers and inhibitors.

Issue 10: " What are the Processes Enabling and Inhibiting Alignment?"

Neo, 1988; King et al., 1989; Luftman, 1996 and Kanungo and Chouthoy, 1999 have contributed to the understanding of the processes that may enable or inhibit alignment. The important enablers include Executive's support, Close relationship between IT and non-IT people, IT department prioritizes the workload well and sharing of IT resources. The inhibitors include IT department prioritizes the workload poorly, power & politics within the Firm, IT department does not meet its commitments.

After establishing the Critical Success Factors the next important issue is determining the focus of alignment.

Issue 11: "What is the focus of alignment?"

Hussain et al. (2002) argued that different researchers have focused on different parts of the Henderson and Venkatraman (1989) model, either process or content. They include achieving alignment through social element (involved people) and intellectual element (Methods and techniques). Reviewing a large number of articles relating to fit the authors have concluded that there is little consensus regarding the factors involved. They conclude that there is a need to research into processes associated with alignment.

After knowing the focus of alignment, the unit of analysis in alignment research is quite important.

Issue 12: "What is the Unit of Analysis in the Alignment Research?"

Tallon and Kraemer (2003) examine alignment at process level rather than the Firm level. They tried to establish relationship between executive's perception and reality. They used the notation of IT shortfall (When IT fails to support business strategy) and Strategy shortfall (When strategy fails to use IT). There results indicate that the alignment is highest in production, operations and customer relations and lowest in sales and marketing. They suggest that the benefits in terms of IT pay-offs through strategic alignments are realizable only up to a certain critical level. The authors feel that more research is required to analyze the unit of analysis.

The discussion of the important research issues has shown that there is a clear need for further research into the Strategic alignment area. The chapter provides an overview of the business and IT alignment and highlights the gaps in the research.

References

1. Aggarwal, H., Goyal, D.P. and Bansal, P.K. (2005), "A Conceptual Model of the Challenges in Successful Information Technology to Businesses: A Human Centered Approach", Indian Management Studies Journal, Vol. 9, No.1, pp. 53–72.

2. Allnoch, A. (1997) 'IS executives emphasize alignment of technology, corporate goals', IIE Solutions, Vol. 29,pp. 1213.

3. Ansoff, H.I. (1965) Planning and Control Systems: A Framework for Analysis, Boston,Harvard Business School, MA.

4. Atkins, M. (1994), "IT and IS Perspectives of Business Strategy", Journal of Strategic Information Systems, Vol. 3, No.2, pp. 123–125.

5. Avison, D., Jones, J. Powell, P. and Wilson, D. (2004) "Using and validating the strategic alignment model", Journal of Startegic Information Systems, Vol.13,pp. 223-246.

6. Avison, D.E., Cuthbertson, C and Powell, P. (1999a) "The paradox of information systems: Strategic val- ue and low status", Journal of Strategic Information Systems, Vol. 8, No. 4,pp. 419–445.

7. Avison, D.E., Lau, F., Myers, M. and Nielsen, P. (1999b), "Action Research", Communications of ACM, Vol. 42, No.1,pp. 94–97.

8. Bakos, J.Y. and Treacy, M.E. (1986), "Information Technology and Corporate Strategy: A Research Perspective," MIS Quarterly, Vol.10, No.2, pp. 107–119.

9. Bakos,Y.(1 998), "The Emerging Role of Electronic Marketplaces on the Internet". Communications of the ACM, Vol. 41, No. 8,pp. 35–42.

10. Ball, N.L. and Adams,C.R. (2003) 'Overcoming the elusive problem of IS/IT alignment: conceptual and methodological considerations', Americas Conference on Information Systems, Tampa, FL, USA.

11. Barney, J.B. (1994),."'Competitive Advantage from Organizational Analysis", Texas A&M university, College Station: Working paper.

12. Brancheau, J.C. and Wetherbe,J.C. (1986) "Information Architectures: Methods and Practice", Information Processing and Management, Vol. 22, No.1,pp. 443-453 Brynjofsson, E. (1993), "The Productivity Paradox of Information Technology", Communications of ACM, 36(12), 67–77.

13. Burn, J. (1997), "Information System Strategies and Management of Organizational Change", Journal of Information Technology, Vol. 8 ,pp. 205-216.

14. Cecil, J. and Goldstein, M. (1990), "Sustaining Competitive Advantage from IT", McKinsey Quarterly,Vol. 4,pp. 20–27.

15. Chan, Y.E.; Huff, S.L., Barclay, D.W. and Copeland, D.G. (1997), "Business Strategy Orientation, Information Systems Orientation and Strategic Alignment", Information Systems Research, Vol. 8, No. 2, pp. 125–150.

16. Chang, H.H. (2006) "Technical and management perceptions of enterprise information system importance, implementation and benefits", Information Systems Journal,Vol.16, pp. 263292.

17. Ciborra, C. (1 997), "De Profundis? Deconstructing the Concept of S t r a t e g i c Alignment", IRIS conference (http://www.iris.imformatik.gu.se/reference/iris20/60.htm) DeJager, P. (1 995), "Are Computers boosting Productivity? No!" Computer World, March, 27, 128–130.

18. Earl, M. (1989) Management strategies for Information Technology, Hemel Hempstead, Prentice-Hall,UK Eid, R., Trueman, M. and Ahmed, A.M. (2002) "A cross industry review of B2B critical success factors", Internet Research: Electronic Networking Applications and Policy,Vol. 12, No. 2, pp. 110–123.

19. Galliers, R. and Newell, S. (2003), Strategy as data + sense making in Cummings ,S, Wilson, D. (Eds.) Images of strategy, Blackwell Oxford, 164–196.

20. Galliers, R.D. (1991), "Strategic Information Systems Planning: Myths, Reality and Guidelines for Successful Implementation", European Journal of Information Systems, Vol.1, No. 1, pp. 5564.

21. Giaglis, G.M. (1999) "Focus issue on Legacy Information Systems and Business process Change: On the Integrated Design and Evaluation of Business Processes" Communications of Association of Information Systems, Vol. 2, No. 5, pp. 1–33.

22. Godhue, D.L., Kirsch, L.J., Quillard, J.A. and Wybo, M.D.(1992), "Strategic data planning: Lessons from the field", MIS Quarterly, Vol. 16, No. 1, pp. 11–34.

23. Hansen, G.A. (1994), Automating Business Process ReEngineering: Breaking the TQM Barrier, Prentice-Hall: Englewood Cliffs, NJ.

24. Head, B. (2000), Organizational Issues, CIO Magazine, 3440.

25. Henderson, J.C. and Venkatraman, N.(1989), Strategic Alignment: A Framework for Strategic Information Technology Management, Center for information Systems Research, CISR Working paper, Massachusetts Institute of Technology, Cambridge, MA.

26. Henderson, J.C. ;and Venkatraman, N.(1999), "Strategic Alignment: Leveraging Information Technology for Transforming Organizations", IBM Systems Journal, Vol. 38, No.1/2,pp. 472–484.

27. Henderson, J.C. and Venkatraman, N.(1993), "Strategic Alignment: Leveraging Information Technology for Transforming Organizations," IBM Systems Journal, Vol. 32, No.1, pp. 4–16.

28. Hirschheim, R.; and Sabherwal, R. (2001), "Detours in the path towards strategic IS alignment", California Management Review, Vol. 44,No. 1, pp. 1–15.

29. Hsaio, R. and Ormerod, R. (1998), "A New Perspective on the Dynamics of the IT Enabled Change', Information Systems Journal, Vol. 8, No. 1, pp. 1 –12.

30. Hussain, H.; King, M.; and Cragg, P. (2002), "IT alignment in Small Firms", European Journal of information Systems, Vol.11, pp. 108–127.

31. Ives, B. ;and Learmonth, G.P. (1984), "The Information System as a Competitive Weapon", Communications of ACM, Vol. 27, No. 12, pp. 1193–1201.

32. Kanungo, S. ;and Chouthoy, M. (1998), "IT Planning in India: Implications for IT Effectiveness", Information Technology for Development, pp.71–87.

33. Kennedy, L. (2000), Come Together, Right now, CIO Magazine, http://www.idg. com.au King, W.R., Grover, V. and Hufanagel, E.H. (1989), "Using Information and Information Technology for Sustainable Competitive Advantage: Some Empirical Evidences", Information and Management, Vol.17, pp. 87–93.

34. Labovitz,G. and Rosansky,V. (1 997), The Power of alignment, John Wiley & Sons.

35. Laosethakul, K and Boulton, W (2007) "Critical success factors e-commerce in Thailand: cultural and infrastructural influences", The Electronic Journal of Information Systems in Developing Countries, Vol. 30, No. 2, pp. 1-22, [Online] Available at: http://www.ejisdc.org. Lederer, A.; and Mendelow, A. (1 989), "Co-ordination of the Information System Plans with Business Plans", Journal of Management Information Systems, 6(2), 5–19.

36. Lederer, A.L. and Mendelow, A.L. (1986), "Co-ordination of Information System Plans with Business Plans", Journal of Management Information Systems, Vol. 6, No. 2, pp. 5–19.

37. Loveman, G.W.(1994), An Assessment of the Productivity Impact of Information Technologies: Research Studies, Cambridge MA, MIT Press, 84–111.

38. Luftman J.D. (1996), Competing Information Age: Practical Applications of the Strategic Alignment Model, New York:. Oxford University Press

39. McFarlan F.W. (1 984), "Information Technology Changes the Way You Compete', Harvard Business Review, Vol. 62, No. 3, May-June, pp. 98–103.

40. Mieritz, L. (2004) Bridging the gap between business and IT through value articulation, Gartner Consulting, San Francisco, CA.

41. Miles, R.; and Snow, C. (1978), Organizational strategy, structure and process, McGrawHill, NewYork,NY. Mintzburg, H. (1987) "Crafting strategy", Harvard Business Review,July-August, 66–75.

42. Neo, B. S. (1988), "Factors Facilitating the Use of Information Technology for Competitive Advantage: An Exploratory Study", Information and Management, Vol. 1 5, pp. 191–201.

43. Papp, R. (1999), "Business IT alignment: Productivity Paradox Payoffs", Industrial Management and Data System, Vol. 99, No. 8, pp. 367–373.

44. Papp, R. (2001), Strategic Information Technology: Opportunities for Competitive Advantage, Idea Publishing Group.

45. Porter, M.E. (1987), "From Competitive Advantage to Corporate Strategy", Harvard Business Review, pp.15-31. Porter, M.E. (1996), "What is strategy?", Harvard Business Review, November-December, 61–78.

46. Rai, A., Parnayakuni, R. and Parnayakuni, N. (1996), "Refocusing where and how IT value is realized: An empirical investigation", Omega International Journal of Management Science, Vol. 3, No. 4, July-August, pp.399–412.

47. Rayner, B. (1995), "Management matters", Computerworld Premier 100, October, 9, pp. 7–10.

48. Reich B.H. and Benbasat, I. (1996), "Measuring the Linkage Between Business and Information Technology Objectives", MIS Quarterly, Vol. 20, No. 1, pp. 55–81.

49. Reich, B. H. and Benbasat, I. (2000), "Factors that Influence the Social Dimension of Alignment Between Business and Information Technology Objectives", MIS Quarterly,Vol. 24, No. 1, pp. 81–11 3.

50. Sabherwal, R. and Chan, Y.E. (2001), "Alignment Between Business and IS Strategies: A Study of Prospectors, Analyzers and Defenders", Information Systems Research, Vol.12, No. 1, pp. 11–33.

51. Smaczny, T. (2001), "IS an Alignment between Business and IT the appropriate paradigm to manage IT in Today's organization?", Management Decision, Vol. 39, No. 10, pp. 797–802.

52. Stepanek, M. (2002) 'Management matters', CIO Conference Report on Business IT Alignment. New York, NY: Ziff Davis Media.

53. Steven, L. (1992)," Font-line Systems", ComputerWorld, 26, 61–63.

54. Tainor, E. (2003), From the President's Desk, SIM Top Ten List (http://www.simnet.org).

55. Tallon,P. Kraemer,K. and Gurbaxani, V. (2000), "Executives' perceptions of Business value of IT", Journal of Management Information Systems, Vol. 16, No. 4, pp. 145–172.

56. Tallon,P. ; and Kraemer, K. (2003), Investigating Relationship between Strategic Alignment and Business Value, Idea Publications, Hershy, PA, 1–22.

57. Tallon,P; Gurbaxani, V. ;and Kraemer, K.L. (1998), "Fact or Fiction: The Reality Behind the Executive Perceptions of IT Business Value", Working paper, University of California, Irvine.

58. Venkatraman, N. (2000) "Five steps to dot-com strategy: How to find your Footing on Web", Sloan Management Review,Vol. 41, No. 3, pp.15–28.

59. Venkatraman, N. (1997), "Beyond Outsourcing: Managing IT Resources as a value Center", Sloan Management Review, Spring, Vol. 38, No. 3,pp. 51–64.

60. Venkatraman, N.(1989), "Strategic Orientation of Business Enterprises: The Construct Dimensionality and Measurement", Vol. 35, No. 8, pp. 942–962.

61. Weil,S. (2001), Managing- Surveys Underscore CIO Frustrations, CIO Magazine, http://www.idg.com.au

62. Weill, P. ; and Broadbent, M. (1 998), Leveraging the New Infrastructure, Harvard Business School Press.

63. Wiseman, C. (1985), "Strategic vision", ComputerWorld, 1 9(20), 1–1 7.

64. Wiseman, C. (1988), Strategic Information Systems, Irwin, Homewood, II.

65. Woolfe, R. (1993), "The Path of Strategic Alignment " Information Strategy: The Information Journal, Vol. 9, No. 2, pp. 13–23.

☺☹☹

2

MIS in Banking System

A.K. Saini[1] and Deepak Tandon[2]

The Indian Economy is booming on the back of strong economic policies and a healthy regulatory regime. The effects of this are far- reaching and have the potential to ultimately achieve the high growth rates that the country is yearning for. The banking system lies at the nucleus of a country's development robust reforms are needed in India's case to fulfill that. The BASEL III accord from the Bank of International Settlements attempts to put in place sound frameworks of measuring and quantifying the risks associated with banking operations by 2019. The chapter seeks to showcase the changes that will emerge as a result of banks adopting the international norms and whether they will be able to sustain the pressures and shocks of the changing scenarios. This enables one to discern the complete scenario that will emerge in the years ahead. The Risk Management scenario will strengthen owing to the liberalization, regulation and integration with global markets. Management of risks will be carried out proactively and quality of credit will improve, leading to a stronger financial sector. The authors have emphasized the dire need of Altmann Z Score, Merton Model, KMV Model and Value at Risk Model for the Banks in a more sophisticated manner through caselets.

KEYWORDS Risk Metrics | Banking System | Expected Loss [EL] | Capital Adequacy Requirement [CAR] | KMV Model

2.1 INTRODUCTION

Risk management has assumed increased importance from the regulatory compliance point of view. Credit Risk being an important component of risk, can be viewed at two levels—at the level of an individual asset or exposure and at the portfolio level. Credit risk management tools therefore have to work at both individual and portfolio levels. Traditionally the tools of credit risk management include loan policies, standards for presentation of credit proposals, delegation of loan approving powers, multi-tier credit approving systems, prudential limits on credit exposures to companies and groups, stipulation of financial covenants, standards for collaterals, limits on

---

[1] University School of Management, GGS Indraprastha University, Delhi, India
[2] Lal Bahadur Shastri Institute of Management, (LBSIM), Dwarka, New Delhi, India

asset concentrations and independent loan review mechanisms. Monitoring of non-performing loans has however a focus on remedy rather than advance warning or prevention. Banks assign internal ratings to borrowers, which will determine the interest spread charged over PLR. These ratings are also used for monitoring of loans. Some central banks like the Reserve Bank of India have suggested the use of rating models like Altman's Z score models at individual loan/company level and risk models like Credit Metrics and Credit Risk+ at the portfolio level.

2.2 OVERVIEW

Credit Risk is defined as "The inability or unwillingness of the customer or counter party to meet commitments in relation to lending, hedging, settlement and other financial transactions." Hence Credit Risk emanates when the counter party is unwilling or unable to meet or fulfill the contractual obligations / commitments thereby leading to defaults. Risk management activities will be more pronounced in future banking because of liberalization, deregulation and global integration of financial markets. This would be adding depth and dimension to the banking risks. As the risks are correlated, exposure to one risk may lead to another risk, therefore management of risks in a proactive, efficient & integrated manner will be the strength of the successful banks. In the current norms of Basel

II accord, under Pillar 1, the framework offers three distinct options for computing capital requirement for credit risk. These approaches for credit risks are based on increasing risk sensitivity and allow banks to select an approach that is appropriate to the stage of development of bank's operations. The approaches available for computing capital for credit risk are Standardized Approach, Foundation Internal Rating Based Approach and Advanced Internal Rating Based approach.

Standardized Approach is the basic approach which banks at a minimum have to use for moving to Basel II implementation. It is an extension of the existing method of calculation of capital charge for credit risk. The existing method is refined and made more risk sensitive by:

Introducing more number of risk weights thus aiding finer differentiation in risk assessment between asset groups.

Assignment of Risk weights based on the ratings assigned by External Credit rating agencies recognized by RBI, in case of exposures more than `5 crores.

Recognizing wide range of collaterals (securities) as risk mitigants and netting them off while determining the exposure amount on which risk weights are to be applied.

Introducing Retail portfolio with total exposure up to Rs.5 crores and yearly turnover less than Rs.50 crores as a separate asset group with clear cut definition and criteria.

Assignment of Risk weight for NPA accounts. The rating assigned by the eligible external credit rating agencies will largely support the measure of credit risk. Unrated exposures will normally carry 100% risk weight. But for the financial year 2008-09, all fresh sanctions or renewals in respect of unrated borrowers in excess of ₹50 crores will attract a risk weight of 150%. From 2009–10 onwards, unrated borrowings in excess of 10 crores will attract risk weight of 150%.

The standardized approach was implemented by 31st March 2010, and the forward-looking banks would be in the process of placing their MIS for the collection of data required for the calculation of Probability of Default (PD), Exposure at Default (EAD) and Loss Given Default (LGD). The banks are expected to have at a minimum PD data for five years and LGD and EAD data for seven years.

CRM {Credit Risk Mitigation} refers to permitted methods of netting the exposure value for computing Risk Weights by using Collateral, Third party guarantee (Guarantee) and On-balance sheet netting. CRM is available subject to several conditions. Before netting, Exposure Value (EV) and Collateral Value (CV) are to be adjusted for volatility and possible future fluctuations. EV to be increased for volatility (premium factor) and CV to be reduced for volatility (discount factor). These factors are termed as 'Haircuts' (HC).

Therefore,

$$\text{EV after risk mitigation} = (\text{EV After HC} - \text{CV After HC})$$

However, for banks and financial institutions, credit risk is the most important factor to be managed. Credit risk may take various forms, such as:

- EV after Risk mitigation will be multiplied by the Risk Weight of the customer to obtain Risk-weighted asset amount for the collateralized transaction.
- Presently most Indian banks do not possess the data required for the calculation of their LGDs. Also the personnel skills, the IT infrastructure and MIS at the banks need to be upgraded substantially if the banks want to migrate to the IRB Approach.

However, for banks and financial institutions, credit risk is the most important factor to be managed. Credit risk may take various forms, such as:

- In the case of direct lending, that funds will not be repaid;

↵ In the case of guarantees or letters of credit, that funds will not be forthcoming from the customer upon crystallization of the liability under the contract;

↵ In the case of treasury products, that the payment or series of payments due from the counterparty under the respective contracts is not forthcoming or ceases;

↵ In the case of securities trading businesses, that settlement will not be effected;

↵ In the case of cross-border exposure, that the availability and free transfer of currency is restricted or ceases.

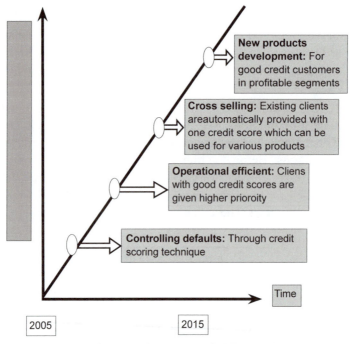

New products development: For good credit customers in profitable segments

Cross selling: Existing clients areautomatically provided with one credit score which can be used for various products

Operational efficient: Cliens with good credit scores are given higher priorioty

Controlling defaults: Through credit scoring technique

Time

2005   2015

Fig. 2.1   Strategic Continuum of M Scoring Models

Source: *http://www. moodyskmv.com*

The more diversified a banking group is, the more intricate systems it would need, to protect itself from a wide variety of risks. These include the routine operational risks applicable to any commercial concern, the business risks to its commercial borrowers, the economic and political risks associated with the countries in which it operates, and the commercial and the reputational risks concomitant with a failure to comply with the increasingly stringent legislation and regulations surrounding financial services business in many territories. Comprehensive risk identification and assessment are therefore very essential to establishing the health of any counterparty.

2.3 COMPONENTS OF CREDIT RISK

As per the existing Standardized approach, Risk Weight (RW) is assigned based on the "External Rating" of the borrowers for "Corporate" asset class and differential (concessional) risk weight of 75% is applicable for "Retail" exposures. Basel Committee taking into account the following elements has determined the risk weights:

- Frequency of Default (Probability of Default - PD)
- Severity of Default (Loss Given Default - LGD)
- Outstanding/modifiers for off balance sheet items (Exposure at Default)
- Maturity adjustment (M)

More advanced approaches provide banks with the following two options for measurement of credit risk:

- **Foundation:** Internal Rating Based (FIRB) - Under the foundation approach, as a general rule, banks provide their own estimates of PD and rely on supervisory estimates for other risk components.
- **Advanced:** Internal Rating Based (AIRB) - Under the advanced approach, banks provide more of their own estimates of PD, LGD and EAD, and their own calculation of M, subject to meeting minimum standards.

Ideally, the more suited approach shall be AIRB as under FIRB, the regulator provides LGD and EAD and it may not be appropriate to calibrate and benchmark these risk components to our portfolios.

AIRB is a highly data intensive approach and requires granular level information on all the aforesaid risk elements. The minimum number of years for which the historical data is to be collected, analysed, calibrated and validated for measurement of capital adequacy is specified below:

- PD: 5 yrs
- LGD and EAD: 7 yrs
- Maturity: Effective maturity based on cash flows

Basel II guidelines stipulates that the risk elements shall cover one full economic cycle so as to iron out the fluctuations in its measurement and computing capital adequacy in a more meaningful manner while possibly covering the economic downturn.

2.4 SUMMARIZING THE CREDIT RISK MODELS

2.4.1 KMV Model

This model was developed by KMV Corporation based on Merton's (1973) analytical model of firm's value. This model uses stock prices and the capital structure of the firm to estimate its probability. The starting point of this model is the proposition that a firm would default only if its asset value falls below certain level (default point), which is a function of its liability. It estimates the asset value of the firm and its asset volatility from the market value of equity and the debt structure in the opinion theoretic framework. Using these two values, a metric (distance from default or DFD) is constructed that represents the number of standard deviation that the firm's asset value is away from the default point. Finally, a mapping is done between the default values and actual default rate, based on historical default experience. *The resultant probability is called Expected Default Frequency (EDF)*. Thus EDF is calculated in the following three steps:

- Estimation of asset value and asset volatility from equity value and volatility of equity return.

- Calculation of DFD as (Asset value – Default point)/(Asset value* Asset volatility)

- Calculation of expected default frequency.

2.4.2 Credit Metrics Model

Credit Metrics is a statistical model developed by J.P Morgan, the investment bank, in the year 1995 for internal use, but now it's being used all around the world by hundreds of banks including Indian banks like the ICICI bank. This model works on the statistical concepts like probability, means, and standard deviation, correlation, and concentrations.

Credit Metrics is a tool for assessing portfolio risk due to changes in debt value caused by changes in obligor credit quality. This model includes the changes in value caused not only by possible default events, but also by upgrades and down grades in credit quality, because the value of a particular credit varies with the corresponding credit quality. Credit Metrics also assess the Valu-at-risk (VAR)—the volatility of value- not just the expected losses. The model assesses the risk within the full context of a portfolio addressing the correlation of credit quality moves across obligors. This allows to directly calculating the diversification benefits or potential over concentrations across the portfolio.

The transition table for the various categories of bonds is determined and then joint probability for both these under different combinations. Then the

NPV of the portfolio is determined for all the combinations and a probability distribution is constructed. These probabilities are actually an analysis of past migrations and same is the case with default probability. In the case of default a recovery rate is taken as the portfolio value. This distribution gives us 2 measures of credit risk: standard deviation and percentile level. This model has some limitations regarding the data availability but it doesn't require any changes as such for application in the Indian scenario.

2.4.3 VAR Model

This model is being used in some of the banks currently in India. Value at risk (VAR) is a statistical risk measure, which is used extensively for measuring the market risk of portfolios of assets and/or liabilities. Suppose a portfolio's value at risk is 2Mn$ with a 95% confidence level, then it means that the portfolio is expected to loose a maximum of 2Mn$ 95% of the times. The Value at risk is calculated by constructing a probability distribution of the portfolio values over a given time horizon. The values may be calculated on the daily, weekly or monthly basis.

2.4.4 Altmann Z Score

Altman's Z score predicts whether or not a company is likely to enter into bankruptcy within one or two years. Edward Altman developed the model by examining 85 manufacturing companies in the year 1968. Later, additional "Z-Scores" were developed for private manufacturing companies (Z-Score - Model A) and another for general/service firms (Z- Score - Model B). The Z-Score combination.

The algorithm has been consistently reported to have a 95 % accuracy of prediction of bankruptcy up to two years prior to failure on nonmanufacturing firms as well. There have been many other bankruptcy predictors developed and published. However, none has been so thoroughly tested and broadly accepted as the Altman Z-Score.

The Altman Z-Score variables influencing the financial strength of a firm are: current assets, total assets, net sales, interest, total liability, current liabilities, market value of equity, earnings before taxes and retained earnings.

The model can be used for a quick check about the health of a company. It however cannot be used for individuals. The value of Z is given by the following equation:

$$Z = 0.012X1 + 0.014X2 + 0.033X3 + 0.006X4 + 0.999X5$$

where,

X1 = working capital/Total assets

X2 = Retained earnings/Total assets

X3 = Earnings before interest and taxes/Total assets

X4 = Market value of equity/Book value of total liabilities

X5 = Sales/Total assets

A "Z" value above 1.8 is supposed to be quite safe, while the value below 1.8 indicates a high probability of bankrupt

2.5 CREDIT STRATEGY, POLICIES AND PROCEDURES

The credit risk strategy should provide continuity in approach, and will need to take into account the cyclical aspects of any economy and the resulting shifts in the composition and quality of the overall credit portfolio. This strategy should be viable in the long run and through various credit cycles. An organisation's risk appetite depends on the level of capital and the quality of loan book and the magnitude of other risks embedded in the balance sheet. Based on its capital structure, a bank will be able to set its target returns to its shareholders and this will determine the level of capital available to the various business lines.

Keeping in view the foregoing, a bank should have the following in place:

- Dedicated policies and procedures to control exposures to designated higher risk sectors such as capital markets, aviation, shipping, property development, defence equipment, highly leveraged transactions, bullion etc.

- Sound procedures to ensure that all risks associated with requested credit facilities are promptly and fully evaluated by the relevant lending and credit officers.

- Systems to assign a risk rating to each customer/borrower to who credit facilities have been sanctioned.

- A mechanism to price facilities depending on the risk grading of the customer, and to attribute accurately the associated risk weightings to the facilities.

- Efficient and effective credit approval process operating within the approval limits authorized by the Boards.

- Procedures and systems which allow for monitoring financial performance of customers and for controlling outstanding within limits.

➤ Systems to manage problem loans to ensure appropriate restructuring schemes. A conservative policy for the provisioning of non-performing advances should be followed.

➤ A process to conduct regular analysis of the portfolio and to ensure on-going control of risk concentrations.

The credit policies and procedures should necessarily have the following elements:

➤ Banks should have written credit policies that define target markets, risk acceptance criteria, credit approval authority, credit origination and maintenance procedures and guidelines for portfolio management and remedial management.

➤ Banks should establish proactive credit risk management practices like annual/half yearly industry studies and individual obligor reviews, periodic credit calls that are documented, periodic plant visits, and at least quarterly management reviews of troubled exposures/weak credits.

➤ Business managers in banks will be accountable for managing risk and in conjunction with credit risk management framework for establishing and maintaining appropriate risk limits and risk management procedures for their businesses.

➤ Banks should have a system of checks and balances in place around the extension of credit which are:

➤ An independent credit risk management function

➤ Multiple credit approvers

➤ An independent audit and risk review function

➤ The Credit Approving Authority to extend or approve credit will be granted to individual credit officers based upon a consistent set of standards of experience, judgment and ability.

➤ The level of authority required to approve credit will increase as amounts and transaction risks increase and as risk ratings worsen.

➤ Every obligor and facility must be assigned a risk rating.

➤ Banks should ensure that there are consistent standards for the origination, documentation and maintenance for extensions of credit.

✦ Banks should have a consistent approach toward early problem recognition, the classification of problem exposures, and remedial action.

✦ Banks should maintain a diversified portfolio of risk assets in line with the capital desired to support such a portfolio.

✦ Credit risk limits include, but are not limited to, obligor limits and concentration limits by industry or geography.

✦ In order to ensure transparency of risks taken, it is the responsibility of banks to accurately, completely and in a timely fashion, report the comprehensive set of credit risk data into the independent risk system

2.6 TYPICAL ORGANISATIONAL STRUCTURE

At organizational level, overall risk management should be assigned to an independent Risk Management Committee or Executive Committee of the top Executives that reports directly to the Board of Directors.

The purpose of this top level committee is to empower one group with full responsibility of evaluating overall risks faced by the bank and determining the level of risks which will be in the best interest of the bank.

The function of Risk Management Committee should essentially be to identify, monitor and measure the risk profile of the bank. The Committee should also develop policies and procedures, verify the models that are used for pricing complex products, review the risk models a development takes place in the markets and also identify new risks. Internationally, the trend is towards assigning risk limits in terms of portfolio standards or Credit at Risk (credit risk) and Earnings at Risk and Value at Risk (market risk).

A prerequisite for establishment of an effective risk management system is the existence of a robust Management Information System (MIS), consistent in quality. The existing MIS, however, requires substantial up gradation and strengthening of the data collection machinery to ensure the integrity and reliability of data.

The risk management is a complex function and it requires specialized skills and expertise. Banks have been moving towards the use of sophisticated models for measuring and managing risks. Large banks and those operating in international markets should develop internal risk management models to be able to compete effectively with their competitors.

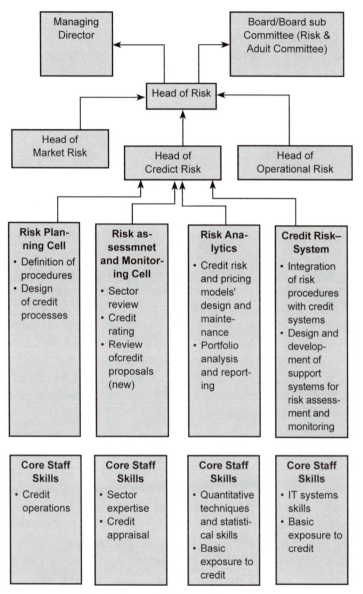

Fig. 2 Loan Policies and procedures

As the domestic market integrates with the international markets, the banks should have necessary expertise and skill in managing various types of risks in a scientific manner. At a more sophisticated level, the core staff at Head Offices should be trained in risk modeling and analytical tools. It should, therefore, be the endeavor of all banks to upgrade the skills of staffs.

Given the diversity of balance sheet profile, it is difficult to adopt a uniform framework for management of risks in India. The design of risk management functions should be bank specific, dictated by the size, complexity of functions, the level of technical expertise and the quality of MIS. The proposed guidelines only provide broad parameters and each bank may evolve their own systems compatible to their risk management architecture and expertise.

Internationally, a committee approach to risk management is being adopted. While the **Asset-Liability Management Committee (ALCO)** deals with different types of market risk, the **Credit Policy Committee (CPC)** oversees the credit/counterparty risk and country risk.

Banks could also set up a single Committee for integrated management of credit and market risks. Generally, the policies and procedures for market risk are articulated in the ALM policies and credit risk is addressed in Loan Policies and procedures.

Currently, while market variables are held constant for qualifying credit risk, credit variables are held constant in estimating market risk. The economic crises in some of the countries have revealed a strong correlation between unhedged market risk and credit. Forex exposures, assumed by corporate who have no natural hedges, will increase the credit risk which banks run vis-a-vis their counterparties. The volatility in the prices of collateral also significantly affects the quality of the loan book. Thus, there is a need for integration of the activities of both the ALCO and the CPC and consultation process is established to evaluate the impact of market and credit risks on the financial strength of banks. Banks may also consider integrating market risk elements into their credit risk assessment process.

2.7 MEASUREMENT OF RISK & CREDIT RATING SCORING

- ↢ Quantifying the risk through estimating expected loan losses i.e. the amount of loan losses that bank would experience over a chosen time horizon (through tracking portfolio behavior over 5 or more years) and unexpected loss (through standard deviation of losses or the difference between expected loan losses and some selected target credit loss quantile);
- ↢ Risk pricing on a scientific basis; and
- ↢ Controlling the risk through effective Loan Review Mechanism and portfolio management.

The credit risk management process should be articulated in the bank's Loan Policy, duly approved by the Board. Each bank should constitute a high level Credit Policy Committee, also called Credit Risk Management Committee or Credit Control Committee etc. to deal with issues relating to credit policy and procedures and to analyze, manage and control credit risk on a bank wide basis. The Committee should be headed by the Chairman/CEO/ ED, and should comprise heads of Credit Department, Treasury, Credit Risk Management Department (CRMD) and the Chief Economist. The Committee should, inter alia, formulate clear policies on standards for presentation of credit proposals, financial covenants, rating standards and benchmarks, delegation of credit approving powers, prudential limits on large credit exposures, asset concentrations, standards for loan collateral, portfolio management, loan review mechanism, risk concentrations, risk monitoring and evaluation, pricing of loans, provisioning, regulatory/legal compliance, etc.

Concurrently, each bank should also set up Credit Risk Management Department (CRMD), independent of the Credit Administration Department. The CRMD should enforce and monitor compliance of the risk parameters and prudential limits set by the CPC. The CRMD should also lay down risk assessment systems, monitor quality of loan portfolio, identify problems and correct deficiencies, develop MIS and undertake loan review/audit. Large banks may consider separate set up for loan review/audit. The CRMD should also be made accountable for protecting the quality of the entire loan portfolio. The Department should undertake portfolio evaluations and conduct comprehensive studies on the environment to test the resilience of the loan portfolio.

Credit Risk may be defined as the risk of default on the part of the borrower. The lender always faces the risk of the counter party not repaying the loan or not making the due payment in time. This uncertainty of repayment by the borrower is also known as default risk.

The credit approval process should aim at efficiency, responsiveness and accurate measurement of the risk. This will be achieved through a comprehensive analysis of the borrower's ability to repay, clear and consistent assessment systems, a process which ensures that renewal requests are analyzed as carefully and stringently as new loans and constant reinforcement of the credit culture by the top management team.

Banks must have a MIS, which will enable them to manage and measure the credit risk inherent in all

The broad objectives of studying the Credit risk Management evolving the Bank's credit risk policy are on- and off- balance sheet activities. The MIS should provide adequate information on the composition of the credit portfolio, including identification of any concentration of risk. Banks should price their loans according to the risk profile of the borrower and the risks associated with the loans.

2.8 OBJECTIVES OF THE STUDY

- To build a high quality portfolio in line with the Bank's risk appetite and strategy.
- To identify, measure, monitor, manage and control risk effectively and to ensure that the Bank gets compensated for the risk assumed

- ↬ To maximize Bank's Risk-Adjusted Return by maintaining credit risk exposure within acceptable parameters.
- ↬ To develop a greater ability to recognize and avoid potential problems.
- ↬ To support sustainable business growth within the overall Risk appetite of the Bank.
- ↬ Diversifying the risk profile among different segments of Products, Geographies, Group etc in order to minimise the concentration risk and maximise returns.

2.9 SCOPE

The scope of our study is to build a high quality portfolio in line with the Bank's risk appetite and strategy and to support sustainable business growth within this appetite. By building upon the model of transition matrix we have tried to identify measure, monitor, manage and control risk effectively and to ensure that the Bank gets compensated for the risk assumed. Diversifying the risk profile among different segments of Products, Geographies, Group etc in order to minimise the concentration risk and maximise returns and to maximize Bank's Risk- Adjusted Return by maintaining credit risk exposure within acceptable parameters.

2.10 METHODOLOGY

The authors have devised Credit Risk Transition matrix in a New Generation Private Sector Bank {IndusindBank} which can help as against qualitative/ structural approaches as follows:

2.10.1 Transition Matrix

Default probability is measured using risk factors. The change in the default probability or the volatility in PD is measured through Transition Matrix (TM) While PD measurement helps in measuring risk at the instrument level, PD volatility helps in measuring risk at the portfolio level. The likelihood of a customer migrating from its current risk-rating category to any other category within the time horizon is frequently expressed in terms of rating TM. TM is expressed in a Matrix form.

The transition matrix including probabilities to move from one rating to another rating represents the kernel of many credit risk and rating calculations. Following the requirements of Basel II financial engineers need software tools allowing for adjustment of transition matrices provided by rating agencies to the economic cycles and to generate transition matrices according to the local financial and economic conditions. The generated transition matrixes are the basis for calculation of credit risk of counterparts using a set of internal (Credit Metrics, Credit Risk and Basel II Standard, Foundation and Advanced Approaches) evaluation models. The estimation of credit risk involve cumulative and marginal default probabilities for future periods used to calculate expected and unexpected losses (Credit VAR) within a multi-period credit exposure model. The results of transition matrix estimation of Data Supporter Module are used by Risk Evaluator to calculate credit risk of single counterparts and various aggregates based on sub portfolios, concern structures and other grouping criteria such as branches and countries.

One limitation of this method is the size of the pools. Most banks do not have large enough credit portfolios to be able to estimate PDs with accurate granularity. The smaller number of obligors, the more volatile the PD estimation will be.

Another limitation is given if PDs are calculated once a year (at year end); changes in the PDs cannot be foreseen in time. A monthly estimation and comparison of PDs on a year-to-year basis is therefore helpful to extend the time series and calculate the credit risk and expected losses on current data.

Using the method of pseudo-pooling, banks can compute transition probabilities or cumulated multi-year PD. For multi-year estimations, it is crucial that the pool remains "static" or "frozen" with respect to the obligors in it, so that the time period is equal for all the obligors in the respective pool. In other words, it will be incorrect - say 5-year PDs, if some obligors have been in the pool for 5 years and some for only 4 or 3 years. However to overcome this problem two types of pools are used.

2.10.2 Dynamic Pool

A dynamic pool of a year is a set of pool of companies where in the membership of the pool does not remain static/constant but keeps on changing based on additions and withdrawals from the pool. Here the companies which withdraw or default in between will be considered and not be taken as addition or outstanding. That is why it is known as dynamic pool.

Unlike the static pool the ratings are not constant throughout the period. It will be dynamic or flexible in nature

2.10.3 Static pool

A static pool of a year is a set or pool of companies having an outstanding rating at the beginning of the year. The membership of the pool remains static /constant over a period of time. For a company to be included in an n year static pool, it has to be outstanding throughout those entire n years. Companies that withdraw or default in between will remain withdrawn of defaulted for the remaining years. A company that gets a rating subsequently, or recovers from default, is considered a new company in that static pool. A company that remains rated for more than one year is counted as many times as number of years over which it was rated. This assumes all ratings are kept current through an on going surveillance process.

2.10.4 Process of Static Pool

- The no of columns for static pools will depend upon the start year, end year and the minimum horizon.
- The software should count the number of rated accounts under each category, for a finalized assessment done between two particular dates.
- If there is any case, which has be clicked for "Default" the ratings of those accounts should not be included in the static pool. Similarly any withdrawn cases should also be excluded from the count.
- If there are more than 1 finalized assessment for a particular case the rating of that assessment which has
- the latest Assessment date should be considered for counting.
- After Static Pool we have to observe the behavior of the company i.e. the Transition of the company for the defined horizon.

2.11 OBSERVATIONS

The main findings of the project are:

- IndusInd Bank uses a robust Risk rating framework for evaluating credit risk of the borrowers. The bank uses segment specific rating models equipped with transition matrix capabilities.
- The software should count the number of rated accounts under each category, for a finalized assessment done between two particular dates.
- If there is any case, which has be clicked for "Default" the ratings of those accounts should not be included in the static pool. Similarly any withdrawn cases should also be excluded from the count.
- If there are more than 1 finalized assessment for a particular case the rating of that assessment which has the latest Assessment date should be considered for counting.
- After Static Pool we have to observe the behavior of the company i.e. the Transition of the company for the defined horizon.

Table 2.1 Rating migrations over a period of 4 years for capital broker model

Customer ID	Year 1	Year 2	Year 3	Year 4
CAPITAL 1	B 2	B 3	B 3	B 3
CAPITAL 2	B 5	D	D	D
CAPITAL 3	B 1	B 1	B 1	B 1
CAPITAL 4	B 2	B 2	B 2	B 2
CAPITAL 5	B 3	B 2	B 2	B 2
CAPITAL 6	B 2	B 2	B 2	B 2
CAPITAL 7	B 7	B 7	B 6	B 7
CAPITAL 8	B 1	B 1	B 2	B 2
CAPITAL 9	B 2	B 2	B 2	B 2
CAPITAL 10	B 3	B 3	B 2	B 2
CAPITAL 11	B 7	B 7	B 7	B 7
CAPITAL 12	B 2	B 2	B 3	B 3
CAPITAL 13	B 4	W	W	W
CAPITAL 14	B 3	B 3	B 3	B 3
CAPITAL 15	B 2	B 2	B 2	B 2
CAPITAL 16	B 2	B 2	B 2	B 2
CAPITAL 17	B 8	B 8	B 8	B 8
CAPITAL 18	B 4	B 4	B 3	B 3
CAPITAL 19	B 2	B 2	B 2	B 2
CAPITAL 20	B 5	B 5	B 5	B 5
CAPITAL 21	B 3	B 3	B 3	B 3
CAPITAL 22	B 4	B 4	B 4	B 4
CAPITAL 23	B 2	B 2	B 2	B 3
CAPITAL 24	B 3	B 3	B 3	B 2
CAPITAL 25	B 4	B 4	B 3	B 3
CAPITAL 26	B 1	B 1	B 1	B 1
CAPITAL 27	B 4	B 5	B 5	B 5
CAPITAL 28	B 6	B 6	W	W
CAPITAL 29	B 5	B 5	B 4	B 4
CAPITAL 30	B 6	B 6	B 6	B 6
CAPITAL 31	B 3	B 3	B 3	B 3
CAPITAL 32	B 7	B 7	B 7	B 7
CAPITAL 33	B 1	B 1	B 1	B 1
CAPITAL 34	B 5	B 5	B 5	B 5
CAPITAL 35	B 4	B 4	B 4	B 5
CAPITAL 36	B 3	B 3	B 4	B 4
CAPITAL 37	B 6	B 7	D	D
CAPITAL 38	B 5	B 5	B 5	W
CAPITAL 39	B 8	D	D	D
CAPITAL 40	B 6	B 6	B 6	B 6

CAPITAL 41	B 6	B 6	B 6	B 6
CAPITAL 42	B 8	B 8	B 8	D
CAPITAL 43	B 3	B 3	B 3	B 3
CAPITAL 44	B 4	B 4	B 4	B 4
CAPITAL 45	B 1	B 1	B 1	B 1
CAPITAL 46	B 5	B 5	B 6	B 6
CAPITAL 47	B 7	D	D	D
CAPITAL 48	B 1	B 3	B 3	B 3
CAPITAL 49	B 1	B 1	B 1	B 1
CAPITAL 50	B 1	B 1	B 1	B 1
CAPITAL 51	B 1	B 1	B 1	B 1
CAPITAL 52	B 1	B 1	B 1	B 1
CAPITAL 53	B 1	B 1	B 1	B 1
CAPITAL 54	B 4	B 4	B 4	B 4
CAPITAL 55	B 4	B 4	B 4	B 4
CAPITAL 56	B 4	B 4	B 4	B 5
CAPITAL 57	B 4	B 4	B 4	B 4
CAPITAL 58	B 4	B 4	B 4	B 4
CAPITAL 59	B 4	B 4	B 4	B 4
CAPITAL 60		B 7	B 7	B 7
CAPITAL 61		B 7	B 7	B 8
CAPITAL 62		B 8	D	D
CAPITAL 63		B 5	B 5	B 5
CAPITAL 64			B 3	B 4
CAPITAL 65			B 8	B 8

Table 2.2 Values Values Year 1 and Year 2

Count of Year 1	Year 2										
Year 1	B1	B2	B3	B4	B5	B6	B7	B8	W	D	Grand Total
B 1	10		1								11
B 2		8	1								9
B 3		1	7								8
B 4				11	1						13
B 5					5						6
B 6						4	1				5
B 7							3			1	4
B 8								2		1	3
Grand Total	10	9	9	11	6	4	4	2	1	3	59

Values Year 2 and Year 3

Count of Year 2	Year 3										
Year 2	B1	B2	B3	B4	B5	B6	B7	B8	W	D	Grand Total
B 1	9	1									10
B 2	1	8	1								9
B 3		1	7	1							9
B 4				2	9						11
B 5					1	5	1				7
B 6						4	1				5
B 7							3			1	4
B 8								2		1	3
Grand Total	10	10	9	11	5	5	4	2	1	2	59

Values Year 3 and Year 4

Count of Year 2	Year 3										
Year 2	B1	B2	B3	B4	B5	B6	B7	B8	W	D	Grand Total
B 1	9										9
B 2		9	1								10
B 3		1	9	1							11
B 4				9	2						11
B 5					4				1		5
B 6						4	1				5
B 7							3			1	4
B 8								2		1	3
Grand Total	10	10	9	11	5	5	4	2	1	2	59

Count of Year 3	Year 4										
Year 3	B 1	B 2	B 3	B 4	B 5	B 6	B 7	B 8	W	D	Grand Total
B 1	100.00	0.00	0.00	0.00	0.00	0.00	0.00	0.00	0.00	0.00	100
B 2	0.00	90.00	10.00		0.00	0.00	0.00	0.00	0.00	0.00	100
B 3	0.00	9.09	81.82	9.09	0.00	0.00	0.00	0.00	0.00	0.00	100
B 4	0.00	0.00	0.00	81.82	18.18	0.00	0.00	0.00	0.00	0.00	100
B 5	0.00	0.00	0.00	0.00	80.00	0.00	0.00	0.00	20.00	0.00	100
B 6	0.00	0.00	0.00	0.00	0.00	80.00	20.00	0.00	0.00	0.00	100
B 7	0.00	0.00	0.00	0.00	0.00	0.00	75.00	25.00	0.00	0.00	100
B 8	0.00	0.00	0.00	0.00	0.00	0.00	0.00	66.67	0.00	33.33	100
Grand Total	100.00	99.09	91.82	90.91	98.18	80.00	95.00	91.67	20.00	33.33	800.00

Count of Year 1	Year 2										
Year 1	B 1	B 2	B 3	B 4	B 5	B 6	B 7	B 8	W	D	Grand Total
B 1	90.91	0.00	9.09	0.00	0.00	0.00	0.00	0.00	0.00	0.00	100
B 2	0.00	88.89	11.11		0.00	0.00	0.00	0.00	0.00	0.00	100
B 3	0.00	12.50	87.50	0.00	0.00	0.00	0.00	0.00	0.00	0.00	100
B 4	0.00	0.00	0.00	84.62	7.69	0.00	0.00	0.00	7.69	0.00	100
B 5	0.00	0.00	0.00	0.00	83.33	0.00	0.00	0.00	0.00	16.67	100
B 6	0.00	0.00	0.00	0.00	0.00	80.00	20.00	0.00	0.00	0.00	100
B 7	0.00	0.00	0.00	0.00	0.00	0.00	75.00	0.00	0.00	25.00	100
B 8	0.00	0.00	0.00	0.00	0.00	0.00	0.00	66.67	0.00	33.33	100
Grand Total	90.91	101.39	107.70	84.62	91.03	80.00	95.00	66.67	7.69	75.00	800.00

Count of Year 2	Year 3										
Year 2	B 1	B 2	B 3	B 4	B 5	B 6	B 7	B 8	W	D	Grand Total
B 1		10.00	0.00	0.00	0.00	0.00	0.00	0.00	0.00	0.00	100
B 2	11.11	88.89	0.00		0.00	0.00	0.00	0.00	0.00	0.00	100
B 3	0.00	11.11	77.78	11.11	0.00	0.00	0.00	0.00	0.00	0.00	100
B 4	0.00	0.00	18.18	81.82	0.00	0.00	0.00	0.00	0.00	0.00	100
B 5	0.00	0.00	0.00	14.29	71.43	14.29	0.00	0.00	0.00	0.00	100
B 6	0.00	0.00	0.00	0.00	0.00	75.00	0.00	0.00	25.00	0.00	100
B 7	0.00	0.00	0.00	0.00	0.00	16.67	66.67	0.00	0.00	16.67	100
B 8	0.00	0.00	0.00	0.00	0.00	0.00	0.00	66.67	0.00	33.33	100
Grand Total	101.11	110.00	95.96	107.22	71.43	105.95	66.67	66.67	25.00	50.00	800.00

Count of Year	Year										
Year	B 1	B 2	B 3	B 4	B 5	B 6	B 7	B 8	W	D	Grand Total
B 1	95.00	5.00	0.00	0.00	0.00	0.00	0.00	0.00	0.00	0.00	100.00
B 2	34.01	59.63	6.36	0.00	0.00	0.00	0.00	0.00	0.00	0.00	100.00
B 3	0.00	36.36	56.90	10.10	0.00	0.00	0.00	0.00	0.00	0.00	100.00
B 4	0.00	4.17	35.23	54.55	6.06	0.00	0.00	0.00	0.00	0.00	100.00
B 5	0.00	0.00	0.00	32.97	53.04	4.76	0.00	0.00	9.23	0.00	100.00
B 6	0.00	0.00	0.00	0.00	27.78	51.67	6.67	0.00	8.33	5.56	100.00
B 7	0.00	0.00	0.00	0.00	0.00	32.22	53.89	8.33	0.00	5.56	100.00
B 8	0.00	0.00	0.00	0.00	0.00	0.00	25.00	44.44	0.00	30.56	100.00
Grand Total	67.04	69.70	62.59	66.04	56.54	61.98	53.89	75.00	15.00	38.89	566.67

Banks and financial institutions are lending to individual borrowers on an ongoing basis. Credit risk management is a vital link between the borrowers and the institution. Identifying, measuring, monitoring and control lead to credit risk mitigation. Correlation and volatility of credit portfolio have a direct effect on one or the other. Transition matrix for probability of default helps top to bottom approach of the ratings calculations. It includes using credit risk, Basel II standards, foundation and advanced approaches and evaluation models. This model is a better model than value at risk (VAR) and it overlooks the limitations of VAR model (Delta method, historical simulation, Monte-Carlo method).

This chapter raises the awareness of VAR versus transition matrix in a heteroscedastic world within the framework for Basel II, accounting issues, tax issues. In case the limitations of this transition matrix can be improvised and the value of the credit event can be maximized it is worthwhile proposition to adopt transition matrix.

References

1. Bidani S.N., (2010), "Managing Non-Performing Assets in Banks", Vision Books publishers, Ref:#8-02-06-12, pp.71-74.

2. Paul Jusin , Suresh Padmalatah (2008) — Management of Banking & Financial services , Pearson Education

3. Dun & Bradstreet (2009) - Financial risk Management, Tata McGraw Hill Professional

4. Harrington, Niehaus (2007) Risk Management & Insurance, Tata McGraw Hill

5. Bell David E, Schleifer Jr, Risk Maqnagement (2004). Thomson Press, New Delhi

6. Timolthy WKoch, (1998), "Bank Management", Library of Congress Cataloging-in-Publication data

7. Timothy W Koch, (1998), "Bank Management - Overview of credit policy and loan characterstics", Third Edition, The Dryden Press, Harcourt Brace College Publishers, pp. 431-440

8. RBI (2007b). Indian Financial Sector Reforms: Address by V Leeladhar Deputy Governor Reserve Bank of India at the Annual Washington Conference of the Institute of International Bankers on March 5, 2007 www.rbi.org.in.

9. Levine, Ross, 1996. "Foreign banks, financial development and economic growth", in Claude

10. E. Barfield, ed., International Financial Markets (Washington, D.C., AEI Press).

11. Hoffman, Douglas G. Managing Operational Risk. New York: John Wiley & Sons, Inc., 2002.

☺☹☺

3

ICT & Internet

Jashwini Narayana[1], Anshu Mala[2] and Rajiv Naidu[3]

ICT and the Internet are correctly said to significantly contribute towards an increasingly globalised world. In Tiji, quite a number of researchers have investigated into/around this ICd industry but predominantly focused either on education or tourism needs. Ihe objectives and strategies for the ICd industry has been formulated at a national and policy level, but what is being done in implementing these polices by the relevant agencies, is an aspect to further delve into. Since the ICd industry is at its infancy, the overall progress of this industry until now will be noteworthy for further policy implications, dftis country and industry specific research findings suggest that diji has just but passed the infancy stage thus, remains very young in terms of ICddevelopment.

KEYWORDS   Fiji | ICT Industry | Pacific Island Nation | ICT | E-commece

3.1 INTRODUCTION

The fast-paced evolution of computing technologies such as the world wide web and internet based interfaces have brought businesses and countries together like never before. Quintessentially, we are living in an era of technology where mobile phones, computers, the internet and so forth mark our success or failure. The ability to communicate has not only been revamped, it has been revolutionised. The ADB report regards Information Communication Technology (ICT) as a powerful integrative tool for the widely dispersed, thus this sector is considerably, an important market for almost all countries but what works for the developed countries may not be workable for developing nations 3. Effectively then, in any national ICT strategy, such policies must be closely linked to domestic policies in order to create a favourable environment for the development and the deployment of ICT. ICT does hold great promises for the developing economies in Asia and

[1,2] School of Management & Public Administration, University of the South Pacific, FIJI

[3] FIJI Trades & Investment Board, Suva, FIJI

the Pacific-promises of: better educated workforce, empowerment of citizens, decentralisation of information, greater accessibility and communication, increased potential for research and development, and stronger integration with the global economy. However, government's need to recognise the potential of ICT and subsequently enact appropriate policies and regulations to encourage its widespread adoption in order to exploit the maximum benefit of these different and diverse technologies. In the contemporary geopolitical map, there remains significant disparity in terms of technology distribution. While some countries are world leaders, others lag far behind.

Nonetheless, the good news is that ICT has penetrated the Asia Pacific region and is growing rapidly. So much so that by the end of 2001, the region had the highest growth than any region in the world, a fifty-fold increase over 1995. Whilst small island states such as those in the Pacific region seek to increase their development and their standing in the global community, they are increasing plagued with a myriad of other problems when attempting to harness ICT progression such as the general lack of enforcement of intellectual property rights, the lack of infrastructure for e-commerce, insufficient communications infrastructure to connect rural areas and to connect to international gateways and so forth.

The fast-paced evolution of computing technologies such as the world wide web and internet based interfaces have brought businesses and countries together like never before. Quintessentially, we are living in an era of technology where mobile phones,

3.2 LITERATURE REVIEW

A number of authors have directed their attention to ICT related activities in the Pacific. In our perusal of current local literature, we noted that current work particularly dealt with education or tourism related matters. For instance, McMaster et al. and Doorne have talked around tourism opportunities. Robbins and Williams et al. have looked into educational opportunities. Chand et al. examined the impact of ICT on rural development in the Solomons. We next, give brief outlines of the work of writers who have researched around the ICT industry in Fiji and/or South Pacific.

Williams' research showed that the state of libraries, archives and museums has not improved in the past five years. Libraries and archives do have a role in education. She furthered that on the contrary, the library situation in Fiji, Papua New Guinea (PNG) and Solomons have worsened due to poor government financial support which makes purchase of ICT equipment unattainable.

In their research on the economic impact of internet usage in promoting small-scale budget tourist accommodation businesses in Fiji, Samoa and Tonga, McMaster et al. reported that most locals have limited knowledge/

exposure to ICT compared to expatriate owners who have higher skill and experience levels. They concluded that if given proper design and promotion, internet can be an effective marketing tool for tourism for Small to Medium Enterprises (SMEs) in the South Pacific.

Doorne, from his research on community integrated tourism development in the South Pacific stated that communities should be actively involved in the management and control of their resources and to facilitate community integration, basic computer training and resource management practices are required.

Another evaluative research on computer science curriculum in secondary schools in Fiji by William et al. highlighted that IT education needs improvement hence the need for a curriculum update, review and change. They believe that this is imperative now and even more so in the future given the rapid development in technology.

Minges and Gray concluded that a more liberalised telecom environment with lower prices for ICT services will provide better quality and more innovation. They stressed that Fiji compares well in terms of knowledge and affordability given the relatively high literacy and school enrolment and flat rate local call pricing for dial-up Internet access. However, they argued that Fiji does less well in infrastructure, usage and quality.

Rahiman and Naz argued that public awareness of e-governance is critical - there is a need to gauge public perception and to increase awareness. They also raised the issue of community involvement in dialogue and decision making.

Mistry and Rodrigues contended that ICTs and the right to information strategies should be developed in a coordinated fashion to open up channels of communication between Pacific Island governments and their disparate populations. They furthered that the more recent ICTs such as computers are not yet widely entrenched throughout the Pacific, hence could be effectively coupled with older ICTs, such as radios.

Thus far, very few studies have been carried out on a wider industry level for ICT development in Fiji, since it is still at developmental and/ or experimental stages. Fiji has also realised, albeit late, the importance of this sector. To this end, the respective ICT stakeholders are putting in their best efforts to further develop this sector. Their efforts seek to give the sector a much more national role rather than the niche role it currently has. The objectives and strategies for the ICT industry have been formulated at a national and policy level in Fiji's Strategic Development Plan (SDP) 2007-2011, but what is being done in implementing these polices by the relevant agencies, is an aspect to further delve into. The overall progress of this industry until now will be noteworthy for further policy implications. As it is, the current regime in Fiji is tapping into the potential niche industries like ICT industry in addition to the 'cash cow' industries of Fiji. It is of no surprise that the ICT industry in Fiji is 'green' in a sense that it has just but passed the infancy stage. This research will help to advance understanding into the current status of ICT developments in Fiji. It is our hope that, our study will open up some directions for future research - to factor a holistic and intrinsic discourse into the said topic. Secondly, it is in our premise that this area remains largely 'under-researched' locally, hence one of the aims of this chapter is to contribute to the current body of limited literature. Further usefulness of the study lies in its timeliness, given that Fiji has started working towards ICT development (though in a sluggish fashion), and the process is still very much in the making.

3.3 RESEARCH METHODS

The study used multiple qualitative research methods to collect data. Inductive strategy was followed which commenced with data collection, went onto data analysis and finally helped in the formation of generalisations. In doing so, reliance was placed on both the primary and secondary sources, which were interviews with primary document survey and secondary document survey, respectively.

Research was mainly conducted by semistructured interviews. Questions asked were in an open-ended manner. We acknowledge that certain information might have been withheld during the interviews due to security and confidentiality matters. The topics selected for interviews evolved around: how Fiji commenced with ICT projects; what we are doing now; what Fiji plans to do in the immediate future and much later; what are the approved structure/agency fully involved in the project and what are the possible hindrance, solutions and opportunities in this sector. The aim of the interviews was to extract information from interviewees about the process, their experiences, opinions and commitments towards the practicality of the process.

These topics allowed for the fulfilment of the reason for this study. The institutional reports, departmental documents, reports and submission targets, institution/ministerial correspondences, those that were made available wherever possible were examined on the ICT sector development in Fiji for actual intentions and effectiveness of ICT programs. Additionally, cabinet decisions, ministerial speeches and other related meaningful reports were sought to view the direction and commitment of the government towards the emerging sector. The secondary sources included journal articles, conference proceedings, newspapers and the internet. Both the published as well as the unpublished sources were referred to. Newspapers were merely used to track down more reliable information.

Data gathering from all relevant sources mentioned in references ceased at the end of June 2007. There may have been further developments or up-dates after this date.

3.4 THE MAKING OF THE ICT SECTOR

Fiji has slowly begun to realise that an increased use of ICT is vital for socio-economic development. Appendix 1 gives details on Fiji—country report. Stakeholders in Fiji clearly understand that ICT can contribute towards productivity improvements, especially in the public sector. The state has ensured that specific strategies and actions are contained in the National Strategic Development Plan to address this. Statistically, the communication sector reported an increase in its contribution to Fiji's GDP from 2.7 per cent of GDP in 1989 to 3.6 per cent by 2005; expectation remains around 3.5 per cent until 2008. Overall, while access to traditional ICT like radio and television is all time high, there is a rise in Internet usage.

The need for ICT development in Fiji is apparent. From a country perspective, it is important for Fiji to be at par with other nations. In so doing, it must engage in such developments. "ICT development could be thought of as a measure of the development of a culture in the scope of Globalisation." Fiji is a developing country and over the last 30 years or so, many businesses and academic institutions have been established. Furthermore, a greater portion of the populace is now focused on education. The combination of these factors has been the driving force behind ICT developments in Fiji. Fundamentally, with globalisation came improvement in ICT and its subsequent benefits.

An example of such a benefit is Quest, a regional call centre of the ANZ Banking Group based in Fiji. It provides state of art facilities and customer services to users of specific banking products and has become one of the premier employers of the country. In turn, it has attracted investment and recognition to the country as a whole. Fiji holds optimistic views on the development of the ICT industry, as a development tool for its economic growth. Government showed the earliest initiative towards ICT by establishing an ITC (Information Technology and Computing Services) department. Progress on further development has been slow and even stagnant at times but the year 1995 witnessed the introduction of Internet in Fiji which brought about many developments later. Major developments started with the connection to the Southern Cross Fiber Optic undersea cable. The Southern Cross Cable - a link to the world was somewhat a milestone in the history of Fiji's ICT.

In February 2002, the Cabinet SubCommittee on Investment (CSI) decided on the compilation of the ICT policy statement of specific strategies and actions to ensure the development of the sector. In June 2002, a two-day national

ICT strategy workshop was held. Later in January 2003, new members were appointed to the Information Technology Advisory Council (ITAC), after which the Ministry organised a workshop on the theme "Creating Information Economy for Fiji" with the objective of an early draft on the ICT Development Policy. Then in July 2003 an assessment of the Telecommunications, Post and Information Technology Sector was carried out by the World Bank Group. Issues raised in this assessment report are similar to those raised in the Strategic Development Plan (SDP) 2003–2005.

How did ICT development in Fiji take-off? There are many ways to answer this question. For starters, Fiji has a good strategic location, that is, it is the hub of the South Pacific. Fiji is somewhat the center of all trade in the Pacific. We also house the regional university in the Pacific (one of only two in the world). And many in Fiji are literate. Furthermore, there has been a marked increase in computer competency amongst the populace since the last decade. Unfortunately, while taking into account the fact that Fiji is a developing nation, there really has not been leaps and bounds progress in ICT sector in the past decade. A factor could be the sheer costs involved in exploiting such technology. For instance, "Fiji's mobile phone charges are among the highest in the world with the industry being monopolised" . Given this, for a country like Fiji which has a low wage rate and struggling labour market, this cost structure can be described as non-conducive for ICT development in general.

ICT development commenced with the automation of manual tasks - tasks which were time consuming and prone to errors. The actual process started with the advent of Analogue Voice Technologies with manual switch (board) operators. These electronic processes later became digitised, thus developing the local ITC even further. Specifically, the National ICT Development Policy identified the following applications as priorities:

- e-Filing of income tax
- Company office search/registration
- Drivers license
- Births, death & marriage registrations
- Immigration

These were particularly record keeping systems—systems which keep track of birth/death/marriage details and the immigration system which records flight details and passenger information and so forth. Keeping records in physical files is not practical any longer considering the volume of data that is involved with such applications, in view of the fact that data storage is just but one aspect. For efficient work practices, the stored data must allow easy retrieval and that too, with minimum delays. Also, the data needs to be updated with back-up for future use. Such factors gave rise to ITC development. Moreso, there is a move from the government to be citizen centric, that is, the plan is to take service to the citizens instead of asking citizens to make an effort to come to the service providers hence making things easier, convenient as well as cheaper for the public. There is, however, a process to all this. The process of ICT development commences with the identification of a need and the cost savings associated with ICT projects. Following the determination of the scope of the project, a blueprint is formulated. A team is then created to conduct a business analysis of the projects before the commencement of any development or design. At the macro level, though, there are many operational models suggested by various organisations, many of which involve a "lifecycle" approach. ICT development as a whole is a continuous process with new technologies and processes being developed. The trend remains the same with most technologies that are implemented.

The current Fiji Government is tapping into the potential niche industries like ICT industry in addition to the 'cash cow' industries of Fiji. To this end, much is owed to Fiji's connectivity to the Southern Cross Cable securing its chances to be promoted and marketed as an ICT destination abroad. Fiji boasts of a strong national ICT plan that is to unfold over the next 10 years. But, the liberalisation of the telecommunications sector must come sooner to allow for continuous development if such a plan is to materialise in the desired fashion. Further, government (in collaboration with other providers) needs to establish new units or restructure other services to monitor and support the non-formal sector.

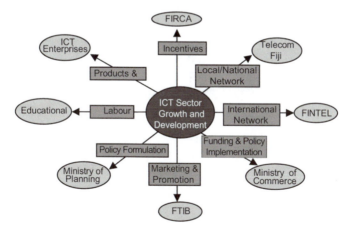

Fig. 3.1   The stakeholders and their roles in ICT sector development in Fiji
Source: *Narayan, Mala, & Naidu developed for this chapter*

The relevant ICT industry stakeholders as illustrated in Figure 3.1 have a crucial role to play. The arrows in the diagram represent the role of major stakeholders to the development of the ICT sector in Fiji. There are many factors that determine ICT development. The controlling agency in Fiji is the government. The Ministry of Information gives specific licenses for ICT related technologies. The Ministry of Commerce, Business Development & Investment (MCBDI) is responsible for the e- commerce program to inform, provide advice and to assist Fiji's Private Sector businesses to adopt e-commerce and increase competitiveness. ICT funding comes from the Ministry of Finance. This Ministry is responsible for setting developmental standards. ICT in turn looks after the IT infrastructure across government departments and ministries, and is responsible for local IT capacity building.

There are universal standards and bodies that govern aspects of ICT. Fiji (and the Pacific) has been adopting standards and technologies of the more developed countries, gaining from their successful experiences and knowledgebase. Normally, the Head Units/Offices based overseas implement new technology first, upon success, same is then transferred to their other branches in smaller countries. The model does become country specific to some extent as it depends on internal as well as factors outside our state.

ICT processes are ongoing and evolving. In particular, Fiji is trying to follow the e-citizen paradigm set by Singapore. It is engaging experts from China and Singapore to aid with the e-government plan—putting our services online. There is in place a National ICT Development Policy with the theme "e-Fiji, empowering our people." The document's policy aims to encourage, facilitate, and support development and growth of the ICT industry. While the policy is theoretical, the practical success is realised via an ICT Development Implementing Agency to ensure the implementation of the action plan leading to e-Fiji. Effectively, the concept entails two networks, intranet and extranet physically separated for security reasons. The intranet carries information concerned with national confidentiality and the governmental internal office automation, as such is not for public consumption. Whereas, extranet faces public directly, providing various e- government services to the public. Figure 3.2 illustrates this concept.

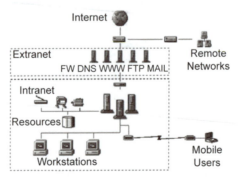

Fig. 3.2 IT Platform Intranet vs. Extranet

Source: *http://www.pcnet.idv.tw/pcnet/network/network_what_is.html*

The remaining key players are Data3—a Microsoft Partner residing in Australia, Fiji International Telecommunications Limited (FINTEL),

Amalgamated Telecom Holdings (ATH-TELECOM FIJI, CONNECT, TRANTEL, VODAFONE) UNWIRED, KIDANET, DIGICEL, Investors, private IT sectors and private sectors undertaking back office operations. Players outside Fiji are Australian Government, Japanese Government (Financial Aid), Cisco (initiatives for education), Australia and New Zealand ISPs/Telecoms. It is, as a matter of fact, the government's shares in strategic players and the oversight in early monopolistic licensing that has led to the loss or delay of developments in the ICT industry. A key strategic player, ATH has very heavily and is continuing to invest in the much needed infrastructure to enhance growth of ICT industry in Fiji.

Nonetheless, some progress is evident and cannot go unnoticed. The success of ICT programs is one such relevant factor when noting progress. The outcome of the projects or programs indicates how well the project had been implemented with respect to accomplishing set goals. Success, to a great extent is measured through cost savings. Basically, work processes should become more efficient, secure and reliable. Micro-business efficiency assessment involves fast, timely service (quick turnaround time associated with delivery of services to customers), cost cutting, sales output, customer acceptance, network traffic, increased profit, decreased cost of doing e-business, staff survey, customer survey and improved quality of life. It is also measured by the point of sale machines at supermarkets, resultant being better shopping experience for customers. Further, e-banking is making it easier to pay bills online and to access associated services online. Lack of awareness or lower usage rate in this area could be due to lack of education or a feeling of insecurity when using machines. Fiji's border control at the airports is also more efficient and secure. Exchange of information between departments within companies has become easier. So much so that we are now moving towards consolidating data so that it can be used as the single point of truth instead of having bits and pieces sitting with different departments.

The favourable macro-environment created generates more investment from abroad, increases economic growth and further enhances communication technologies. But this is still a new concept since full implementation is in process. The installation of the Southern Cross cable has introduced high speed and broadband Internet connection.

Schools are now introducing computing at lower secondary school levels. A number of ministries have information based websites. Introduction of mobile devices such as blackberry and mobile GPS systems has reached our shores. Citizens enjoy access to satellite television with Fiji TV and Pacific Broadcasting Services (PBS). Fiji has direct communication with the outside world with video conferencing and such. National ICT department is creating lots of improvements in the technological sector. Government is now thinking of implementing e-voting system. Essentially, while ICT in Fiji is still in its development phase, all these developments were unheard of, some years ago in Fiji. Fiji's ICT industry is definitely developing in the area of hardware suppliers and technical support services. It was the realisation of government that led to the set up of an ICT Park that instigated the importance ICT played in today's IT world and the benefits developing countries could foresee from IT parks.

Essentially, effective 1 January 2006 for a period of 7 years until 31 December 2012, approved new and existing ICT industries including Software Development and Call Centers will be provided the following tax incentive in the event of significant increase in capacity and the number of employees:

- 80% Income Tax exemption for business employing more than 101 employees
- 60% Income Tax exemption for business employing 60–100 employees
- 40% Income Tax exemption for business employing 10–59 employees

Further, the importation of computer equipment and accessories (hardware) will be exempted from fiscal and excise duty in an attempt to make these items more affordable and to facilitate growth in IT business and education in this discipline. Software attracts a low levy of 3 per cent. Ten year tax holidays are also available to companies operating in the temporary studio city zone. To date, government has signed off three studio city zones in Suva for Tele-Business Park to be set up within the zone. These are Kalabo Tax Free Zone (TFZ), ATH and University of the South Pacific (USP). More to this, the 2007 revised Budget makes available incentives to investors in Kalabo area whereby: the ICT business location must be in the kalabo ICT Economic Free Zone, employ more than hundred workers and where 60% of sales is exported. This speaks well on the commitment of current regime towards ICT development. BUT, overall, we are still way behind in terms of development. The good news is that it doesn't seem that far away. We have made some progress despite the common constraints.

Table 3.1 Rural telecommunications November 2003

Villages	Households	Population	Provided Access	Percentage
1,671	73,168	415,582	950	56.83
Division	Villages	Households	Population	Provided Access
Central	400	14,295	82,979	250
Eastern	274	6,936	37,02	189
Northern	428	17,835	109,465	213
Western	569	34,103	186,114	298

Source: *Ministry of Information, Communications and Media Relations, 2004:37*

It is true that the general public or majority of the population have no idea what ICT is and what it can do for us. This is due to the lack of information provided concerning ICT and also the level of education in this field. Also the way this industry is being handled in Fiji is not up to the standards it should have been.

A reality check on this industry in Fiji says that, it has not reached the level of success it should have compared to the amount of resources employed for its success. A look at the time and money spent on the resources signals that Fiji is still way behind than most of the developing countries around the world. Development is occurring but is rather slow and not at the speed at which most countries have developed. For one, Fiji is said to have the highest mobile rates in the world. But this is improving, given the recent entry of a competitor-Digicel. Comparatively, Tonga and Samoa have better mobile services than Fiji. While Vodafone Fiji proudly announces that it has attained about 25 per cent of the population as mobile users, they are silent on the fact that they do not have the capabilities to handle that much traffic. Second is the broadband connection in Fiji - the amount of money the public spends for the ISP services is way too high compared to the level of service provided by these sectors. The speed is too slow. The entire nation does not have the range to accommodate the signal. This results in signals being so weak that they advertise it as high speed internet yet it can be compared with dial up. It has been slow but is picking up pace. Progress is largely due to the growing need for access to information and communication using Internet. Undoubtedly, while the demand for ICT skills remains high, the problem is that of retention of highly skilled professionals. Awareness remains a knotty area. Generally, whatever developments and innovations eventuate in Fiji, are only known by people who are actually working in the industry. It cannot be denied that a proportion of Fiji's population do not get proper education. Because of this, they are also seriously computer illiterate. Many don't have access to internet. Still many do not have computers at home. With respect to education and training, computer literacy at pre-tertiary level is rather low, especially in rural areas due to very limited access to computers. Table 3.1 and Figure 3.3 illustrate these statistically.

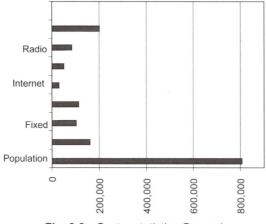

Fig. 3.3 Sector statistics General

Source: *Ministry of Information, Communications and Media Relations, 2004:34*

With the progress to-date, what have been witnessed overall are: the introduction of networked systems, serious computerisation of public and private services and higher speed Internet access. But progress is very much hindered by political upheavals and lack of resources in terms of both finance and labour. Skilled workers continue to leave for greener pastures. The monopoly status enjoyed by the ISP further hinders ICT growth. Now, given that competition is lacking, service providers enjoy profits at the expense of the public who have no choice but to accept services at higher prices, that is those who can afford such services. Lack of education as mentioned prior also hinders growth. Computer literacy has only increased recently but there still exists a vast gap. Funding is yet another of the bigger issues. Fiji as it is, as a nation is stringent on all expenses. Given the December 5 coup, assistance from some donors is also not forthcoming which aggravates resource availability. Other hinderances include problems associated with deregulation of the market, IT staff salary and poor public awareness on automated systems and services.

Even so, all is not at odds. Fiji did come up with the following objectives specific to telecommunications:

- To consolidate and amend the law relating to posts and telecommunications.
- To abolish the exclusive privilege of government regarding telecommunications.
- Constitute a new regulator, Telecommunications Authority of Fiji (TAF), providing for its operation, amends and consolidation of the law relating to telecommunications and radio communication.
- Transfer to TAF most of the functions at present conferred on the Minister as regulator and repeals and re-enacts with minor modifications as to language relevant provisions of the Posts and Telecommunications Decree 1989.

Communities such as schools, villages, government, public and private sector are required. Fiji Institute of Technology and the USP do offer various IT related training, yet, this is still insufficient compared to the demand for IT professionals. To fill this training gap, there are also a number of private sector firms which provide training but there is a need to establish quality of such training. Further, there are other technical institutes which provide specialised training in IT/IS and also run specific programs as per client specifications. Opportunities are many and do exist for and in this industry.

There will definitely be a huge demand for IT graduates in the years to come given the ICT projects lined up for the coming years. They might even command their desired salary. This will somewhat curtail IT 'brain-drain' as IT experts experience job satisfaction. Job opportunities created in this industry will lead to positive rippling effects on the economy - economic growth. Should international companies be willing to outsource part of their projects to Fiji, this will bring in revenue to the country instead of Fiji having to outsource most of its ICT projects as has been the case in the past years. With appropriate funding and skilled personnel, ICT can be developed in both public and private sectors in Fiji. New technologies should be explored to improve on the current ICT standards.

3.4 KEY FINDINGS

There is consensus between the interviewees on the 'age of ICT sector' in Fiji. All agree that, Fiji has progressed though in a slow fashion (due to mentioned constraints). Fiji has just but passed the infancy stage and remains 'green', it is yet to achieve much more. There is also agreement on the major constraints of high costs given the monopoly status of Telecom, lack of public awareness on the importance of this sector, difficulty in retaining highly qualified personnel, financial constraints (this is no surprise given the tight country budget Fiji is employing at present), political developments which affect donor country aids to Fiji, training schemes and costs of latest ICT mediums which are generally not that affordable to many especially in the rural areas. That being said, Fiji is still at the forefront of ICT development when compared to her regional neighbours and this is mainly due to the double blessings of being at a centrally ideal location and also having the Southern Cross cable and relatively good infrastructure at its disposal.

This research in particular focussed on the progress in Fiji's ICT industry until now. The preceding commentary indicates that Fiji has passed the infancy stage but remains very young in terms of general ICT development. Market is neither adequately deregulated nor completely efficient. However, the picture may vary within next seven to ten years if progress is kept at a steady flow and there are no disruptions, particularly socio-political disorder such as the coups Fiji has befallen. These unfortunate events set back technological development by a decade or more, based on its severity. Fiji's ICT sector still has a long way to go and there is a lot of catching up to do. The good news is that, like the previous government, the current regime is also showing its commitment towards this sector. So while we are behind many countries, we can still progress. However, the current constraints need to be handled effectively.

The government objectives on telecommunications are encouraging and signals towards further deregulation. In light of the constraints and the current status of Fiji, it is recommended that a private-public partnership be developed between the government and the private sector. Government through FTIB gives a number of incentives to the existing and the very new in this sector.

Conditions included in these incentives can be: companies to assist in general ICT public awareness in anyway they can. As good corporate citizen companies can be asked to run promotional programs in areas where ICT holds little understanding. Companies can also donate computers to schools and institutions as part of the corporate social responsibility (CSR) programmes. For companies that show interest in this respect, state can identify a number of schools particularly in the rural areas that need computers, in such a way that all schools at a certain point in time are equipped. There are certain large multinational companies as well as some NGOs and diplomatic corps which have been actively carrying this out and it is indeed a positive contribution towards the general development of the ICT industry.

Secondly, since highly qualified people have been leaving Fiji for greener pastures in droves, new students can be given scholarships to study IT in various educational institutes in Fiji after which they be bonded for a number of years and be requested to serve in rural schools with understudies. Still on the educational institutes—such institutes should work together with the Education Ministry and Labour Ministry to identify which degree programs lead to bloated graduates with poor employment prospects and those that Fiji really requires. Together, they can act to balance out student intake in such courses. For instance, there are often complains of excess graduates in the education degree who remain unemployed after graduating. At the same time, there are chronic shortages of IT personnel in different levels and sectors of the industry. The education degree can also be upgraded to incorporate IT knowledge. Fiji can also explore how it can best maximise from the dot com phenomenon as has been done by the government of Tuvalu which holds exclusive rights to the domain TV and this has been leased by them to various companies who pay millions of dollars a year to administer and sublease the domain. This is an example of how a Small Island Developing State (SIDS) in the region has exploited a niche area in this very dynamic and young industry.

Third, companies which now go online should run one-off awareness programs throughout Fiji as part of their CSR programmes. It is one thing to come up with an e-location which gives the general public some idea on a company's scope of work, it is entirely another issue whereby the users actually know how to use the e-site. Many types of interface should be made available online and the experience to the visitor must be maximised. Some companies, such as Fiji Water, Pure Fiji, Vodafone Fiji, etc... have invested a lot of time and money to ensure that their respective sites do this. It does not make sense to have an e-site where customers still have to visit the company premises for more information, to request and to fill out a number of forms. Instructions should also be simple for clear understanding. It is also noted that the senior citizens are not that comfortable while 'talking on or to machines', they are more at ease with human contact. But this is not something confined to only senior citizens of the region, it also afflicts many who fall in the Generation X category. It might be a little too ambitious but for Fiji to become e-Fiji, it should also take this group into account whereby, certain educational institutions can offer crash courses on the very basics of computers/use of internet only for this group. Once again, due to cost constraints on the state, this may require private, public and educational institute partnership. In this way the different parties share costs, resources and in turn also benefit from each other. Government can assist in terms of incentives offered to such institutes and the private sector while such sectors assist the government in moving the ICT sector forward.

What this will quintessentially attain over a sustained period is a highly versatile and technologically competent populace, where there is empowerment through knowledge and education via the mediums of the ICT industry. A succinct advantage of this would be holistically harmonious environment in which business and the state can mutually thrive. Another recommendation is that there is a need for more drive and investment in the ICT sector from all stakeholders in order to transform the current niche form status to one which can be a nationally realised sector - accessible to those who seek it. This could be facilitated via ICT parks (which is being advanced by the state and the private sector), tax concessions and incentives to companies which venture into this industry with strong CSR programmes aimed at expanding the sector.

Essentially, Fiji still has a fair way to go insofar as its fledgling ICT industry is concerned. It is important that ongoing research on similar topics be conducted to contribute to its progress. Such continual research will keep creating better understanding and enhance new knowledge as well as reflect on policies as Fiji gains maturity in ICT.

Organisation	Production Computers	Admin. Computers	Internet Computers	Computers 3+ Years old	Broken Computers
USP	1200	500	1000	300	20
Fiji TV	3	49	34	31	1
Archives	0	5	1	5	1
Museum	6	6	1	4	0

First, a similar analysis can be undertaken after seven or ten years to note progress—periodic research. Given that the sector of ICT is very much in the making, in seven to ten years time, the stance will be much different from its earlier state of affairs. Second, a comparative study can be undertaken between island nations. This will help uncover the approaches taken by different islands and help reveal complexities, similarities, differences etc. The scope of this kind of research may be too broad but can be narrowed down to observe specific elements such as the role of government in developing the sector.

Sincere acknowledgement is accorded to the following for their contribution towards the completion of this chapter:

- Faculty of Business & Economics Research Committee of University of the South Pacific for funding.

- All interviewees namely, Rajneil Raj - a Systems Analyst/Applications Architect at ITC Services - government; Ushneesh Yadav - a Research Assistant (Ministry of Reconciliation) at the Parliament of Fiji, Sandeep Chand—a Network Administrator at the Parliament of Fiji; Rishan Goundar—a Network and Computer Engineer with Exceed Pasifika; Ronal Nair—a Lecturer in Computing at APTECH and Ashneel Kamal Narayan—a Technical Manager at Kris Myer (Fiji) Limited. In addition to this list, one of the interviewees (Government employee) requested for anonymity. His wish is respected but we do acknowledge his contribution as well. The interviewees provided valuable information particularly in a pragmatic sense - what Fiji did, what it is doing in actuality compared to what it proposed towards the 'making of the ICT sector'.

- Research Assistant—Rajiv Naidu who later joined as a co-author of this chapter. We thank him for his complete and timely efforts towards collection of relevant data via internet and interviews.

APPENDIX 1. FIJI*: COUNTRY REPORT

A. COUNTRY INFORMATION	Population: 775,000
B. ICT EQUIPMENT	
Access to Internet Services	Access to the internet is less than 25% of the population at all access points. The exception is the office environment which is between 25 and 50% of the population
Connectivity	Telephone, Fax, e-mail, and WWW are used by all of the organisations greater than once a day. Audio-conferencing, video-conferencing, and V- SAT terminals are used greater than once a day by the University but used only occasionally by the other organisations. PEACESAT are never used. The University and the Fiji Museum use low speed data connections greater than once a day while the other organisations do not use them at all. The University also uses a high speed data connection greater than once a day. No organisations use LEOS satellites
Computers	

Organisation	Total staff	Staff Confident with ICT and Computers	Staff Recently Trained	Staff Learning Computer Skills on Job
USP	800	750	60	10
Fiji TV	65	65	0	65
Archives	19	10	3	3
Museum	22	17	0	15

Pages	Three of the four respondents to the survey—USP, Fiji Television, and the Fiji Museum—have a home page on the Internet
Staff Usage of Internet	USP, Fiji Television, and the Fiji Museum have more than 75% of their staff using e-mail in their work. USP also has more than 75% of staff using the internet. For Fiji Television and the Museum between 26% and 50% access the internet. Listserve, Usenet, Online Ordering, and Web Publishing are never used. The one exception is the University which has less than 10% of staff using these facilities
Internet Applications	USP: Websites are used for staff and student research. List servers are only used for specific staff and student groups. Fiji Television: Mostly news and current-affairs related sites.
Staff Training	

C: E-GOVERNANCE	
ICT Equipment and Services	No figures have been supplied.
E-Governance Applications	The Internet is used to provide a list of government agencies, national statistics, national events, regional events, and for the counting of election votes. The Museum also uses public access kiosks and allows ordering online
Government Initiatives	A seminar on E-Governance has been organized by the Ministry of Information in Suva
Government Websites	www.fiji.gov.fj is a government website offering general information
ICT Policy	fully implemented ICT policy, but respondents did not know if central Government had one.
Access to Government Services	rchives of Fiji advise that training of public officials takes place and that ICT is reinforced through training institutes and universities
Government Access	The following departments use faxes, e-mail, and the internet: Administrative, Economic Development, Education, Electoral, Foreign Affairs, Museums, and Police. All other departments use faxes and e-mail
Legislation	Fiji has some Copyright law in place
Inhibitors	The cost of Internet Services, slow connections, a lack of digitised government information, equipment costs, and the ownership of Telecom services have been cited as major inhibiting factors in the development of e- governance Other factors identified include a lack of political and staff awareness of the opportunities presented by e- governance
Barriers	The cost of equipment, ISPs, bandwidth, and the cost of domestic and international telecommunication have been cited as major barriers constraining the use of ICT in the organisations Other barriers identified include a reliable power supply, access to telephone networks, a lack of online resource material, and staff understanding as to the value of ICT
Development Plans	USP has a strategic IT development plan in place Fiji Television is planning to upgrade the company's ISP connection to a "dedicated link"' of 28.8 kbps The National Archives of Fiji have made a request to Government for funding for the automation of the national archives The Museum plans to link all computers to the internet instead of just the one (as is the current situation)

Source: *Zwimpfer Communications Ltd (2002: 51-54)*

References

1. Adriaanse, A. and Voordijk, H., Interorganizational communication and ICT in construction projects: a review using meta triangulation, http://www.emeraldinsight. com/Insight/viewPDF.jsp?contentTyp e=Article&Filename=html/Output/ Published/EmeraldFullTextArti cle/Pdf/3330050302.pdf, Construction Innovation: Information, Process, Management 5 (3): 159-177 (2005)

2. April, D., Information and communications technologies statistical overview: Defining the information and communication technology sector: Adoption of the OECD definition an d introducing the North American industry classification system, http://strategis.ic.gc.ca/infotech (1999).

3. Asian Development Bank (ADB), Information and communication technology for development in the Pacific: The role of information and communication technology (ICT) in fostering poverty reduction efforts and socioeconomic development in the Pacific region, ADB (2003).

4. Banuri, Asian Forum on ICT Policies and e-Strategies "Session 1 ICT, PRSPs, and MDGs" (No Date stated).

5. Chand, A., Leeming, D., Stork, E., Agassi, A. and Biliki, R., The impact of ICT on rural development in Solomon Islands: The PFNET case, Prepared for ICT capacity building at USP project, Mar. (2005).

6. Chand, S., Network Administrator, Parliament of Fiji, Personal Communication, 21 June (2007).

7. Doorne, S., Community integrated tourism development in the South Pacific, Prepared for the ICT capacity building at USP project, Sept. (2004)

8. Draft Pacific Islands Regional Information And Communication Technologies Policy, (No Date stated).

9. Engineering, Construction and Architectural Management 12 (1): 21-37 (2005).

10. Fiji Trades Investment Board (FTIB), IT Overview in Fiji, Unpublished paper (2004).

11. Fink, D. and Disterer, G., International case studies: To what extent is ICT infused into the operations of SMEs? http://www.emeraldinsight.com/Insight/ viewPDF.jsp?contentTyp e=Article&Filename=html/Output/Published/ EmeraldFullTextArti cle/Pdf/0880190603.pdf, Journal of Enterprise Information Management 19 (6): 608-624 (2006).

12. FTIB, Incentives for Investing in the Fiji Islands, www.ftib.org.fj (2007).

13. Galloway, L. and Mochrie, R., The use of ICT in rural firms: a policy-orientated literature review, http://www.emeraldinsight.com/Insight/ viewContentItem.do?con tentType=Article&contentId=1464974 Journal of Info 7 (3): 3346 (2005).

14. Giordano, T., Library co-operation on ICT in Italy: an overview . http://www.emeraldinsight.com/Insight/viewContentItem.do?con tentType=Article&contentId=862421 Electronic library and information systems 36 (3): 144-151 (2002).

15. Goundar, R., Engineer, Computer and Networking (TFL), Datec Training Center, Personal Communication, 6 May 2007.

16. ICT and Trade Development in the Pacific Islands Region: UN- ESCAP, Regional Summary, Nov. (2001).

17. IT Policies in Asia and the Pacific: Theory, Practice and Way Forward, Address by G.H.P.B. Van Der Linden, VicePresident, Knowledge Management and Sustainable Development, Asian Development Bank To Development Gateway Forum 2005, Beijing, "Information Technology and Collaborative Development", 17 Sept. (2005).

18. Journal of Educational Administration 41 (2): 158-170 (2003).

19. King, S., McMenemy, D. and Poulter, A., Effectiveness of ICT training for public library staff in the UK: Staff views, http://www.emeraldinsight.com/Insight/viewContentItem.do?con tentType=Article&contentId=15581 13.

20. Kokkonen, P. and Anja, T., The International Journal of Entrepreneurship and Innovation 8 (1): 44-52(9) (2007).

21. Lan, Y. and Unhelkar, B., Global enterprise transitions: Managing the process, US, UK: Idea Group Publishing (2005).

22. Martey, A., ICT in Distance   Education in Ghana. http://www.emeraldinsight. com/Insight/viewContentItem.do?con   tentType=Article&contentId=861479, Library Hi Tech News, 21(5): 16-18 (2004).

23. McKenzie, D.J., Youth, ICT Ministry of Information, Communications and Media Relations, ICTs and Development, (2004).

24. Mcmaster, J., Kato, M. and Khan, N., Economic impact of e- commerce on small tourism enterprises, Prepared for the ICT capacity building at USP project, Mar. (2004).

25. Minges and Gray, Bula internet: Fiji ICT case study, International telecommunication (2004).

26. Ministry of Information, Communications and Media Relations, Subregional symposium on ICT for development in Pacific Islands Developing Countries, Suva, 6-9 Dec. (2004).

27. Mistry and Rodrigues, E-Governance in the Pacific Islands: Entrenching Good Governance & Sustainable Development by Promoting ICT Strategies Based on The Right to Information, IIDS Conference on Governance and Development, 1-3 Dec., Suva: University of the South Pacific (2005).

28. Naidu and Jansen, Pacific Island Countries (No Date stated) Nair, R., Lecturer in Computing, Suva: APTECH, Personal Communication, 20 June (2007).

29. Narayan, A.K., Technical Manager, Kris Myer (Fiji) Limited, Personal Communication, 14 June (2007).

30. OECD, Annex 1B, OECD definition of the ICT sector, www.oecd.org/dataoecd/49/44/35930616.pdf, (2006, revised 2007).

31. Pacific Islands Forum Secretariat, Forum Information and Communications Technologies Ministers Meeting, Summary Outcomes (2006).

32. Pacific Islands Forum Secretariat, Pacific Plan Background Papers, (2005).

33. Pacific Islands Forum Secretariat, The Pacific Plan, For Strengthening Regional Cooperation and Integration (2005) Peansupap, V. and Walker, D., Factors affecting ICT diffusion: A case study of three large Australian construction

contractors, http://www.emeraldinsight.com/Insight/viewContentItem.do?contentType=Article&contentId=1465091.

34. Peansupap, V. and Walker, D.H.T., http://www.emeraldinsight.com/Insight/viewContentItem.do?con tentType=Article&contentId=1563216 Engineering, Construction and Architectural Management 13 (4): 364-379 (2006).

35. Rahiman & Naz, Digital Divide Within Society: An Account of Poverty, Community and E-Governance in Fiji (2005).

36. Raj, R., Systems Analyst/Applications Architect, ITC Services - Government, Personal Communication, 19 June (2007).

37. Robbins, C., Educational multimedia for the South Pacific: Research Report for the ICT capacity building at USP project entitled "Maximising the benefits of ICT/Multimedia in the South Pacific: Cultural pedagogy and usability factors," Prepared for ICT capacity building at USP, Aug. (2004).

38. Sarshar, M. and Isikdag, U., A survey of ICT use in the Turkish construction industry, http://www.emeraldinsight.com/Insight/viewContentItem.do?con tentType=Article&contentId=845834, Engineering, Construction and Architectural Management 11 (4): 238-247 2004).

39. Shiels, H., McIvor, R. and O'Reilly, D., Understanding the implications of ICT adoption: insights from SMEs, http://www.emeraldinsight.com/Insight/viewContentItem.do?con tentType=Article&contentId=852241 Logistics Information Management 16 (5): 312-326 (2003).

40. Siriwongworawat, S., Use of ICT in Thai libraries: An overview, http://www.emeraldinsight.com/Insight/viewContentItem.do?con tentType=Article&contentId=862435 Electronic Library and Information Systems 37 (1) :38-43 (2003).

41. Spacey, R., Goulding, A. and Murray, I., ICT and change in UK public libraries: does training matter? http://www.emeraldinsight.com/Insight/viewContentItem. do?con tentType=Article&contentId=859071 Library Management 24 (1/2): 61-69 (2003).

42. Strategic Development Plan (2003-2005).

43. Strategic Development Plan (2007-2011).

44. Teltscher, S., Asian Forum on ICT Policies and e-Strategies, "Session 2: Globalization and WTO: ICT, Trade and Competitiveness", DRAFT, United Nations Conference on Trade and Development The Electronic Library 24 (2): 265-276 (2006).

45. Wainwright, D., Green, G., Mitchell, E. and Yarrow, D., Towards a framework for benchmarking ICT practice, competence and performance in small firms, http://www.emeraldinsight.com/Insight/viewContentItem.do?con tentType=Article&contentId= 1465048 Performance Measurement and Metrics 6 (1): 39-52 (2005).

46. Williams, E., Digital community services: Pacific libraries and archives: Future prospects and responsibilities, A report, Sept. (2002).

47. Williams, E., Kato, M. and Khan, N., Evaluation of computer science curriculum: In Fiji secondary schools, Prepared for the ICT capacity building at USP project (2004).

48. World Bank, ICT at a glance, Fiji (2005).

49. Yadav, U., Research Assistant (Min. of Reconciliation), Parliament of Fiji, Personal Communication, 20 June (2007).

50. Yuen, A.H.K., Law, N. and Wong, K.C., ICT implementation and school leadership: Case studies of ICT integration in teaching and learning, http://www.emeraldinsight. com/Insight/viewContentItem.do?con tentType=Article&contentId=839261

51. Zwimpfer Communications Ltd, Internet Infrastructure and e- Governance in Pacific Islands Countries, A Survey on the Development and Use of the Internet (2002)

☺☹☹

Web Quality in IT Industry

Sarita Kanaujiya[1], Preeti Gusain[2], Neha Agarwal[3] and Soni Wadhwa[4]

The enhanced internet penetration and the increased usage of the facilities provided by the e-commerce websites, and thus generate the urge to find out the best amongst the options and the factors determining it. This chapter tries to explore the optimally performing e-commerce websites in the Indian context based on the evaluation parameters highlighted by WebQual. The issue of website quality is tackled from the perspective of 'Voice of the Customer'. In this chapter an online survey is administered through questionnaire with a sample of 60 respondents in Delhi & NCR, to examine the customers' satisfaction level involved with website quality that is influenced by a series of quality dimensions which hinder in delivering the best web quality in IT industry. To observe the questionnaire WEBQUAL instrument was used and response was taken to examine the different aspects associated with customer's satisfaction level. It is tested with the help of regression analysis.

KEYWORDS | Assurance | Empathy and Responsivenessd | IT Sector | Reliability | WEBQUAL

4.1 INTRODUCTION

Information technology is playing an important role in India today as it has changed the image from a slow growing economy to the place of innovative entrepreneurs.

The IT sector in India has opened up the opportunity of employment by 2.5 million. India is now one of the biggest IT capitals of the world.

4.1.1 Industry Segmentation

IT industry can be broadly classified into three sectors:

⤻ Software IT Services

⤻ IT enabled Services (ITeS)-BPO

[1,2,3,4] Maharaja Agrasen Institute of Technology, Delhi, India

◀ Present Industry Structure

The Indian IT industry comprises of well established firms as well as the emerging players that have just started up. The industry is fragmented yet concentrated. In terms of Small and Medium Enterprise (SMEs) and their offerings, they can be termed as fragmented. But, on the other hand, the leading players, their earnings and their offerings, the industry can be termed as concentrated.

The industry can be categorized as follows:

Tier I Players	Tier II Player	Offshore Golbal Service Provider
Pure Play BPO Providers	Captive BPO Units	Emergine Players

Tier I Players

The number of players in this category is very low (5-7).They account for almost 45 per cent of IT Services and 4-5 percent of BPO exports. These firms have increased their sales due to their strong management capabilities and Global Delivery Model (GDM). These factors have helped them to mark their presence globally. They have started new services like IT consulting, Research and Development (R & D), testing etc.

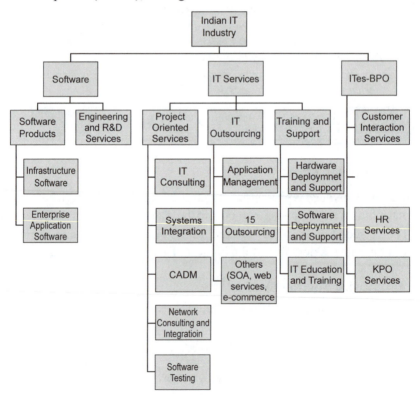

Fig. 4.1 Hierarchy of India IT Industry.

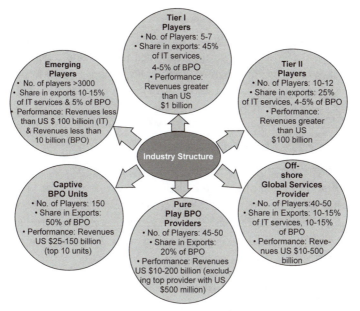

Fig. 4.2 Industry Structure.

Tier II Players

Their revenue is greater than US $ 100 billion. The number of player are low (10-12). They account for 25 per cent of IT services and 4-5 per cent of BPO exports. Due to limited number of clients and verticals, these players have registered a lower growth rate then the Tier I players.

Offshore Global Service Providers

This category has around 30-40 players who registered their sales revenue of US $ 10-500 billion. These players are recording inorganic growth through acquisitions in low cost destinations including India. But, due to complex local market conditions, they are facing challenges in integrating Indian operations.

Pure Play BPO Providers

The number of players in Pure Play BPO providers has hanged around 40-50. They account for around 20 per cent of BPO exports. These providers are facing serious challenges in terms of increasing customer expectations in quality and delivery of service.

Captive BPO Units

There are about 150 players in Captive BPO Units. They account for 50 per cent of BPO exports. They are also increasing their presence in Tier II cities, firstly for cost and resource considerations.

Emerging Players

The number of players which are emerging in this category is over 3000. They account for about 10-15 per cent of IT services exports and 5 per cent of BPO. These players are facing problems as they have limited access to markets.

4.2 ADVANTAGE INDIA

4.2.1 Technically Skilled Professionals

There is a huge reservoir of technically skilled manpower in India. This has been proved to be as one of the most critical success factors for IT sector. The main reason behind this growth is the demographic profile of India, where over 50 per cent of the population is below 25 years of age. The growing number of world class educational institutions along with the policy for educational loans, have geared the growth of the industry.

4.2.2 English Speaking Population

The medium of education in India is primarily English due to India's emigrant past and this has proved to be boon to the industry. After USA, India is the largest nation in the world in terms of English speaking population.

4.2.3 Robust Telecom Infrastructure

The telecom Industry in India is well established. The telecommunication network in India is the third largest network in the world and the second largest among the emerging notions in Asia. The availability of superior, robust and reliable telecom connectivity has added to the success of the whole industry in India.

4.2.4 Rendering Customized, End to End and Niche Services/Solutions

Indian firms have slowly graduated from giving customized solutions to the end services and also niche solutions/services, due to the increasing pervasiveness of IT and huge potential for earning foreign exchange.

4.2.5 Low Costs of Offshore Outsourcing

The first driver for off shoring to India was cost. But, India has proved to render quality services at affordable costs. According to off shoring to India results in saving 25-60 per cent base cost.

4.2.6 Favourable Government Policies

Entry barriers for foreign investors have been removed in India after the liberalization of Indian economy. Therefore, liberalized FDI policies, tax exemptions, basic infrastructure, subsidies etc. from the government has definitely provided a boost to the establishment of the IT industry in India.

4.2.7 Quality Orientation

Indian companies are certifying themselves with ISO 9001, Six Sigma, Just in Time, COPC certificate to attract foreign clients.

4.2.8 Established IT hubs in India

- Bangalore
- Hyderabad
- NCR-Delhi
- Kolkata
- Mumbai
- Pune
- Chennai

4.2.9 Emerging IT Hubs in India

Slowly and steadily the Tier 2 and Tier 3 cities are also emerging to become IT hubs. The major advantages which these cities provide are:

- Higher savings in administration
- Lower infrastructural costs
- Large pool of talents in the form of skilled professionals

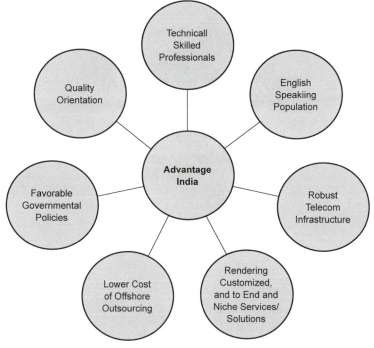

Fig. 4.3 India's competitive advantage.

Fig. 4.4   Established IT Hubs In India.

Fig. 4.5   Emerging IT Hubs In India.

4.3 WEBSITE QUALITY

"WebQual is an instrument for assessing the usability, information, and service interaction quality of Internet web-sites, particularly those offering e-commerce facilities" To identify and check the website quality provided by the company WebQual is used with respect to the customer's satisfaction level. The five dimensions of QUALITY are:

- ◁ Tangibility: includes physical facilities, equipment, personnel and communication materials.
- ◁ Reliability: is the ability to work dependably and accurately for the promised services.
- ◁ Responsiveness: is willingness on the part of service providers for helping the customers and providing service.
- ◁ Assurance: is employee's knowledge, courtesy and ability to convey trust and confidence.
- ◁ Empathy: is giving attention to the individual customers.

4.3.1 Objectives of the Study

The objective of the research done for the company was to know about the website quality provided by Pintwire Infomatics to their customers. Moreover the secondary aim was also to find out the quality of the website service provided by the company over some pre-setted parameters by getting response from the customers who are currently using Pintwire's website service. However, if looked into the questionnaire the purpose of finding out the website quality provided by Pintwire Infomatics was a quite successful exercise.

4.4 RESEARCH METHODOLOGY

The questionnaire was administrated using WebQual instrument. The design used for the study is descriptive under conclusive design. It is a quantitative design where the defined hypothesis is tested on the basis of primary data which is collected with the help of a structured tool called questionnaire.

The study was done with a sample size of 60 respondents. The respondents were selected for the study from the various customers of Pintwire Infomatics. A random sampling was taken.

The research instrument or tool used for the preparation of this project is Questionnaire. A questionnaire consists of a list of questions printed in a definite order on a form to be asked from respondent.

4.4.1 Data Collection

The approach used for the data collection is Survey Method.

There are two sources of data collection:

- ◁ Primary Data: Data collected for the purpose of this project is through:
- ◁ Observations
- ◁ Survey through Questionnaire

✦ Secondary Data: Secondary data collected through:

✦ Websites

✦ Books

4.4.2 Hypothesis

✦ Hypothesis is a supposition or proposed explanation made on the basis of limited evidence as a starting point for further investigation.

✦ It is a proposition made as a basis for reasoning, without any assumption of its truth.

✦ The hypothesis for this study is constructed below on the basis of dimensions of quality:

H_1	Customers perceived 'Reliability' of website of Pintwire Infomatics leads to customer satisfaction.
H_2	Customers perceived 'Performance' of website of Pintwire Infomatics leads to customer satisfaction.
H_3	Customers perceived 'Responsiveness' of website of Pintwire Infomatics leads to customer satisfaction.
H_4	Customers perceived 'Durability' of website of Pintwire Infomatics leads to customer satisfaction.
H_5	Customers perceived 'Features' of website of Pintwire Infomatics leads to customer satisfaction.

4.4.3 Analysis

Table 4.1 showing the regression analysis among customer satisfaction through responsiveness, reliability, empathy & assurance. to examine the relationship between these variables (responsiveness, reliability, empathy, assurance) multiple regression has been run.

Table 4.1 Regression analysis of customer satisfaction through responsiveness, reliability, empathy & assurance

	Model 1	Model 2	Model 3	Model 4
Responsiveness	0.812*	−0.111	−0.056	−0.070*
	0.082	0.169	0.099	0.031
Reliability		0.996*	−0.232	0.039
		0.171	0.189	0.061
Empathy			1.265*	−0.104
			0.165	0.099
Assurance				1.132*
				0.069

Note: Here * denotes the value of p is level.
less than 0.05 which represents the significance

Dimension–Responsiveness (Model 1)

Model 1 shows the relationship between customer satisfaction and responsiveness. Here the value of p is less than 0.05. Hence, responsiveness is significant to the customer satisfaction. It implies that customer satisfaction is achieved through responsiveness.

Dimension–Reliability (Model 2)

Model 2 shows the relationship between responsiveness and reliability through customer satisfaction which implies that when customer satisfaction is measured then only reliability is satisfying the customers. Here in the Table 4.2 the value of p in reliability is less than 0.05. Hence, it means only reliability is significant and responsiveness is insignificant to the customer satisfaction.

Table 4.2 R square

	Model 1	Model 2	Model 3	Model 4
R Square	0.75	0.88	0.96	0.99

Dimension–Empathy (Model 3)

This model examines the relationship between responsiveness, reliability and empathy. It implies that when responsiveness, reliability & empathy are measured through customer satisfaction then only empathy is satisfying the customers. Here the value of p in empathy is less than 0.05. Hence, it means that only empathy is significant and responsiveness, reliability is insignificant with respect to the customer satisfaction.

Dimension–Assurance (Model 4)

This model examines the relationship between responsiveness, reliability, empathy and assurance. It implies that when responsiveness, reliability, empathy and assurance is measured through customer satisfaction then only two variables responsiveness & assurance are satisfying the customers. Here the value of p in responsiveness and assurance are less than 0.05. Hence, it means that only responsiveness and assurance are significant to the customer satisfaction. However responsiveness & reliability are insignificant with respect to the customer satisfaction.

From all the above analysis we conclude that responsiveness and assurance is the two main predictor of the customer satisfaction with respect to the website quality of Pintwire Infomatics Pvt. Ltd.

4.5 LIMITATIONS OF THE STUDY

- ◁ The very first limitation of this study is the small sample size because it was provided by the company itself.
- ◁ The second limitation of this study is that the sample size is confined to Delhi & NCR.
- ◁ The results of this study cannot be generalized because the samples were heterogeneous in nature and this can be also stated as a limitation for this study.
- ◁ The next limitation is the time constraint because the duration of training was short, due to which it was difficult to collect data.
- ◁ Another limitation has been the cost, as it involves the collection of primary and secondary data, therefore the cost incurred was much more.
- ◁ Sometimes customers don't used to share the true information because of ignorance and their busy schedule.

Finally, winding up this chapter, we conclude that customers are the most important asset of any organization. The success of any organization ultimately depends on how efficient and effectively its customer is being satisfied. Therefore the main aim of the organization must be to satisfy its customers for longer time duration. In this study I found that Responsiveness and Assurance are fully satisfying the customers but rest of the parameters are not satisfying the customers. So the other parameters such as Reliability & Empathy need to be improved in order to satisfy the customers. Moreover it would improve reputation of the company, retain the current customers and bring new customers. Broaden their outlook, capacity and potential with the effective utilization of website quality.

We would like to thank Ms. Nitika Sharma, Assistant Professor, Department of Management for her constant enthusiastic encouragement and valuable suggestions without which this chapter would not been successfully completed.

We would also like to thank our classmates who were ready with positive comments all the time, whether it was an off-hand comment to encourage us or a constructive piece of criticism and a special thank to the faculty of Maharaja Agrasen Institute of Technology who arranged a good environment for us.

References

1. Available from: http://www.webqual.co.uk
2. Available from: http://www.pintwire.com
3. Available from: http://www.pintwire.co.in

☺☻☹

IT Deployment in Banks through DEA

Sanjay Dhingra[1]

This chapter evaluates the efficiency of IT deployment of Public sector banks (PSBs) in India for the period 2003 to 2009 using a technique known as Data envelopment analysis (DEA). DEA technique is a non-parametric method used for evaluating the relative efficiency of similar units like banks. The input variables selected for DEA are computerization expenditure to operating expenditure, fully computerized branches to total branches, number of ATMs, PCs per employee, core banking branches to fully computerized branches, while the output variables chosen are business per employee, business per branch and operating profits per employee. The CCR model with output orientation and BCC model with output orientation have been applied separately on the same data to calculate the efficiency of each bank. Results indicate that average technical efficiency of IT deployment of PSBs has gradually improved during the study period. It has also been observed that banks have considerably improved their scale efficiency over the same period.

KEYWORDS   Data Envelopment Analysis | Public Sector Banks | Technical Efficiency | Scale Efficiency

5.1 INTRODUCTION

In tune with global trends and practices, IT innovations in the last few years have changed the landscape of banks in India. Banks in India too started perceiving information technology as a crucial component to achieve strategic and operational goals. Today, information technology seems to be the prime mover of all banking transactions. Trends show that banks in India have been endeavoring to leverage technology to bring about improvements in; quality of customer services, scale and specialization in products, alternative sources of income particularly from fee-based services, geographical reach through communication networks and electronic delivery channels, risk management practices, housekeeping, internal control systems and regulatory compliance, cost efficiencies, and scale economies. To achieve the improvement, banks have taken several technological initiatives such as telebanking, mobile

---

[1] University School of Management Studies, G. G. S. Indraprastha University, Delhi, India

banking, net banking, Automated Teller Machines (ATMs), credit cards, debit cards, smart cards, Customer Relationship Management (CRM) software, electronic payment systems, data warehousing and data mining solutions, which have totally transformed the banking industry. An indication of the extent of investment and percolation of IT in different categories of banks is evident from the data presented in Table 5.1.

Table 5.1   IT percolation in banks in India (as on March 2009)[6]

Parameter	Nationalized banks	State bank group	Old private sector banks	New private sector banks	Foreign banks
Banks	19	07	15	08	31
Branches	39,376	16,062	4,673	4,204	293
ATMs	15,938	11,339	2,674	12,646	1,054
ATMs per branch	0.40	0.71	0.57	3.0	3.6
Fully computerized branches (%)	92.9	100	—	100	100
IT expenditure (in crores incurred between September 1999 and March 2009)	11,802	6,095	—	—	—

It is clear from Table 5.1 that banks have invested heavily over the years in IT systems. Looking the dependence of banks on IT, there is no doubt that, IT over the years has become business driver rather than a business enabler.

IT is considered to be an important tool in improving the efficiency of banks, therefore this chapter evaluates the efficiency of IT deployment of Public Sector Banks (PSBs) in India for the period 2003 to 2009. The period 2003 to 2009 is selected as most of computerization of the banks has happened in this period only. The public sector banks have been selected for the study due to the dominant position enjoyed by these banks and their contribution towards socio-economic development of the country. The efficiency of banks has been calculated using the CCR and BCC models of DEA technique.

5.2 DATA ENVELOPMENT ANALYSIS

Charnes et al. first proposed DEA as an evaluation tool to measure and compare the DMU's productivity. After that this tool has been extensively used in banking and other areas to measure the DMU's relative productivity. Data Envelopment Analysis is an approach of comparing the efficiency of organizational units such as bank branches, schools, hospitals and other similar instances where there is a relatively homogenous set of units. The analysis will measure output(s) achieved from the input(s) provided and will compare the group of DMUs by their strength in turning input into output. At the end of analysis, the DEA will be able to say which units are (relatively) efficient and which are (relatively) inefficient.

It is a method for mathematically comparing different Decision-Making Units' (DMUs) productivity based on multiple inputs and outputs. The ratio of weighted inputs and outputs produces a single measure of productivity called relative efficiency. DMUs that have a ratio of 1 are referred to as efficient, given the required inputs and produced outputs. The units that have a ratio less then 1 are less-efficient relative to the more efficient unit(s). Because the weights for input and output variables of DMU are computed to maximize the ratio and are compared with similar ratios of best performing DMUs hence the measured productivity is referred as relative efficiency.

5.2.1 DEA Model Selection

One of the basic choices in selecting a DEA model is to decide, whether to use an input-orientation or an output-orientation. The difference is subtle but important and can typically be best understood by considering whether a DMU emphasize on reducing inputs while achieving the same level of output or emphasize on producing more output given the same level of input.

DEA offers three possible orientations in efficiency analysis:

- Input-oriented models are models, where DMUs are deemed to produce a given amount of output with the smallest possible amount of input.
- Output-oriented models are models, where DMUs are deemed to produce the highest possible amount of output with the given amount of input.
- Base-oriented models are models, where DMUs are deemed to produce the optimal mix of input and output.

Return to Scale

Return to scale refers to increasing or decreasing efficiency based on size. For example, a manufacturer can achieve certain economies of scale by producing thousand integrated circuits at a time rather than one at a time. It might be only 100 times as hard as producing one at a time. This is an example of Increasing Returns to Scale (IRS).

On the other hand, the manufacturer might find it more than trillion times difficult to produce a trillion integrated circuits at a time because of storage problems and limitations on the worldwide silicon supply. This range of production illustrates Decreasing Returns to Scale (DRS). Combining the extreme two ranges would necessitate Variable Returns to Scale (VRS).

Constant Return to Scale (CRS) means that the producers are able to linearly scale the inputs and outputs without increasing or decreasing efficiency.

This is a significant assumption. The assumption of CRS may be valid over limited ranges but its use must be justified. But, CRS efficiency scores will never be higher than that of VRS efficiency scores. In a CRS model, the input-oriented efficiency score is exactly equal to the inverse of the output-oriented efficiency score. This is not necessarily true for inefficient DMUs in the case of Variable Return to Scale (VRS) assumption. The CRS version is more restrictive than the VRS and yields usually a fewer number of efficient units and also lower efficient score among all DMUs. In DEA literature, the CRS model is typically referred to as the CCR model after the seminal publication, by Charnes et al.

The CCR Model of DEA

DEA is a linear programming based technique for measuring relative performance of DMUs. CCR model, which was initially proposed by Charnes et al., can be represented as a fractional linear programming problem:

$$E_o = \frac{u_1 y_{1o} + u_2 y_{2o} + \cdots u_s y_{so}}{v_1 x_{1o} + v_2 x_{2o} + \cdots v_m x_{mo}}$$

Subject to

$$\frac{u_1 y_{1j} + u_2 y_{2j} + \cdots u_s y_{sj}}{v_1 x_{1j} + v_2 x_{2j} + \cdots v_m x_{mj}} \le 1 \ (j = 1, ..., n)$$

$$v_2, x_2 \cdots v_m \ge 0$$

$$u_1, u_2 \cdots u_s \ge 0$$

where E_o = the efficiency of the oth DMU,

y_{so} = s^{th} output of oth DMU,

u_s = weight of sth output

x_{mo} = m^{th} input of the oth DMU

v_m = weight of mth input

Here the DMUj to be evaluated on any trial be designed as DMUo where o ranges over 1,2, ..., n.

The constraints meant that the ratio of "virtual output" to "virtual input" should not exceed 1 for every DMU. The above fractional program can be replaced by the following linear program:

Maximize $E_o = u_1 y_{1o} + v_2 x_{2o}. + ... + u_s y_{so}$

Subject to $v_1 x_{1o} + v_2 x_{2o} + ... + v_m x_{mo} = 1$

$u_1 y_{1j} + u_2 y_{2j} + ... + u_s y_{sj} \le v_1 x_{1j} + v_2 x_{2j} + ... + v_m x_{mj} \ (j = 1, ..., n)$

$v_1 v_2 .... v_m \ge 0$

$u_1 u_2 .... u_s \ge 0$

The DEA model is a fractional linear program but may be converted into linear form in a straight forward manner by normalizing either the numerator or the denominator of the fractional program objective function, so that the methods of linear programming can be applied. The weighted sum of the inputs is constrained to be unity in the linear program. As the objective function is the weighted sum of outputs that has to be maximized, this formulation is referred to as the output maximization DEA program.

In the model the weights are treated as unknown. They can be obtained by solving the fractional programming problem to obtain values for the input weights (v_i) $(i = 1, ..., m)$ and the output weights $(u_r)(r = 1, ..., s)$. The value obtained of these weights will maximize the efficiency of the oth target unit.

The BCC Model of DEA

Banker et al. published the BCC model whose production possibility set PB is defined by:

$$P_B = \{(x, y) \mid x \geq X\lambda, y \leq Y\lambda, e\lambda = 1, \lambda \geq 0\}$$

where, $X = (x_j) \in R^{m*n}$ and $Y = (y_j) \in R^{s*n}$ are a given data set, $\lambda \in R_n$ and e is a row vector with all elements equal to 1. The BCC model differs from the CCR model only in the adjunction of the condition $e\lambda = \sum_{j=1}^{n} \lambda_j = 1$. Together with the condition $\lambda_j \geq 0$, for all j, this imposes a convexity condition on allowable ways in which the n DMUs may be combined.

The output-oriented BCC model can be written as

Max. η_B
Subject to $X\lambda \leq x_o$
$\eta_B y_o - Y\lambda \leq 0$
$e\lambda = 1$
$\lambda \geq 1$

This is the envelopment form of the output-oriented BCC model.

5.3 RESEARCH METHODOLOGY

In order to find the efficiency of IT deployment, the required data for the study period on input variables i.e. computerization expenditure to operating expenditure, fully computerized branches to total branches, number of ATMs, PCs per employee, core banking branches to fully computerized branches and output variables i.e. business per employee, business per branch and operating profits per employee required for applying DEA technique has been compiled from secondary sources such as RBI trend and progress reports from 2003 to 2009 and Prowess database, a corporate database developed by Center for Monitoring of Indian Economy (CMIE). The Punjab and Sind Bank has been excluded from the study on account of very low investment in information technology. Expenditure made by the bank on computerization between September 1999 and March 2009 is just '69 crores, which is the minimum expenditure incurred by any of the public sector bank. IDBI has been excluded because it became public sector bank in the year 200405 and hence its data was not comparable with other public sector banks. Production approach is being used for choosing the input and output variables. The production approach considers the efficiency, with which inputs (physical variables such as manpower, ATMs, IT expenditure etc) are converted into outputs. DEA-Solver software has been used to solve linear programming model.

In the application of DEA, inadequacy of data or sample size may impair results. The DEA is said to be computationally more convenient when the number of DMUs are larger than the total number of inputs and outputs by at least three times. In the present study, 26 PSBs have been selected which are more than three times that of number of inputs and outputs. The data for the period 2003 to 2009 is being considered for the study, as this was the transformation phase for the public sector banks in terms of IT deployment. Most of the computerization like full computerization of branches, core banking, and ATMs deployment has happened during this period only. On each year of data, CCR output-oriented model (output maximization) and BCC output-oriented model (output maximization) have been applied. Efficiency scores between 0 and 1 have been obtained for every bank, for the each year. The average efficiency of all the banks for each year has been computed.

5.4 RESULTS

The technical efficiency, management efficiency and scale efficiency obtained by applying CCR model and BCC model of DEA technique are summarized in Table 5.2, Table 5.3 and Table 5.4 respectively.

Table 5.2 DEA efficiency score of banks with CCR output orientation model

DMU	Eff03	Eff04	Eff05	Eff06	Eff07	Eff08	Eff09
Allahabad Bank	1.00	1.00	1.00	1.00	1.00	1.00	1.00
Andhra Bank	0.55	0.56	0.63	0.57	0.75	0.81	0.71
Bank of Baroda	1.00	1.00	0.82	1.00	1.00	1.00	1.00
Bank of India	1.00	1.00	1.00	1.00	1.00	1.00	1.00
Bank of Maharashtra	0.73	0.93	1.00	0.54	0.58	0.68	0.75
Canara Bank	0.77	0.89	1.00	1.00	1.00	1.00	1.00
Central Bank of India	0.89	1.00	1.00	0.80	0.81	0.71	1.00
Corporation Bank	0.46	0.46	0.71	0.73	0.85	1.00	1.00
Dena Bank	0.54	0.56	0.52	0.83	1.00	1.00	0.85
Indian Bank	0.56	0.60	0.56	0.61	0.80	0.82	0.82
Indian Overseas Bank	0.92	1.00	1.00	1.00	1.00	1.00	1.00
Oriental Bank of Commerce	1.00	1.00	1.00	1.00	1.00	1.00	1.00
State Bank of India	1.00	0.99	1.00	0.78	0.79	0.84	0.92
State Bank of Bikaner & Jaipur	0.60	0.50	0.50	0.55	0.72	0.66	0.68

State Bank of Hyderabad	0.80	0.85	0.75	0.79	1.00	0.87	0.93
State Bank of Indore	1.00	1.00	0.83	0.82	1.00	1.00	1.00
State Bank of Mysore	1.00	0.62	0.63	0.70	0.83	0.91	0.88
State Bank of Patiala	0.69	0.77	0.74	0.92	1.00	1.00	1.00
State Bank of Saurashtra	1.00	0.84	0.89	0.75	0.89	0.97	*
State Bank of Travancore	0.85	0.75	0.94	0.95	1.00	1.00	1.00
Punjab National Bank	1.00	0.99	1.00	0.74	0.90	0.78	0.79
Syndicate Bank	1.00	1.00	1.00	1.00	0.59	0.78	0.71
UCO Bank	1.00	1.00	1.00	1.00	1.00	1.00	1.00
Union Bank of India	1.00	1.00	1.00	1.00	1.00	0.97	0.83
United Bank of India	1.00	0.99	1.00	1.00	1.00	1.00	0.91
Vijaya Bank	0.74	1.00	1.00	1.00	1.00	0.91	0.88
Average	0.85	0.86	0.87	0.85	0.90	0.91	0.91

Notes: * State Bank of Saurashtra was merged with State Bank of India in year 2008-09
1. Eff03 to Eff09 represents the technical efficiency for each year for the period 2003 to 2009.

Table 5.3 DEA efficiency score of banks with BCC output orientation model

DMU	Eff03	Eff04	Eff05	Eff06	Eff07	Eff08	Eff09
Allahabad Bank	1.00	1.00	1.00	1.00	1.00	1.00	1.00
Andhra Bank	0.67	0.75	1.00	0.83	0.92	0.83	0.72
Bank of Baroda	1.00	1.00	1.00	1.00	1.00	1.00	1.00
Bank of India	1.00	1.00	1.00	1.00	1.00	1.00	1.00
Bank of Maharashtra	0.74	0.94	1.00	0.79	0.81	0.79	0.80
Canara Bank	1.00	1.00	1.00	1.00	1.00	1.00	1.00
Central Bank of India	0.98	1.00	1.00	1.00	1.00	1.00	1.00
Corporation Bank	1.00	0.96	1.00	1.00	1.00	1.00	1.00
Dena Bank	0.71	0.72	0.97	1.00	1.00	1.00	0.96
Indian Bank	0.63	0.73	0.84	0.74	0.90	0.85	0.82
Indian Overseas Bank	0.92	1.00	1.00	1.00	1.00	1.00	1.00
Oriental Bank of Commerce	1.00	1.00	1.00	1.00	1.00	1.00	1.00
State Bank of India	1.00	1.00	1.00	0.90	0.83	0.85	0.96
State Bank of Bikaner & Jaipur	0.69	0.50	0.84	0.59	0.82	0.68	0.69
State Bank of Hyderabad	0.81	0.85	0.96	0.84	1.00	0.87	0.93
State Bank of Indore	1.00	1.00	0.92	0.98	1.00	1.00	1.00
State Bank of Mysore	1.00	0.62	0.79	0.80	0.85	0.91	0.88
State Bank of Patiala	0.83	0.85	1.00	1.00	1.00	1.00	1.00
State Bank of Saurashtra	1.00	0.84	0.93	0.84	0.89	0.98	*
State Bank of Travancore	0.91	0.94	1.00	0.99	1.00	1.00	1.00
Punjab National Bank	1.00	1.00	1.00	0.74	0.90	0.78	0.79
Syndicate Bank	1.00	1.00	1.00	1.00	0.76	0.78	0.74
UCO Bank	1.00	1.00	1.00	1.00	1.00	1.00	1.00
Union Bank of India	1.00	1.00	1.00	1.00	1.00	1.00	0.83
United Bank of India	1.00	1.00	1.00	1.00	1.00	1.00	1.00
Vijaya Bank	0.99	1.00	1.00	1.00	1.00	0.96	0.93
Average	0.92	0.91	0.97	0.92	0.95	0.93	0.92

Notes: * State Bank of Saurashtra was merged with State Bank of India in year 2008-09
1. Eff03 to Eff09 represents the pure technical efficiency for each year for the period 2003 to 2009.

5.4.1 Outcome of CCR Output Orientation Model

CCR model works on CRS assumption. It assumes that all the DMUs are operating at optimal scale. CCR model output results in measure of efficiency, called Technical Efficiency (TE), which is affected by Scale Efficiencies (SE). Therefore results of CCR model reflect the overall efficiency of banks. The BCC model assumes VRS specification, permits the calculation of TE, without the SE effects. TE obtained from BCC model, without the SE effect is known as pure technical efficiency.

Table 5.4 Scale inefficiency in percentage

DMU	Ineff03	Ineff04	Ineff05	Ineff06	Ineff07	Ineff08	Ineff09
Allahabad Bank	0.00	0.00	0.00	0.00	0.00	0.00	0.00
Andhra Bank	18.45	25.63	37.13	30.51	18.54	2.50	0.97
Bank of Baroda	0.00	0.00	18.19	0.00	0.00	0.00	0.00
Bank of India	0.00	0.00	0.00	0.00	0.00	0.00	0.00
Bank of Maharashtra	0.49	0.89	0.00	31.45	27.79	14.32	5.85
Canara Bank	23.15	11.00	0.50	0.00	0.00	0.00	0.00
Central Bank of India	8.40	0.00	0.00	20.10	19.00	28.99	0.00
Corporation Bank	54.03	51.96	29.34	27.27	14.73	0.00	0.00
Dena Bank	23.44	21.87	47.12	17.04	0.00	0.00	11.14
Indian Bank	11.37	17.95	32.90	18.13	10.62	3.47	0.00
Indian Overseas Bank	0.02	0.00	0.00	0.00	0.00	0.00	0.00
Oriental Bank of Commerce	0.00	0.00	0.00	0.00	0.00	0.00	0.00
State Bank of India	0.00	1.12	0.00	13.51	5.18	0.26	4.22
State Bank of Bikaner & Jaipur	13.60	0.66	39.73	7.69	12.34	2.38	0.86
State Bank of Hyderabad	1.20	0.31	22.26	6.51	0.00	0.12	0.70
State Bank of Indore	0.00	0.00	9.33	16.02	0.00	0.00	0.00
State Bank of Mysore	0.00	0.67	20.75	12.79	2.32	0.37	0.17
State Bank of Patiala	16.71	9.48	26.49	8.49	0.00	0.00	0.00
State Bank of Saurashtra	0.00	0.25	4.54	10.01	0.17	0.64	*
State Bank of Travancore	6.81	20.42	5.88	3.86	0.00	0.00	0.00
Punjab National Bank	0.00	1.20	0.00	1.04	0.02	0.31	0.08
Syndicate Bank	0.00	0.00	0.00	0.00	22.44	0.01	4.43
UCO Bank	0.00	0.00	0.00	0.00	0.00	0.00	0.00
Union Bank of India	0.00	0.00	0.00	0.00	0.00	2.75	0.00
United Bank of India	0.00	1.08	0.00	0.00	0.00	0.00	8.53
Vijaya Bank	24.43	0.00	0.00	0.00	0.00	4.96	5.64
Average	7.77	6.33	11.31	8.63	5.12	2.35	1.70

Notes: * State Bank of Saurashtra was merged with State Bank of India in year 2008-09 1.
Ineff03 to Ineff09 represents the scale inefficiency for each year for the period 2003 to 2009.

CCR output oriented model is applied on each year of data for the period between 2003 and 2009 using the selected input and output variables. The results of the model are presented in the Table 5.2.

From the Table 5.2, which represents output of CCR model with output orientation, it is clear that average IT efficiency of the banks has improved from 0.85 in year 2003 to 0.91 in the year 2009. This means, that average inefficiency of the public sector banks have decreased from 15 percent to 9 percent during the period. Also lowest relative efficiency score of 0.46, which has been achieved by a bank in year 2003 improved to 0.68 in the year 2009. This shows that technical efficiency of PSBs has improved with the deployment of IT over a period of time. This also suggests that, by adopting best practices, PSBs can, on an average further increase their output of business per employee, business per branch and operating profits per employee by at least 9 percent keeping the same level of inputs.

5.4.2 Outcome of BCC Output Orientation Model

In order to find scale inefficiency, management inefficiency or pure technical inefficiency the BCC model has been applied. Pure technical inefficiency (obtained from BCC model) i.e. technical inefficiency devoid of scale effects, is totally under the control of management and results directly due to management errors. Thus it is also called management inefficiency. It occurs when more of each input is used, than is required to produce a given level of output. BCC output oriented model is applied on each year of data for the period between 2003 and 2009 using the selected input and output variables. The performance of DMUs is summarized in Table 5.3.

From the Table 3, which represents output of BCC model with output orientation, it is clear that average IT efficiency of the banks remained more or less same during the period 2003 to 2009 i.e. 0.92. This implies an inefficiency of 8 percent in handing the IT inputs. Allahabad Bank, Bank of Baroda, Bank of India, Canara Bank, Indian Overseas Bank, Oriental Bank of Commerce, UCO Bank and United Bank of India are found to be efficient through out the study period. This indicates that these banks have used their IT resources optimally through out the study period. The results of CCR model reported above, shows an improvement in average IT efficiency (technical efficiency) from 0.85 to 0.91 during the study period, while BCC model results reported that average IT efficiency (management efficiency) of the banks remained more or less same during the study period i.e. 0.92. This implies that an improvement in technical efficiency has been due to improvement in scale efficiency rather than due to management efficiency or pure technical efficiency.

5.4.3 Scale Inefficiencies

Scale efficiency is obtained by dividing the efficiency score obtained from CCR model with the efficiency score of BCC model. The percentage inefficiency is obtained by subtracting the score of scale efficiency from unity and multiplying the result with 100. The scale inefficiency calculated for the period 2003 to 2009 is shown in Table 5.4.

Results show that overall average scale inefficiency of PSBs has reduced from 7.77 percent in the year 2003 to 1.7 percent in the year 2009. This shows that scale inefficiency of PSBs has decreased with the deployment of IT over a period of time. The exceptionally high inefficiency of 11.31 percent, obtained in the year 2005, may be due to heavy investment in core banking by banks. Results clearly show that banks have used the IT successfully to reduce the scale inefficiency by properly deploying ATMs and bringing the branches under core banking.

Results of the study show that the average efficiency (technical efficiency obtained by applying CCR model) of the banks' with respect to IT has improved gradually from 0.85 in year 2003 to 0.91 in the year 2009 (Table 5.2). From the result of BCC model with output orientation, it is clear that average IT efficiency(management efficiency) of the banks remained more or less same during the period 2003 to 2009 i.e. 0.92 (Table 5.3). This suggests that improvement in average efficiency (technical) for the period 2003 to 2009 is due to improvement in scale efficiency rather than of management efficiency. This calls for proper utilization of IT resources such as finding proper locations of ATMs where they can be maximally utilized and ensuring the minimum downtime of the IT systems. It is also observed that overall average scale inefficiency of PSBs has been reduced from 7.77 percent in the year 2003 to 1.7 percent in the year 2009 (Table 5.4). This suggests that computerization particularly deployment of ATMs and core banking solution has helped the banks to become scale efficient. Overall it can be concluded that banks have used the IT successfully to reduce the scale inefficiency by properly deploying ATMs and bringing the branches under core banking. However the almost stagnancy of pure technical efficiency or management efficiency observed in banks is still an area of concern to the bankers.

This work has been carried out as part of my Ph.D. work.

References

1. Dhingra S. Measuring IT effectiveness in banks of India for sustainable development.
2. BVICAM's International Journal of Information Technology.2011; 3(2):19—22.
3. Charnes A, Cooper W, Rhodes E. Measuring the efficiency of decision making units. Eur J Oper Res. 1978; 3:429-44.

4. Charnes A, Cooper W, Lewin, YA, Seiford M L. Data envelopment analysis: Theory, methodology and application. Boston: Kluwer Academic Publishers; 1994.

5. Banker RD, Charnes A, Cooper W. Some models for estimating technical and scale inefficiencies in data envelopment analysis. Manag Sci.1984; 30:1078-92

6. Dyson RG, Allen R, Camanho AS, Podinosky VV, Sarrico CS, Shale EA. Pitfalls and protocols in data envelopment analysis. Eur J Oper Res.2001; 132(2): 245-59.

7. India. Report on trend and progress of banking in India. Mumbai: Reserve Bank of India; 2009.

☺☹☹

6

Volatility Clustering in IT Index

Anurag Agnihotri[1]

The volatility in the stock market creates the opportunity for the investor and their uncertainties also cause the risk for the investor. Keeping this in mind this chapter has looked in to the volatility and with specific reference to IT Index in Indian stock market. For this purpose we have used the closing price of the BSE-IT Index for estimation of volatility using GARCH are from 1-04-05 to 31-03- 2013.This chapter tries to find out if there is volatility clustering in the BSE IT (Information Technology) index in the stock market using the ARCH/GARCH Model to indicate the volatility in the stock market. The closing prices considered. After fitting the GARCH model in the data, analysis on the findings will be done. Following which the concluding part of the chapter, in which the limitations of this model along with further suggestions will be elucidated. It was found that GARCH 1,1 has proved the time varying volatility in the IT sector.

KEYWORDS   BSE | Clustering | GARCH | Stock Market | Volatility

6.1 INTRODUCTION

The Indian IT sector is the major sector which has played an important role in the growth and decline of Indian stock market. The BSE IT index is the true representative of the Indian stock market. The stock market is exposed to a high degree of volatility; prices fluctuate within minutes and are determined by the demand and supply of stocks at a given time. In addition the international trading and investment exposure has made it imperative to better operational efficiency. With the view to improve, discipline and bring greater transparency in this sector, constant efforts are being made and to a certain extent improvements have been made. Due to previous trends, informed investors realise that the nature of the stock market is volatile. Volatility is the most important variable in valuating derivative instruments. It has central role in risk management, asset valuation and investment in general. Actually modern risk management practices rely on volatility of asset and correlation of assets. However, it must be borne in mind that volatility is not the same

---

[1] College of Vocational Studies, Delhi University, India

thing as risk. Risk management and correct hedging are hugely important and valuable businesses and misconceptions can have disastrous effects. Therefore since volatility has such a wide scope, it may be beneficial for an investor to study it. The IT and IT enabled services industry in India has recorded a growth rate of 22.4% in the last fiscal year. Out of this figure, the domestic IT market in India accounted for 900 billion rupees. Volatility in the stock market may be attributed to several reasons. Many technical experts are confidently assuring them that the stock markets will go to higher levels in a short period of time. Due increasing volatility, analysis of stock market trends has become increasingly important.

6.2 INFORMATION TECHNOLOGY SECTOR

6.2.1 Review of Literature

Gertler and Hubbard revealed that business investment spending is also influenced by stock return Volatility. Schwert characterized the changes in Stock Market Volatility through time. The Stock Volatility increased by a factor of two or three during this period compared with the usual level of the series. There is no other series that experienced the similar behavior. The relationship between Stock Volatility and several measures of corporate profitability was also analysed. Akgiray discovered that daily series exhibited much higher degrees of statistical dependence than that had been reported in previous studies. Schwert explained that volatility measured by the standard deviation of rates of return to a broad Stock Market index such as the Standard and Poor's 500. Bailey and Chang found that investors tend to change with risk premium return of their portfolios with regard to changing macroeconomic fundamental like inflation, interest rate, exchange rate and industrial production, which evolve the long-term trend of volatility. Sias and Starks associate the day of the week effects in explaining the volatility. Some researchers relate interest rate and inflation with fluctuations in the stock market. Bekaert observes that in segmented capital markets, Volatility is a critical input in the cost of capital. Volatility can also be used as a decision making criterion. Chowan and Shukla have tried to analyse the following questions like, has the Stock Market Volatility increased? Has the Indian Stock Market developed into a speculative bubble due to the emergence of New Economy stocks? Why is this Volatility pronounced? They tried to unearth the rationale for those weird movements. Poon *et al.* Volatility has a wide sphere of influence including investment, security valuation, risk management and policy making. They also put emphasis on the importance of Volatility forecasting in various things such as options pricing, financial risk management etc. Karmakar measured the Volatility of daily stock return in the Indian Stock Market over the period of 1961 to 2005. Using GARCH model, he found strong evidence of' time varying Volatility. Parikh had thrown flash that effect of the events on the markets are basically short lived, unless if it has the long-term implications. Joshi and Pandya, observed that Volatility in the stock market has important bearing on earnings of individuals investors and the efficiency of stock market. The relatively small value of error coefficient of GARCH (1, 1) implied that large market surprises induced relatively small revisions in future volatility. Chou, have found on the estimation using GARCH the analysis implied a deep drop in stock price. Therefore identification of sources of uncertainty was important. More serious attention should be paid towards takeovers and computer programmed trading as they cause sizable disturbances. Marko Rinaten conducted a research on implied volatility measures; those can be interpreted as the market's perception on the future volatility of the underlying asset. Implied volatility seems even to bare eye present higher memory thus suggesting that higher order GARCH model would be suitable. However with only rolling n day measure as volatility proxy is inadequate to perform reliably more deep going analysis, and it was not in the original scope of this chapter which was only meant to learn and test out the procedures related to volatility forecasting with ARCH/ GARCH models.

Volatility is an area of research for many academicians, and most of the studies have been conducted on the major stock indices like NIFTY and SENSEX. While the studies conducted on the volatility of the sectoral indices are very few, therefore the present study seeks to analyse the volatility of the IT sector volatility based BSE IT Index.

6.2.2 Objective

The objective behind this chapter is to check for volatility in the BSE-IT (Information Technology) index, through ARCH/GARCH (Generalised Auto Regressive Conditional Heteroskedasticity) model. The aim is to theorize the statistical results to understand the behaviour of this stock market index.

6.2.3 Scope and Coverage

The study of volatility using ARCH/GARCH has a very wide scope. Understanding volatility is very important. In this chapter volatility has been studied in the closing prices of the previous years from (2005-2013) using the ARCH/GARCH model.

However this model can also be used in volatility forecasting. Volatility also has a pronounced role in modern finance as it is used in multiple risk management solutions.

6.2.4 Data Research and Methodology

The data considered for estimation of volatility using ARCH/ GARCH is the closing price of BSEIT index from 1-04-05 to 31-08-2013.

The GARCH Model

The GARCH is a time-series technique that allows users to model the serial dependence of volatility. GARCH modelling builds on advances in the understanding and modelling of volatility in the last decade. It takes into account excess kurtosis and volatility clustering, two important characteristics of financial time series. It provides accurate forecasts of variances and covariance's of asset returns through its ability to model time-varying conditional variances. Therefore, GARCH models can be applied to such diverse fields term structure of interest rates, Portfolio management and asset allocation, Option pricing, Foreign exchange, Risk management

Unit Root Test (Stationarity Test)

A unit root test has been applied to check whether a series is stationary or not. Stationarity condition has been tested using Augmented Dickey Fuller (ADF) [Dickey and Fuller (1979, 1981), Gujarati (2003), Enders (1995)].

6.2.5 Empirical Estimation

As mentioned above volatility will be checked for the closing price of BSEIT index for the period of 1-4-05 to 31-3-13.The necessary tests along with analysis and interpretation have been conducted:

The Graph 1 shows that the closing prices of the IT index are fluctuating and not uniform in nature. In the Table 6.1, observed that since chi square value is zero, it implies that heteroskedasticity is there, therefore this series is not stationary we will now examine stationarity with the help of correlogram and unit root tests.

The Table 6.2 finds that the spikes in the ACF and PCF at some lags are sticking out of the bars so the series is not stationary. After examining the p value of LCLOSE in the above tests, we see that it is greater than alpha, the level of significance which is taken to be 10%. So we accept the null hypothesis that LCLOSE has a unit root. So LCLOSE is not stationary.

Therefore, we shall take the first difference of the LCLOSE time series and then conduct unit root test and observe the Correlogram. Table 6.6 observed that spikes lie within the bars therefore LCLOSE is stationary. Furthermore, we superimpose the plots of our actual and simulated time series. The aforementioned rigorous analysis and statistical testing support the conclusions concerning the results. Volatility in the stock market has important bearing on earnings of individual investors and the efficiency of stock market in general for channelising resources for its productive uses. Present study attempts to get insight into behaviour of the volatility in Indian Stock Market.

The model with large value of lag coefficient shows that the volatility in the both markets is highly persistent and is predictable. The relatively small value of error coefficient of GARCH (1, 1) implies that large market surprises induce relatively small revisions in future volatility. Table 6.9 explains that we can find that the p value of D(LCLOSE) is 0.00 is less than the level of significance so the null hypothesis is rejected. This means that D(LCLOSE) doesn't have a unit root. Hence, it is stationary. Now we shall generate a series on DLCOSE which is the first difference of LCLOSE.

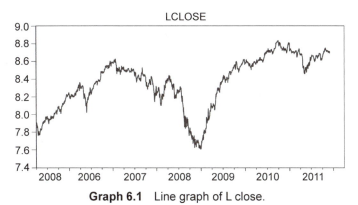

Graph 6.1 Line graph of L close.

The Graph 6.2 of the series Dlclose shows that there is very high volatility. There are very large and sudden variations. Table 6.10 explain chi square value of DLCLOSE is greater than level of significance so the Null Hypothesis (there is no Heteroskedasticity) is accepted. So the problem of Heteroskedasticity is solved.

The series DLCLOSE is stationary. We will now fit the ARCH model till it fails. Since the p-value is greater than the level of significance, we can see that the ARCH model fails at (4,0). We will now fit the corresponding GARCH models. Only the models that fit the required criteria (p-value of resids and garch should be less than level of significance) have been shown. Table 6.5 found that P-value of GARCH term<level of significance so the Null Hypothesis (beta2, the coefficient of RESID(-1)^2 is zero) is rejected. So there is significant GARCH effect and volatility is present. Thus the GARCH effect at (1,1) can be observed in the Graph 6.3.

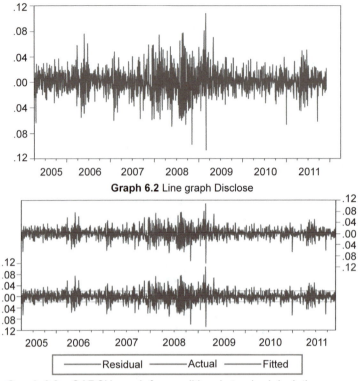

Graph 6.2 Line graph Disclose

Graph 6.3 GARCH graph for conditional standard deviation.

GARCH 2, 1 show that since all the spikes are within the bars, the model has been properly fitted (Table 6.11). GARCH 2,1 shows that since P-value is less than level of significance, we can see that GARCH effect is present (Table 12). GARCH 2,2 present that Since P-value is less than level of significance, we can see that GARCH effect is present (Graphs 6.4 and 6.5). Therefore we have fitted the GARCH model at (1,1), (2,1) and (2,2). We failed in fitting the model at (1,2), (2,3) and (3,1). In order to determine the best model out of the above, we will be taken the following parameters into consideration:

- R^2 and adjusted R^2 should be maximum.
- Akaike info criterion should be minimum.

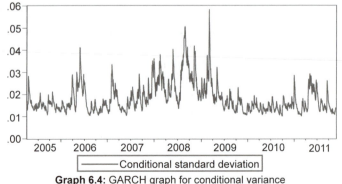

Graph 6.4: GARCH graph for conditional variance

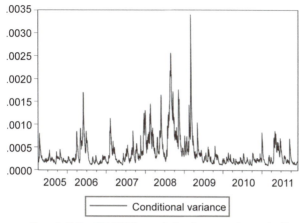

Graph 6.5 GARCH graph for time varying volatility.

3. Schwarz criterion should be minimum.

4. Durban Watson criterion should be closest to 2.

According the above criteria the GARCH (1,1) model is the best fit out of the above models.

It can be concluded that the BSE IT is a volatile index where time varying volatility is present as provided by the GARCH 1,1 and GARCH 2,1. After looking at the behaviour of the BSE-IT index and the volatility clustering associated with it one can come to the conclusion that volatility persists within this index. We observed that the GARCH effect was there when we fit the data within the model. However though we have completed our objective, there are a few limitations in this chapter as well No focus has been given to the forecasting of future values using the GARCH model. Another drawback is not taking into consideration any other variables from the index whose impact may be of a certain degree of importance. Finally, due to the study of data only between April 2005 and March 2013 we were unable to note down and study the effects before and after these dates.

References

1. Gertler ML, Hubbard RG. Financial factors in business fluctuations. NBER Working Papers 2758, National Bureau of Economic Research, Inc; 1989.

2. Akgiray V. Conditional Heteroskedasticity in Time series of Stock Returns: Evidence and Forecasts. Journal of Business. 1989; 62(1):55-80.

3. Bailey W, Chung YP. Exchange rate fluctuation, political risk and stock market returns: some evidences from an emerging market. Journal of Financial and Quantitative Analysis. 1995; 30(4):541-61.

4. Schwert WG. Why does stock market volatility change over time? J Finance. 1989; XLIV(5); 1115-53.

5. Schwert WG. Stock market volatility. Financial Analysts Journal. 1990 May-Jun. 23-34.

6. Bekaert. Emerging equity market volatility. J Financ Econ. 1995; 43:29-77.

7. Ray Yeutien Chou, Volatility Clustering ARCH/GARCH.

8. Poon et al. The jump-risk premia implicit in options: evidence from an integrated time-series study. J Financ Econ. 2003; 63:3-50.

9. Karmakar M. Stock market volatility, roots and results. Vikalpa. 2006 Jan-Mar; 20(1):7-48.

10. Joshi K, Pandya R. Study of volatility in Indian stock markets to understand the reasons for turbulence in the last two years- Volatility in Indian stock market. XIM, Bhubaneswar; 2000.

Appendix for GARCH/ ARCH/UNIT ROOT TEST tables

Note: Only relevant tables are given here.

Table 6.1   Heteroskedasticity Test: ARCH

F-statistic	62.37867	Prob. F(1,1736)	0.0000
Obs* R-squared	60.28437	Prob. Chi-Square(1)	0.0000

Test Equation:
Dependent Variable: RESID^2
Method: Least Squares
Date: 11/08/13 Time: 11:00
Sample (adjusted): 4/06/2005 3/30/2013
Included observations: 1738 after adjustments

Variable	Coefficient	Std. Error t-Statistic	Prob.
C	4977.922	318.0004 15.65382	0.0000
RESID^2(−1)	0.186274	0.023585 7.898017	0.0000
R-squared	0.034686	Mean dependent var	6115.255
Adjusted R-squared	0.034130	S.D. dependent var	13027.08
S.E. of regression	11820.05	Akaike info criterion	21.59413
Sum squared resid	2.43E+11	Schwarz criterion	21.60042
Log likelihood	−18763.30	Hannan-Quinn criter.	21.59646
F-statistic	62.37867	Durbin-Watson stat	2.025141
Prob(F-statistic)	0.000000		

Table 6.2 Correlogram at level

Correlogram of LCLOSE

Date: 11/05/12 Time: 19:24
Sample: 4/01/2005 3/30/2012
Included observations: 1741

Autocorrelation	Partial Correlation		AC	PAC	Q-Stat	Prob
		1	0.997	0.997	1732.5	0.000
		2	0.993	−0.009	3454.3	0.000
		3	0.990	0.046	5166.6	0.000
		4	0.987	0.034	6870.2	0.000
		5	0.985	0.005	8565.2	0.000
		6	0.982	−0.026	10251.	0.000
		7	0.979	−0.002	11928.	0.000
		8	0.976	−0.011	13595.	0.000
		9	0.973	0 023	15252.	0.000
		10	0.969	−0.039	16899.	0.000
		11	0.966	−0.036	18534.	0.000
		12	0.962	−0.022	20158.	0.000
		13	0.958	−0.003	21771.	0.000
		14	0.955	0.013	23372	0.000
		15	0.951	0.011	24963	0.000
		16	0.948	0.005	26543	0.000
		17	0.944	−0.009	28112	0.000
		18	0.940	−0.050	29670	0.000
		19	0.936	−0.015	31215.	0.000
		20	0.932	−0.040	32747.	0.000
		21	0.928	0.036	34267.	0.000
		22	0.924	−0.007	35775.	0.000
		23	0.920	−0 002	37271.	0.000
		24	0.917	0.032	38755.	0.000
		25	0.913	0.007	40229.	0.000
		26	0.909	−0.021	41691.	0.000
		27	0.905	−0.010	43142.	0.000
		28	0.901	−0.010	44580.	0.000
		29	0.897	0.002	46006.	0.000
		30	0,893	0 004	47421.	0,000
		31	0.889	0.016	48824.	0.000
		32	0.886	0.028	50217.	0.000
		33	0.882	0.017	51600.	0.000
		34	0.879	−0.010	52973.	0.000
		35	0.875	−0.009	54335.	0.000

Table 6.3 Unit root test of LCLOSE at level(intercept)

Null Hypothesis: LCLOSE has a unit root Exogenous: Constant Lag Length: 0 (Automatic based on SIC, MAXLAG=24)		
	t-Statistic	Prob.*
Augmented Dickey-Fuller test statistic	−1.560279	0.5028
Test critical 1% level values:	−3.433905	
5% level	−2.862997	
10% level	−2.567593	

Augmented Dickey-Fuller Test Equation
Dependent Variable: D(LCLOSE)
Method: Least Squares
Date: 11/03/13 Time: 22:00
Sample (adjusted): 4/04/2005 13/02/2011
Included observations: 1740 after adjustments

Variable	Coefficient	Std. Error	t-Statistic	Prob.
LCLOSE(-1)	−0.002479	0.001589	−1.560279	0.1189
C	0.021190	0.013292	1.594142	0.1111
R-squared	0.001399	Mean dependent var		0.000463
Adjusted R-squared	0.000824	S.D. dependent var		0.019325
S.E. of regression	0.019317	Akaike info criterion		−5.054481
Sum squared resid	0.648550	Schwarz criterion		−5.048204
Log likelihood	4399.399	Hannan-Quinn criter.		−5.052160
F-statistic	2.434472	Durbin-Watson stat		1.957282
Prob (F-statistic)	0.118876			

Table 6.4 Unit root test of LCLOSE at level(trend and intercept)

Null Hypothesis: LCLOSE has a unit root Exogenous: Constant, Linear Trend Lag Length: 0 (Automatic based on SIC, MAXLAG=24)		
	t-Statistic	Prob.*
Augmented Dickey-Fuller test statistic	−1.747481	0.7296
Test critical values: 1% level	−3.963326	
5% level	−3.413394	
10% level	−3.138140	

* MacKinnon (1996) one-sided p-values.
Augmented Dickey-Fuller Test Equation
Dependent Variable: D(LCLOSE)
Method: Least Squares
Date: 11/11/13 Time: 23:15
Sample (adjusted): 4/04/2005 3/30/2013
Included observations: 1740 after adjustments

Variable	Coefficient	Std. Error t-Statistic	Prob.
LCLOSE(-1)	−0.003387	0.001938 -1.747481	0.0807
C	0.027985	0.015675 1.785365	0.0744
@TREND (4/01/2005)	9.20E-07	1.13E-06 0.818185	0.4134

R-squared	0.001783	Mean dependent var	0.000463
Adjusted	0.000634	S.D. dependent var	0.019325
R-squared			
S.E. of regression	0.019319	Akaike info criterion	-5.053717
Sum squared resid	0.648300	Schwarz criterion	-5.044301
Log likelihood	4399.734	Hannan-Quinn criter.	-5.050235
F-statistic	1.551718	Durbin-Watson stat	1.956259
Prob(F-statistic)	0.213177		

Table 6.5 Unit root test of LCLOSE at first difference (intercept)

Null Hypothesis: D(LCLOSE) has a unit root Exogenous: Constant
Lag Length: 1 (Automatic based on SIC, MAXLAG=24)

		t-Statistic	Prob.*
Augmented Dickey-Fuller test statistic		−31.72531	0.0000
Test critical values:	1% level	−3.433910	
	5% level	−2.862999	
	10% level	−2.567594	

Augmented Dickey-Fuller Test Equation
Dependent Variable: D(LCLOSE,2)
Method: Least Squares
Date: 11/03/13 Time: 22:09
Sample (adjusted): 4/06/2005 13/02/2011
Included observations: 1738 after adjustments

Variable	Coefficient	Std. t-Statistic Error	Prob.
D(LCLOSE(-1))	−1.062711	0.033497 -31.72531	0.0000
D(LCLOSE(-1),2)	0.084351	0.023932 3.524561	0.0004
C	0.000498	0.000463 1.075846	0.2821
R-squared	0.493511	Mean dependent var	1.64E-05
Adjusted R-squared	0.492927	S.D. dependent var	0.027067
S.E. of regression	0.019274	Akaike info criterion	−5.058408
Sum squared resid	0.644521	Schwarz criterion	−5.048983
Log likelihood	4398.757	Hannan-Quinn criter.	−5.054923
F-statistic	845.2727	Durbin-Watson stat	2.007839
Prob(F-statistic)	0.000000		

Table 6.6 Heteroskedasticity Test: ARCH

F-statistic	0.470662	Prob. F(1,1737) Prob.	0.4928
Obs*R-squared	0.471076	Chi-Square(1)	0.4925

Test Equation:
Dependent Variable: WGT_RESID^2
Method: Least Squares
Date: 11/13/13 Time: 14:51
Sample (adjusted): 4/05/2005 3/30/2013
Included observations: 1739 after adjustments

Variable	Coefficient	Std. t-Statistic Error	Prob.
C	0.984962	0.050355 19.56027	0.0000

WGT_RESIDA^(-1)	0.016460	0.023992 0.686048	0.4928
R-squared	0.000271	Mean dependent var	1.001424
Adjusted R-squared	-0.000305	S.D. dependent var	1.845831
S.E. of regression	1.846113	Akaike info criterion	4.065190
Sum squared resid	5919.921	Schwarz criterion	4.071471
Log likelihood	-3532.683	Hannan-Quinn criter.	4.067513
F-statistic	0.470662	Durbin-Watson stat	1.999519
Prob (F-statistic)	0.492774		

Table 6.7   ARCH (1,0)

Dependent Variable: D(LCLOSE)
Method: ML - ARCH (Marquardt) - Normal distribution
Date: 11/13/13 Time: 15:52
Sample (adjusted): 4/04/2005 3/30/2013
Included observations: 1740 after adjustments
Convergence achieved after 7 iterations
Presample variance: backcast (parameter = 0.7)
GARCH = C(2) + C(3)*RESID(-1)^2

Variable	Coefficient	Std. Error	z-Statistic	Prob.
C	0.000988	0.000416	2.376424	0.0175
	Variance Equation			
C	0.000263	8.06E-06	32.61008	0.0000
RESID(-1)^2	0.297770	0.032327	9.211302	0.0000
R-squared	-0.000740	Mean dependent var		0.000463
Adjusted R-squared	-0.001893	S.D. dependent var		0.019325
S.E. of regression	0.019344	Akaike info criterion		-5.143574
Sum squared resid	0.649939	Schwarz criterion		-5.134157
Log likelihood	4477.909	Hannan-Quinn criter.		-5.140092
Durbin-Watson stat	1.957943			

Table 6.8 ARCH (2,0)

Dependent Variable: D(LCLOSE)
Method: ML - ARCH (Marquardt) - Normal distribution
Date: 11/13/13 Time: 15:53
Sample (adjusted): 4/04/2005 3/30/2013
Included observations: 1740 after adjustments
Convergence achieved after 7 iterations
Presample variance: backcast (parameter = 0.7)
GARCH = C(2) + C(3)*RESID(-1)^2 + C(4)*RESID(-2)^2

Variable	Coefficient	Std. Error	z-Statistic	Prob.
C	0.001176	0.000360	3.265006	0.0011
	Variance Equation			
C	0.000191	9.11E-06	20.95882	0.0000
RESID(-1)^2	0.274295	0.028839	9.511321	0.0000
RESID(-2)^2	0.245465	0.030841	7.959009	0.0000

R-squared	-0.001364	Mean dependent var	0.000463
Adjusted R-squared	-0.003094	S.D. dependent var	0.019325
S.E. of regression	0.019355	Akaike info criterion	-5.196699
Sum squared resid	0.650344	Schwarz criterion	-5.184143
Log likelihood	4525.138	Hannan-Quinn criter.	-5.192056
Durbin- Watson stat	1.956724		

Table 6.9 GARCH (1,1)

Dependent Variable: DLCLOSE
Method: ML - ARCH (Marquardt)-Normal distribution
Date: 11/03/13 Time: 22:28
Sample (adjusted): 4/04/2005 13/02/2011
Included observations: 1740 after adjustments
Convergence achieved after 9 iterations
Presample variance: backcast (parameter = 0.7)
GARCH = C(2) + C(3)*RESID(−1)A2 + C(4)*GARCH(−1)

Variable	Coefficient	Std. Error z-Statistic	Prob.
C	0.001340	0.000361 3.432397	0.0006
	Variance Equation		
C	1.44E-05	2.52E-06 5.707458	0.0000
RESID(-1)A2	0.138932	0.017693 7.852315	0.0000
R-squared	-0.001621	Mean dependent var	0.000463
Adjusted R-squared	-0.003351	S.D. dependent var	0.019325
S.E. of regression	0.019358	Akaike info criterion	-5.275220
Sum squared resid	0.650510	Schwarz criterion	-5.262664
Log likelihood	4593.441	Hannan-Quinn criter.	-5.270577
Durbin- Watson stat	1.956223		

Table 6.10 Correlogram Q-statistics

Date: 11/12/12 Time: 16:08
Sample: 4/04/2005 3/30/2012
Included observations: 1740

Autocorrelation	Partial Correlation		AC	PAG	Q-Stat	Prob
		1	0.041	0.041	2.8938	0.089
		2	−0.043	−0.044	6.0734	0.048
		3	−0.031	−0.027	7.7069	0.052
		4	0.006	0.006	7.7679	0.100
		5	−0.008	−0.011	7.8757	0.163
		6	−0.018	−0.013	8.4696	0.206
		7	0.001	0.002	8.4701	0.293
		S	−0.003	−0.005	8.4879	0.387
		9	0.009	0.009	8.6456	0.471
		10	0.034	0.033	10.628	0.387

Table 6.11 GARCH (2, 1)

Dependent Variable: D(LCLOSE)
Method: ML - ARCH (Marquardt) - Normal distribution
Date: 11/13/13 Time: 16:16
Sample (adjusted): 4/04/2005 3/30/2013
Included observations: 1740 after adjustments
Convergence achieved after 10 iterations
Presample variance: backcast (parameter = 0.7)
GARCH = C(2) + C(3)*RESID(-1)^2 + C(4)*RESID(-2)^2 + C(5)*GARCH(-1)

Variable	Coefficient	Std. Error	z-Statistic	Prob.
C	0.001315	0.000362	3.356416	0.0008
Variance Equation				
C	1.04E-05	2.32E-06	4.504452	0.0000
RESID(-1)A2	0.169010	0.027300	6.190837	0.0000
RESID(-2)A2	−0.060303	0.028165	−2.141023	0.0323
GARCH(-1)	0.864147	0.019644	43.99135	0.0000
R-squared	−0.001516	Mean dependent var		0.000463
Adjusted R-squared	−0.003825	S.D. dependent var		0.019325
S.E. of regression	0.019362	Akaike info criterion		−5.275253
Sum squared resid	0.650443	Schwarz criterion		−5.259558
Log likelihood	4594.470	Hannan-Quinn criter.		−5.269449
Durbin-Watson stat	1.956427			

Table 6.12   GARCH (2, 2)

Dependent Variable: D(LCLOSE)
Method: ML - ARCH (Marquardt) - Normal distribution
Date: 11/13/13 Time: 16:19
Sample (adjusted): 4/04/2005 3/30/2013
Included observations: 1740 after adjustments
Convergence achieved after 11 iterations
Presample variance: backcast (parameter = 0.7)
GARCH = C(2) + C(3)*RESID(-1)^2 + C(4)*RESID(-2)^2 + C(5)*GARCH(–1) + C(6)*GARCH(–2)

Variable	Coefficient	Std. Error	z-Statistic	Prob.
C	0.001390	0.000362	3.566971	0.0004
	Variance Equation			
C	5.82E-07	3.39E-07	1.719979	0.0854
RESID(-1)^2	0.160953	0.024037	6.695984	0.0000
RESID(-2)^2	–0.152869	0.022782	–6.710016	0.0000
GARCH(-1)	1.677141	0.062875	26.67438	0.0000
GARCH(-2)	–0.686809	0.058684	–11.70349	0.0000
R-squared	-0.001833	Mean dependent var		0.000463
Adjusted R-squared	-0.004722	S.D. dependent var		0.019325
S.E. of regression	0.019371	Akaike info criterion		-5.277564
Sum squared resid	0.650649	Schwarz criterion		-5.258730
Log likelihood	4597.480	Hannan-Quinn criter.		-5.270600
Durbin- Watson stat	1.955807			

☺☻☹

7

Competitiveness through ICT Contribution

Sara Cepolina[1]

The chapter addresses a new holistic organization paradigm along the garment val-ue chain, covering the main advanced technology innovation solutions at the aim to foster industry sustainability and competitiveness. The proposed manufacturing sys-tem will allow the garment industry to fully satisfy the final customer requirements in terms of functionality, comfort and fashion while increasing industry sustainability and competitiveness through its implications in terms of productivity, time to market and wastes reduction. The framework and the method developed for garment industry is presented and two ICT based innovative solutions regarding product tracking and virtual prototyping are analysed.

KEYWORDS Garment Industry | Competitiveness | Sustainability | SCM | ICT

7.1 INTRODUCTION

"... In future, winning companies will be the ones able to connect with consumers and optimise their in-store experience thanks to an integrated business and product planning. The latter should speed-up design and development while integrating sourcing, supply and logistic partners with the aim of improving companies service strategies and create unique flow paths" (Mrs Ern-Stockum–Managing Director, Kurt Salmon).

"... (the) experience has shown that, when suppliers and retailers cooperate, exchange information on stock levels and sales and, more generally, create solid and long-lasting relationships as business partners, both parties can achieve much better results than if they deal with each other merely as suppliers and buyers." (Mr. Massoletti–AEDT VicePresident)

These two considerations emerged during the recent European Apparel and Textile Confederation (EURATEX) annual general assembly well summarize the European industrial approach to the hypercompetition (D'Aveni, 1994)

---

[1] Università di Genova, Italy

characterizing the garment industry and underline the relevance and the future expectations for ICT technology applications into the garment supply chain.

The garment industry has been subject to different reconfiguration processes to adapt itself to the changing political, environmental, economic and competitive factors. Old economic trends have been added recently by newer globalisation trends which affect deeply the apparel supply chain modifying its configuration and intensifying the industry competitive pressure (Cepolina & Scarsi, 2011). The emerging garment value chain is high disperse and is composed by numerous different players all over the world. In these globally networked organizations, a firm's competitive advantage lies not so much in being "the best", but in its ability to co-create with others and to orchestrate this process of co-creation in the most efficient, effective (Daiser, 2009) and sustainable way. At this aim enterprises have to develop new competencies and capabilities.

Emerging concepts of garments as made-to- measure fashion items or technical clothes like protective equipment, medical appliance, wearable computer etc. require a reconfiguration of the overall customer-vendor relationships, a paradigm change in customer service and customer relationship management with a focus on value-adding product- services and sustainability (Binder, Janicke & Petschow, 2001). In other words new management of product complexity, new attention should be paid to customisation and personalisation taking into account sustainability issues like: resources sparing, environment protection, and cleaner utilisation, waste re-cycling. This situation criticality looks for new policies in the market of products, to lower tangibles spoilage, by value-chain paradigms turned on intangibles. This chapter addresses appropriate management concepts building on knowledge and technological tools integrated within a seamless common architecture, purposely developed for benefitting this industry. The proposed framework—the Extended Smart Sustainable Organization (xSSO)—is suggested to become the new networking oriented, integrative framework for the organization of flexible garment manufacturing of the future (Abernathy, Volpe & Weil, 2006).

7.2 THEORICAL FRAMEWORK

7.2.1 Smart Organization

The organization is knowledge-driven, internetworked, dynamically adaptive to new organizational forms and practices, learning and able to create and exploit the opportunities offered by the new economy (Abernathy, Volpe & Weil, 2006).

The idea that today all companies are more or less working in networks of various types leads to some implications (Filos & Banahan, 2000). To work effective in communities a company has to change its understanding about its environment: the organization should recognise the value of partner contribution and use it for the wellbeing of the community; the organization should not seek to control its environment but recognise that any such attempt would at best, fail, and at worst, stifle the creativity and imagination necessary to support innovation (Matheson & Matheson, 1998); the organization should realise that trust is a key issue in determining the success of relationships in the digital economy (Camarinha-Matos, Afsarmanesh & Erbe, 2000) and seeks to prove it, in the way it interacts.

To achieve this new understanding, companies need collaborative and networking competencies (Grant, 1996; Lorenzoni & Lipparini, 1999). These competencies can be reached by the evolution of the companies in the field of ICT networking, organizational networking and knowledge networking.

7.2.2 Sustainable Organization

The sustainability is becoming urgent demand. The World Commission for Environment and Development (WCED) clearly stated the new economic paradigms for sustainable development, which meets the needs of the present population without compromising the needs of future generations (Carr, 2001).

Sustainable organization introduces constraints aimed at lowering material and energy depletion intensity (at production, use and dismissal);—avoiding toxic dispersion and lower pollution; enhancing using renewable resources and re-using of exhausted tangibles;—increasing the service intensity (by artefacts sharing, by functions dispensing, etc.);—increasing recycling efficiency, with profitability of the new business aiming at the tangibles reverse logistics (from waste, to 'raw' materials); increasing energy efficiency (World Commission on Environment and Development, 1987). Company's competitiveness will turn towards the ability of offering to the customer expected product functions with proper satisfaction and nonrenewable resource balance. xSSO concept is based on research work developed within the Leapfrog European research project. The concept, there developed by the technical and scientific perspectives, is here enriched with the sustainability component and it is faced by the managerial perspective with attention to its implications in terms of firms' competitiveness. Technical aspects are briefly introduced to show system functionalities and any further information can be found in (Walter, Kartsounis & Carosio, 2009).

7.3 XSSO FRAMEWORK

The xSSO concept is based on different theories coming from numerous research fields (smart organization, ICT, knowledge management, relationship marketing and cluster analysis, supply chain management and innovation management (Nonaka, 1991; Pilat, 2004; Handfield & Nochols, 1999; Chopra & Meindel, 2003; Shapiro, 2001; Gronros, 1987;

Gummeson, 1987; Hakansson, 1979; Kang & Kang, 2009; Gupta, Raj & Wilemon, 1986; Chesbrough, 2003) offering an original, holistic and new integration framework able to support strategic behaviour of enterprises operating in the sector. Each company could query the software and receive different options to improve its competitive positioning. The options could refer to many firm's areas, like: logistics, quality system, supply chain management, networking etc.. The enterprise will adopt and include in its own xSSO the options considered most relevant and coherent with its corporate strategy (Cepolina, 2011).

The application of the xSSO concept is aimed to modernise and transform the garment sector into a flexible knowledge-driven sustainable high- tech industry by:

- ◁ a leap in productivity and cost efficiency in the garment manufacturing process,
- ◁ a radical move towards rapid customised manufacturing,
- ◁ a coherent life cycle sustainability assessment and
- ◁ a paradigm change in customer service and customer relationship management with a focus on value-adding product-services.

The integration of all innovations and new processes/services requires a new holistic organizational paradigm along the value chain, covering efficient life-cycle design (Bendell, 2000), production, use and recovery. Garment development and production have to be done in flexible, dynamically interoperating networks of enterprises (Anderson-Connell, Ulrich, & Brannon, 2002), flexibly adaptive to new emerging production technologies and business models, fully adaptive regarding customized market requirements and new technologies (Mo & Nemes, 2001). The novel manufacturing system has to enable the garment to suit the final customer use in terms of functionality, comfort and fashion effects while increasing productivity and reducing time to market. Much more flexibility and dynamism than currently in the traditional, complicated, resource and waste intensive textile and clothing value chain is required.

This holistic organizational framework with related conceptions, methods and operational tools will allow the garment industry to develop and produce extended garment products in flexible, dynamically interoperating networks of enterprises. It enables an integrated management of existing and new products and processes for garments within new business models of the factory of the future. Moreover the proposed approach has positive implications also by the demand side. In fact, the high and early customer involvement into the design and concept steps allows achieving a high rate of customer satisfaction, minimizing returns of goods and restraining waste (Luttropp & Lagerstedt,1999; Candi, 2006). The consequent cost reductions benefit enterprise and customers as well.

The xSSO framework is the basic framework for modelling organizational networks with the constituting elements and their relationships, the dynamic behaviour in terms of stability, control structures, flexibility, self-adaptivity and robustness properties for the targeted knowledge-based, integrated garment production processes. It refers to suitable visualization and navigation software tools for selecting, designing and operating network instances, also including functionality and sustainability testing structures.

xSSOs are implementing and applying elements of both the dimensions of smartness (knowledge-base) and sustainability (ecoconsistency) networked by powerful ICT structures in a trans-disciplinary environment including engineering, economics and social perspectives (Vieira, 2009).

The xSSO application framework consists of the model set the repository and a configurator, whose main aspects are outlined in the next sections, and various implementation sets besides the operational systems. These elements are interacting with the goal to support garment companies enabling the establishment of smart organizations. An overview of the interactions is given in Figure 7.1, describing the principle sequence of interaction.

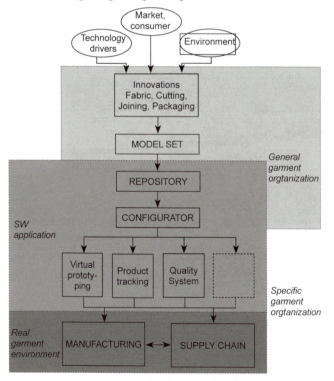

Fig. 7.1 Context of the xSSO framework

7.4 MODEL SET

The Model Set is the first step of the research and comprises the analysis of competitive behaviour of firms operating in the garment industry and their abstraction into models. The out coming models refer to all aspects of operational activity in the garment manufacturing and garment supply chain. A set of model types aligned in a concise structure has been developed, based on state-of-the-art frameworks for enterprise and ICT modeling (Porter, 1998). Following the xSSO conception the Model Set allows creating a consistent, comprehensive integrated set of models of enterprise acting in the garment value chain (Nordas, 2004).

The modelling subjects range from representing data to representing conceptions and ideas from organizational aspects to product aspects. The xSSO Model Set supports various levels of abstraction and innovations. It also supports various specific views of an organization. Model types of various levels of abstraction but with the same scope can be combined.

The xSSO Model Set constitutes the comprehensive knowledge about the structural needs of different emerging areas, like new materials, new flexible automation cells, new garment virtual prototyping, in a sustainable organization framework. A model consisting of three layers and views corresponding to respectively the rows and columns in the overview in Figure 7.2 was implemented.

SMART SUSTAINABLE ORGANIZATION			
xSSO	*Organization view*	*Processing View*	*Product view*
Knowledge asset later	Knowledge about organizational Structures	Knowledge about Process and Resources	**Knowledge about Products**
Sustainability layer	Sustainability constrains on organization	Sustainability issues on process and resources	**Sustainability issues on products**
Organization layer	Business model	Business process	**Business service**
ICT layer	**ICT architecture**	**Information flow**	**Product data**

Fig. 2 Overview of the xSSO model set

7.5 REPOSITORY

The repository is the concretization of the model set activity, cataloguing all the models developed in the previous research's step. Its main objective is to allow data storage and reuse from the Configurator. The repository is specifically designed to store models related to traditional issues and innovative solutions as they are created and developed. These models are then used as basis to start the analysis required to applying these technologies to the actual configuration of the industry, suggesting the areas where a major effort in modifying the status is required.

The model development is, actually, based on GME (General Modelling Environment) that is an open source application, developed by the Institute for Software Integrated Systems of the Vanderbilt University. XML format is the source of information used by the repository.

The design of the repository starts from the xSSO Model Set in order to separate the data structure from the application (GME) that uses it.

This choice allows changing the application platform without loss of information or models.

The implemented structure is very simple and do not investigate the intrinsic nature of the component: all objects are similar, only common characteristics are used: the object has a name, a description, some attributes, a position in the diagram and connections with other objects.

Different components have different associated rules and a graphical aspect that differentiate each other. The rules and the graphical aspect refer to a metamodel that is common to all models Rules describe the behaviour of a component, for example how to connect with another component, how many component of each type can be inserted in a model and so on.

The xSSO Repository is a relational database that stores the GME model and collaborates with the Configurator. Also, the xSSO has some simple web interfaces to manage the inserted model, user information and rights. It can be easily connected with web publication tools, like Java servlets or PHP pages, or with remote application through a secure socket.

7.6 CONFIGURATOR

The Configurator is a software tool which enables firm to query the repository in an easy to use and user-friendly way. It enables the selection of best suitable innovations for the design and operation of individual enterprise in smart networks. After the selection, in fact, each proposed innovation is visualised together with current situation of the (extended) enterprise. The configurator's outcome is not only a set of possible innovations to improve firm's competitiveness and efficiency but it offers ready to use and customised software.

To improve the usability for the user, the models of the innovations and their relationships are presented graphically. Navigation within these models is possible, based on the relations in and between models.

Navigation is very important for the user to quick find and assesses suitable innovations. Therefore a navigation based on classifications is applied. There should be no restrictions for creating classifications. The classifications suitable for navigations are created as a tree because circular relations between navigations will irritate the user. The classifications should be extendable without the need to change the classification of existing innovations. All data concerning the models are stored in the xSSO Repository and all data necessary for evaluation of models are stored in the xSSO Configurator.

Due to the strict splitting of data and evaluation logic, the Configurator accesses the model data with the help of high-level functions provided by the Repository. For sake of portability these high-level functions are designed to be independent from the technical implementation of the data pool to allow an easy change of the data delivery system. The evaluation logic should also be independent from the Model Set, so that changes to the Model Set do not require a redesign of the evaluation logic but only marginal changes should be needed.

The selected system allows the flexible design of objects which are used for the evaluation logic. Each object has a freely defined set of attributes helping the navigation and allowing, without additional configuration effort, to make a full-text search or an attribute-specific search. Therefore the configuration of the system is mainly focused on creating the necessary objects to realise the classifications, navigation and evaluation logic.

7.7 CASE STUDIES

The over outlined xSSO framework allows modelling of and analysis of an existing network for innovation and production, and it let to select and configure appropriate measures in order to improve the integration of activities and actors. ICT technology plays a strategic role supporting the garment supply chain management and networking, allowing integration between different actors along the chain, supporting information-sharing (Kollberg & Dreyer, 2006). ICT plays also an important role in the strengthening and reinforcing the sustainability efforts giving a greener face to the fashion value-chain (Sahni, 2010).

Radio Frequency Identification technology (RFID), virtual prototyping and design, Computer integrated manufacturing (CIM) as well as vendor managed inventory (VMI) and collaborative planning, forecasting and replenishment (CPFR) are examples of ICT based solutions improving efficiency by sharing information related to matching demand and supply such as short- and long-term production planning, demand forecasting, materials and capacity planning. The first two solutions are standalone analysed in the following sections.

7.8 PRODUCT TRACKING

7.8.1 Technology Background

Product tracking technology is gaining increasing importance due to the globalization process and to the resulting global and complex supply chain's configuration. The markets of the modern world are characterised through an increasing globalisation and rapid technology changes.

This situation asks for ICT technologies and applications which enable the identification of products as single items, of item working resources (e.g. cut, sewing machines), of logistic entities (e.g. transport units, boxes, cartons) by attaching different information (e.g. status values, quality control information, progress messages) to the single items in an inter-firm way. This information has to be readable from different players in the value chain.

To identify goods along the value chain, the RFID technology has been selected, being a contact-less and reliable identification technology (Wang, Tang, Sheng & Wang, 2006).

Typical RFID mobile device uses client-server architecture. Because the device runs in a web browser, every computer with an internet connection serves as client. A hand-held RFID scanner can be connected to this computer enabling to collect RFID data from the scanned tags. The data is then transferred via the internet connection to the prototype server instance where it could be processed.

7.8.2 Economic Implications

Globalization process results in an increasingly intense competition, as new producers and merchants gain access to previously well limited markets (D'Aveni, 1994). Innovation, the increase of productivity and the optimisation of business processes are keys to survive and prosper in this environment (Porter, 2001).

The RFID system could support companies' competitive challenge supporting garment supply chain integration, offering a quick and transparent order, manufacturing and delivery process to the customers ordering, with positive implications in terms of quality and efficiency. Additional benefits of RFID relate to the production phase in terms of logistics and security, improving available information through the supply chain, and in terms of networking configuration of production, allowing information exchange between commissioning industries and suppliers. The increased reliability given by the RFID traceability properties makes the possibility to match apparel parts (trousers and jackets), realised by different suppliers, much easier then previously.

RFID could, for examples, enhance the process of create and verify the delivery notes. Through scanning of objects tagged with an RFID label it is possible to automatically add and verify the goods that are packed for transportation and automatically assign carton numbers. Compared to other methods this modified process yields the potential to save time and costs, especially for the actors in later steps of the chain, like transportation service providers or customers.

Fig. 7.3 RFID Based inventory
Courtesy Salpomec Oy.

Customer driven integrated manufacturing tracking systems allow individualized web orders to be processed in 'real-time' and 'tracked' throughout the supply chain. Straight forward CAD/CAM processing technology interlinking web frontend 3D configuration processes and e-shops with backend weavers and manufacturers generates automatically BoL/BoM embedded into the SCM system "TXTChain". Both B2B and B2C tracking tools are available from order input until home delivery, info for the latter the customers can trace in his e- account on the retailers website.

Concerning the sustainability issue, RFID achieves higher efficiency which leads to sustainability through its positive implications in inventory productivity and accuracy and operating efficiency. The technology helps in errors location, in loss prevention, in unnecessary truck deliveries minimization, in cloth life cycle management, in stolen items control and in reduction of customers' trips to store for items that were out of stock during their initial visit. It could works also on the consumer behaviour, raising consumer awareness of the apparel life cycle and communicating how each garment rates in terms of overall sustainability (Treanor, 2011).

Moreover RFID technology and product tracking solutions are fundamental pillars in the evolution of digital clothing supply chains, from design to retail, that minimize returns and reduce waste.

7.9 VIRTUAL PROTOTYPING

7.9.1 Technology Background

CAD tools have greatly evolved and new techniques and capabilities were introduced allowing the 3D representation of soft material in a dynamic environment. So today the most updated ICT technologies can be applied to the design and evaluation of garment new collection in terms of virtual, instead of physical prototypes in a collaborative manner (Magnenat-Thalmann, 2010; Apeagyei 2010). Design and prototyping are critical activities in order to meet consumers demand, to reduce wastes and to address sustainability issues. The key innovative concepts are based on ICT technical developments offering a comprehensive methodology for garment design performed directly in 3D, replacing virtual prototypes instead of physical prototypes, contributing to reduce the timeconsuming tasks of design and prototyping. Recent CAD processes allow to represent typical body shapes integrating representative female and male morphotypes derived from hierarchical statistical clustering of Anthropometric Survey data or based on specific customer sample data acquired through three-dimensional (3D) body scanners (Zulck, Koruca & Borkircher, 2011).

The development of a web platform enabling e- collaboration between potential users of 3D design and Virtual Prototyping, such as product managers, designers, modelists and sales and marketing personnel in a scenario intended to speed up and enhance creativity and effectiveness represents a further important key opening new challenges to enhance sustainability in clothing supply chain. This platform can be linked to other satellite web- delivered services, such as a fabrics library, a cost estimation module and a real-time animation module, offering visualisation of animated virtual mannequins 'dressed' with the new creations and allowing the customer himself to virtual dress the garment for appreciating its look and for feeling its comfort.

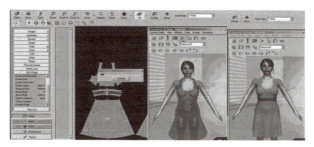

Fig. 7.4 Interface of a platform for garment virtual fit testing *Courtesy Bronzewear*

7.9.2 Economic Implications

Virtual prototyping application has strong economic implication in terms of efficiency improvement and cost reduction as well as in terms of customer satisfaction and customer relationship management (CRM).

The simulation introduction all along the design process and the virtual prototyping allow garment companies to adopt postponement strategy and just in time strategy. This ICT based solutions linked to the e-business make it possible to assembly the final product only when customer has just acquired it. Economic benefits relate to stock and waste reduction, inventory lower costs thanks to lean production adoption, improved quality levels and compressed production cycle time. Furthermore this technology could support the control over the manufacturing and development process of garments, thanks to its easy integration into existing production plant and in the future flexible automation production.

Considering the customer point of view, he is deeply involved since the design and concept phases till to the production and logistic ones (Abecassis-Moedas, 2006). Customers are able to design their personnel ideal garment matching at the same time the hand made comfort and fit evaluation benefits with affordable costs levels and delivery time. Concerning the sustainability issue, virtual prototyping supports the digitalization process of the garment supply chains, through e-configurators, digital design toolkits, online dressing facilities and the development of "controlled" virtual shopping communities. The digital assessment of fit forms is more accurate in 3D; this has positive effects on sample budgets and therefore means fewer physical samples, lower transport costs, less material use and, above all, time savings. It is a keystone in developing a garment sustainable supply chain, allowing the product to remain in digital form until later in the process. At least in fact it is more sustainable to create and buy a garment in a digital form, because whenever a physical sample is created, waste is introduced into the process.

7.9.3 Concluding Remarks

The xSSO is a web-based decision support system, enabling visualisation and navigation for identifying, selecting and designing innovative methods and technologies for the garment industrial sector, in order to improve the integration of activities and actors. The interactive overall platform allows to reach a high integration level of the entire supply chain, from the front-end collaborative design toolkit up to manufacturing and e-fulfilment, thanks to ICT technology. The two ICT based solutions analysed show the technology contribution in terms of variety synchronisation from design to production, from sale, delivery and post sale.

By the economic perspective, the xSSO framework allows to minimize stock and its related costs and to achieve important competitive advantages both in terms of cost and diversification advantages. The xSSO is also a Consumer Driven Manufacturing business model which reduces stock wastes and promotes a real sustainable supply chain. These savings result in a win-win situation for all the players involved in the supply chain.

Thanks to ICT and internet application, the process integration of CAD-CAM is accelerated and optimized in a global CDIN (Computer Driven Intelligent Network), where the consumer becomes producer (prosumer), driving the fully integrated supply and manufacturing chain by him or herself. I would like to acknowledge the research team of the Leapfrog European project for the kind support and collaboration

References

1. Abecassis-Moedas C. (2006). Integrating design and retail in the clothing chain: An empirical study of the organisation of design. *International Journal of Operations and Production Management, 26(4),* 412–428.
2. Abernathy, F. H., Volpe A. & Weil D. (2006). The future of the apparel and textile industries: prospects and choices for public and private actors. *Environment and Planning, 38(12),* 2207–32.
3. Anderson-Connell, L. J., Ulrich, P. V. & Brannon E. L. (2002). A consumer-driven model for mass customization in the apparel market. *Journal of Fashion Marketing and Management, 6(3),* 240–58.
4. Apeagyei P.R. (2010). Application of 3D body scanning technology to human measurement for clothing Fit. *International journal of digital content technology and its applications, 4(7),* 58–67.
5. Bendell J. (2000). *Terms of endearment: business, NGOs and sustainable development* Sheffield: Greenleaf Publishing Limited.
6. Binder M., Janicke M., Petschow U. (2001). *Green industrial restructuring international case studies and theoretical interpretations.* New York: Springer Verlag Press.
7. Camarinha-Matos L. M., Afsarmanesh H., Erbe H.H. (2000). *Advances in networked enterprises: virtual organisations balanced automation and systems integrations.* Dordrecht: Kluwer Academic Press.
8. Candi, M. (2006). Design as an Element of Innovation: Evaluating Design Emphasis in Technology-Based Firms. *International Journal of Innovation Management,* 10(4), 351-374.
9. Carr G. (2001). *The digital enterprise: how to reshape your business for a connected world.* Harvard: Harvard Business School Press.
10. Cepolina S. (2011), Extended Smart Sustainable Organization in Garment industry, in Lather, Saini, Khatri, *Strategies and innovations for sustainable organizations,* McMillan publisher India Ltd

11. Cepolina S., Scarsi R. (2011), Apparel supply chain management: ICT contribution to networking sustainability and competitiveness, in Bartolo H. et al. *Proceedings of SIM 2011 Sustainable Intelligent Manufacturing,* 1ST Press Lisbona.

12. Chesbrough, H. W. (2003). *Open Innovation: The new imperative for creating and profiting from technology.* Boston: Harvard Business School Press.

13. Chopra S., Meindel P. (2003). *Supply Chain Management: Strategy, Planning, and Operation.* New Jersey: Pearson Prentice Hall Press.

14. Daiser R. (2009). *Designing the Smart Organization: how breakthrough corporate learning initiatives, drive strategic change and innovation.* San Francisco: Jossey Bass/Wiley Press.

15. D'Aveni, R. A. (1994). *Hypercompetition: Managing the Dynamics of Strategic Maneuvering.* New York: The Free Press.

16. Filos E., Banahan E. (2000). Will the Organisation Disappear? The Challenges of the new Economy and Future Perspectives. In L. M. Camarinha-Matos, H. H. Afsarmanesh, Rabelo (eds), *E-Business & VirtualEnterprises* (pp. 3–20). Dordrecht: Kluwer Press.

17. Grant, R. M. (1996). Prospering in dynamically- competitive environments: Organizational capability as knowledge integration. *Organization Science, 7(4),* 375387.

18. Gronros C. (1987). Marketing redefined. *Management decision, 28(8),* 5–9.

19. Gummeson E. (1987), The new marketing: developing long-term interactive relationships. *Long range planning, 20(4)*, 10–20.

20. Gupta A. K., Raj S. P. & Wilemon D. (1986). A Model for Studying R&D-Marketing Interface in the Production Innovation Process. *Journal of Marketing,* 50 (April), 7–17.

21. Hakansson H. (1979). *Corporate technological behaviour: cooperation and networks.* London: Routledge Press.

22. Handheld R. B., Nochols E. L. (1999). *Introduction to Supply Chain Management.* New Jersey: Pearson Prentice Hall Press.

23. Hilger J., (2008). The apparel industry in West Europe. Copenhagen Business School, *Creative Encounters Working Papers, 22.*

24. Kang K., Kang J. (2009). How do firms source external knowledge for innovation? Analysing effects of different knowledge sourcing methods. *International Journal of Innovation management, 13(1),* 1–8.

25. Kollberg M., Dreyer H. (2006). Exploring the impact of ICT on integration in supply chain control: a research model, *www.sintef.se/prqject/SMARTLOG*

26. Lorenzoni G., Lipparini A. (1999). The leveraging of interfirm relationships as a distinctive organizational capability: a longitudinal study. *Strategic Management Journal, 20(4),* 317–338.

27. Luttropp C., Lagerstedt J. (1999). Customer benefits in the context of life cycle design. *Eco-Design '99: 1st Inti. Symp. on Environmental Conscious Design and Inverse Manufacturing, Tokyo.* Feb. 1999.

28. Magnenat-Thalmann, N. (2010). *Designing and Animating Patterns and Clothes, Modeling and Simulating Bodies and Garments.* Springer Publisher.

29. Mahadevan B. (2000). Business models for internet-based e-commerce: an anatomy. *California Management Review, 1(July)*, 55–69.

30. Matheson D., Matheson J. E. (1998). *The smart organization: creating value through strategic R&D.* Cambridge: Harvard Business School Press.

31. Mo J. P. T., Nemes L. (2001). *Global engineering, manufacturing and enterprise networks.* Dordrecht: Kluwer Academic Publishing.

32. Nonaka I. (1991). The knowledge creating company. *Harvard Business Review. 69 (6 Nov-Dec)*, 96–104.

33. Nordås H. K. (2004). The global textile and clothing industry post the agreement on textiles and clothing. *World Trade Organization discussion Paper, 5*, Geneva, Switzerland.

34. Pilat, D. (2004). The ICT Productivity Paradox: Insights from Micro Data. *OECD Journal: Economic Studies, 38*, 37–65.

35. Porter M.E. (1998). Clusters and the new economics of competition. *Harvard Business Review, 1(Nov.)*, 77–90.

36. Porter M.E. (2001). *Competition in global industries.* Harvard: HBS Press Book.

37. Sahni H. (2010), Towards Sustainable Fashion - Computer Technology Integration for a Green Fashion Value-Chain. *www.fibre2fashion.com*

38. Shapiro J. F. (2001). *Modeling the Supply Chain.* Pacific Grove, CA: Duxbury Thomson Learning Press.

39. Treanor Z. (2011). Sustainable Apparel: Integrating Global Commerce and Increasing Consumer Awareness.

40. Vieira V.A. (2009). An extended theoretical model of fashion clothing involvement. *Journal of Fashion Marketing Management, 13(2)*, 179-200.

41. Walter L., Kartsounis G. A., Carosio S. (2009). *Transforming clothing production into a demand-driven, knowledge-based, high-tech industry.* London: Springer-Verlag Press.

42. Wang Z., Tang R., Sheng W., Wang G. (2006). Research on RFID-Based Production Logistics Management Techniques with Application in Garment Industry. *International Technology and Innovation conference 2006*, Hangzhou, China, June 2006.

43. World Commission on Environment and Development (1987). *Our Common Future.* Oxford: Oxford University Press.

44. Zulch G., Koruca H.I. & Borkircher M. (2011). Simulation-supported change process for product customization—A case study in a garment company, *Computers in Industry*, Vol. 62, 568—577.

☺☹☺

8

Obstacles in Information System Success

Bikram Pal Kaur[1] and Himanshu Aggrawal[2]

To gain better competitive advantage in the market, the organization are using information systems. Most of the organizations either have established the information system or they upgrade their information system. But still there are lots of hurdles for gaining information system success. There have been a large number of analyses of critical success factors of information system projects in the literature, but there is shortfall in research efforts in studying failures globally and particularly in India. Therefore this chapter attempts to study empirically the obstacles coming in Information system success. A questionnaire survey has been conducted to know the failures factors for not updating the information system timely. The survey has been done on two prominent telecommunication organization, one having successful IS (Reliance Communication) due to its continuous updation with respect to time, industry and executives other (Puncom, Mohali) don't have. As India is the second largest country in terms of mobile users in the world therefore the study of this industry is strategically and economically important due to its high potential for the growth of the country.

KEYWORDS Information System (IS) | Critical Success Factors (CSFs) | Continuous Updation | Indian Telecommunication Industry

8.1 INTRODUCTION

Information system is a suite having different software modules that integrates different functional departments in an organization. It provides the support for collaborating the different departments from planning, manufacturing to customer service, and finally to achieve the business goals. The market of various corporate information systems has grown tremendously. However, the implementation process of information systems is not only complex, but also organizationally disturbing and resource exhaustive. Many information system implementation projects gains incomplete success or the failures. The causes of failures are comprehensive which can be attributed to insufficient planning, stabilization, requirements and continuous updation of the system both at

---

[1] Computer Science and Engineering, Department, Chandigarh Engineering Colleges, Punjab
[2] Computer Science and Engineering Department, Punjabi University, Punjab, India

the business and project levels. Incompetent project management, minimum support from the corporate management etc. are also the contributory failure factors. The complexity in information system implementation has attracted much attention both from academic researchers and industrial practitioners. The reason behind this is that most of the studies conducted focus themselves on the success factors and neglect failure factors. Therefore study of the failures is equally important and yet not highlighted.

In this chapter, the author attempted to discover the underlying critical success and failure factors of an information system projects if they are not updated continuously. A questionnaire survey of two information systems of telecommunication industry was conducted and analyzed.

8.2 LITERATURE REVIEW

The study suggests that during the past two decades, investment in Information technology and Information system have increased significantly in the private and public sector organization whereas the rate of failure remains quite high.

The various factors responsible for IS failures are:

- Lack of top management commitment to the project;
- Poor user commitment;
- Inadequate user involvement;
- Requirements not well understood;
- Failure to manage the expectation of users;
- Changing scope;
- Lack in skills;
- New technology;
- Insufficient Staffing;
- Lack of organizations' commitment to a systems development methodology;
- Poor estimation techniques;
- Inadequate people management skills;
- Failure to adapt to business change;
- Failure to manage the plan.

The Standish Group prepared a report of a survey in which 365 IS executives participated. The reports suggests that IS/IT failures were covered up, ignored, and/or rationalized by IS/IT personnel. They advocate that the CEO's role in IS/IT planning and development should be:

- Quantify the business value of the IT by measuring its overall economic value to the business.
- Recentralize control of IT spending while maintaining flexibility.

- Communicate the results one expects in clear
- Financial terms.
- Keep the IT architecture/infrastructure simple.
- Be firm on rigorous pilot testing.
- Make sure that the new system has the capacity to handle the required number of transactions that need to be processed.
- Closely monitor what IT suppliers are using to run their own businesses.
- Avoid succumbing to hasty decisions based on the urgency of the situation.

New requirements are influencing the business processes as the business needs are changing very fast. Therefore to keep pace with the global market and to achieve the competitive advantage, the company has to react immediately and improve the quality of the adopted IS...

Turban et al. reviews yearly Datamation (a leading practitioner journal of information systems) and then suggests why IS are important for a business organization.

The information systems are required for the following reasons:

- For the business process reengineering.
- To meet the company's goals and objectives.
- Better decision making.
- For the development of productivity.
- Enhancing the quality of product.
- Enhancing the quality of product.
- Building the competitive edge.
- Retention of change management environment.
- Creation of Research and Innovation

According to Turban et al., the IS projects can be classified into four categories:

- Commercial e.g. customer relationship management (CRM), e-commerce, knowledge management
- Strategic e.g. re-engineering, information architecture
- Organizational e.g. centralization vs. decentralization, outsourcing, resource management;
- Technological e.g. database, internet and intranet.

Diniz, proposed a three dimensional model for the evaluation of virtual business environments from the user's perspective by doing the case study of three banks in a Brazil. The studies include the services offered, functionality, reliability, security of transactions on the sites and also the user's transaction quality. This evaluation approach is useful to known the quality of the sites used for Internet banking.

All the studies predict that during the past two decades, investment in Information technology and Information system have increased significantly in the organization. But the rate of failure remains quite high. Therefore an attempt is made to prepare the continuous updation model for the prediction of the success or failure of the organization taking into consideration the telecom sector. The current empirical study is particularly important as it may contribute in forming a model for the Indian telecom industry.

8.3 OBJECTIVES AND SCOPE OF THE STUDY

⤙ To study the causes of failures of ISs due continuous non-up gradation of IS.

⤙ To study the critical success factors of continuous up gradation of IS especially for the Indian telecom industry.

The objective of study is to analyze the failure and success factors of Information System due to non-up gradation and also pinpoint the most important factors. Also, the study focuses on testing the relevance of the factors existing in literature in the Indian Telecom Industry.

In view of the certain constraints like time and money, the study is confined to the two organizations, namely, Reliance Communication Chandigarh, Punjab Communication Limited, Puncom, and Mohali.

Table 8.1   Sampling Plan

Organization	Management Level	Population	Sample	Actual Response	%age of Response Size
Puncom	Top Level	14	11	10	90.90
	Middle Level	20	14	13	92.85
	Lower Level	210	146	136	93.15
Total		244	171	159	92.30
Reliance	Top Level	12	10	9	90
	Middle Level	42	32	29	90.62
	Lower Level	77	57	42	73.68.
Total		131	89	80	84.76
	Grand Total	375	270	239	88.53

These enterprises are selected because they have extremely good business performance and high Employment generators and early adopters of IT with functional ISs. This industry is strategically and economically important for the growth of the country as India is the second largest country in using the mobile services in the world. Among these organizations, Reliance Communication is an upstream company concerned with telecommunication products and services. The other companies is also a telecommunication unit having manufacturing unit as well as service unit and are responsible for supplying finished products to consumers, i.e. the downstream company.

8.4 RESEARCH METHODOLOGY

A. For the Organization

- Universe of study: Telecommunication industry comprises of Reliance Communication, Vodafone, Essar, Idea, and Bharti-Airtel.
- Sample Selection: Reliance Communication Chandigarh, and Punjab Communication Ltd (Puncom) Mohali.

B. For the Respondents

- Universe of study: All managers working at the three levels of the selected organizations.
- Sample Selection: A number of respondents based on proportional stratified sampling from all of these organizations are selected. The respondents are identified from various levels / business functions in each organization such as top management, ARE management, functional heads, and ARE staff and users. The primary data is collected via questionnaires cum interviews with the selected respondents. Statistical Package for the Social Sciences (SPSS) statistical tool is used for the statistical analysis. The norms are formalized for the choice of respondents from the participating organizations on the basis of detailed discussions with a number of academicians, researchers and industrial experts. It is observed that increase in sample size will affect the results only marginally, whereas effort for it is considerable. The sample size from a stratum is determined on the basis of the following criterion:

  70% of the population where sample size > 100

  50% of the population where sample size < 100.

8.4.1 Data collection tools

Primary data has been collected through a questionnaire-cum-interview method from the selected respondents. The questionnaire is designed based on the literature survey, and detailed discussion with many academicians, professionals and industry experts

8.5 INTRODUCTORY CONTINUOUS UPDATION COMPONENT

27 variables related to continuous updation of IS are selected for the study relating to failure and success factors of Information System. Quantitative analysis is performed by using various testing models, Anova F, T-tests are applied to check importance and to identify CFF & CSF between Puncom & Reliance.

8.5.1 Continuous Updation System

The analysis had been made on the basis of the mean scores. The responses of the managers of the two companies differ significantly in terms of their mean scores. Among these companies, Reliance Communication Ltd. has been pioneer in continuous updating full-fledged Information System (IS) with fully automated procedures, processes and practices. The Puncom has a function-wise domestic IS, that is not well-integrated. IS is only being used as a support tool by the Puncom managers. The Figure 8.1 explains the mean scores of both the companies.

From the mean scores, it can be depicted in Puncom there is very less up gradation in the ttechnology innovative factors that leads to its IS failure. Their market research at the global level is very low which its critical failure factor becomes. The project planning, monitoring factors are also very slow which leads to the failure of IS. However employee's awareness, knowledge, understands of advanced technology and methodology is found to be sufficient in Puncom. This high managerial expectations are prevalent in Puncom because the company has been the player among the public sector telecommunication and managers of the company strongly feel that tremendous improvement in IS functioning should be done by updating the in-house IS to global IS.

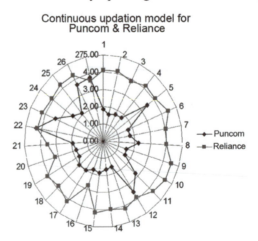

Fig. 8.1 Continuous Updation Model

The mean scores, also depicts that the managers of Reliance give maximum importance to the 'Marketing related' factors which leads to its IS success. However on other hand, the managers of Reliance do not have such high aspirations as the company has already has fully fledged Information System implemented. The global IS continuous updation in Reliance is found to be efficient as it has a potential for the decision making process.

8.5.2 Validity of the model

This has been tested by performing the following tests:

Measures of goodness

Content validity

The various views/sub-views and the factors / variables has been identified on the basis of extensive survey and study of literature.

The users of the Information systems has attained at the three levels of the management in the two participant organizations with rigorous consultation and discussions. This revealed that the questionnaire has been comprehensive and useful for the organizations.

Scale reliability

Reliability of the scale has been studied for Continuous Updation using Alpha method of scale reliability. The Cronbach's Alpha was calculated for both Puncom & Reliance which is discussed in detail in Table 8.2

As depicted from the Table 8.2, the value of the Cronbach's Alpha was found to be greater than the standardized value of 0.6.This means the data is reliable. Hence both Puncom & Reliance had attained value of 0.811 & 0.822 respectively and overall 0.985. This establishes the reliability of the scale.

Table 8.2 Reliability of scale

	Puncom Reliance	Cronbach's Alpha Reliability			
Continuous Updation Process	No. of item	No. of item	PunCom	Reliance	Overall
	27	27	.811	.822	0.985

8.5.3 Continuous Updation Process for Information System

The respondent has been divided into three levels i.e. top level, middle level and operational level. Responses to factors and variable has given in the tabular form and also explained graphically. A conclusion has been drawn from these tables and graphs. Firstly the data have been tested by using mean Scores at top management, middle management and lower management level has been tabulated in Table 8.3 and Fig. 8.3 and Fig. 8.4 for Puncom and

Reliance. The responses of the managers of two companies differ significantly in terms of From Table 8.2 it was analyzed that the mean score of Puncom are near to 2 whereas in Reliance the overall mean is greater than or equal to 4. Further on the basis of mean score overall average of extremely important factors were identified in both the companies mean score. From the above results it had been concluded that Reliance has been sincere in continuously updating fully fledged Information System with fully automated procedures processes and practices .This shows that the variable identified as in Table 8.3 are first planned then executed in the right direction whereas in Puncom there is a need for flexible model and still a huge scope of improvement & integration is possible.

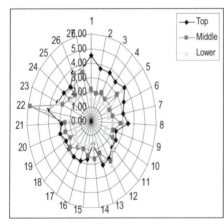

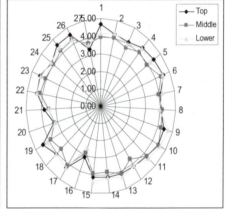

Fig. 8.2 Comparative of Continuous Updation Model of Puncom at

Fig. 8.3 Comparative of Continuous Updation Model of Reliance at three levels

Table 8.4 Mean Scores (Puncom, Reliance)

S. No.	Factor	Puncom				Reliance			
		Top	Middle	Lower	Total	Top	Middle	Lower	Total
1	Price	4.50	2.15	1.63	1.85	4.67	3.93	4.12	4.11
2	Brand Image	3.70	1.92	1.38	1.57	4.22	4.00	4.26	4.16
3	Selection of	3.70	2.15	1.54	1.72	4.11	3.72	3.95	3.89
4	Market Position	3.50	1.92	1.64	1.78	4.33	4.03	4.26	4.19
5	Online and	3.80	3.00	3.47	3.45	4.44	3.86	4.19	4.10
6	Sales force	3.30	1.85	1.55	1.69	4.56	4.34	4.50	4.45
7	Delivery of	3.00	2.08	1.63	1.75	4.00	3.90	4.17	4.05
8	Flexibility to	3.40	2.77	2.07	2.21	4.00	4.10	3.95	4.01
9	Support	2.40	2.15	1.43	1.55	4.44	4.24	4.71	4.51
10	Quality to	2.60	2.31	1.44	1.58	4.44	4.45	4.60	4.53
11	Quality to	2.70	2.92	2.78	2.79	4.22	4.21	4.40	4.31
12	Quality of	3.10	3.31	3.60	3.54	4.11	3.59	4.05	3.89
13	RD centre	3.20	2.38	1.38	1.58	4.11	4.10	4.29	4.20

14	Market research	1.60	2.62	1.57	1.66	4.11	3.79	4.14	4.01
15	Market	2.60	2.38	1.73	1.84	4.11	3.90	4.38	4.18
16	Authority of	2.90	2.08	1.67	1.78	3.11	2.83	2.60	2.74
17	Clarity of	2.90	2.15	1.93	2.01	4.22	4.07	4.24	4.18
18	Formal and	2.80	2.69	1.90	2.03	4.00	3.59	4.00	3.85
19	Quality &	2.70	2.23	1.63	1.75	4.44	3.86	4.14	4.08
20	Information	3.00	2.54	1.60	1.76	3.22	3.21	3.14	3.18
21	Firm assests	2.80	2.46	1.79	1.91	3.78	3.48	3.50	3.53
22	Organizational	4.10	5.85	4.21	4.34	4.33	4.14	4.33	4.26
23	Marketing	3.40	2.92	3.35	3.31	4.44	4.03	4.33	4.24
24	Technological	3.20	2.54	2.38	2.44	4.11	3.93	4.14	4.06
25	Innovational	3.00	2.31	2.03	2.11	4.56	4.14	4.33	4.29
26	Marketing	3.70	3.54	3.67	3.66	4.56	4.21	4.24	4.26
27	Low	3.70	3.46	3.85	3.81	3.33	3.66	3.57	3.58

Table 8.5 *t* test for 3 levels of puncom and reliance

Factors	Top-Top		Middle-Middle		Lower-Lower	
	t	Sig. (2-tailed)	t	Sig. (2-tailed)	t	Sig. (2-tailed)
Price of IS	.383	.708	6.773	.000**	19.232	.000**
Brand actual	1.237	.241	7.372	.000**	22.930	.000**
Selection of services /products	.927	.371	5.059	.000**	16.023	.000**
Market Position	2.041	.063	7.941	.000**	27.152	.000**
Online and offline promotion/ advertising and offline	2.421	.027*	3.595	.001**	6.613	.000**
Sales force	2.576	.022*	9.302	.000**	22.304	.000**
Delivery of products/services	2.301	.036*	5.395	.000**	23.431	.000**
Flexibility to support optimization of business procedure	1.309	.210	4.831	.000**	11.050	.000**
Support dynamically changing process	4.372	.001**	6.834	.000**	33.494	.000**
Quality to support products or services	3.945	.001**	8.092	.000**	29.347	.000**
Quality to support business efficiency and staff productivity	3.787	.002**	5.154	.000**	15.176	.000**
Quality of Communication in different	1.796	.090	.890	.386	2.889	.005**
RD centre	1.899	.075	4.870	.000**	21.763	.000**
Market research at global level for up to date IS.	6.049	.000**	4.276	.000**	17.938	.000**
Market research at global level for up to date IS (or worldwide) electronic presence of brands	3.640	.003**	3.744	.002**	18.968	.000**
Authority of the project manager actual	.459	.652	2.497	.025	9.459	.000**
Clarity of organizational goals	2.816	.012*	6.167	.000**	16.733	.000**
Formal and strict rules for employees	2.979	.009**	4.162	.000**	13.818	.000**
Quality & commitment of business and product	3.712	.002**	5.871	.000**	16.739	.000**

Information exchange between the IS team and	.598	.558	2.493	.020	13.064	.000**
Firm assests ac tual	2.392	.030*	3.730	.001**	14.451	.000**
Organizational assets	.814	.428	-.746	.470	.929	.357
Marketing assets	3.576	.003**	5.098	.000**	9.458	.000**
Technological assets	2.705	.021*	5.910	.000**	13.323	.000**
Innovational differentiation	4.050	.001**	6.587	.000**	13.870	.000**
Marketing differentiation	2.988	.010*	2.093	.045*	3.300	.002**
Low cost strategy actual	−1.000	.338	.676	.506	−1.995	.052

For the significant finding the difference in the three levels are calculated by using T-test as depicted in a Table 8.4.

Hypothesisl (H1): There is a significant difference in the levels individually(Top of Puncom to Top of Reliance, Middle of Puncom to Middle of Reliance, Lower of Puncom to Lower of Reliance) of the selected companies on the basis of mean scores (T-test).

Table 8.4 examined the differences existing in the two companies in context to ISs continuous updation activities... If the value of the significance is more than 0.05 those variables are not significantly contributing towards the model, it was found that the variables selected by application of T test at three different level of both the companies showed that the variables contributing are significantly different therefore alternate hypothesis is accepted. At various level variables identified are

Top Level: Online and offline promotion/advertising through IS, Sales force, Delivery of products/services, Support dynamically changing process, Quality to support products or services, Quality to support business efficiency and staff productivity, Research and development in the organization, national wide, actual, Clarity of organizational goals to employees, Formal and strict rules for employees to follow, Quality & commitment of Business & Product consultant of IS, firm assets, Marketing assets, Technological assets, Innovational differentiation, Marketing assets factors contributes significantly in the study .

Middle Level: Price, Brand Image, Selection of services/products, Market Position, Online and offline promotion/advertising and offline promotion/ advertising, Sales force, Delivery of products/services, Flexibility to support optimization of business proc, Support dynamically changing process, Quality to support products or services, Quality to support business efficiency and staff productivity, Quality of Communication in different organizational units comm. actual, Research and development in the organization, Market research at global level for up to date IS at global level for up to date IS, Market research at global level for up to date IS (or worldwide) electronic presence of brands, Authority of the project manager, Clarity of organizational goals to employees, Formal and strict rules for employees to follow, Quality & commitment of Business & Product consultant of IS, Information exchange between the IS team and other employee, firm assets actual, Marketing assets, Technological assets, Innovational differentiation, Marketing differentiation factors contributes significantly in the study.

Operational Level: Price , Brand Image, Selection of services/products, Market Position, Online and offline promotion/advertising and offline promotion/advertising, Sales force, Delivery of products/services, Flexibility to support optimization of business proc, Support dynamically changing process, Quality to support products or services, Quality to support business efficiency and staff productivity, Quality of Communication in different organizational units, Research and development in the organizational , Market research at global level for up to date IS at global level for up to date IS, Market research at global level for up to date ISs(or worldwide) electronic presence of brands, Authority of the project manager, Clarity of organizational goals to employees, Formal and strict rules for employees to follow factors contributes significantly in the study.

Following are the observation for the three levels of Puncom and Reliance

◆ In Reliance, Chandigarh a full-fledged ERP based IS is in place and is fully operational and their business largely depends on it. The manual procedures, practices and processes have been largely replaced by the IS and the day-to-day working of managers is through the IS only.

◆ In Puncom, Mohali, some functional managers are the users of IS but not all the managers are well acquainted to using an IS. IT is more a support tool rather than a driver in the company. The in-house IS exists but more as function-wise and level-wise information systems that are not very well integrated.

Table 8.6 F scores of reliance and puncom

Factors	Reliance		Factors	Puncom	
	F	Sig.		F	Sig.
Price of IS	3.557	.033*	Price of IS	66.345	.000
Brand Image	1.069	.348	Brand Image	71.503	.000
Selection of services/pro	.835	.438	Selection of	45.282	.000
Market Position	1.839	.166	Market Position	29.930	.000
Online and offline promotion	3.443	.037*	Online and offline promotion	5.930	.003
Sales force	.428	.653	Sales force	26.967	.000
Delivery of products/service	1.611	.206	Delivery of products/service	12.781	.000
Flexibility to support optimization of business	.242	.786	Flexibility to support optimization of business	8.801	.000

Support dynamically changing	3.728	.028*	Support dynamically	12.301	.000
Quality of Communicat	.569	.568	Quality of Communic	18.331	.000
Quality to support	.718	.491	Quality to support	.262	.770
Quality of Communication	3.348	.040*	Quality to Communication	1.072	.345
Research and	.462	.632	Research and	28.141	.000
Market research at	1.391	.255	Market research	10.205	.000
Market research at	3.041	.054	Market research	5.129	.007
Authority of the project manager	4.263	.018*	Authority of the project	12.756	.000
Clarity of organization	.335	.717	Clarity of organizati	7.137	.001
Formal and strict rules	1.997	.143	Formal and strict	14.894	.000
Quality & commitment	1.791	.174	Quality & commitme	13.560	.000
Information exchange	.086	.917	Information	23.343	.000
Firm assets actual	.510	.602	Firm assets	14.762	.000
Organization al assets	.607	.548	Organizational	2.941	.056
Marketing assets	2.328	.104	Marketing assets	3.886	.023
Technologic al assets	.589	.557	Technolog ical assets	12.410	.000
Innovational differentiation	.730	.485	Innovational	9.005	.000
Marketing differentiation	.395	.675	Market differentiation	.346	.708
Low cost strategy	.483	.619	Low cost strategy	4.152	.018

H2: Puncom & Reliance (Level-wise comparisons based on one way Anova F-Test) are significantly different in IS system Continuous Updation (ANOVA)

Table 8.6 examined the differences existing in the two companies in context to ISs continuous updation activities... If the value of the significance is more than 0.05 those variables are not significantly contributing towards the model ,it was found that the variables like Quality to support business efficiency and staff productivity, Marketing assets, Organizational assets, Clarity of organizational goals to employees are neither contributing in Reliance nor in Puncom. So these are excluded from the present study. Further variables whose significance value is less than 0.05 were considered relevant for developing IS model as shown in Table 8.6.

This proved that the model is significantly different in Reliance and Puncom as the alternate hypothesis was rejected.

8.5.4 Reliance Communication

Following factors play a great role in the Critical Success factors of IS in Reliance.

The various marketing related factors like information of the competitive services, prices and promotion of the products for the encouragement of the customers to purchase and negotiate through the IS in the global market is existing in IS.

In general, IS playing a great role in the online services for the delivery of products and services. IS supports various dynamically changing processes of the organization.

Quality of communication existing in the different organizational units through IS is very high. Every employee is answerable for their own domain of work through IS.

Authority of the project manager for updating the employees regarding the organizational goals from time to time is the normal activity of the Reliance.

This company provides a large services and product selection as the customers are more likely to find what they are looking for from the IS of Reliance.

Online and offline promotion/advertising have been encouraged through global IS because the majority of online vendors needed their trade immediately. An online ordering service allowed them to place an order at any time without waiting for a sales person.

Reliance has integrated their Information system with the web sites having their back-end operation, thus allowing customers to keep track of product availability and provide accurate information about it on their web sites.

Business clients also needed assurance that goods are available and would be delivered on time. It offers a services and products delivery anywhere in the world within 48-72 hours.

Employees follow the formal and strict rules for IS implementation.

The consultants of IS find to be highly committed to quality and the business product. Regular information exchange between the IS team and other employee leads to the success for IS failures.

Research and development centre is existing in the organization.

Market research at global level for up to date IS is in vogue. Nationwide (or worldwide) electronic presence of brands is available which is the continuously updated.

8.5.5 Puncom

Following factors play a great role in the Critical Failure Factors in IS of Puncom

   ◄ The various marketing related factors like information of the competitive services, prices and promotion of the products for the encouragement of the customers to purchase and negotiate through the IS in the global market is found to be missing.

↵ In general, a brand starts lagging in the global market and hence customer awareness declines. Due to non availability of the online services through IS for the delivery of products /services is missing as the organization is a public undertaking in which a lot of formal chapter work is required to be processed in parallel.

↵ Sales force (marketing, promoting online services).Puncom rely on sales force rather than on the IS. Puncom should use its sales force, which had strong relationships with vendors, to encourage them to place orders through an online system.

↵ Puncom needs to form long-term relationship with vendors for facilitating the transition from the old to the new system, with strong customer support provided through the company's sales force and online training. Puncom required its vendors to change their purchasing system and practices.

↵ While vendors had to put more effort into learning how to use a new system to place online orders themselves, the sales force put more time and effort into developing marketing programs for them.

↵ Flexibility to support optimization of business processes using global IS is the requirement of current market. IS must support dynamically changing process to give the competitive advantage. But Puncom's IS lags in it.

↵ Quality of Communication in different organizational units is lacking in the in-house IS of Puncom.

↵ Research and development in the organization's R & D centre actual is just on cards and is not properly functional.

↵ Market research at global level for up to date IS is lagging.

↵ Worldwide electronic presence of brands is missing.

↵ Authority of the project manager for implementing the new IS is lacking.

↵ No clarity of organizational goals to employees.

↵ Firm assets regarding the global ARE need to be employed in the organization.

8.5.6 Recommendations

Due to the high rate of failures of IS, it has been found that the organization which is lagging in IS online services, online customers, there is a real challenge in conducting business in the global market. They are not able to compete with other online competitors, therefore to convince customers to shop online or use online services some international standardized based IS for handing their business is required only then the company can have good business performance.

The researchers also observed that, Reliance is having a service-oriented culture than Puncom. Reliance encourages personal communication with customer services or sale personnel and develops relationships with them, and in return, their interests will be looked after in forms of extra care, extra service, and even discount.

This explains that the organization focusing its effort on customer service and customer relationships or human-touch activities. By providing a call center, sales support, and online chat, customers could have or maintain.

Direct communication with a company and feel that online shopping/business purchasing from Reliance is more personal and less individualistic processes. Besides this there is tremendous potential of further growth due to the introduction of 3G and Internet based Technology by the Reliance.

The study of this sector is of great importance for the employability, economic and business.

The study has identified and examined CSFs and CFFs related to continuous updation in the information system. The organizations must be highly concerned about that online security and privacy, their brand name recognition and reputation, customer support, relationship and delivery. Organizations need to understand the behavior of online customers.

The researchers found that all successful companies put effort into collecting customer profiles and conducting market research in order to understand their target customers. Organizations must support fully integrated IS development. As the survey is based on private(Reliance) versus public(Puncom)sector organizations, this studies concludes that the private sector organization are illustrious in their strength for gaining competitive advantage by having effective IS and hence the public sector organization must try to replicate the same.

This CSFs and CFFs guideline could also be applied to other developing countries with similar business and Information System related infrastructures and national culture mostly in developing countries.

References

1. Benjamin I. P. Rubinstein, Peter L. Bartlett, and J. Hyam Rubinstein, Shifting, One-Inclusion Mistake Bounds and Tight Multiclass Expected Risk Bounds, in Advances in Neural Information Processing Systems 19 (NIPS 2006), 2007.
2. Bentley, L.D. and Whitten, J.L. (2007). System analysis and design for the global enterprise, McGrawHill, Boston.

3. Standish Group . 2001. Extreme Chaos. http://www.standishgroup.com/ sample_research/PDFpa ges/extreme_chaos.pdf. 2004. Third Quarter Report 2004.http://www.standishgroup.com/sample_research/P DFpages/q3-spotlight. pdf

4. DeLone, W.H., and McLean, E.R. 2004. "Measuring E- Commerce Success: Applying the DeLone & McLean Information systems Success Model," International Journal of Electronic Commerce (9:1), fall, pp 31-47. Turban, E. & McLean, E. & Wetherbe, J. (2005). Information Technology for Management: Transforming Organizations in the Digital Economy (5th Ed.). New York: John Wiley & Sons, Inc.

5. Diniz E, Porto R & Adachi T, September-2005. "Internet Banking in Brazil: Evaluation of Functionality, Reliability and Usability", Electronic Journal of Information Systems Evaluation, Vol. 8, Issue 1, pp 41-50 J Jay Liebowitz , "A look at why information systems fail Department of Information Systems," Kybernetes, Vol. 28 No. 1, 1999,pp. 61-67, © MCB University Press,0368-492X, University of Maryland-BaltimoreCounty, Rockville, Maryland, USA .

6. Flowers, S. (1997), "Information systems failure: identifying the critical failure factors," Failure and Lessons Learned in Information Technology Management: An International Journal, Cognizant Communication Corp., Elmsford, New York, NY, Vol. 1 No. 1, pp. 19-30.

7. DeLone, W.H., and McLean, E.R. 2004. "Measuring E- Commerce Success: Applying the DeLone & McLean Information Systems Success Model," International Journal of Electronic Commerce (9:1), Fall, pp 31-47.

8. Bruce Curry and Luiz Moutinho, "Neural networks in marketing: Approaching consumer responses to advertising stimuli", European Journal of Marketing, Vol 27 No 7, 1993 pp 5- 20.

9. Demuth, H. B., Beale, M., 2004. User's Guide for Neural Network Toolbox (version 4) for use with MATLAB 6.1. The Math Works Inc., Natick, MA.

10. Kweku Ewusi Mensah, "Critical issues in the abandoned information system development projects", Loyola Marymount University, Los Angeles, CA, Volume 40, Issue 9(September 1997) pages 74-80, 1997, ISSN: 00017082.

11. Angeliki Poulymenakou1 and Vasilis Serafeimidis2, Volume1, number 3, 1997, "Failure & Lessons Learned in Information Technology Management", Vol. 1, pp. 167177.

☺☺☹

PART 2

Enterprise Resource Planning and Sustainability

9

Web Based ERP for Entrepreneurs

Chaudhry Muhammad Nadeem Faisal[1]

Software as services is link to the concept of cloud computing is a style of computing where information technologies enable business products, services and solutions as a service over the internet. The concept of SAS (software as services) is currently in very early stages of development. There are a lot of researches being carried out in this area. Authors focus to analyze the SAS and also to propose a concept based on qualitative studies for business process integration and Industrial collaboration, in the context of small businesses. The primary aim of their research work is to integrate process not only within the organization but also with the partners and customers.

KEYWORDS	Software as Services (SAS)	SMEs	Business Process Integration	Cloud Computing	B2B Collaboration

9.1 INTRODUCTION

Enterprises are increasingly in use with rapid business environments that requiring the need to respond to fast moving windows of opportunities and respond to challenges and growth possibilities and shorter lead-time for decision making. Swift environmental changes, diverse business developments and continuous improvement in their information system, many organizations think to enhance their business processes through integration and B2B (business to business) collaboration. The enterprises today are forging ahead with the effort of integrating information systems across corporate boundaries to unite the customers, suppliers and any other business partners with which they interact. They use the information regarding their finances, employees, and to manage the items or assets they own.

The focus of this study is to make the structure, constant and smooth flow of information with help of Web based services in efficient manners to support SMEs in textile sector with uniform graphics interface, as the interface is the gauge for the success of applications. As in SMEs, the textile manufacturing process is divided into clusters e.g. ginning, spinning, weaning, processing and made ups. Only few corporate level industries possess their own complete

---
[1] The University of Faisalabad, Pakistan

units for manufacturing. SMEs sector majorly faces the problem due to dis-integration and cluster based industry in different geographical locations. As they have to support each other in value addition process of a product.

9.2 BACKGROUND

Small Businesses have been facing tremendous changes within economic, commercial and technological environments. It is evolving an urgent problem for them how to utilize information technology and to build an effective information system. The poor performance is only due to limited resources and unawareness about the Information system capabilities, poor implementation, lack of business processes integration and industrial collaboration.

Due the limited resource and lack of IT expertise most of the organization do not have their own complete information system. As the installing, developing and maintenance of ES (Enterprise system) is very expensive as only the big or corporate level organization can bear the cost. Pakistani entrepreneurs have been facing tremendous changes within economic, commercial and technological environments e.g., excessive regulation, energy shortage, water shortage, difficulties in marketing and selling the products, unawareness about the technology, lack of expertise in information technologies, obsolete technology, limited R&D (Research and Development) support, lack of capital and financial resources, low skill mix of the labor/work force, limited productivity of works and rising competition due to imported products.

9.3 SMES IN PAKISTAN

Small Medium Enterprise sector is the backbone of Pakistan economy, as it plays vital role in the social and economical development of the Pakistan. According to the statistics collected from SMEDA (Small Medium Enterprise Development Authority), there are about 3.2 million business enterprises in Pakistan, (44% Rural & 56% Urban), where they produce a wide range of goods and services, provide employment for a large number of skilled and semi-skilled workers, account for a substantial proportion of manufacturing output, and make a major contribution to the country's balance of payments. Author focus of attention on the textile manufacturing related SMEs is, specifically in Faisalabad. As Faisalabad is the third largest city of Pakistan having 45932 SMEs manufacturing units, from them 22378 related to business of textile sector.

Table 9.1 Total Number of SMEs in Textile clusters in Faisalabad

Textile Sector	Units:
Gining	26
Spinning	44
Weaving	21,842
Printing	192

Apparel & Made Ups: 1200 registered	300
Small & Medium	274
Large Units	250,000

Table 9.2   Survey results on SMEs

Entrepreneur's Education: Only 49% entrepreneur in SMEs sector having college or graduate level qualification.
Technical Training: 70% entrepreneur in SMEs sector had not obtained any training.
Computer Usage: only 46% have computer. While from them 57 % SMEs it for just maintaining books of accounts while 43 % for letter writing/email/internet.
Power Outages: 62% did not have their own power generation mechanism.

9.4 CLOUD COMPUTING IMPLICATIONS

It is a style in which all the information technology related capabilities are providing services and transferring technology, data and software applications from local systems thought network into Clouds. According to the "the aims of the cloud computing is the migration of users", data and processing from desktop PCs (client system) and corporate servers to the cloud. It is also defined by why not just move all processing power to the cloud and walk around with an Ultra-light input device with a screen? The Cloud computing brought a lot of services i.e. database, storage, backup, data replication, data protection and maintain the security of the services. Cloud computing in simple words is the delivery of services or capabilities over the network and it is segregated into three following entities.

- Software as a service (SaaS): Applications based services delivered over the network.
- Platform as a service (PaaS): A software development framework/ components all delivered on the network on demand, the users have to pay.
- Infrastructure as a service (IaaS): An integrated environment of computing resources, storage and network fabric delivered to network users have to pay for usage model.
- Hardware as Layer (HaaS)
- Virtualization as Layer (VaaS)

9.5 SAS BASED ERP

Software as a service is link to the concept of cloud computing a new paradigm e.g., Google apps. The paradigm focuses on sharing data and computation power over the scalable network nodes. Nodes include the end user computer, data center and web services. Software as a service term is used to provide software and application based services to users on their demand. It is also defined by today most of services we use on the web, are not just the web pages but are the web based applications that we access through network using a browsers. It is increasingly prevailing distribution model based on applications that are hosted by provider to customer through the network. It is a mature and a new development approach. A lot of IT expertise companies offers this SOA (Service oriented architecture) through web where the user has to pay against the desired services e.g., SAS based ERP, E- supply chain management, CRM. As ERP (enterprise resource planning) changed from traditional Client/Server environment to the web based and Internet/Intranet network computing support environment along with user oriented approach for usability perspective. Web based services are the new breed of web based applications. These services performed different functions from simple to complex business processes.

A great benefits of SAS based ERP is that remote user like executive and sale person, can access the data with the help of browser. It removes the problems from the investment towards the maintences of server and other hardware's. It also removes your problems for new add-one feathers, upgrades, easier management, compatibility, effective collaboration and global accessibility.

Different companies provide similar service oriented architecture through browsers in order to solve the enterprise problems and to derive their perspective solutions. BScaler enterprise recourse Manager™, Black Soft and Web ERP™, Salesforce.com and Sugar CRM provides SAS based ERP to Small and medium level industries which include Business 2 Business (B2B), CRM and e-supply Chain services. SaaSplus, Inc is also SAAS ERP providers in USA, also offering ERP based applications.

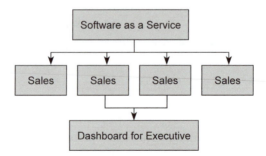

Fig. 9.3 Flow of Information and Business Process Integration

9.6 USER INTERFACE

Interface of application play an important role for the adoptability and efficiency of the application. The interface describes the function between the things, this term related to engineering technology used to describe the equipment, components and components connections,. User satisfaction is one evaluation mechanism for gauging system success. There is need to evaluate, the efficacy of user characteristics and fitness factors as determinants of ERP success. The technological products always relied upon the User Interface Design (UID) to elevate their complexity and usability. Technology its self may not win user acceptance and satisfaction. The usability, and user experiences on the end product, is the key to acceptance/satisfaction. Engineer's always focus on the technology aspects while the usability specialists focus on the interface at which user interact. When applied to computer software and web based applications, User Interface Design is known as Human-Computer Interaction (HCI).

Interface Design in terms of computers refers to many products where the application user's interacts with controls/displays. The best user interface designing always requires the systematic approach and to ensure optimum performance, usability Testing is required for evaluations. This empirical testing/investigations permit the application users to provide data that use to design optimized interface.

9.7 FINDINGS

The purposed concept of computing is derived from the real world service model to give out the processing time to SMEs in textile sector to mange their business processes individually. So this requires the deployment of datacenter and storage which must be in control of government and at a place where the uninterrupted power supplies i.e. electricity or solar panel are available. SMEs can freely access the desired business applications accordingly. Here the focus is on the cloud based services oriented infrastructure (SAAS Based ERP) that will not only facilitate the SMEs to manage their business activities, but also to develop fastest supply chain with smooth flow of information between different cluster of SMEs where they exist demographically at different locations.

The division of this service oriented model for E-government into three levels as given in Figure 9.4 First part is to manage the business resources and transaction individually, in second to make collaboration between business to business (B2B) in different cluster of SMEs. The third phase to provide the service oriented architecture (SAAS Based ERP) with uniform graphic interface based applications (UUGI) for better understanding, memorability and adoptability as discuss later.

The Web Based ERP possesses tremendous potential to meet the above mentioned challenges as its goals to obtain better resources, utilization of ES capabilities and also to provide the cost effective services. It will help to produce a valuable product or services with concrete flow of work, material, and information. The informational/ functional integration and collaboration within the different clusters of SMEs facilitate them in planning, which involves demand forecasting, level of inventory, manufacturing and production planning. This level of integration between the different clusters of SMEs in textile value chains makes fastest the supply chain process to reduce the emission of carbon. It can also raise the utilization rate of resource and reducing the electricity cost and consumption as Pakistani SMEs facing now a days.

This will help to resolve the biggest issue in Pakistani textile sector, that is the workers as well as entrepreneurs are not very much familiar with software and computer based applications. It is also costly for the entrepreneurs to spend time and money for training. Web based ERP with uniform graphic interface will enhance the workers adaptability, memorability and thy can work consistently. Application with single graphic Interface could also reduces the human mistake and builds confidence in them

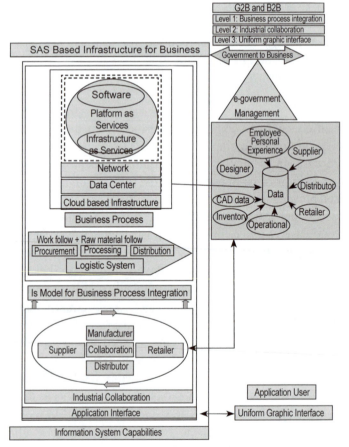

Fig. 9.4 Conceptual Diagram for SAS based ERP to Support Textile Sector

This chapter discusses how to make an organizational process and information centric with cloud based application. It suggests to the government to offer such application to entrepreneurs so they can reduce their operational cost. To develop this cloud computing infrastructure there are high prioritiy needs i.e. complete support of Government authorities and the support of the autonomous bodies that are directly responsible for the development of SMEs in Pakistan. Pakistan is a developing country where no any organization is ready to take the initiatives to promote the awareness and capabilities of information technologies in entrepreneurs. This way government can supply the business communities with enterprise application via cloud computing and can raise the utilization of data center considerably to reduce the consumption of energy. Therefore, cloud computing is the best Environment to establish the e-government The Ministry of Industries, commerce, science and technology, and the Small and Medium Enterprise Development Authority (SMEDA). The authors have recommended that there should be some actions taken by the government officials to regulate, promote and to create cloud computing environment for textile SMEs in Pakistan.

References

1. Lizhe Wang, Jie Tao, Marcel Kunze "Scientific Cloud Computing: Early Definition and Experience", Proceedings of the 2008 10th IEEE International Conference on High Performance Computing and Communications—Volume 00 Karlsruhe, Germany, pp. 825–830, 2008.
2. H, Steve, "Cloud computing made clear", Business Week, Issue 4082, pp.59–59, May, 2008.
3. B. Hayes, "Cloud computing', Communications of the ACM, Vol. 51 no, pp.9–11, May, 2008.
4. A. Weiss, "Computing in the Clouds", networker, vol. 11, no. 4, p.18, Dec, 2007.
5. R. Buyya, A. Sulistio, "Service and Utility Oriented Distributed Computing Systems: Challenges and Opportunities for Modeling and Simulation Communities", Simulation Symposium, pp. 68–81, 2008.
6. Geva Perry, "How Cloud & Utility Computing Are Different, at GigaOm." [Online] [Cited Nov 21, 2008] Available: http://gigaom.com/2008/02/28/how-cloud-utilitycomputing-are-different.
7. Small & Medium Enterprises Department State Bank of Pakistan, SME Finance Quarterly Review First Quarter, 2008
8. http://www.smeda.org/ SMEDA, Small and Medium Enterprise Authority
9. Chaudhry Muhammad Nadeem Faisal, Muhammad Sheraz Arshad Malik "Usability evaluation of Software as Service from Individuals perspective" Vol. II No. 7 (March 2011). ISSN: 1697-9613 (print)-1887-3022 (online). www.eminds.uniovi.es

10. B Scaler enterprise recourse Manager, available online at: http://www.bscaler. com/retrieved (02–02–2011)

11. B Scaler, available online at: http://www.bscaler.com/saasplus/index_ saasplus.htm retrieved (02–02–2011)

12. Chaudhry Muhammad Nadeem Faisal, Issues in Cloud Computing: Usability evaluation of Cloud based application, LAP LAMBERT Academic Publishing, Germany, ISBN–10: 3838362829, ISBN–13: 978–3838362823, PP, 34.

13. http://www.w3.or~R/2004/NOTE-ws-arch-2004021 I /

14. Weihong Li, Lifang Peng, Upgrade ERP from C/S to B/S Based on Web Service, 0-7803-8971-9/05/$20.00 02005 IEEE

15. Evan Asfoura, the Classification of Business Model for the Exchange of Distributed Components of Federated ERP Systems on the Basis of Web Services,

16. Holsapple, Clyde W., Wang, Yu-Min and Wu, Jen-Her (2005): Empirically Testing User Characteristics and Fitness Factors in Enterprise Resource Planning Success. In International Journal of Human-Computer Interaction, 19 (3) pp. 325–342

17. Li Hong1, Ye Feng 2, The Applied Research of ERP in Logistics Management of Petroleum Company, 978-1-4244-7330-4/10/$26.00 ©2010 IEEE 49

18. Qing Chen, Yang Wang, Enterprise Collaborative Business Systems Based on Web Services Technology, 2010 International Conference on E-Business and E-government, 978-0-7695-3997-3/10 $26.00 ©2010 IEEE, DOI 10.1109/ ICEE.2010.16

19. http://cloudcomputing.sys-con.com/node/1200642

20. Brockhoff K, Hauschildt J. Schnittstellen managementkoordination ohne Hierarchie , Zeitschrift Fuehrung und Organisation, 1993,6 (2): 396–403S

21. Renping Xu1, Interface Management for Industrial Design, 978-1-4244-5268- 2/09/$25.00 ©2009 IEEE

22. Holsapple, Clyde W., Wang, Yu-Min and Wu, Jen-Her (2005): Empirically Testing User Characteristics and Fitness Factors in Enterprise Resource Planning Success. In International Journal of Human-Computer Interaction, 19 (3) pp. 325– 342

23. http://www.usernomics.com/user-interface-design.html

☺☺☹

10

Advance Manufacturing Technologies MSME

Brijesh Singh[1]

10.1 INTRODUCTION

Micro, Small and Medium Enterprises (MSMEs) play a pivotal role in the development of national economy by contributing significantly in nation's Gross Domestic Product (GDP), employment generation and exports. The growth of these enterprises is particularly important for developing countries because they provide not only large employment at comparatively lower capital cost in comparison to large enterprises, but also help in industrialization of the rural and backward areas. They also contribute in reducing regional imbalances and assure more equitable distribution of national income and wealth.

To support the significant contribution of MSMEs, few recent examples are presented here. At the start of 2014, there were an estimated 5.2 million businesses in the United Kingdom (UK) which employed 25.2 million people and had a combined turnover of more than £3,500 billion. In UK, small enterprises accounted for 99.3% of all businesses, 47.8% of employment and 33.2% of turnover in private sector. Further, across the European Union (EU), there were 21.2 million Small and Medium Enterprises (SMEs) in the non-financial business sector in 2013 and accounted for 99.8% of all enterprises, 66.8% of total employment and 57.9% of total value added generated[9]. In India, the size of the registered MSMEs was estimated to be about 46.756 million (about 31.8% MSMEs of manufacturing nature, whereas 68.2% MSMEs were engaged in the services) that employed approximately 106.152 million of persons and contribute nearly 7.28% of the country's GDP, 37.52% of the total manufacturing output and 34% of the exports. As elucidated in these reports, it is thus well accepted that MSMEs are the backbone of a nation's sustainable economic development.

[1] Associate Professor, Department of Mechanical Engineering, Galgotias College of Engineering and Technology, Greater Noida, India

SMEs have played tremendous role in manufacturing sector all over the worldas these are manufacturing products for sale to customer, offering services and producing raw materials for big enterprises. To solve some of the existing manufacturing problems which existed in the form of low labour productivity, low machine utilization, high labour absenteeism, high rejection rate, high cost of production and high inventory, adoption for Advance Manufacturing Technologies (AMT) is required. AMT plays a major role in quality and flexibility improvements in SMEs. Further, to increase competitiveness and productivity in SMEs, the use of AMT is one alternative. The motivating forces for AMT proposals may also include obtaining financial benefits, countering skill deficiency and enhancing enterprise image. However, marketing and manufacturing that included workforce skills and capabilities and workforce participation have larger effect on enterprise performance. In addition to this, development in Information and Communication Tools (ICT) provides the opportunity for SMEs to expand their business into foreign market.

India's GDP, although growing at a rate greater than 5% per annum during the last two decades, still lags other emerging economies such as China's GDP. As discussed above, one important way to improve India's competitiveness would be to drive innovation in MSMEs which currently have several barriers as identified and analyzed in this research. Keeping this in mind, a comprehensive study was conducted in this work to understand the role that MSMEs can play in India's growth potential. It is also important to point out here that previous studies on SMEs/MSMEs considered these enterprises as a whole and later classified these with variety of products. Hence, in order to broaden the understanding of the issues pertinent to specific industry sectors, the three sectors namely; glassware, shoe/footwear and lock manufacturing enterprises were considered in this study. These sectors were chosen as they affect daily life of all the consumers in India, and thus would have the utmost benefit to Indian economy if we would impart these sectors on a high growth path. Furthermore, the utility of AMT in growing these sectors has not been clearly understood so far. Thus, the research presented herein, performed a careful investigation of the willingness of these sectors to adopt new technologies. With this, the underlying challenges preventing their growth can be addressed. This is particularly important for a developing nation like India as it is necessary to develop innovative ways to accelerate and maintain growth while providing high quality products; and a range of AMT can provide such a pathway for MSMEs.

This research allowed us to identify key weaknesses in their current business strategies and inherent barriers for their growth. This would help us in providing guidance on future business strategies that MSMEs should focus on. The next contribution of research presented here is a clear understanding the role and current state of Human Resource (HR) related affairs on the success of MSMEs - this topic has not obtained sufficient attention in existing literature, especially in the Indian context. The final outcome of this research is detailed investigation of the adoption of Information Technology (IT) tools in MSMEs, again something that has been poorly addressed in literature in Indian context. Overall, we believe that the inferences drawn from this research will be valuable to future growth of these important sectors forming MSMEs, so that they can drive innovation leading to a future India that can successfully compete on a global scale and deliver high quality products at low cost while providing good employment to its large populace.

10.2 METHODOLOGY AND DEMOGRAPHIC OF MSMEs

Methodology covers the detailed procedure for entire research. For the purpose of the survey to collect the responses, a structured questionnaire (questions on five point Likert scale) was framed and was sent to the enterprises involved in manufacturing of glassware and allied products (94 enterprises), shoe/footwear (96 enterprises) and locks (81 enterprises). A total of 84 responses (31% response rate) were collected. Personal visits were also conducted to improve the response rate. About 57% of the total respondents belong to manager's level, whereas remaining were either owner or partners.

Initial findings are discussed on the basis of descriptive statistics using mean, Standard Deviation (SD) and frequency distribution for which Statistical Package for Social Sciences (SPSS) Version 16.0 is employed to analyze the data collected through duly filled in questionnaire. For validity and reliability of collected responses, Cronbach's Alpha is computed. The framed hypotheses are validated and tested statistically by employing one-way ANOVA and t-test. Further, to establish relationship (or to know the impact) of few identified variables with performance parameters, factor analysis and correlation analysis (Pearson's correlation coefficient) is done.

Nature and characteristics of MSMEs surveyed is presented in the demographic profile. About 20% enterprises surveyed belong to micro (0-9 employees), 35% enterprises belong to small (1049 employees) and 45% enterprises belong to medium (50-249 employees) enterprises. Hence, it reflects that all the enterprises surveyed are of MSMEs nature, not only in Indian respect, but also in global respect. Further, there is nearly equal participation of all the three sectors in this survey.

10.3 FINDINGS OF THE RESEARCH

From the conducted research, it was observed that more than a quarter of MSMEs (about 30%) were involved in export and were having annual sales turn-over of more than Rupees 500 lakhs (10 lakh = 1 million). More than half of the surveyed enterprises were having about 10% of sales growth and it was expected that the same would be maintained for the next three years. The state of availability of automated machines was very poor in MSMEs. Material handling in almost all the enterprises was done by manual means. A few enterprises employed sales promotion techniques. About one-third enterprises were involved in allocation of funds/budget preparation. Almost all the enterprises were referring competitors' product cost while fixing their products' cost. The largest numbers of orders were received by customers directly. Cancellation, modification in address, change in quantity/product etc. was generally acceptable. Unfortunately, none was offering after sales service. Almost none of the enterprises used to communicate with their customers and never collected any data related to customers' need, improvement in product etc.

It was observed that approximately 10% of enterprises encountered with the problem of disobeying payment agreements or terms for maximum of about one tenth of the orders. The top three order winning criteria included quality, product durability and product cost that not only help in retaining the customers but also help in improving sales. Almost all the enterprises outsourced the transportation whereas about 10% were using own shipment. Shipment in alliance with transporters was observed to be highly reliable and had its high trustworthiness as its delivery was safe. Payments were mostly received by cheques and by demand drafts. However, substantial amount of cash transaction and business on credit could not be ruled out. It was investigated that the procurement of raw material was either regular or done within a week time, just after accepting the order. During the procurement, poor attention was paid towards related issues that included record of suppliers, comparative charts, quality of items, transportation cost and safety and trustworthiness of procurement. The lead time of supply was quite high as about 40% respondents reported for lead time of more than 15 days. Almost all the enterprises (about 95%) maintained huge inventory of raw materials and brought out parts as holdings were for more than 15 days as high inventories were assumed to be the solution of fluctuating market. For generating production schedules, most of the enterprises considered the quantity of confirmed order. Further, most of the enterprises considered make to order, followed by make to stock, as prominent manufacturing strategy.

The most prominent pollutant generated were $CO/CO_2/NO_x/SO_2$, followed by noise pollution, mixing of chemicals in water, mixing of residuals in water and discharge of hot water. None was adopting any prescribed method for solid waste disposal. Supply of power was poor and most of the enterprises were facing power crises and thus employed alternative power source or power backup, which was largely a generator. Non-availability of power generally made the product costlier and might also cause delay in meeting the due date of supply. However, many of the enterprises suggested that non-availability of power never affect the rate of production and in meeting quality standards because they knew it very well that electricity would not be available and therefore did not rely on regular electricity supply for production. Instead, they used to employ generator to meet- out the targeted production. About one-third enterprises never took any kind of loan from any of the banks and run the entire business from funds arranged on their own. Nearly half of the respondents reported that they did not experience any problem in getting the loan (from sanction to disbursement). However, respondents told that the major hindrance in getting loan was the "Security/Assets/Collateral Deposits". Further, the most adverse situation was created by fluctuation taking place in the cost of raw material, cost of fuels like Compressed Natural Gas (CNG)/ Liquefied Petroleum Gas (LPG)/Diesel etc. and non availability of benefits of Tax and Special Economic Zone (SEZ).

About 40% enterprises were producing the products of excellent quality (fit for export), while about 90% enterprises were manufacturing the products of good quality (fit for Indian market) and 31% enterprises were producing the products of satisfactory quality (fit for rural market). These MSMEs were manufacturing more than one type of quality standards (as per order received). Surprisingly, very few enterprises reported for total rejection rate of less than 5% for which the major influencing factors included problem of supplied raw material, operator's problem and machine problem. So, there is a strong need to reduce the rejection rate, need for rework and rejection as scrap. Successful adoption of suitable AMT could offer significant improvement as the performance of MSMEs could be improved by improving product quality, employing automated machines for production and reducing cost of production. Product quality and reliability, increase in annual turn-over, reduction in product cost, increase in return on investment, meeting due dates of supply and production with zero defects were observed as the potential competitive priorities and business objectives among all the MSMEs. Most of the respondents were not aware of the latest developments taking place in the area of AMT. This research observed that only owner/partner or proprietor took the initiative for adoption of suitable AMT for most of the times as he/ she was the supreme power of decision making and thus, it had least level of its opposition. Workers never got involved in idea generation for adoption of AMT, thus, they might resist. It was observed that MSMEs have invested and adopted Numerically Controlled (NC)/Computerized Numerically Controlled (CNC)/Automated machines, followed by Office Automation (OA) and Computer Aided Design (CAD). In general, all sectors of MSMEs were still willing to adopt NC/CNC/Automated machines in near future. Improved quality, increased sales, lowering production cost, reduction in rejection/ re-work/scrap, reduction in labour cost and reduction in labour were among the top five benefits that attracted adoption of AMT.

There was no process champion or technological expert. It was observed that the most common risks during AMT adoption were opposition by workforce, inadequate training of workers, production interruptions during AMT installations and failure in meeting financial objectives. The performance of enterprises was generally evaluated by increase in profit, sales and orders. The most of the enterprises neither evaluated employees' performance nor employed benchmarking in any area. Overall state of availability of welfare facilities and its effectiveness was poor in MSMEs. Miss-happening in terms of minor accidents was reported by almost all the enterprises. Availability of Doctor in MSMEs was rare. The most favourable five ergonomic aspects included approach to hand tools, availability of stair cases, availability of sun light, floor condition and ventilation. The most adverse five conditions included non-availability of smoking zone, non availability of canteen/tea and snacks, improper rest between shifts, existing sweating condition and back/body ache problems. Participation of employees for activities like for problem solving during machine failure/breakdown, cleaning of self work places, housekeeping and for preventive maintenance was somewhat poor. During planning of AMT investment, workforce should be involved from its initial idea generation to actual working phase, including post evaluations, as employees of various sectors of MSMEs were generally not willing to accept the adoption of newer technologies and used to oppose and motivate others to oppose. They forced to accept the introduction of new/latest technologies/AMT only because of fear of loss of job.

Employees' of various sectors of MSMEs were always bothered for reducing waste, improving the quality, effective utilization of resources, reducing the power requirement and reducing the pollution. MSMEs were generally operative for all week days with one or more shift working per day and were employing over-time with a provision of extra wages. State of leave was poor as more than one weekly off without deducting salary was given by very less number of enterprises. Enterprises generally offered gifts/ bonus at the time of festivals. Effective loan facility was missing. Most of the workforce employed in MSMEs was unskilled and generally recruited with personal contact and/or with the reference of working employees. Most of the employees left the job because of more salary, better environment and due to personal problems. When an employee leaves the job, only due Provident Fund (PF) was generally paid.

Except 15% of enterprises, all were equipped with computer and printer. Internet was available in three quarter of enterprises. However, overall observations reflected that MSMEs were having poor IT related infrastructure and hence would not be exploitable to the potential benefits of IT to compete in present era of global market. The maximum use of computer/IT/Electronic Commerce (EC) was reported for billing and collection followed by three more areas as payroll/HR, suppliers' information and in research and development. Documents used in MSMEs were generally manually prepared. About one-third enterprises were having their web-sites with poor updating frequency and only about 10% respondents reported that the user might place the order or they receive/get orders for supply of products through web-site. Regarding the problem faced by the enterprises when orders were received through Internet either via e-mail or website, about 15% respondents reported for problem faced in identity confirmation, address confirmation, payments, delivery of products and trustworthiness of customer, while about 13% respondents reported for problem faced in shipment. Respondents said that whenever they got order (either by phone, fax or by e-mail), they usually made a phone call for confirmation of identity. The most commonly used modes of payment receiving were cheques, demand draft and cash. About 60% respondents told that they used to accept cash on delivery.

10.5 WEB-BASED ORDER-SUPPLY SYSTEM

A web based application system is proposed that can be prepared in a customized manner and can be hosted on web-server. Its development and successful adoption may enable the enterprises for (1) Marketing - Globally, (2) Order Receiving and Supply - Globally with shipment in alliance, (3) Communication with Customer, (4) Communication with Vendors - for the supply of raw material and sub-contracted parts, as and when required, and (5) Communication with Dealers - who are responsible for sales of products to customer, along with online transactions in real time.

10.6 DISCUSSION

Technology adoption is a catalyst not only for growth among India's MSMEs but for the growth of the Indian economy on the whole. Many stakeholders, including the Government of India, technology enterprises and MSME leaders recognize that roadblocks relating to infrastructure, technology and skilled labour must be eliminated to sustain the growth of MSMEs and ensure their continued contribution to India's industrial production, economic growth and employment. Most of the MSMEs of India, at present, are not able to produce quality products, at par with global standards. Rejection is also appreciable that needs to be reduced. To grow, more orders are required and thus, more customers are required. To satisfy customer, high quality products are to be offered for sale to customer in an earliest possible time. These products must be reliable and cost effective. Lack of affordable and continuous power supply is hindering the functioning of MSMEs and thus, affecting quantity, quality and cost of produced products. Further, prevailing fluctuating markets are creating threats potentially in terms of cost of raw materials. Entire set of findings advocate for adoption of suitable AMT so as to explore its lucrative benefits, not limited to improved quality, less rejection, less inventory, less production cost and better performance of the products. Hence, adoption of suitable AMT, IT tools and improving workforce state (by training, motivation and offering favourable and ergonomic working conditions) is essentially needed for MSMEs of India so as to achieve their accelerated growth.

Further, Government of India is aware of most of the problems faced by the MSMEs and is taking appropriate measures. In order to boost the MSME sector, several schemes are operational that include Technology Centre Systems Programme, India Inclusive Innovation Fund, Credit Linked Capital Subsidy, Credit Guarantee Scheme, Prime Minister's Employment Generation Programme, Micro and Small Enterprises (MSE) Cluster Development Programme and Scheme for Extension of non tax benefits to MSMEs for three years. The Government has also notified the Public Procurement Policy that mandate that every central ministry/department/public sector-undertaking shall set a minimum annual procurement goal of 20% of total product purchases from MSEs from financial year 2012-13 onwards, in a period of three years.

This research, on the basis of surveyed MSMEs of India, concluded that the largest numbers of orders are received by customers directly and the prominent order winning criteria (quality, product durability and product cost) not only help in retaining the customers but also help in improving sales. Significant amount of cash transaction and business on credit is in place. The lead time of supply is quite high and almost all the enterprises maintain huge inventory as holdings are for more than 15 days. Enterprises employed manufacturing strategy as make to order, potentially, followed by make to stock. The pollutants generation cannot be ignored as none is adopting any prescribed method for solid waste disposal. The supply of power is poor and enterprises are facing power crises and thus use alternative power source or power backup, which is largely a generator. About one-third enterprises run the entire business from funds arranged on their own. Nearly half of the respondents told that "Security/ Assets/Collateral Deposits" is the major hindrance/problem in getting the loan.

Almost all the enterprises reported for total rejection rate of more than 5% and quality of produced product is generally not suitable for export. So, there exists a strong need to reduce the rejection rate. Successful adoption of suitable AMT can offer potential improvement in this respect. MSMEs have invested and adopted NC/CNC/Automated machines followed by OA and CAD and in general, these are still willing to adopt NC/CNC/Automated machines. The top benefits of adoption of AMT include quality improvement, increase in sales and reduction in production cost, rejection, labour cost and in labour. While adopting AMT, opposition by workforce, inadequate training of workers, production interruptions and failure in meeting financial objectives are observed as the most common risks. The performance of enterprises is generally evaluated by increase in profit, increase in sales and increase in orders, while there is no evaluation of employees' performance and they are not using benchmarking in any of the areas. Except 15% of enterprises, all are equipped with computer and printer and Internet is available in three quarter of enterprises. However, overall observations reflect that MSMEs are having poor IT related infrastructure and hence could not exploit the potential benefits of IT to compete in present global market. With this, greater emphasis on adoption of IT tools including suggested web-based order supply system in manufacturing sector is also needed.

On the basis of research conducted, not only to retain faith of customers, but also to satisfy the customer and to increase the customer base, it is recommended that all the entrepreneurs may be educated to adopt practices including allocation of funds/budget preparation, sales promotion techniques, communicating with customers, after sales service etc. More orders can be obtained by offering quality products with high level of durability at a lower cost in a shorter period. MSMEs should participate in seminars and trade fair so as to remain update from newer technologies and to open new opportunities. Suitable type of AMT should be adopted by MSMEs so as to improve product quality, reduce product costs, increase throughput, to reduce rejection and to increase flexibility, as needed to survive and grow. Skill deficiency of workforce is prone that results in more rejections with less wages/salaries. While planning for adoption of AMT, an enterprise may involve its entire workforce at various levels of adoption, even from the level of idea generation. All the employees should be considered as a team/family of enterprise and should be encouraged for training/re-training and for skill enhancement. Service of a technical consultant is needed even to educate entire workforce as adoption of newer technology is not for their job loss, but it will help in increasing their earnings. Skill level of entire workforce will improve and thus, new opportunities will be generated as markets are global. All the enterprises should emphasize on various welfare facilities including first aid facility, hospitalization, Employee's State Insurance Corporation (ESIC) scheme and training/re-training along with safety of employees. Working conditions must be designed ergonomically so that the life/health of workforce will not be in jeopardy. The state of leaves, leave rules, salary, wages, bonus, awards, PF, recruitment, trainings, payment of salary after leaving the lob and retirement benefits may be as per governing rules and should be implemented with true and humanitarian spirit. Evaluation of employees as well as enterprises may be carried out that can be in terms of accepted production rate, reduction in rejection and increase in turn-over/sales.

Supply of power at normal rates for entire working hours should be made available to all the enterprises. The pollution generated by enterprises should be reduced and proper treatment/waste management should be employed to save ground, water, air and ultimately, the environment. In this regard, governing laws should be amended with its strict enforcement. Cash transaction/credit should be avoided. Financial assistance in terms of loan at cheaper interest rates is essentially needed for MSMEs. Loan procedures should be simplified with elimination of personal borrowings. The state related to cost of fuels like CNG/LPG/Diesel, cost of raw material and Government policies related to taxation should be addressed at policy makers' level. Further, all the enterprise should be equipped with computer, printer and Internet. Each enterprise must have a web-site with real time database connectivity so that orders and transactions can be processed along with customers' communication at any time from any geographic location, and should adopt EC/IT/ICT/software.

This study is based on responses of participated MSMEs of India and to broaden the aspect and coverage, the study must be planned in much larger way. Future studies and researches in this regard will help the manufacturers, policy framers and researchers to reach to a common consensus.

References

1. Abdullah NAHN, Zain SNM. The internationalization theory and Malaysian small and medium enterprises (SMEs). International Journal of Trade, Economics and Finance. 2011; 2(4):318–22.
2. Demeter K, Kolos K. Marketing, manufacturing and logistics: an empirical examination of their joint effect on company performance. International Journal of Manufacturing Technology and Management. 2009; 16(3):215–33.
3. Gill HS, Singh H, Singh S. Effectiveness of advanced manufacturing technologies in SMEs of auto parts manufacturing. Proceedings
4. of the 2010 International Conference on Industrial Engineering and Operations Management; 2010 Jan 9–10; Dhaka, Bangladesh.
5. Kakati M. Strategic evaluation of advanced manufacturing technology. International Journal of Production Economics 1997; 53:141–56.
6. Orr S. A comparison of AMT strategies in the USA, South Africa and Germany. International Journal of Manufacturing Technology and Management. 2002; 4(6):441–454.
7. Rose AMN, Deros BMd, Rahman MNAb, Nordin N. Lean manufacturing best practices in SMEs. Proceedings of the 2011 International Conference on Industrial Engineering and Operations Management; 2011 Jan 22–24; Kuala Lumpur, Malaysia. p. 872–7.
8. Taha Z, Tahriri F. Critical success factors for advanced manufacturing technology (AMT). International Conference on Mechanical and Electrical Technology; 2009. p. 38. Available from http://ebooksasmedigitalcollection.asme.org/content.aspx?bookid=301&sectionid=38780683 [Accessed on April 23, 2013].
9. Small business statistics, issued by federation of small business, UK. Available from http://www.fsb.org.uk/stats [Accessed on January 06, 2015].

10. Annual report on European SMEs 2012/13: a recovery on the horizon. Available from http://ec.europa.eu/enterprise/policies/sme/facts-fig-ures-analysis/performance-review/files/supporting-documents/2014/annual-report-smes-2014_en.pdf [Accessed on January 06, 2015].

11. Annual report 2013–14, Ministry of MSMEs, Government of India. Available from http://msme.gov.in/WriteReadData/DocumentFile/ANNUALREPORT-MSME-2013-14P.pdf [Accessed on January 06, 2015].

12. Economic Survey 2013–14, Government of India. Available from http://indiabudget.nic.in/es2013-14/echap-09.pdf [Accessed on January 06, 2015].

13. Export promotion, development commissioner, Ministry of MSMEs, Government of India. Available from http://www.dcmsme.gov.in/ sido/export.htm [Accessed on January 07, 2015].

☺☹☹

11

ERP Implementation Barriers

Manu Sharma[1], Sudhanshi Joshi[2] and Vinod Kumar Singh[3]

The purpose of this study is to investigate and determine factors and barriers that organizations have encountered during the implementation of Enterprise Resource Planning (ERP) systems.

KEYWORDS ERP | Integrated System

11.1 INTRODUCTION

Problem Statement—There are numerous factors affecting successful implementation of an ERP system in an organization that have not yet been fully identified and described. The intent of this study was to identify, analyze, and investigate the factors affecting the implementation of an ERP system. Consequently, results of the data collection and analysis resulted in recommendations that can help companies make better decisions about future ERP systems implementation.

Significance of the Study—To help organizations to gain a better understanding of ERP and the factors that could prevent successful implementation of an ERP system. Organizations can benefit from this study by learning from other businesses' past barriers to successful installation and not repeating these same mistakes themselves.

Research Questions—The following research questions were framed that affect the implementation of ERP:

- ◁ What problems and issues have companies encountered while implementing an ERP system?
- ◁ What has been top management's involvement with the ERP implementation Process?
- ◁ What kind of, and how much, training have the employees been given on an ERP system?

---

[1] Lecturer, Department of Management Studies, Graphic Era University, Dehradun
[2] Petroleum University Dehradun
[3] Assistant Professor, MHE, Oman

Research objectives—A Survey of the NSE/BSE100 companies was the research methodology for this study. This survey was designed to complete three objectives. The first objective of the survey was to identify important issues, problems, and factors encountered by companies during the ERP implementation process. The second objective of the survey was to determine what involvement top management had with the implementation. Finally, the third objective of the survey was to determine what kind of training, if any, employees received for operating the ERP system before the "Go Live" date.

Research Assumption—First, the researcher assumed that organizations of different financial and physical sizes would respond equally to the questions, since the ERP process and ERP implementation is similar for all organizations. Second, the researcher also assumed that each participant in the sample would answer the questionnaire honestly. Third, the researchers assumed that the study findings would be truly representative of the organizations selected.

Design/Methodology—The population for this study was the 676 senior executives of BSE/NSE top 100 companies belongs to service and manufacturing industry. Of these, 131 respondents with a return rate of 19.4%. The standard deviation and analysis of the variance (ANOVA) were the statistical tests used to analyze the data.

Research Limitations—The barriers this study found were lack of top management involvement, improper training of employees, monitoring the information received in developing the application management strategy, application errors, and outage repairs of an application management. Since this study is limited to few companies based on BSE/ NSE enlisting (as on 15th April 2007), it is possible that the results are not generalized and only apply to these companies. Perhaps the survey instrument used for this study was not sufficient since it did not cover all the issues and barriers related in the literature review. Research Implications-With the response rate of 19.4%, about 58% were in the manufacturing sector (the reason behind is the evolution of MRP II from manufacturing setup). All the respondents had implemented at least one of the ERP modules, 67% had implemented at least two modules, 30% had implemented at least three modules and 20% had implemented four modules.

Since most of the organization is already implemented an ERP system, recommendations and guidelines can be obtained which can be used to assist other companies in overcoming barriers to successful implementation.

11.1 REVIEW OF LITERATURE

The current global business dynamics which is characterized by customer-driven markets, shorter product life cycles, and narrow e-niches generates the need for all organization to work together (Blue ocean Stretegy) to gain the competitive benefits. To meet international competition, One performance enhancing tool is advanced technologies implementation (Kremers & Van Dissel, 2000).

As much as technology has enabled improvements such as higher productivity, it has also made the business process more complex because of many different computer software systems used within all the different functions of an organization (Honig, 1999).

Competition is now based on delivery, lead time, flexibility, greater integration with the customers and suppliers, and higher levels of product differentiation. ERP can help with this make-to-order environment (Honig, 1999).

ERP system evolved to help organizations manage information throughout the company, from the plant to the back office, and now the front office (Oliver, 1999). Demand for expand functionality led to the current ERP system (Appleton, 1997; kapp, Latham & Ford Latham, 2000; Markus, Tanis & Fenema, 2000).

MRP is computerized methodology to the scheduling of materials purchase for assembly. It has usually been associated with distinct manufacturing operations and is not compatible to continous process industries. MRP rotates about the Bill of Materials (BOM) and the Master Production Schedule (MPS) (Kapp, Latham, & Ford- Latham, 2000). In the BOM, every product is broken down into progressively lower levels until reaching a raw material or brought kept (Kapp, Latham, & Ford-Latham, 2000). The MPS is a spreadsheet that forecasts demand for each product of organization over time. The core of MRP starts will a Bill of Materials Processor (BOMP). This helps plan the necessities of each part, materials and assembly (Kapp, Latham & Ford- Latham, 2000).

There are many benefits to be realized to be realized with the implementation of an ERP system, and this is the reason they are becoming so significant to business (Shanks,2000). Some of the benefits are:

- ERP allows integrated information system, which lead to more efficient business processes that cost less than unintegrated systems.
- ERP facilitates easier global integration. Barriers such as currency exchange rates, languages and cultural differences can be bridged automatically, allowing date to be more easily integrated.
- ERP integrates people and data, and eliminates updating and repairing of many separate computer systems.
- ERP allows management to manage operations, not just monitor them. When the system is implemented properly, these benefits can help the company achieve increased profitability and productivity.

- ERP allows employees to share information, query data, and run reports. This eliminates the need to store duplicate information in more than one place and reduces the amount of work necessary to gather and analyze information.

- ERP systems increase efficiency by freeing employees from performing time consuming, manual work. For example, legacy systems often require hours or days to run reports. With ERP, reports can be produced in seconds. These efficiencies allow employees to spend time on other tasks, reducing operating expenses (Shanks, 2000).

There exist two approaches for ERP Implementation—Incremental deployment or Big Bang Approach.

The Big bang Approach is not the best technique for every organization to use (Songini, 2000). There exist some critical point that requires top management's involvement is critical, communication with the employees is vital, and extensive training of staff is essential.

There is lot many of research on Survival strategies for an effective ERP implementation. According to Vowler (2000), ERP has spread like a "purple tide" across corporate businesses. Survival tricks identified by Shupe Consulting (2001) that are required during ERP Implementation.

11.1.1 Research Methodology

A Survey Instrument (Appendix A) was selected for NSE/BSE Enlisted top 100 companies. One objective of the survey was to determine if the companies had implemented an ERP system. Another objective of the survey was to identify issues, problems and factors that encountered with the implementation process. Aside to this the survey also asked if and how top level management has involved with the ERP project (through open ended comments (Appendix B).

11.1.2 Data Collection

We e-mailed 676 survey instruments with 30 questions in two sets. The questionnaire was mailed to BSE enlisted top 50 companies, as on 15th April 2007. The next set of questionnaire was sent to 176 senior executives of NSE (Nifty- fifty and Junior Nifty) enlisted top 50 companies, as on 15th April 2007.

11.1.3 Data Analysis

We used the statistical package for social Sciences (SPSS) software to analyze the data from the survey.

11.1.4 Method of Data Analysis

The Statistical techniques used to compare different variables were the mean, standard deviation, and analysis of variance (ANOVA). When the mean and standard deviation were too close in numerical value to make a determination of which factor had the largest impact on the ERP implementation, the ANOVA was used to make the decision. Frequencies and percentages were also used to analyze some of the survey questions. After frequencies were calculated they were converted to percentages. The purpose of this was to determine which responses received the most replies and what impact they have on ERP Implementation.

A total of three categories were analyzed and compared by means of the ANOVA: (1) The effectiveness of the information received in developing application management strategy, (2) labor hours spent on repairs to ERP Applications, and (3) Percentage of application errors. The factors in these groups were analyzed and compared to determine which factor within each group had the largest impact on an ERP Implementation.

SPSS was used to analyze the data from the survey instrument for the calculation of the mean, standard derivation, and ANOVA.

11.1.5 Survey Information

A Self administered questionnaire was mailed to 676 top executives at the NSE/BSE top 100 companies. When Mailing the survey instrument to the exchange enlisted companies,duplicate companies (those on both lists) were eliminated, since they had previously been surveyed. Examples of the survey instrument, cover letter, and follow-up letter can be viewed in Appendix A. Each survey question had a different number of responses. The initial mailings and subsequent follow-ups resulted in 131 responses, a response rate of 19.4%. This was an acceptable response rate given that the individuals in the targeted organizations were extremely busy top executives with high-level responsibilities.

11.1.6 Demographics of the Respondents

Respondent's Job Title—The respondents reported their job titles as follows-CIO numbered 71(54%), CTO's numbered 38 (29%), Director, Manager, Supervision of IS numbered 14 (11%), and the category of "other" numbered eight (6%).

Functional Area—The respondents' functional areas were reported as follows: Application development numbered 12 (9%), system integration numbered three(2%), IT senior management numbered 76 (58%), application implementation numbered four (3%), and Enterprise Management numbered 38 (28%).

Number of employees—The number of employees in the respondents' organization were as follows: 500 or fewer numbered two (1.5%), 501-1000 numbered three (2.3%), 1001-2500 numbered four (3%), 2501-5000 numbered nine (6.8%), 5001-7500 numbered 10 (7.6%), 7501-10,000 numbered four (3.1%), 10,001-20,000 numbered 31 (23.7%), and over 20,000 numbered 68 (52%).

11.1.7 Organization's Business Activities

The Business activities of the respondents' organizations were as follows:

With globalization being one of the main buzzwords for the new millennium, there will be numerous changes in technology. One of these technological changes has been the implementation of an ERP system. According to Schneider (2000), "doing the homework" on the implementation of an ERP system is one of the best ways to prevent problems and overcome the barriers to and issues of successful installation. A strong infrastructure is the key to successfully completing the ERP system installation process.

One of the barriers organanizations experiences dealt with top managemment's involvement with the ERP system's.

Recommendation

The following are study-based recommendations that should be considered before deciding to implement an ERP system.

1. Appoint a project team with a strong leader that can help employees understand the options offered by an ERP system.
2. Implement a "Train the Trainer" program. This program trains a person, the trainer, on the ERP system by the ERP software vendor. The trainer would then be responsible for training the employees.
3. Educate the project team and allocate an employee training budget. A dedicated training room is essential for employee
4. Identify the business goal and objectives of the company.
5. Establish a clear vsison
6. Understanding all the functions of an ERP system. Extensive planning and understanding of the concepts of an ERP system saves time.
7. Choose the ERP features that the organization needs, and do not install the whole ERP system if it is not needed.

Future Researc

We are highly:

    ⇝ The correlation between ERP failure and non-use of Total Quality Management (TQM) principles in ERP system design and development.

- ✦ Integrating ERP in the business school curriculum.
- ✦ The cost and benefits of system implementation.
- ✦ The impact of ERP system on the accounting and auditing profession.
- ✦ Determination of how top management can help with the change management resulting from an ERP implementation.
- ✦ Determination of the proper amount of training employees need before the "go-live" date.
- ✦ Determination of additional barriers to successful implementation that the study did not uncover.

References

1. Appleton, E. (1997). How to survive ERP. Datamation, 43, 50
2. Brown,J.(2001). ERP doomed by poor planning. Computing Canada, 27(3),11.
3. Cliffe, S. (1999). ERP Implementation. Harward Business Review, 77(1), 16.
4. Honig, S. (1999). The changing landscape of computerized accounting system. The CPA Journal, 69(5), 14–19.
5. Kapp,M., Lathan,B., 5 Ford-latham,H. (2000). Learning requirements planning: A model for developing enterprise wide training and education. Production 5 inventory management Journal, 41(3), 52.
6. Kremers, M., 5 Van Dissel,H. (2000). ERP system migrations. Communication of the ACM, 43(4), 22.
7. Lee, A(2000). Researchable directions for ERP and other new information technologies. MIS Quarterly, 24(1), 6.
8. S. Markus,L., Tanis,C.,5 Fenema, P. (2000). Multisite ERP implementations. Communication of the ACM, 43, 42.
9. Romeo, J. (2001a). ERP: On the rise again—The reports of ERP's demise were greatly exa
10. Schnieder, I. (2000). Information please. Bank Systems 5 Technology, 37(12), 46–47.
11. Schmenner, R. (1998). Operations Management. Business Horizons, 41(3), 3-4.
12. Songini,M.(2000). Despite odds. Georgia hits it big with ERP system,Computer World, 10–11.

☺☺☹

12

Enterprise Resource Planning

Amit Gautam[1]

In the present business environment, role of a financial analyst is considered to be very important and inevitable. Financial analyst as managers, consultants, advisors or auditors plays an important role in controlling, managing, and supporting the business. As business needs are very complex in nature, the implementation of an ERP package needs financial analyst with functional skills for evaluation, Business Process Reengineering (BPR), Mapping of Business requirements, Report designing, ensuring Business controls, customization of the package for the specific requirements, Documentation etc., Sooner or later a financial analyst without the knowledge of ERP may feel as if he is a fish out of the bowl. By this article it is attempted to highlight various aspects of ERP and specific areas of ERP that are relevant for financial analysts.

KEYWORDS   ERP | Organization | Planning | Design | Finance

12.1 INTRODUCTION

Enterprise Resource Planning is the latest high-end solution information technology has lent to business application. The ERP solutions seek to streamline and integrate operation processes and information flows in the company to synergize the resources of an organization namely men, material, money and machine through information. Initially implementation of an ERP package was possible only for very large Multi National Companies and Infrastructure Companies due to high cost involved. Today many companies in India have gone in for implementation of ERP and it is expected in the near future that 60% of the companies will be implementing one or the other ERP packages since this will become a must for gaining competitive advantage.

12.1.1 Evolution of ERP

In the ever-growing business environment the following demands are placed on the industry:

    ↲ Aggressive Cost control initiatives

---
[1] Associate Professor, School of Management Sciences, Varanasi

◆ Need to analyze costs/revenues on a product or customer basis

◆ Flexibility to respond to changing business requirements

◆ More informed management decision making

◆ Changes in ways of doing business

Difficulty in getting accurate data, timely information and improper interface of the complex natured business functions has been identified as the hurdles in the growth of any business. Time and again depending upon the velocity of the growing business needs, one or the other applications and planning systems have been introduced into the business world for crossing these hurdles and for achieving the required growth. They are:

◆ Management Information Systems (MIS)

◆ Integrated Information Systems (IIS)

◆ Executive Information Systems (EIS)

◆ Corporate Information Systems (CIS)

◆ Enterprise Wide Systems (EWS)

◆ Material Resource Planning (MRP)

◆ Manufacturing Resource Planning (MRP II)

◆ Money Resource Planning (MRP III)

The latest planning tool added to the above list is Enterprise Resource Planning.

12.1.2 Need for ERP

Most organizations across the world have realized that in a rapidly changing environment, it is impossible to create and maintain a custom designed software package, which will cater to all their requirements and also be completely up-to-date. Realizing the requirement of user organizations some of the leading software companies have designed Enterprise Resource Planning software which will offer an integrated software solution to all the functions of an organization.

12.1.3 Features of ERP

Some of the major features of ERP and what ERP can do for the business system are as below [Antweiler Werner and Trefler Daniel, 2002]:

◆ ERP facilitates company-wide Integrated Information System covering all functional areas like Manufacturing, Selling and distribution, Payables, Receivables, Inventory, Accounts, Human resources, Purchases etc.,

◆ ERP performs core corporate activities and increases customer service and thereby augmenting the Corporate Image.

◆ ERP bridges the information gap across the organization.

- ERP provides for complete integration of Systems not only across the departments in a company but also across the companies under the same management.
- ERP is the only solution for better Project Management.
- ERP allows automatic introduction of latest technologies like Electronic Fund Transfer (EFT), Electronic Data Interchange (EDI), Internet, Intranet, Video conferencing, E- Commerce etc.
- ERP eliminates the most of the business problems like Material shortages, Productivity enhancements, Customer service, Cash Management, Inventory problems, Quality problems, Prompt delivery etc.,
- ERP not only addresses the current requirements of the company but also provides the opportunity of continually improving and refining business processes.
- ERP provides business intelligence tools like Decision Support Systems (DSS), Executive Information System (EIS), Reporting, Data Mining and Early Warning Systems (Robots) for enabling people to make better decisions and thus improve their business processes. [Gupta, Anil & Govindarajan, V, 2002]

12.1.4 Components of ERP

To enable the easy handling of the system the ERP has been divided into the following Core subsystems:

- Sales and Marketing
- Master Scheduling
- Material Requirement Planning
- Capacity Requirement Planning
- Bill of Materials
- Purchasing
- Shop floor control
- Accounts Payable/Receivable
- Logistics
- Asset Management
- Financial Accounting

12.1.5 Suppliers of ERP

There are many numbers of ERP suppliers who are very active in the market. Some of the companies offering renowned international ERP products include:

- Baan
- CODA
- D&B
- IBM
- JD Edwards
- Marcarn
  - Oracle
  - Peoplesoft
  - Platinum
  - Ramco
  - SAP
  - SMI
  - Software 2000

12.1.6 BPR and ERP

Business Process Reengineering is a pre-requisite for going ahead with a powerful planning tool, ERP. An in depth BPR study has to be done before taking up ERP. Business Process Reengineering brings out deficiencies of the existing system and attempts to maximize productivity through restructuring and reorganizing the human resources as well as divisions and departments in the organization. [Sahay S, Walsham G, 2002]

Business Process Engineering evolves the following Steps:

- Study the current system
- Design and develop new systems
- Define Process, organization structure and procedure
- Develop customize the software
- Train people
- Implement new system

The principle followed for BRP may be defined as USA principle (Understand, Simplify Automate) i.e., Understanding the existing practices, Simplifying the Processes and Automate the Process. Various tools used for this principle are charted below:

- *Understand Simplify Automate*
- Diagramming Eliminating EDI
- Story-boarding Combining ERP
- Brain storming Rearranging

12.1.7 Change and BPR

BPR is inevitable not only for ERP but as far as any business process is concerned. BPR becomes the first step in the process of ERP implementation. Business process reengineering is taken to conduct feasibility study and other restructuring exercises. Nothing can be done to prevent change. The best way to manage change is to adopt it. Time and again it has been proved that imposing change of any magnitude all on a sudden is not the proper way. There needs to be a proper method to bring about it. Business process reengineering is one scientific study that helps organizations largely to analyse the viability of not only ERP but any other dynamic change. BPR ERP is interrelated. [Verma, S, 1998]

BPR does not necessarily stop with the process of identifying the possibility. It also suggests a series of steps that needs to be executed, for ERP to find a place in the organization. BPR is the first step that comes prior to ERP implementation. The reason is simple. Many parameters are taken while preparing ERP. This includes the assumption of Predefined functions. Hence ERP software will be preconceived to perform those set of functions. On the other hand companies expect ERP to function in such a way that it coincides with the regular business process. BPR ERP can be the biggest challenge for the vendor and the company as such. BPR ERP forms an important part of ERP study.

12.1.8 Solving BPR-ERP Clash

There are two alternatives that will help the companies to combat this menace. The company can either restructure the business process itself or customize the ERP system so that it suits the business process. Deciding this is paramount to ERP implementation. BPRERP has lot of conflicts. The pros and cons of each of them are explained in the following paragraphs:

12.1.9 Implementing ERP Software to Suit Business Needs

When the company demands particular ERP software they have to make compromises on the budget because reworking modules and supplying an ERP Software would definitely be a costly affair. This is because of the complications involved in doing the same. Apart from finance this also calls for persons with greater working knowledge to design the systems. This means the process is not going to be unambiguous. The process will also require frequent updations. This is going to be difficult taking into account the several changes that has already been inflicted on the system to make it business friendly.

12.1.10 Restructuring the business process to be ERP Friendly

This method also requires lots of monetary outlay because of the major change in business process. The customers will not be receptive to changes in business process. It is possible to train the employees but whereas in the case of customers they cannot be expected to stay in tune in tune with the whims and fancies of the organization. It is possible to train the employees. The likelihood of them to adapting to the change at the immediate outset is very much limited. This will cast a spell on the revenue of the business and unless ERP does not make it good in the later days the voluminous investment cannot be justified. [Christie W, 2001]

12.1.11 Selection of ERP

Once the BPR is completed the next task is to evaluate and select a suitable package for implementation. Evaluation of the right ERP package is considered as more crucial step. Evaluation and selection involves:

- checking whether all functional aspects of the Business are duly covered
- checking whether all the business functions and processes are fully integrated
- checking whether all the latest IT trends are covered
- checking whether the vendor has customizing and implementing capabilities
- checking whether the business can absorb the cost
- checking whether the ROI is optimum

12.1.12 Implementing an ERP

Implementing an ERP package has to be done on a phased manner. Step by step method of implementing will yield a better result than big-bang introduction. The total time required for successfully implementing an ERP package will be anything between 18 and 24 months. [Chase, Richard B., and Nicholus J. Aquilano, 2006]

The normal steps involved in implementation of an ERP are as below:

- Project Planning
- Business & Operational analysis including Gap analysis
- Business Process Reengineering
- Installation and configuration
- Project team training
- Business Requirement mapping
- Module configuration
- System interfaces
- Data conversion
- Custom Documentation
- End user training

- Acceptance testing
- Post implementation/Audit support

The above steps are grouped and subdivided into four major phases namely

- Detailed discussions,
- Design & Customization,
- Implementation and
- Production

12.1.13 Benefits of ERP

The benefits accruing to any business enterprise on account of implementing are unlimited. According to the companies like NIKE, DHL, Tektronix, Fujitsu, Millipore, Sun Microsystems, following are some of the benefits they achieved by implementing ERP packages:

- Gives Accounts Payable personnel increased control of invoicing and payment processing and thereby boosting their productivity and eliminating their reliance on computer personnel for these operations.
- Reduce chapter documents by providing on-line formats for quickly entering and retrieving information.
- Improves timeliness of information by permitting, posting daily instead of monthly.
- Greater accuracy of information with detailed content, better presentation, fully satisfactory for the Auditors.
- Improved Cost Control
- Faster response and follow up on customers
- More efficient cash collection, say, material reduction in delay in payments by customers.
- Better monitoring and quicker resolution of queries.
- Enables quick response to change in business operations and market conditions.
- Helps to achieve competitive advantage by improving its business process.
- Improves supply-demand linkage with remote locations and branches in different countries.
- Provides a unified customer database usable by all applications.
- Improves International operations by supporting a variety of tax structures, invoicing schemes, multiple currencies, multiple period accounting and languages.
- Improves information access and management throughout the enterprise.

◅ Provides solution for problems like Y2K and Single Monitory Unit (SMU) or Euro Currency

12.1.14 Significance of ERP Implementation

Companies have to clearly know what enterprise resource is planning before thinking of implementing them. The catch word of ERP implementation is speed. The faster it is implemented the quicker and better are the advantages and delivery in terms of results. This early process has another hold. The returns are sought at a shorter period. This deviation from the conventional practice has become the order of the day as far as many companies are concerned. Formerly Business process re-engineering played a vital role with respect to implementation. It is important to know the components of Enterprise resource planning .Merely defining enterprise resource planning will not help in this.

This naturally paved way to development of gaps between the actual results and the one derived during the process of foreseeing. Tuning ERP as per the whims and fancies of the practices followed in the company became a routine affair. This led to slogging and dragging beyond the time limits permitted. It was monetarily pinching and played havoc in the customer's trust. It is also necessary to understand that mere ERP planning does not guarantee the benefit of ERP. It has to be implemented as planned after understanding the components of enterprise resource planning.

In spite of having improved the implementation issues what remains static and unfettered is the manner in which companies go ahead with ERP implementation. In fact they don't even check the desirability of going into ERP. Some issues that an organization has to address after defining enterprise resource planning are:

◅ Popular information systems |
◅ Likelihood of fluctuations in the choice of technology
◅ The ability of market players to stay in tune with it
◅ The ways and means to implement a business applications like ERP
◅ To benefit from the same so as to gain a competitive edge
◅ Their usage and services
◅ The necessity for innovating software applications

If an organization is able to answer these questions without any ambiguity and substantiate the results then it can be said that it has a path or up focus in taking ERP. The questions mentioned above are crucial and will even decide the business model of the company. ERP implementation is a vital in the whole process of ERP. They can take place only if one understands "What is enterprise resource Planning" and defining enterprise resource planning in their organization. [Bruce, Harry J, 2005]

12.1.15 Current Approach

It is essential to have an overview of the current approach. The current approach is claimed to be relatively successful. The current approach more popularly referred to as "baan" has two underlying principles:

The idea which concentrates on molding the business: This category is prominent when the organizational unit calls for a radical restructuring process by all means. This process will be carried in all aspects of the business .Some of them include strategic maneuver, operation of trade and the circumstances that call for change and adaptability. Defining enterprise resource planning in context to the concerned organization will help to decide on this issue.

The plan which lays more emphasis on technical parameters: Here business takes the back seat. The thrust lies on technical dimensions. This does not ignore the commercial viability as such but they occupy seat only in the due course of time more so when operations are triggered in full stream and not at the initial stage itself. The advantage with this type is that it does not call for an immediate modification of the business structure. However it is essential to know the components of enterprise resource planning.

12.1.16 ERP Implementation Life Cycle

The process of ERP implementation is referred as d as "ERP Implementation Life Cycle". The following are the steps involved in completing the lifecycle.

12.1.17 Shortlist on the basis of observation

Selecting an ERP package for the company can nevertheless be compared with the process of "Selecting the right Person for the Right Job". This exercise will involve choosing few applications suitable for the company from the whole many.

12.1.18 Assessing the chosen packages

A team of Experts with specialized knowledge in their respective field will be asked to make the study on the basis of various parameters. Each expert will not only test and certify if the package is apt for the range of application in their field but also confirm the level of coordination that the software will help to achieve in working with other departments. In simple terms they will verify if the synergy of the various departments due to the advent of ERP will lead to an increased output. A choice is to be made from ERP implementation models. [Greene, James H, 2005]

12.1.19 Preparing for the venture

This stage is aimed at defining the implementation of ERP in all measures. It will lay down the stipulations and criteria have to be met. A team of officers will take care of this, who will report to the person of the highest hierarchy in the organization.

12.1.20 Gap Analysis

This stage helps the company to identify the gaps that has to be bridged, so that the company's practice becomes akin to ERP environment. This has been reported as an expensive procedure but it is inevitable. The conglomerate will decide to restructure the business or make any other alterations as suggested by GAP analysis in order to make ERP user friendly. A choice is to be made from ERP implementation models. [Jetter, Otto, 2006]

12.1.21 Designing the System

This step requires lot of meticulous planning and deliberate action. This step helps to decide and conclude the areas where restructuring have to be carried on. A choice is to be made from ERP implementation models.

12.1.22 In-house Guidance

This is regarded as a very important step in ERP implementation. The employees in the company are trained to face crisis and make minor corrections as well because the company can neither be at liberty nor afford the bounty to avail the services of an ERP vendor at all times.

12.1.23 Checking

This stage observes and tests the authenticity of the use. The system is subjected to the wildest tests possible so that it ensures proper usage and justifies the costs incurred. This is seen as a test for ERP implementation.

12.1.24 The real test

At this stage the replacement takes place viz the new mechanism of operation and administration takes over the older one.

12.1.25 Preparing the employees to use ERP

The employees in the organization will be taught to make use of the system in the day to day and regular basis so as to make sure that it becomes a part of the system in the organization.

12.1.26 Post Implementation

The process of implementation will find meaning only when there is regular follow up and proper instruction flow thereafter and through the lifetime of ERP. This will include all efforts and steps taken to update and attain better benefits once the system is implemented. Hence an organization has to perform ERP implementation safely and correctly.

12.1.27 Financial Analyst (FA) and ERP

A pertinent question one financial analyst may ask is "How does an ERP matter for me?". As mentioned earlier the role of a financial analyst in any business either as a Consultant, Auditor, Advisor or Manager is inevitable.

12.1.28 FA as a Consultant

Implementation of ERP solutions is one of the largest drivers of growth in the consultancy business. The introduction of such a large and complex software like ERP, which enables an organization to integrate their manufacturing, finance and marketing operations at all levels, is in itself a challenge, since it calls for technical and functional skills and a change in user mindsets. And therein comes a role of a consultant. CA as a Consultant will play a major role in implementation of an ERP solution. [Zipkin, Paul H, 2006]

12.1.29 FA as an auditor

Assuming a situation where the client has implemented an ERP solution. If the auditor is aware of ERP he can make use of the features of ERP and thereby:

- Ensures that the internal controls and checks are consistently maintained.
- Ensures that the provisions of Income tax or other fiscal laws are not ignored e.g., one can control the payment of cash in excess of Rs.10000 for expenses or Rs.20000 as loans and advances, The TDS deductions and payments are automated etc.,
- Ensures that the Accounting Standards are consistently followed across the company.
- Improves the quality of the reporting.

12.1.30 FA as an Advisor

As an advisor to a company a financial analyst can participate in various stages of ERP implementation. It goes without saying that advising without the knowledge of the current trends and modern management techniques will prove to be a wrong advice and may have a negative impact on the growth of the client.

12.1.31 FA as a Manager

By now one should know that the ERP is a high end sophisticated software solution that reduces the pressure and work load of the Managers and provides accurate, timely information for taking appropriate business decisions. Financial analyst as managers with knowledge of ERP will be able to achieve their targets and goals by proper implementation of ERP system in their organization. In fact Managers are expected to translate the business rules and requirements for mapping them into ERP software. Managers as representatives of the Organization have to coordinate with Vendors, Consultants, Auditors etc., for a proper implementation of ERP package.

The growing information needs of an enterprise make it imperative to improve or replace old systems. Especially under the present Indian business environment, where the globalization has been initiated, full convertibility is coined, Infrastructure Projects are nearing completion, and it is expected that the whole business system will undergo a major shift. Thus by being a proficient ERP consultant, financial analyst will prove their commitment to the business world and modern management.

Reference

1. Antweiler Werner and Trefler Daniel: ERP: A view from trade, The American Economic Review, March 2002.
2. Gupta, Anil with Govindarajan, V., "Building Global Presence Through Enterprise Resource Planning," The Financial Times, January 30, 2002.
3. Sahay S, Walsham G, 'Information Technology in Companies: A Need for Theory Building' Business Standard, 14 Oct. 2002
4. Verma, S , "Room for ERP", Business India, 12 January, 1998.
5. Christie W, 'Concept Behind ERP', Economist, November 2001.
6. Chase, Richard B., and Nicholus J. Aquilano. ERP & Its Implementation, 6th ed. Prentice Hall, 2006
7. Bruce, Harry J. ERP Handbook, Tata McGraw Hill, 2005.
8. Greene, James H. Enterprise resource palling, 3rd ed., New York, McGraw Hill, 2005.
9. Jetter, Otto, ERP and BPR, Upper saddle River, NJ, Prentice Hall, 2006.
10. Zipkin, Paul H. Foundations of ERP Management, New York, Mc Graw Hill, 2006

☺☻☹

Chapter-12

13

Decision Supporting Systems in Decision Making

Shatha Yousif AL-Qassimi[1] and Akram Jalal Karim[2]

The dynamic improvement in banks and other financial provider obligated BAH-RAIN COMMERCIAL FACILITIES COMPANY (BCFC) to implement the concept of Business Process Re-engineering (BPR). This was to provide innovative product and services and decrease the gap between BCFC and other banks or financial service provider. This research's object is to evaluate the impact of BPR on business performance and discover how BPR will affect (cost, quality, and time cycle) of products and services provided. Data obtained from secondary and primary sources, and analysis done through simple percentage analysis and regression analysis. This research concludes that BPR is not risk-less, and failed to be perfectly implemented to the following reasons: lack of executive leadership, and organizational resistance.

KEYWORDS Decision Support Systems | Knowledge-based Systems | Decision Making Process | Bahrain Banks

13.1 INTRODUCTION

In a world progressively more motivated by the three Cs (Customer, Competition and Change), companies are paying attention for new solutions for their business problems. Lately, some of the more booming companies in the world seem to have an incredible solution, Business Process Re-engineering (BPR).

13.1.1 Overview of BPR

An information technology takes a major function in re-engineering the majority of business processes. Efficiency of processes, communications, and teamwork among responsible people will significantly increased all the way through speed, information processing capacities, and the use of computers and internet technology.

[1,2] College of Business and Finance, Ahlia University, Manama Kingdom of Bahrain

13.1.2 Goal of BPR

These issues dictate business enterprise of Business Process Re-engineering into the large strategy for persistent competition advantage, check costs, and distinguish products and effective price management with superior force and then faultless execution.

13.1.3 What to re-engineer

Reference to various in the BPR territory re-engineering supposed to center the attention on processes and not be restricted to thinking about the organizations, a business process is a chain of stepladder intended to create a product or a service. It comprises all the activities that carry specific outcome for a given customer, processes are currently hidden and unnamed for the reason that people consider the entity divisions more frequently than the procedure and process with which all of them are concerned. So companies that are considering a process in term of department such as marketing must switch to names those processes that they do. These names should involve all the work that engaged from start to finish.

The importance of processes not just limited to include organization diagram, they must also contain what are named process maps to provide an image of how work flows all the way through the company. Process mapping presents tools and a verified line for recognizing your exist As-Is business processes and can be used to present a To- Be outline for re-engineering your product and service functions. It is the vital link that your BPR team can concern to enhanced understanding and radically develop your business processes and performance. Recognizing and drawing the processes, choosing which ones required to be reengineered and in which arrange is the critical question. No company can take up the undesirable task of re-engineering all the processes at once. Generally they make their selections based on three criteria:

Table 13.1   Selection Based on Three Criteria

Dysfunction	Importance	Feasibility
The worst functioning process.	The main serious and powerful to customer satisfaction.	The processes those are most likely to be successfully re-engineered.

13.1.4 Re-engineering Stages

- ⊲ The Envision stage: the company reviews the existing strategy and business processes and based on that review business processes for improvement are targeted and IT opportunities are identified.
- ⊲ The Initiation stage: project teams are assigned, performance goals, project planning and employee notification are set.

- The Diagnosis stage: documentation of processes and sub-processes takes place in terms of process attributes (activities, resources, communication, roles, IT and costs).
- The Redesign stage: new process design is developed by devising process design alternatives and through brainstorming and creativity techniques.
- The Reconstruction stage: management technique changes occur to ensure smooth migration to the new process responsibilities and human resource roles.
- The Evaluation stage: the new process is monitored to determine if goals are met and examine total quality programs.

13.1.5 Research Objective

This research will investigate the impact of BPR on business performance in the financial sector and will test the relationship between (cost, quality, and time cycle) with business performance under the BPR solutions. Interviews will be conducted with key people who experienced this process and performance will be evaluated based on speed, quality of service provided, and cutting cost by utilizing the minimum required resources.

13.1.6 Research Structure

First, we will have a general review on previous literatures, and elements of re-engineering. After discussing that part will explain our research methodology and present our research questions, hypothesis, and the research design. Some challenges of BPR were discussed before going to analyzing the results. On the final stage, we discussed the result that obtained to come to our conclusion.

13.2 LITERATURE REVIEW

The idea of re-engineering sketches its origin back to management theories built-up in the early of nineteenth century. The aim of BPR is to revamp and modify the on hand business practices or process to attain remarkable development in organizational performance. Organizational development is a nonstop process but the rapidity of adjust has improved in manifolds. In an unstable global world, organizations improve competitive advantage BPR by completely redesigning chosen processes.

Since its initiation two decade ago, BPR has become a buzz word to carry about innovative initiatives and cultural changes in the business world. Many companies deployed BPR and achieved new competitive advantages in the global marketplace. Sharma (2006) posited that business process re-engineering implies transformed processes that together form a component of a larger system aimed at enabling organization to empower themselves with contemporary technologies business solution and innovations. Organizational valuable performance has turn out to be a catchphrase in contemporary business; as consequences there are unavoidable pressures for Business Process Re-engineering.

According to Stoddard and Jarvenpea (1995) Business Process are simply a set of activities that transformed a set of inputs into a set of outputs (goods or services) for another person or process using people and equipments. Business process entails set of logically related tasks performed to achieve a defined business output or outcome. It involves a wide spectrum of activities procurement, order fulfillment, product development, customer service and sale (Sharma 2006). Thus, Business Process Re-engineering becomes an offshoot of Business Process.

BPR relies on a diverse school of ideas. It accepts as true the on going process development, re-engineering believe that existing procedure is unconnected and there is necessity to originate a new one. Such a fresh plan will allow the designers of BPR to spotlight on innovative process. Business Process Re-engineering in the genuine brains, have mixed achievements therefore, business process re-engineering projects intend to transform incompetent effort process. Henceforth, organizations required to optimize outcome from this form in actual business circumstances.

Business process re-engineering (BPR) does not appear to qualify as a scientific theory because among other things, it is not duplicable and it is limited in scope (Maureen et al, 2005). Recently organizational improvement is a nonstop progression however the rapidity of change had enlarged in many ways. Which means that in these spirits surrounding organizations will improve its readiness for action in its process, if it successfully design and apply Business Process Re-engineering (BPR) on the chosen procedure.

According to Huang and Palvia (2001), change management and corporate culture have played significant roles in BPR and ERP acceptance in various countries. Aspects affecting BPR execution outcomes can be classified into two categories: national & environmental and organizational & internal. National & environmental factors include such variables as economy and economic growth, infrastructure, and government regulations. Organizational & internal factors describe such firm specific aspects as information technology (IT) maturity, BPR experience, and computer culture. On the one hand, information technology, such as ERP, enables and reinforces firms' innovative behavior as one of the key success factors for BPR and change management. The Conference Board (2004) reports that "IT systems that don't mesh, making it difficult to consolidate data cross the organization" as one of the key obstacles to innovation and BPR. On the other hand, BPR is measured as one of the fundamentals for a successful ERP implementation.

In learning national differentiation and execution practices, Sheu *et al.* (2003) find that culture and language, government and corporate policies, management style, and government regulations are among the key aspects that have to be taken into consideration to successfully implement BPR & ERP in the global marketplace. Moreover, Martinsons (2004) reports that even in the same country using the same information technology, four private (non-state) ventures (PVs) that he studied performed significantly better than four state-owned enterprises (SOEs) in implementing ERP in China.

Thus, he considers that dissimilar types of organizations even within a single country may behave differently due to social, cultural, and government policy influences. Based on a study of 150 enterprises in China, He (2004) finds via a resource-based viewpoint that BPR is one of the critical success factors (CSFs) of ERP implementation along with executive support, ERP-SCM vision, and ERP Communications of the IIMA 25 2005 Volume 5 Issue 1 Comparative Study of BPR in China Xin James He concept. While high costs, high complexity are considered the most commonly encountered obstacles of ERP implementation both in China and in USA, insufficient IT infrastructure, lack of well-trained workers, lack of incentives for the state-owned enterprises (SOEs), and different corporate culture are China specific obstacles to ERP implementation (He, 2004).

Aremu and Saka (2006) argued that Information technology (IT) is a strategic resource that facilitates major changes in competitive behavior, marketing and customer service. In essence, IT enables a firm to achieve competitive advantages. IT should be viewed as more than an automating or mechanizing force; to fundamentally reshape the way business is done. Information technology (IT) and Business Process Re-engineering (BPR) have recursive relationship. IT capabilities should support business processes and business should be in terms of the capabilities IT can provide.

13.2.1 Elements of Re-engineering in an Organization

Ezigbo (2003), the essential element or principles of re-engineering include the following:

Table 13.2 Essential element or principles of re-engineering

• Rethinking the theory of the business.
• Challenging old assumptions and discharging old rules that are no longer applicable.
• Breaking away from conventional wisdom and the constraints of organizational boundaries.
• Externally focus on c lients and the age group of superior value for clients.

• Encourages training and development by building creative work environment.
• Consider and carry out as much activity as feasible horizontally, focusing on f lows and processes through the organization.

13.3 RESEARCH METHODOLOGY

There are number of phases involved in the production of research document, however we used empirical and descriptive method to reach our objective in this research. According to Hammer & C hampy (1993) 'Re-engineering is the basic review and essential redesign of business processes to reach remarkable improvements in critical measures of performance such as cost, quality, service and speed'. Therefore, our dependent variable is Business performance and independent variables are (Speed, Quality, and Cost). Data for this chapter was obtained from primary and secondary sources. The primary source involves the use of questionnaire that was designed considering expert views on business process re-engineering. The chapter further employed personal interview to obtain additional information on the specific areas that the questionnaire mechanism did not cover. The secondary data source is extracted from report, journals, textbooks and other relevant publications.

13.3.1 Research Questions and Hypotheses

We set three questions to be answered through this research as follow:

Table 13.3   BPR Based Hypothesis

•	Do BPR enhance cost cutting in the process of delivering services or products ?
•	Do BPR enhance quality of services or products provided?
•	Do BPR enhance speed and time consumed in delivering services or products?

The following hypotheses formulated to be tested.

Table 13.4   Hypothesis Formulated

H_1.	There is significant relationship between cost and business performance.
H_{o1}.	There is no significant relationship between cost and business performance.
H_2.	There is significant relationship between quality and business performance.
H_{o2}.	There is no significant relationship between quality and business performance.
H_3.	There is significant relationship between time cycle and business performance.
H_{o3}.	There is no significant relationship between time cycle and business performance.

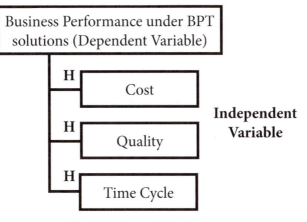

Fig. 13.1: Research Model

13.3.2 Research Design

We followed a quantitative method by distributing questionnaire to staff from various strategic departments of Bahrain Commercial Facilities (BCFC) which already implemented BPR solutions and this will add some qualitative feature. The questionnaire was divided into two parts. The first section asked to the respondents about their views on the impact of business process re-engineering on organizational performance while the second section focuses on the demographic characteristics of the respondents. The data collected were analyzed through simple percentage analysis and regression analysis.

We distributed 80 questionnaires to targeted people and we get back 50 responses only which represent 62.5% of our targeted sample.

13.4 CHALLENGES AND IMPLEMENTING BPR

Companies need to have sufficient motivation to make significant changes for business and performance improvements. However, generally this is difficult to reach due to the resistance of change by the organization culture and the commitment and reliance on the existing processes.

Moreover, high cost of change specifically the cost of high-end technology implementation and its obstacles may stand as barriers to the success of BPR solution, where advance technology needs a professional and well trained human resources in addition to a well stabilized infrastructure or even in many organizational development it will cost to outsource its technology based solutions to a vendor.

As BPR combine tasks and processes to fewer and may reduce human interaction, as a result human allocation, restructuring and downsizing will be a considerable concerns to the company's management and a difficult decision to take. Furthermore, luck of time and deprived planning may lead companies to fail in implementing BPR solution which this will case huge financial losses.

13.5 RESULTS AND FINDINGS

H_1. There is significant relationship between cost and business performance.

This hypothesis laid down to test the relation between (Cost & Business Performance) under BPR solutions and to answer the first question in this research (Do BPR enhance cost cutting in the process of delivering services or products). On the other hand, we set null hypothesis against H_{01}.

When the regression between cost and business performance calculated (sig=0.307, which is greater than 0.05) therefore H_1 rejected while H_{01} accepted which mean the relationship between cost and business performance doesn't exist.

Table 13.5 Research Based on ANOVAs Test-1

ANOVAb

Model		Sum of Squares	Df	Mean Square	F	Sig.
	Regression	.174	1	.174	1.067	.307[a]
1	Residual	7.806	00	.163		
	Total	7.980	49			

a. Predictors: (Constant), Cost
b. Dependent Variable: BP

Coefficients[a]

Model		Unstandardized Coefficients		Standardized Coefficients		
		B	Std. Error	Beta	T	Sig.
1	(Constant)	3.453	.513		6.725	.000
	Cost	.129	.124	.147	1.033	.307

a. Dependent Variable: BP

H_2. There is significant relationship between quality and business performance.

This hypothesis laid down to test the relation between (quality & Business Performance) under BPR solutions and to answer the second question in this research (Do BPR enhance quality of services or products provided). On the other hand, we set null hypothesis against H_{02}.

When the regression between quality and business performance calculated (sig=1.582, which is greater than 0.05) therefore H_2 rejected while H_{02} accepted which mean the relationship between quality of service & products provided and business performance doesn't exist.

Table 13.6 Findings Based on ANOVAs Test-2

ANOVA[b]

Model		Sum of Squares	Df	Mean Square	F	Sig.
1	Regression	.255	1	.255	1.582	.215[a]
	Residual	7.725	48	.161		
	Total	7.980	49			

a. Predictors: (Constant), Quality
b. Dependent Variable: BP

Coefficients[a]

Model		Unstandardized Coefficients		Standardized Coefficients		
		B	Std. Error	Beta	T	Sig.
1	(Constant)	3.593	.313		11.477	.000
	Quality	.106	.084	.179	1.258	.215

a. Dependent Variable: BP

H_3. There is significant relationship between time cycle and business performance.

This hypothesis laid down to test the relation between (Time Cycle & Business Performance) under BPR solutions and to answer the third question in this research (Do BPR enhance speed and time consumed in delivering services or products). On the other hand, we set null hypothesis against H_{03}.

When the regression between time and business performance calculated (sig=0.004, which is less than 0.05) therefore H_3 accepted and H_{03} rejected, which mean the relationship between quality of service & products provided and business performance exist and BPR enhance the time cycle to deliver product and services.

Table 13.7 Research and Findings Based on ANOVAs Test-3

ANOVA[b]

Model		Sum of Squares	Df	Mean Square	F	Sig.
1	Regression	1.266	1	1.266	9.053	.004[a]
	Residual	6.714	48	.140		
	Total	7.980	49			

a. Predictors: (Constant), Time
b. Dependent Variable: BP

Coefficients[a]

Model		Unstandardized Coefficients		Standardized Coefficients		
		B	Std. Error	Beta	T	Sig.
1	(Constant)	5.249	.425		12.346	.000
	Time	−.307	.102	−.398	−3.009	.004

a. Dependent Variable: BP

13.6 DISCUSSION

BPR solution objectives is to help the companies to fundamentally rethink how they do their work in order to dramatically cut operational cost, improve customer satisfaction by the quality of the products and services provided, and speed up the consumed time to provide the products or services. Therefore, BPR aims to enhance business performance and as (Hammer and Champy, 1993) said: "Re-engineering is the fundamental rethinking and radical redesign of business processes to achieve dramatic improvement in critical, contemporary measures of performance such as cost, quality, service, and speed".

In our research we distributed 50 questionnaires to Bahrain Commercial Facilities (BCFC), a company which just experienced the BPR solutions, and from BCFC's experience which is reflected on the questionnaire answers we come to the following results after calculating the linear regression between business performance as an independent and the following variables as dependants (cost, quality, and time).

◁ There is no relationship between cost and business performance after implementing BPR. Although it's known that an important aspect of business performance is the cycle time, and it's know as the total consumed time to accomplish a frequent task. It also may extend this definition to reach the time consumed to come with new ideas of products or services to the customers. Time can be used to measure productivity by comparing time consumed in specific company with benchmarks. Many benefits can reached by reducing time cycle such as product or services can enter and reach market earlier, and enhance profitability.

◁ There is no relationship between quality and business performance after implementing BPR. However we know that the use of operational techniques and activity to maintain a quality of product or service that will satisfy specific needs, the aim of quality is to provide quality that is satisfactory, e.g (safe, and economical) which require an integrating several related steps including proper specification to meet the requirements; production to meet the specification; inspection to determine the degree of conformance to specification; and review of usage to provide for revision of specification. To control quality management and especially top management must have a commitment to TQC, to enhance the quality of products and service provided; where process capabilities and design, ethics, change and development, internal staff relations all should be controlled.

❧ There is a positive relationship between time and business performance after implementing BPR. Many companies beset with extremely long time to deliver a product or services and cannot solve this issue because they have difficulties to bring products and services on idle time.

The causes of long cycle time are broad and diverse, and have a growing impact on operating results. However, recognizing and modifying the source obstacle should be made to attain major enhancements in business performance. The disadvantages of long time cycle can swing between customer dissatisfactions and loss of customer base, drop in sales, high cost because of non value added processes, destroying goodwill, and losing the business. Cycle time always should be pressed in all stages to achieve an idle time cycle from time that order is taken to delivering product and services. The process design must spotlight the customer's needs: high quality, short cycle time, and low cost.

In our interviews with account department we concluded that the new system causing them many errors since it's migrated with the old system, moreover other staff who use the output of account department were complaining about accuracy of work done. Therefore, we come through that account staffs were not well trained on the new system and/or not willing to accept this change.

Moreover, consumer finance department were referring any delay or errors in underwriting loans to the new system which is again show as the lack of knowledge or training to those employees.

These results are not limited to this research only; where in diffident scenarios of BPR implementation the results might be different and the relation between the dependant and the variables may vary due to several factors such as BPR implementation plan, post implementation procedures, organizational culture, management commitment, quality assurance. Etc...

BPR put forward hope of providing such improvement in cost, cycle time, quality, and use of capital to many enterprises. Re-engineering is not riskless, and many have failed to reengineer. There are several victorious stories, like: Ford Motor, and IBM Credit. However, some will fail.

The reasons why re-engineering efforts fail are often due to lack of executive leadership or due to organizational resistance therefore Companies need to have sufficient motivation to make significant changes for business and performance improvements. BCFC management was committed to change; it is ready for change, but information technology support was not up to the standards and the employees were not trained well on the new system and this obstacle mentioned previously in chapter four under challenges as follow high cost of change specifically the cost of high-end technology implementation and its obstacles may stand as barriers to the success of BPR solution, where advance technology needs a professional and well trained human resources in addition to a well stabilized infrastructure or even in many organizational development it will cost to outsource its technology based solutions to a vendor.

The concluded relations reflects BCFC experience in implementing their BPR solution and the inverse relation might be due to a failure of the BPR implementation in any phase of that project.

References

1. Aremu, M. A. and Saka, S. T. (2006) "The Impact of Information Technology on Library Management: A Marketing Perspective" in Advances In Management, A Publication of Department of Business Administration, University of Ilorin, Nigeria, 5 (l): 141–150.
2. Communications of the IIMA 30 2005 Volume 5 Issue 1
3. Conference Board (2004). Making Innovation Work. Research Report 1348-04-RR, April 2004.
4. Ezigbo C.A. (2003). Advanced Management Theory Immaculate Pub, Enugu, pp. 83–90.
5. Hammer, M. and Champy, J. A.: (1993) Re-engineering the Corporation: A Manifesto for Business Revolution, Harper Business Books, New York, 1993.
6. He, Xin James (2004). The ERP challenge in China: A Resource-Based Perspective. Information Systems Journal, 14 (2), 153–167.
7. Huang, Z. and Palvia, P. (2001). ERP Implementation Issues in Advanced and Developing Countries. Business Process Management Journal, 7 (3), 276–284.
8. Martinsons, M.G. (2004). ERP in China: One Package, Two Profiles. Communications of the ACM, 47 (7), 65–68.
9. Maureen W., William W.C, Wan C.L and Vand (2005). Business Process Re-engineering Analysis, and Recommendations, Planning Review, November pg. 22.
10. Sharma M. (2006). Business Process Re-engineering: A Tool to further Bank Strategic Goals. Journal of Management Information Systems 12: 1.
11. Sheu, C., Yen, H. R., & Krumwiede, D. (2003). The effect of national differences on multinational ERP implementation: An exploratory study. Total Quality Management & Business Excellence.

☺☺☹

Software Process Re-engineering in SME's

Ashima[1] and Himanshu Aggarwal[2]

Software Process Re-engineering is the core kernel of software process improvement (SPI). Today, the very promising small scale software enterprises (SME's) are striving for standardization of their software development processes. They are carrying out improvement processes but not a proper set of processes. Lack f experienced process engineers and activities which lead them to have a good CMM level is a big issue to be resolved. There are no underlying problems for large scale software industries due to enough resources like available budget, trained as well as experienced and dedicated software professional's team for software process improvement programs, required set of efficient tools and technology for actual implementation. And top of the all required infrastructure, proper understanding and mindset for applying software re-engineering initiative. Unfortunately, there is limited adoption, absorption, adaptation and assimilation of software process improvement models in SME's due to lack of know-how and available resources in terms of money, time, perceived benefits, quality focus. Unavailability of required automated tool sets, in-house software process assessment. In nutshell, there is limited adoption, absorption, adaptation and assimilation of software process improvement models in SME's due to lack of knowhow and available resources in terms of money, time and perceived benefits. This chapter explores as SPI has evolving nature, there is a need of Cost- effective framework which provide customization of tools and techniques w.r.t prevalent technologies encompassing agility, object orientation, component based modeling and reuse, architecture centric approaches, configuration and risk management, heterogeneous project types and sizes.

KEYWORDS Software Process Re-engineering | SPI | SME's | Software Process Automation | CMM | Software Process Customization

14.1 INTRODUCTION

Software Process Re-engineering is thought of as a vehicle which has the ability to carry the organizations achieves higher capability levels. The efficient and qualitative software project management totally finds its success in managing the triple constraint i.e. scope, time and cost. But, Software

[1] Department of Computer Science and Engineering, Thapar University, Patiala
[2] Department of Computer Engineering, Punjabi University, Patiala.

Process Re-engineering adds some more dimensions to software project management at a higher level of abstraction i.e. at process level. It guides and directs the available set of processes to be re-engineering e.g. adding more effective and efficient software processes, deleting ineffective set of processes, reordering the processes and activities in process set, configuring i.e. adapting and changing the processes according to the project requirements. Therefore SPI is really an indispensible cog in the gears of software process standardization and continuous software quality enhancement. This chapter's objective is to find the state of art in SPI in Small Scale Enterprises SME's, sieve the essential parameters from existing approaches towards SPI which focus on SMEs. Further, these parameters can be studded into SPI which can be used to add a new vision to SPI. The explored factors will be able to characterize the relevant technology, tools, methods, software process automation according to the needs of the SME's. A further objective is that of discussing the significant issues related to this area of knowledge, and to propose different strategies from which innovative research activities can be thought of and planned. As small and medium-sized software enterprises (SMEs) because are not capable of bearing the cost of implementing these software process. Implementation of software engineering techniques is difficult task for SMEs as they often operate on limited resources and with strict time constraints. There are number of methodologies to address these issues. In this chapter, various SPI methodologies for SMEs are discussed. This will lead towards maturity of software process improvement in SMEs and also facilitates in development of automation tools for SPIs in future.

14.2 STANDARD APPROACHES

The evolution of Software Process and Quality Frameworks described by (Sheard, 2001) represented the multitude of frameworks and standards used to derive one from other shows the usage of one framework in developing another. For example, the Systems Engineering Capability Maturity Model (SE- CMM) of EPIC1 developed from the Capability Maturity Model (CMM) for Software, the International organization for standardization (ISO) Software Process Improvement Capability dEtermination (SPICE), MIL-STD-499B (draft), and the Institute of Electrical and Electronics Engineers standard for systems engineering [IEEE 1220]. The SE-CMM was subsequently used in creating the Integrated Product Development CMM [IPD-CMM], the Security Systems Engineering CMM (SSECMM), and a merged Systems Engineering Capability Model (SECM) that is currently being developed with facilitation from the Electronics Industries Association (EIA). Incoming Arrows in following Figure 14.1 shows how one standard is derived from other different SPI standards.

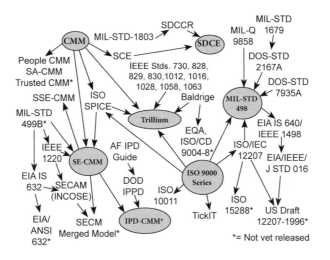

Fig. 14.1 The Frameworks Quagmire (Sheard, 2001)

(a) Capability Maturity Model (CMM)

Capability Maturity Model (CMM) proposed by the US Software Engineering Institute (SEI) to measure a contractor's ability to develop quality software (Humphery W., 1989)

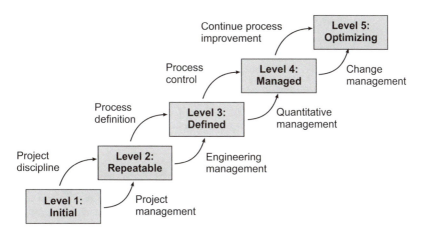

Fig. 14.2 CMM (Adopted from (Humphery W., 1989)

The Capability Maturity Model (CMM) developed at the Software Engineering Institute is based on the premises that maturity indicates capability and to obtain continuous process improvement it is much better to take small evolutionary steps rather than revolutionary innovations. it aims at guiding software organizations in selecting process improvement strategies by first determining their current process maturity before identifying their organization's critical quality and process improvement issues. These five developmental stages are referred to as maturity levels, and at each level, the organization has a distinct process capability. By moving up these levels, the organization's capability is consistently improved.

(b) Capability Maturity Model Integration (CMMI)

Capability Maturity Model Integration (CMMI) is a process improvement approach that provides organizations with the essential elements of effective processes. It is a model that consists of best practices for system and software development and maintenance. The model may also be used as a framework for appraising the process maturity of the organization. CMMI has features like Integration of software engineering and system engineering, Treating an each process very minutely, Focusing on continuous improvement (Crosby, 1979).

Level	Focus	Process Areas
5 Optimizing	Continuous process improvement! and resolution	Organization innovation and development, Casual Analysis
4 Quantitative managed	Quantitative management	Organization process performance Quantitative process management
3 Defined	Process standardization	Requirements development, Technical solution, Product integration. Verification, Validation, Organization process focus. Organization process definition, Organization project management. Integrated supplier management, Risk management, Decision analysis and resolution. Organization Environment for integration, Integrated training
2 Managed	Basic project management	Requirements management, project planning, Project Project monitoring and control. Supplier agreement management. Measurement and analysis. Process and product quality assurance. Configuration Mgmt
1 Performance	None	

Fig. 14.3 CMMI (Adopted from (Crosby, 1979).

(c) Software Process Improvement and Capability Determination (SPICE)

SPICE stands for Software Process Improvement and Capability dEtermination. Capability determination however is concerned with assessing an organization or project in order to determine risks to the successful outcome of a contract, development or service delivery (Dorling, 1993). The objective is to assist the software industry to make significant gains in productivity and quality, while at the same time helping purchasers to get better value for money and reduce the risk associated with large software projects and purchases (Route and Terrence, 1995) Model is depicted in Figure 18.4.

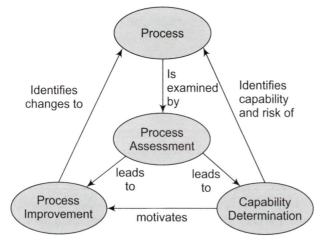

Fig. 14.4   SPICE Adopted from (Route and Terrence, 1995)

(d) BOOTSTRAP

BOOTSTRAP methodology can be applied to small and medium size software companies or software departments within a large organization. A new release (Release 3.0) of the BOOTSTRAP methodology has been developed to assure conformance with the emerging ISO standard for software process assessment and improvement (Hasse, 1994). The BOOTSTRAP methodology explored by (Kuvaja, 1994) provides support for the evaluation of process capability against a set of recognized software engineering best practices, include internationally recognized software engineering standards, identify organization's process strengths and weaknesses, support improvement planning with suitable and reliable results and also support the achievement of the organization's goals by planning improvement actions.

14.3 SOFTWARE PROCESS CUSTOMIZATION

(a) Software Product Line Practices

The software engineering product line practices argued by (Jones, 2002) include those practices necessary to apply the appropriate technology to create and evolve both core assets and products as follows:

Architecture Definition, Architecture Evaluation, Component Development, COTS utilization, Mining Existing Assets, Requirements Engineering, Software System Integration , Testing, Understanding Relevant Domains. Technical management practice: Configuration Management, Data Collection, Metrics, and Tracking, Make/Buy/Mine/Commission Analysis, Process Definition, Scoping, Technical Planning, Technical Risk Management, Tool Support. Organizational Management Practices: Building a Business Case, Customer Interface Management, Developing an Acquisition Strategy, Funding, Launching and Institutionalizing, Market Analysis, Operations, Organizational Planning, Organizational Risk Management.

(b) Software Process Customization

(McCormick, 2001) emphasizes "What's needed is not a single software methodology, but a rich toolkit of process patterns and 'methodology components' (deliverables, techniques, process flows, and so forth) along with guidelines for how to plug them together to customize a methodology for any given project." In (Moitra, 2001) opinion Quality in the Indian software industry is also reflected in the high maturity of Indian software companies. India has the highest number of CMM level 5 companies. More than half of all CMM level 5 companies in the world are located in India. In addition, (Asundi, 1999) finds most Indian software companies have achieved ISO 9001 certification. Other quality certifications such as COPC, SixSigma, and People-CMM have also been achieved by a large number of Indian software companies. It is noticed by (Bhatnagar, 1987)that India has many domestic challenges to overcome such as poverty and illiteracy, the Indian software industry has matured and is predicted to play a significant role in software services and product markets .The existing skilled human resource has remained one of the most important reasons for companies to outsource to India.

(c) The Prime Prelect

The Process Improvement in Multimodel Environments (PrIME) project will span a breadth of topics that are needed for an organization to be successful with process improvement in multimodel environments explored by (SEI). The project will concentrate on several subsets of models and standards that are commonly used in industry, such as Six Sigma, CMMI, Lean, and Agile methods.

(d) Intel's Idea of Customization—Accelerated Software Process

Intel's Information Technology (IT) department (Brodnik, 2008) explored the idea of ASP1 Improvement. They found that small projects which are less than six months have small teams, limited scope, and low risk need not to be appraised like large projects. Small projects should have different set of simplified version software processes clubbed into their software improvement initiatives. So, variety of project sizes should not have a single set of processes. Software processes must be tailored and customized according to the perspective of key stakeholders, engineers, process coaches, and auditors.

(e) Wipro's Idea of Customization—veloci-Q

veloci-Q (Subhramanyam, 2004) enabled the delivery of quality products and services without slowing down the system i.e. in time and quick delivery. In Figure 18.5, the Unified Quality System veloci-Q removed outdated information and duplications that had accumulated over time. Introduction of Six Sigma concepts increased the customer and business focus of project execution processes. veloci-Q complies with the coveted Capability Maturity Model Integration for Systems Engineering, Software Engineering, and Integrated Product and Process Development (CMMI- SE/SW/IPPD), V1.1 and ISO 9001:2000 frameworks.

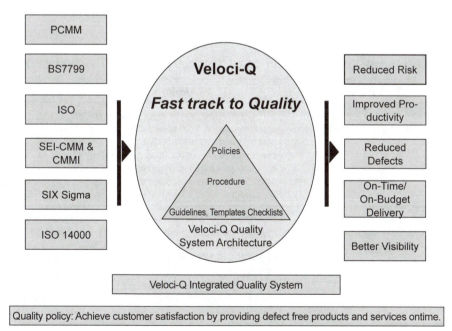

Fig. 14.5 Unified Quality System (Subhramanyam, 2004)

(f) PRISMS Project

Process Improvement for Small to Medium Software enterprises (PRISMS). The model (Commision of Software Standards, 2009) enables individual SMEs to tailor the software process improvement to the organization's business objectives. It works towards identifying key process areas and customizing and assessing these processes on ordinal scale according to their degree of conformance to the defined process. Figure 18.6 shows that assessment methods helps to aims at finding and prioritizing the essential set of processes based upon which the organization works towards maturity.

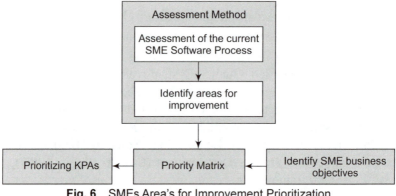

Fig. 6 SMEs Area's for Improvement Prioritization
Framework (Commission of Software Standards, 2009)

Multidimensional Approaches to Software Process Reengineering

Thrust Area	Major Contribution
Software Process Improvement using Service Oriented Approach (Park, 2007)	SIR-CM to store and manage heterogeneous assets which produced from software process improvement tools and adapted the Service Oriented Approach to construct the repository for connecting many different types of software process improvement tools. Configuration management method is also integrated to control and manage the assets.
A Gradual Approach for Software Process Improvement in Small and Medium enterprise (Alexandre, 2006)	The approach proposes a gradual Software Process Improvement framework based on a series of gradual assessments: a micro-evaluation, an OWPL-evaluation and a SPICE or CMM assessment. It allows SMEs to start SPI in a much targeted manner, to quickly progress within a limited budget and, eventually, to reach an acceptable level according to SPI standard models such as CMM and SPICE.

Process and infrastructure oriented improvement initiatives in Small Settings (Montoni, 2007)	Both CMMI and MPS Model-based assessment techniques indicates the TABA Workstation (Process-centered Software Engineering Environment) as a significant strength for the SPI implementations. The main objective of TABA Workstation is to provide an infrastructure to overcome inherent difficulties of SPI implementation initiatives like lack of financial resources. Moreover, the knowledge required for executing the improved processes is captured within the TABA workstation knowledge base.
Requirements Engineering Process Assessment and Improvement (Sommerville & Ransom, 2005)	To generate the greatest increase in RE maturity for the lowest cost without compromising organizational profitability or operations, following pragmatic proposals for maturity improvement: (1) Focus improvements on areas of requirements engineering where the company is weak as suggested by the Area/Strength matrix. (2) Consolidate and standardize practices that are already in use in the company. (3) Only introduce new practices where the cost of introduction is low
Framework-Based Software Process Improvement (Jalote, 2002)	Lessons learned regarding managing the CMM initiative in an organization: -Treat each SPI initiative as a project. -Have a schedule of one year or less for SPI initiative -Manage the risks to the SPI project
Return on Investment for implementing a SPI (Humphery W. S., 1991)	Potential return on investment (ROI) for implementing a continuous software process improvement program can be as much as 8:I within the first 2 years-$8 saved for every $1 invested-thus providing the needed stimulus and motivation.
Organizational-level software process improvement model (O-SPIM) (Xiaoguang, 2008)	SQMSP Software Quality Management and Support Platform (SQMSP), which was used in some medium-sized enterprises in China. Organizational level software process improvement model is an object-oriented model, which mainly supports the software products development and business control from balancing, implementing and supporting the organizational level business. It covers the business processes for multi-product, multi-project comprehensive quality assurance features This model gives solutions for organizational-level requirements assigning, project balancing and resources balancing.
Best practices in implementation of software process improvement (Galinac, 2009)	The SPI implementation strategy consists of 14 best practices deriving from agile methods, exploiting ideas of incremental deliveries, short iterations with frequent reviews and close collaboration with customers, which are intended to be suitable for global software development (GSD) organizations. It also emphasizes that improvement teams implementing the strategy are more likely to have better progress and achieve better effectiveness in terms of improvement deployment within development teams.

Software Quality and IS project performance improvements (Girish, 2007)	IS implementation strategies - executive commitment and prototyping—have a significant impact on both software quality and project performance, training had a significant effect only on software quality and simplicity has a significant effect only on project performance.
Software Release Planning: an evolutionary and iterative approach (Greer & Ruhe, 2004)	EVOLVE uses a genetic algorithm to derive potential release plans within redefined technical constraints to achieve higher flexibility and to better satisfy actual customer requirements. It takes as input a given set of requirements with their effort estimations and their categorizations into priorities by representative stakeholders. .
Goal-Driven Agent-Oriented Software Processes (Cares, 2006)	i* framework represents the software process using an agent-oriented language to model it and a goal- driven procedure to design for improving the quality of software processes which require their explicit representation and management
Measurement Practices at Maturity: Levels 3 and 4 (Alain, 2008)	Evaluation and continuous improvement of software maintenance are key contributors to improving software quality. The software maintenance function suffers from a scarcity of the management models that would facilitate these functions
IT Performance Improvement (Mallette, 2005)	Using COBIT with SEI CMM combines the best of both worlds to improve IT performance and drive the results to the business bottom line. The IT Governance. Institute's Control Objectives for Information and related Technology (COBIT) is generally accepted as the de facto for IT. Sustaining current performance while continuously reducing costs, decreasing exposure to risk and carving out resources to safely improve performance from a budget constantly targeted for cost reduction is the IT challenge.

It has been that small and medium- scale software enterprises hire external Consultants for process appraisals i.e. no in-house software process appraisal .This means higher cost expended for getting appraised from outside consultants. As technology has already come a long way therefore adding process assets reusable libraries, reusable design and code components, reusable verified and validated requirements set and object orientated methods and tools is actually needed to enhance software process improvement small scale enterprises. Agility is another significant feature which can speed up the pace of software development. But to glue agility and reusability of components, design, architecture intact, a process reengineering framework must be developed which can enable process customization according to the project requirement, project scope, project type , size, cost, time and above all quality. Learning modules can be added to the framework to suggest customized set of processes. These learning modules should aim at appropriate process set which can lead the SME's to one higher level of capability in a customized way.

References

1. Sheard, S. A. (2001). Evolution of the Framework's Quagmire. *Computer, 34* (7), 96–98.
2. Humphrey, W. (1989). *Managing the Software Process*. Addison-Wesley.
3. Crosby, P. (1979). *Quality is Free: The Art of Making Quality Certain.* New York: Penguin.
4. Dorling, A. (1993). SPICE Software Process Improvement and Capability Determination. *Software Quality Journal, 2* (4), 209–224.
5. Rout & Terence, P. 1.–6. (1995). SPICE: A Framework for Software Process Assessment. *Software Process Improvement and Practice, 1* (1), 57–66.
6. Haase, V. M. (1994). BOOTSTRAP: Fine tuning process assessment., *IEEE Software, 11* (4), 25–37.
7. Kuvaja, P. (1994). *Software Process Assessment and Improvement the BOOTSTRAP Approach*. UK: Blackwell Publishers, Oxford.
8. Jones, L. G. (2002). *Software Process Improvement and Product Line Practice CMMI and the Framework for Software Product Line Practice*. US: SEI,Carnegie Mellon University.
9. McCormick, M. (2001). Programming Extremism. *Communications of ACM, 44* (6), 110.
10. Moitra, D. (2001). Indias Software Industry. *IEEE Software,* 77–80.
11. Asundi, A. a. (1999, July). Retrieved august 2010, from www.heinz.cmu.edu: http:// www.heinz.cmu.edu/project/india/pubs/nber_iso_jul99.pdf
12. Bhatnagar, S. C. (1997). The Indian software industry: moving towards maturity 12. 277–288. *Journal of Information Technology, 12,* 277–288.
13. Brodnik, M. P. (2008, Feb). Why Do I Need All That Process? I'm Only a Small Project. *CrossTalk.*
14. Subramanyam, V. P. (2004). *An Integrated Approach to Software Process Improvement at Wipro Technologiestveloci-Q.* US: Software Engineering Institute.
15. Commission on Software Standards. (2009, December) *software_process_improvement_standards_specification*. Retrieved July 2010, from http:// nic.gov.sd: http://nic.gov.sd/ar/pdf/software_process_improvement_standards_specification.pdf
16. Park, E. J. (2007). Frameworks of Integration Repository for Software Process Improvement using SOA. *Proceedings of 6th IEEE/ACIS International Conference on Computer and Information Science* (pp. 200–206.). IEEE.
17. Alexandre, S. R. (2006). OWPL: A Gradual Approach for Software Process Improvement In SMEs'. *Proceeding of 32nd EUROMICRO Conference on Software Engineering and Advanced Applications,* (pp. 328–335).

18. Montoni, M. S. (2007). MPS Model and TABA Workstation: Implementing Software Process Improvement Initiatives in Small Settings'. *Fifth International Workshop on Software Quality, (WoSQ07)* , (pp. 57–63).

19. Sommerville, I. &. (2005). An Empirical Study of Industrial Requirements Engineering Process Assessment and Improvement. *ACM Transactions on Software Engineering and Methodology, 14* (1), 85–117.

20. Jalote, P. (2002). Lessons Learned in Framework-Based Software Process Improvement. *Proceedings of Ninth Asia-Pacific Software Engineering Conference,* 261–265.

21. Humphrey, W. S. (1991). Software Process Improvement at Hughes Aircraft. *IEEE Software, 8* (4), 11–23.

22. Xiaoguang Yan, X. W. (2008). Research on Organizational-level Software Process Improvement Model and Its Implementation. *Proceedings of International Symposium on Computer Science and Computational Technology.*

23. Galinac, T. (2009). Empirical evaluation of selected best practices in implementation of software process improvement. *Information and Software Technology, 51* (9), 1351–1364.

24. Girish, H. J. (2007). Software quality and IS project performance improvements from software development process maturity and IS implementation strategies. *Journal of Systems and Software, 80* (4), 616–627.

25. Greer, D. & Ruhe, G. (2004). Software release planning: an evolutionary and iterative approach. *Information and Software Technology, 46* (4), 243–253.

26. Cares, C. F. (2006). Goal-Driven Agent-Oriented Software Processes. *Proceedings of 32nd EUROMICRO Conference on Software Engineering and Advanced Application,* (pp. 336–347).

27. Alain, A. (2008). A Software Maintenance Maturity Model (S3M): Measurement Practices at Maturity Levels 3 and 4' International Workshop on Software Quality and Maintainability. *Electronic Notes in Theoretical Computer Science, 233,* 73–87.

28. Mallette, D. &. (2005). IT Performance improvement with COBIT and the SEI CMM. *Information Systems Control Journal.*

☺☺☹

15

ERP Deployment

Sona Srivastava and Parminder Narula

Globalization presents both business and technology challenges. Companies find there is no silver bullet when responding to the increased complexity of the key performance resulting from globalization. In order to keep pace with the globalization public sector enterprises also adopted ERP which led to the implementation of SAP in PSUs. Enterprise Resource Planning (ERP) is a mission-critical component of any globalization strategy. The information made available through ERP is key to providing visibility to Key Performance. Enterprise Resource Planning systems are the new solution to business systems. These systems provide comprehensive business functionality in an integrated fashion using a state- of-the-art IT architecture. This trend towards enterprise systems in large and mid-sized organizations has a significant impact on IS careers paths. Enterprise systems essentially change fundamental business work processes thus implying that the system that supports these processes, design and development of these systems, also change, which resulted in numerous systems .The ERP system was hence installed in PSU like BHEL. This chapter identifies opportunities for incorporating the ERP body of knowledge into an IS program in BHEL. . This is an exploratory research chapter that tries to identify the effectiveness of ERP deployment in PSU with special reference to BHEL. We therefore conclude that profitable growth is the key consideration in corporate globalization efforts.

KEYWORDS CRM | Supply Chain | Back office systems | Core System | Customization

15.1 INTRODUCTION

ERP is a one-point source of information that can be used within an enterprise for various business functions like manufacturing, supply chain management, financials, projects, human resources and customer relationship management.

Enterprise resource planning (ERP) is a company-wide computer software system used to manage and coordinate all the resources, information, and functions of a business from shared data stores. An ERP system has a service-oriented architecture with modular hardware and software units or "services" that communicate on a local area network. The modular design allows a business to add or reconfigure modules (perhaps from different vendors) while preserving data integrity in one shared database that may be centralized or distributed. Companies that automate and streamline workflows across multiple sites (including suppliers, partners, and manufacturing sites) produced 66% more improvement in reducing total time from order to delivery, according to Aberdeen's 2007 study of the role of ERP in globalization. Those companies that coordinate and collaborate between multiple sites, operating as a vertically integrated organization, have achieved more than a 10% gain in global market share. The majority of companies studied (79%) view global markets as a growth opportunity, but of those companies, half are also feeling pressures to reduce costs. Of those seeking to reduce costs either directly or by providing the necessary flexibility to ship from more cost effective locations, 74% are also seeking growth opportunities.

15.2 OVERVIEW OF ERP SOLUTIONS

Some organizations—typically those with sufficient inhouse IT skills to integrate multiple software products—choose to implement only portions of an ERP system and develop an external interface to other eRp or stand-alone systems for their other application needs. For example, one may choose to use human resource management system from one vendor, and the financial systems from another, and perform the integration between the systems themselves.

This is common to retailers, where even a mid-sized retailer will have a discrete Point-of-Sale (POS) product and financials application, then a series of specialized applications to handle business requirements such as warehouse management, staff rostering, merchandising and logistics. Ideally, ERP delivers a single database that contains all data for the software modules, which would include:

- Manufacturing
- Supply chain management
- Financials
- Project management
- Human resources
- Customer relationship management

ERP systems saw a large boost in sales in the 1990s as companies faced the Y2K problem in their legacy systems. Many companies took this opportunity to replace their legacy information systems with ERP systems. This rapid growth in sales was followed by a slump in 1999, at which time most companies had already implemented their Y2K solution.

ERPs are often incorrectly called back office systems indicating that customer and the general public are not directly involved. This is contrasted with front office systems like customer relationship management (CRM) systems that deal directly with the customers, or the ebusiness systems such as eCommerce, eGovernment, eTelecom, and eFinance, or supplier relationship management (SRM) systems.

ERPs are cross-functional and enterprise wide. All functional departments that are involved in operations or production are integrated in one system. In addition to manufacturing, warehousing, logistics, and information technology, this would include accounting, human resources, marketing and strategic management.

ERP II means open ERP architecture of components. The older, monolithic ERP systems became component oriented EAS—Enterprise Application Suite is a new name for formerly developed ERP systems which include (almost) all segments of business, using ordinary Internet browsers as thin clients. Best practices are incorporated into most ERP vendor's software packages. When implementing an ERP system, organizations can choose between customizing the software or modifying their business processes to the "best practice" function delivered in the "out-of-the-box" version of the software.

Prior to ERP, software was developed to fit the processes of an individual business. Due to the complexities of most ERP systems and the negative consequences of a failed ERP implementation, most vendors have included "Best Practices" into their software. These "Best Practices" are what the Vendor deems as the most efficient way to carry out a particular business process in an Integrated Enterprise-Wide system. A study conducted by Lugwigshafen University of Applied Science surveyed 192 companies and concluded that companies which implemented industry best practices decreased mission- critical project tasks such as configuration, documentation, testing and training. In addition, the use of best practices reduced over risk by 71% when compared to other software implementations.

The use of best practices can make complying with requirements such as IFRS, Sarbanes-Oxley or Basel II easier. They can also help where the process is a commodity such as electronic funds transfer. This is because the procedure of capturing and reporting legislative or commodity content can be readily codified within the ERP software, and then replicated with confidence across multiple businesses that have the same business requirement.

Businesses have a wide scope of applications and processes throughout their functional units; producing ERP software systems that are typically complex and usually impose significant changes on staff work practices. Implementing ERP software is typically too complex for "inhouse" skill, so it is desirable and highly advised to hire outside consultants who are professionally trained to implement these systems. This is typically the most cost effective way. There are three types of services that may be employed for—Consulting, Customization, Support. The length of time to implement an ERP system depends on the size of the business, the number of modules, the extent of customization, the scope of the change and the willingness of the customer to take ownership for the project. ERP systems are modular, so they don't all need be implemented at once. It can be divided into various stages, or phase-ins. The typical project is about 14 months and requires around 150 consultants. A small project (e.g., a company of less than 100 staff) may be planned and delivered within 3-9 months; however, a large, multi-site or multi-country implementation may take years The length of the implementations is closely tied to the amount of customization desired.

To implement ERP systems, companies often seek the help of an ERP vendor or of third-party consulting companies. These firms typically provide three areas of professional services: consulting, customization and support. The client organisation may also employ independent program management, business analysis, change management and UAT specialists to ensure their business requirements remain a priority during implementation.

Data migration is one of the most important activities in determining the success of an ERP implementation. Since many decisions must be made before migration, a significant amount of planning must occur. Unfortunately, data migration is the last activity before the production phase of an ERP implementation, and therefore receives minimal attention due to time constraints. The following are steps of a data migration strategy that can help with the success of an ERP implementation:

- Identifying the data to be migrated
- Determining the timing of data migration
- Generating the data templates
- Freezing the tools for data migration
- Deciding on migration related setups
- Deciding on data archiving

15.2.1 Process preparation

ERP vendors have designed their systems around standard business processes, based upon best business practices. Different vendor(s) have different types of processes but they are all of a standard, modular nature. Firms that want to implement ERP systems are consequently forced to adapt their organizations to standardized processes as opposed to adapting the ERP package to the existing processes. Neglecting to map current business processes prior to starting ERP implementation is a main reason for failure of ERP projects. It is therefore crucial that organizations perform a thorough business process analysis before selecting an ERP vendor and setting off on the implementation track. This analysis should map out all present operational processes, enabling selection of an ERP vendor whose standard modules are most closely aligned with the established organization. Redesign can then be implemented to achieve further process congruence. Research indicates that the risk of business process mismatch is decreased by:

- ↵ linking each current organizational process to the organization's strategy;
- ↵ analyzing the effectiveness of each process in light of its current related business capability;
- ↵ Understanding the automated solutions currently implemented.

ERP implementation is considerably more difficult (and politically charged) in organizations structured into nearly independent business units, each responsible for their own profit and loss, because they will each have different processes, business rules, data semantics, authorization hierarchies and decision centers. Solutions include requirements coordination negotiated by local change management professionals or, if this is not possible, federated implementation using loosely integrated instances (e.g. linked via Master Data Management) specifically configured and/or customized to meet local needs.

A disadvantage usually attributed to ERP is that business process redesign to fit the standardized ERP modules can lead to a loss of competitive advantage. While documented cases exist where this has indeed materialized, other cases show that following thorough process preparation ERP systems can actually increase sustainable competitive advantage.

15.2.2 Configuration

Configuring an ERP system is largely a matter of balancing the way you want the system to work with the way the system lets you work. Begin by deciding which modules to install, then adjust the system using configuration tables to achieve the best possible fit in working with your company's processes.

Modules—Most systems are modular simply for the flexibility of implementing some functions but not others. Some common modules, such as finance and accounting are adopted by nearly all companies implementing enterprise systems; others however such as human resource management are not needed by some companies and therefore not adopted. A service company for example will not likely need a module for manufacturing. Other times companies will not adopt a module because they already have their own proprietary system they believe to be superior. Generally speaking the greater number of modules selected, the greater the integration benefits, but also the increase in costs, risks and changes involved.

Configuration Tables—A configuration table enables a company to tailor a particular aspect of the system to the way it chooses to do business. For example, an organization can select the type of inventory accounting – FIFO or LIFO—it will employ or whether it wants to recognize revenue by geographical unit, product line, or distribution channel.

So what happens when the options the system allows just aren't good enough? At this point a company has two choices, both of which are not ideal. It can re-write some of the enterprise system's code, or it can continue to use an existing system and build interfaces between it and the new enterprise system. Both options will add time and cost to the implementation process. Additionally they can dilute the system's integration benefits. The more customized the system becomes the less possible seamless communication becomes between suppliers and customers.

15.2.3 Consulting services

Many organizations did not have sufficient internal skills to implement an ERP project. This resulted in many organizations offering consulting services for ERP implementation. Typically, a consulting team was responsible for the entire ERP implementation including planning, training, testing, implementation, and delivery of any customized modules. Examples of customization includes additional product training; creation of process triggers and workflow; specialist advice to improve how the ERP is used in the business; system optimization; and assistance writing reports, complex data extracts or implementing Business Intelligence.

15.3 "CORE SYSTEM" CUSTOMIZATION VS CONFIGURATION

Increasingly, ERP vendors have tried to reduce the need for customization by providing built-in "configuration" tools to address most customers' needs for changing how the out-of-the-box core system works. Key differences between customization and configuration include:

- Customization is always optional, whereas some degree of configuration (e.g. setting up cost/profit centre structures, organizational trees, purchase approval rules, etc.) may be needed before the software will work at all.
- Configuration is available to all customers, whereas customization allows individual customer to implement proprietary "marketbeating" processes.
- Configuration changes tend to be recorded as entries in vendor-supplied data tables, whereas customization usually requires some element of programming and/or changes to table structures or views.

↝ The effect of configuration changes on the performance of the system is relatively predictable and is largely the responsibility of the ERP vendor. The effect of customization is unpredictable and may require time-consuming stress testing by the implementation team.

↝ Configuration changes are almost always guaranteed to survive upgrades to new software versions. Some customizations (e.g. code that uses pre-defined "hooks" that are called before/after displaying data screens) will survive upgrades, though they will still need to be retested. More extensive customizations (e.g. those involving changes to fundamental data structures) will be overwritten during upgrades and must be re-implemented manually.

By this analysis, customizing an ERP package can be unexpectedly expensive and complicated, and tends to delay delivery of the obvious benefits of an integrated system. Nevertheless, customizing an ERP suite gives the scope to implement secret recipes for excellence in specific areas while ensuring that industry best practices are achieved in less sensitive areas.

15.4 EXTENSION

In this context "Extension" refers to ways that the delivered ERP environment can be extended with third- party programs. It is technically easy to expose most ERP transactions to outside programs, e.g.

↝ Scenarios to do with archiving, reporting and republishing (these easiest to achieve, because they mainly address static data);

↝ Transactional data capture scenarios, e.g. using scanners, tills or RFIDs, are relatively easy (because they touch existing data);

....however because ERP applications typically contain sophisticated rules that control how master data can be created or changed, some scenarios are very difficult to implement.

15.4.1 Maintenance and support services

Maintenance and support services involve monitoring and managing an operational ERP system. This function is often provided in-house using members of the IT department, or may be provided by a specialist external consulting and services company.

15.4.2 Advantages

In the absence of an ERP system, a large manufacturer may find itself with many software applications that cannot communicate or interface effectively with one another. Tasks that need to interface with one another may involve:

◂ Integration among different functional areas to ensure proper communication, productivity and efficiency

◂ Design engineering (how to best make the product)

◂ Order tracking, from acceptance through fulfillment

◂ The revenue cycle, from invoice through cash receipt

◂ Managing inter-dependencies of complex processes bill of materials

◂ Tracking the three-way match between purchase orders (what was ordered), inventory receipts (what arrived), and costing (what the vendor invoiced)

◂ The accounting for all of these tasks: tracking the revenue, cost and profit at a granular level.

◂ ERP Systems centralize the data in one place. This eliminates the problem of synchronizing changes and can reduce the risk of loss of sensitive data by consolidating multiple permissions and security models into a single structure.

Some security features are included within an ERP system to protect against both outsider crime, such as industrial espionage, and insider crime, such as embezzlement. A data-tampering scenario, for example, might involve a disgruntled employee intentionally modifying prices to below-the-breakeven point in order to attempt to interfere with the company's profit or other sabotage. ERP systems typically provide functionality for implementing internal controls to prevent actions of this kind. ERP vendors are also moving toward better integration with other kinds of information security tools.

15.4.3 Disadvantages

Problems with ERP systems are mainly due to inadequate investment in ongoing training for the involved IT personnel—including those implementing and testing changes—as well as a lack of corporate policy protecting the integrity of the data in the ERP systems and the ways in which it is used.

◂ Customization of the ERP software is limited.

◂ Re-engineering of business processes to fit the "industry standard" prescribed by the ERP system may lead to a loss of competitive advantage.

◂ ERP systems can be very expensive (This has led to a new category of "ERP light" solutions)

◂ ERPs are often seen as too rigid and too difficult to adapt to the specific workflow and business process of some companies—this is cited as one of the main causes of their failure.

- Many of the integrated links need high accuracy in other applications to work effectively. A company can achieve minimum standards, then over time "dirty data" will reduce the reliability of some applications.
- Once a system is established, switching costs are very high for any one of the partners (reducing flexibility and strategic control at the corporate level).
- The blurring of company boundaries can cause problems in accountability, lines of responsibility, and employee morale.
- Resistance in sharing sensitive internal information between departments can reduce the effectiveness of the software.
- Some large organizations may have multiple departments with separate, independent resources, missions, chains-of-command, etc, and consolidation into a single enterprise may yield limited benefits.
- The system may be too complex measured against the actual needs of the customers.
- ERP Systems centralize the data in one place. This can increase the risk of loss of sensitive information in the event of a security breach.

MRP vs. ERP—manufacturing management systems have evolved in stages over the past 30 years from a simple means of calculating materials requirements to the automation of an entire enterprise. Around 1980, overfrequent changes in sales forecasts, entailing continual readjustments in production, as well as inflexible fixed system parameters, led MRP (Material Requirement Planning) to evolve into a new concept : Manufacturing Resource Planning (or MRP3) and finally the generic concept Enterprise Resource Planning (ERP)

15.4.4 BHEL's IT prowess sets example for PSU sector

The company began its IT sojourn at a time when most other private players where still deliberating on whether to take the IT path or not and today boasts of an IT infrastructure that comprises of a Wide Area Network (WAN), usage of CAD/CAM tools in the designing process and a full fledged **ERP system** to be rolled out in the months to come.

BHEL with a product offering comprising of 180 products and offering systems and services catering to the needs of core sectors such as power, transmission, transportation including railways, defence, telecommunication, oil etc was established in Bhopal more than 40 years ago and is considered to be one of the first players in the electrical industry in the country. The company exports its products to more than 50 countries and registered a turnover of Rs 6347.8 crore in the fiscal year 2000–01.

15.4.5 The beginning of IT

Soon after commencement of operations, BHEL realised the power of IT when in 1960 it underwent a massive technology transfer from countries such as USSR, USA and UK. Though the technology at this stage was still rudimentary, almost all units of BHEL underwent a complete makeover. This makeover covered practically every area of operations from design and documentation to manufacturing. As part of this transfer, the company also acquired all related computer programmes allowing it to rewrite codes to suit the India— specific working conditions.

15.4.6 IT in everyday operations

Over the years, the IT tools in the company have been gradually upgraded in accordance with the requirements of the company and in tune with the technology scenario. Each of the company's manufacturing units have a strong functional computerised system base supported by an appropriate IT infrastructure. The company, which was earlier using mainframe computers, has now replaced them with high-end servers and front-end PCs, which are used extensively across the organisation.

In addition to the above systems, being an engineering organisation, the company has been using PDMS, AutoCAD, CAM and other Computer Aided Engineering (CAE) tools. These tools, Jain points out, are acquired from Original Equipment Manufacturers (OEMs) only. The usage of these tools he says have helped in a faster rollout of products and have helped to ensure greater accuracy of the same.

In an effort to tackle the perennial problem of hacking and intrusion attempts, the company has well defined principles for the protection of its infrastructure and data. The company ensures that norms for computer security are defined and adhered to. All the Internet gateways are protected with firewalls, proxy server and intrusion detection systems. BHEL is presently using firewalls from Checkpoint. Anti-virus software provided on all nodes, desktops and servers are updated regularly. At present, the driving force for IT security in the company is the IT Act, e-commerce activities which encompass authentication, integrity, non-repudiation and confidentiality and lastly service availability.

Currently all manufacturing units of the company have a core team of IT professionals who are responsible for the IT infrastructure in their concerned unit. Each of the major operations in the units such as material management and finance also have their own systems professionals. At the corporate level, overall policy coordination is done by the Corporate Information Technology Group. At present, the company has over 1000 IT professionals working for them. In order to meet the business challenges of the future, some of the newer areas that are being considered for absorption into the IT infrastructure include the enterprise-wide computing systems, collaborative and concurrent engineering, simulation modelling and video conferencing.

BHEL unit launches ERP module Connectivity and BHEL on WAN With a huge set up comprising of 14 manufacturing units, 3 distinct business groups (catering to the power industry and international operations), 4 regional power centres, over 100 project sites, 8 service centres and 14 regional offices, one of the main problems faced by the company was connectivity. In an effort to tackle this problem head-on, the company developed and connected all its offices through a wide area corporate data network called 'BHELNET'.

To connect its various facilities, the company adopted various modes of communication. These included leased lines from VSNL, ISDN, PSTN dial-up and point-to-point leased lines and VSATs. Backed by these means, BHELNET supports applications such as e-mail, file transfer, Intranet applications, Web publishing, business applications and engineering of information applications.

At present all manufacturing units, service divisions and some important projects are connected over BHELNET. Together this number 27, with more expected to be connected soon. In addition to BHELNET, each of the major units of the company have their campus-wide backbone network supported by Local Area Network (LAN) for inter office and department connectivity for systems integration. From the mid 1990s, the company started introducing high speed LANs in various units, which include Gigabit and Asynchronous Transfer Mode (ATM) LAN.

15.4.7 B2B

On the Business to Business (B2B) front, BHEL has already initiated steps to facilitate B2B transactions between their manufacturers units and suppliers. This includes the 'Ancillary Development Department' of Trichy unit of BHEL, which has developed a system to carry out e-commerce activities. The various e-commerce systems that can be carried out leveraging this systems are purchase order, supply materials, completion accounting, work in progress (WIP) analysis, bill processing, material accounting and excise duty.

As a by-product of this system, a number of standard subqueries are developed for retrieving data from the online Oracle database. Data that is required to be sent to subcontractors are transferred through e-mail attachments. The subcontractors can send requests for clarifications or assistance through the Web. Initiatives have also been taken up for development of the company level market place for e-procurement and e-sales. At the unit level, the e-commerce framework has been developed for acquirement of spares of specific products such as pulverizes valves, pumps and traction equipment.

15.5 ERP & ITS FUTURE SCOPE IN BHEL

One of the most recent initiatives of the company has been the initiation of ERP implementation. "In order to keep pace with the new economy, the integration of business processes has become a necessity. To this end we decided to adopt a proven ERP package that would cover all our manufacturing units and business sectors." Accordingly, after evaluating a couple of packages, BHEL zeroed in from SAP, mySAP.com with Pricewaterhouse Coopers as the implementation partner. The company implemented the systems on a pilot basis for identified products. As part of this plan, the rollout of the pilot site i.e. the valves plant at the Trichy plant has been going on in full steam and is expected to be complete by the end of the month.

The ERP solution is expected to be cover modules such as financial accounting (FI), treasury management, control, project systems, sales and distribution, logistics, Customer Relationship Management (CRM), materials management, production planning, quality management and plant maintenance. The servers to be used for the ERP system will include development server, ITS Server, integration (quality and testing) server, workplace server, business warehouse server, knowledge warehouse server, CRM server, network for PCs and servers. Along with ERP adaptation in the manufacturing units, plans have also been chalked out for the implementation of CRM in the business sectors at Delhi.

The company has also embarked on a 100 percent IT literacy plan. It has drafted schemes aimed at imparting education at both the local and corporate levels. At the officer level, the IT literacy rate currently stands at 90 percent.

It was found that, "unlike other organisations, there was no resistance from the employees in using IT tools. In fact, the employees have displayed considerable interest in familiarising themselves with the same." The reason behind this is that the company is primarily a learning organisation.

The other factor being that a large number of machines in the company are computer controlled so the familiarity with IT tools is high. The company has also introduced a capsule computer education in all its training programmes for its professionals. As part of its effort to further the cause of IT literacy, the company is also offering soft loans to employees to buy PCs.

15.5.1 Benefits

The Company has to date invested crores of rupees into building up its IT infrastructure. But have there been any tangible benefits of the same? "In today's e-economy, IT plays an important role since each and everything is required in a digitised format. This holds more importance than ever in our case as it operates in the international market. One of the most visible benefits of our IT initiatives has been the better management of our working capital. The other benefits have been an improvement of operational efficiencies, such as production cycle reduction, inventory reduction, better product design and reduction in wastage of material, performance monitoring, customer care and after sales service."

With an aim to become the leading Indian Engineering Enterprise providing quality products, systems & services in the fields of energy, transportation, industry, infrastructure and other potential areas, the company has well-equipped facilities to carry out research. Some important research facilities are:

- Material Sciences Laboratory.
- Turbo-machinery Laboratory.
- Test facilities for clean coal technology.
- Ultra High Voltage Laboratory.
- Centre for Electric Transportation (with UNDP assistance).
- Welding Research Institute (with UNDP assistance).
- Ceramic Technological Institute (with UNDP assistance).
- Pollution Control Research Institute (with UNDP assistance).
- Fuel Evaluation Test Facility– (BHEL-USAID joint project)

15.6 FINDINGS AND CONCLUSION

- Bharat Heavy Electricals Limited (BHEL), hailed as one of the Navaratnas by the
- Government of India is all set to emerge as a global giant. Endowed with distinctive
- Competence in technology absorption, product development and manufacturing technology,
- the Company continues to play a vibrant role in the Indian power plant equipment market
- Even after the liberalization and opening up of the economy. BHEL supplied sets now account
- for 67,000 MW or 65% of the, country's installed power generating capacity. With 14
- manufacturing units and an annual production capacity of over 4000 MW for power plant
- equipment, the Company ranks among the most important power equipment manufacturers in the world.

15.7 ERP (SAP–HR) INAUGURATED IN BHEL BHOPAL UNIT

In a simple programmed was held at IFX conference hall in Bharat Heavy Electricals Limited, (BHEL), Bhopal unit ERP (SAP-HR) was inaugurated by Rk Singh, Executive Director, BHEL, Bhopal. Inaugurating the momentous occasion of GO-LIVE of Systems, Application and Products—HR System, Singh said that this implementation is a matter of pride for our Corporation as this is one of the major HR Initiatives with a company-wide coverage. He said that the growth BHEL is registering today is because of the intensive strength and work culture of the employees of the company. Appreciating implementation of SAP—HR, he said that many of the issues related to organization can be resolved successfully with this kind of tool.

RSV Prasad said that in today's times HR is looking at itself not only as a Service Function but is aggressively trying to be a strategic partner in business. Due to growing complexities of business scenarios it is absolutely essential that all the resources are put to most optimum use. Winning organizations execute its core business functions economically than their competitors. He said that introduction of this system will help in taking quick decisions and strengthen HR Functions in the Company. .The system will improve the business processes, provide agility and speed in the operations to deliver high quality service and thereby enhance customer satisfaction. The Tiruchirappalli complex of. BHEL, comprising the High Pressure Boiler Plant and the Seamless Steel Tube Plant at Tiruchirappalli, the Boiler Auxiliaries Plant at Ranipet and the Industrial Valves Plant at Goindwal has been expanding its product and technology profiles over the last three decades. Set up initially with technology support from Skoda Exports, Czechoslovakia, the plant updated the technology for its various products in the 1970's with a series of collaborations with leading equipment manufacturers in USA, Germany, Sweden and Switzerland. The boiler unit ratings have been steadily increased from 60 MW to 110 MW, 210 MW, 500 MW. BHEL Tiruchi has entered into technical collaboration with a Leading Company in Germany to design, manufacture and supply higher capacity sub/super Critical once- through boilers of range 660 MW and above. Orders for a total of 583 boilers have so far been bagged by the Company of which 525 boilers have already been Commissioned.SNR Softech Limited provides SAP ABAP/4 support to BHEL. In the following areas:

- Programming using ABAP/4.
- Batch Data Communication.
- SAP Script.
- Logical Databases, ABAP Dictionary and ABAP Objects.
- SAP Query

↜ Info type Development

↜ Customer Enhancements—User exits, BADI

↜ HR Form Editor

↜ Development of Classical and Interactive Reports (ALV, List Report)

↜ Smart forms, ABAP Query

15.8 BHEL UNIT IMPLEMENTS ERP PACKAGE

Bangalore, Dec. 22 the electronics division of Bharat Heavy Electricals Ltd (BHEL) here has successfully implemented ERP (Enterprise Resource Planning) software package integrating its core functions.

The ERP software has been sourced from SAP, Germany.

The implementation of the ERP package, as per its Strategic Plan 2007, will be taken up in a phased manner in other units of BHEL leading to an integration of their business processes, with its attendant benefits. Implemented by a team of BHEL engineers with consultancy from Wipro in a record time of about six months, BHEL expects this package to deliver significant returns over the coming years, resulting in enhanced efficiency in execution of projects and improved services.

By enabling the transfer of uniform and accurate information between various departments and functions as well as with customers and vendors, BHEL is looking ahead after this implementation to lead to an effective integration of the business processes. Improved data availability and monitoring are also expected to facilitate quicker decision making process and finally result in improvement of various business results and enhanced customer satisfaction.

The electronics division is an ISO 9001, 14001 and OHSAS 18001 certified unit and is one of the major manufacturing divisions.

It manufactures modern automation systems for power plants and industries at its facilities at Bangalore.

It has diversified into other high technology areas like semi-conductor devices, solar photovoltaic's, telecommunication and defense.

15.9 HYDERABAD, DEC. 31, 2002

BHEL Ramachandrapuram unit has put into operational mode its enterprise resource planning (ERP) module in its gas turbine section. It was formally launched on Tuesday by the Executive Director, Mr A.N. Jagadeeswaran, and representatives of the IBM. BHEL had initiated work on a pilot ERP project named 'PROGRESS' for its gas turbine manufacturing operations in April 2002. The ERP software was sourced from SAP- India, while IBM Business Consulting Services provided the necessary guidance for the implementation. The ERP implementation is expected to lead to improved delivery times, cost control and inventory management apart from providing means to reduce dependence of human inputs, according to a BHEL release.

In order to achieve the above objectives BHEL has intelligently adopted ERP in all the spheres of its operations. It assures us that Public sector units can also become a mile stone for other sectors by taking the best use of Information System. This has redefined working with all the functional groups performing in an integrated manner utilizing a common project and company database.

References

1. www.snrsoftech.com
2. www.twocircles.net
3. http://researchlibrary.mbtmag.com
4. www.expresscomputeronline.com
5. www.bhel.com
6. http://www.blonnet.com
7. www.aberdeen.com
8. Stephen Harwood: Erp the Implementation Cycle Jacobs, F. Robert (Author),
9. Whybark, David Clay (Author), Author Why Erp? a Primer on SAP Implementation India year book 2009

☺☻☹

16

Automation through ERP Initiative

Chaudhry M. Nadeem Faisal[1], Saeed Ahmad[2] and Amjed Javid[3]

The production of top quality materials/products at high speed with less time is only possible through and efficient information systems. Technologies that carries the flow of work has been widely applied in the various industries, such as OA (Office Automation), manufacturing, banking, security, education and research institutions, financial services, telecommucation industy and so on. The basic objective to adopt such technologies is to improve the business processes through automation using information system. In this research work the authors would like to presents the flow of information in an automated manner for knitting of yarn in textile industry, where it is implemented in Masood textile. This automation in information system developed efficiently inhouse ERP (Enterprise Information System).; it not only helps nut also support the management to manage the business processes

KEYWORDS Automation | Enterprise Information | Automated Information | Management System | Business Processes Integration

16.1 INTRODUCTION

Why is Automation very important? During development and manufacturing quick information turn around, that is required to hit the target and also to sustain the speed of process. Process automation has become very much common in industry. Every company that is involved especially the production oriented business use the automation information system for better management and to track the business processes/operational activities. Nowadays automated information system based applications are very much capable in collecting and measuring the required details for manufacturing or manufacturing related processes because process could be complex and the information required is huge.

The systems are based on automation is very simple thought which the information is forward to accomplish the business functions. These systems work

---

[1,2] School of Management Studies, The University of Faisalabad, Faisalabad, Pakistan
[3] School of Textile Engineering, The University of Faisalabad, Faisalabad, Pakistan

on pre-defined procedure and required less humans interaction and maintenance as compare to traditional information system. These AI based applications fetch the information and send it for further operations. The automated system works for government, private and especially in business context e.g. customer satisfaction, sales department and operational tracking.

Automation in business functions provides enterprise integration by passing the information amongst the systems and processes. The integration in business functions enables the systems for both data and flow of work; because to integrate the flow of work operational and functions integration is required. The reason is that information is swap between the applications, systems at different locations in ERP.

The production of top quality materials/products at high speed with less time is only possible through information systems. The ERP system in MTM (Masood Textile Mills) is consists of different applications as per their requirement for manufacturing, tracking and also to manage the resources. Each application has a distinct task and can be adapted separately to specific processes and requirements. An overlook of the system architecture for knitting is shown in figure 2. The objective of this research work is to define the processes for knitting and role of information system to make them fast, automated and efficient for tracking and monitoring during production.

16.2 AUTOMATION

Computer and related technologies are very much efficient and capable of carry out the functions that acquire humans efforts. While the execution of such function through machine or automation is just because, the humans do not wish to perfrom the same function again and again and also can not perform them consistently, accurately and reliably. Mass production is the major cause for the development of such automated system because the humans can not perform the jobs fastly as machine or automated system can.

The automation also offer the economicle benefits at enterprise level is the major cause of attentions towards, the capabilities of automation system. Atutomation is simply defined as atomatic control of manufacturing throught number of successive stages or the use of automative control to replace or reduce the humans efforts.

Process automation is described using the dedicated molding and appropriate drawing tools for work flow. While in transformation, set of rules are defined for the movement of information in the system. Where the data is read and receive from the sources agent and proceed for further operation in an understand format and this level of movement is responsible between the different connected components. The benefits of Business process automation include the work flow, data integration, and reduction of hand written form, human errors and better process flow and also to allow the new services to the customers for real time monitoring in business processes.

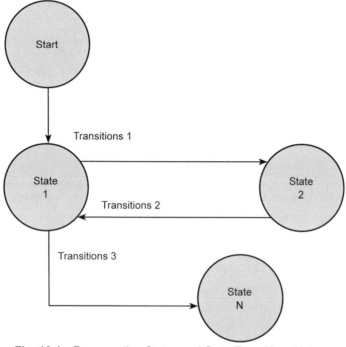

Fig. 16.1 Representing States and State Transitions Using a State Diagram in an automated system

16.3 AUTOMATED INFORMATION IMPLICATION IN TEXTILE INDUSTRY

Information management systems are broad level systems, these systems incorporates huge amounts of data across an organization. Data is entered into systems thought-out the organization. Where it is the responsibility of data management system is to pull these data elements into unified systems. Organizations collect the massive data depends on the nature and size of the organization, and system consist on different software applications with single platform. In order to access and to utilize the information, they need a well-planned and mature information management system.

The given model for automation in information system shown in Figure 16.2 is practically implemented in Masood textile mills. It shows the flow of working and information during knitting process to fabric. As knitting process consists of different processes, different departments play their contribution during manufacturing process. The automated information system divides these processes in different states. Each state has number of transaction. That starts from purchase order originate by the customers and the role of each department till the job completion or final state. Each state is directly or indirectly communicates with the other to describe the flow of process along with information.

MTM (Masood textile mills) have their complete and fully developed ERP system. It almost contain all important applications that provide the vie solutions for textile operation and management. Where the knitting processes is totally based on automation. The AIS (Automated information system) includes different agent's works together in knitting e.g., customer, PPC (production and planning department), Head office, vendors, store, knitting department, third parties manufacturing units.

In (state1) customer originate the PO (purchase order) and system forward it to PPC department (production & planning control department) to check the availability of vacant slot for execution or availability of resources, if not then PO return back to customer with PO status either successful or not.

If resources are available the PO (purchase order) forward towards head office for YD (Yarn Demand). Head office in (state2) generates the inquiries to yarn vendors for YO (Yarn order) and also give the feedback or status of Yarn to the PPC department. Yarn store (state3) receives the yarn as per requirement from vendor or Yarn supplier.

If yarn (State4) does not meet the requirement the store department rejects the order and update the status back to head office. Accepted yarn issues to the knitting department knitting for fabrication. In case (state5) if knitting department reject transaction due to excessive load. The store issues the yarn to third knitting parties or for fabrication.

After the (State6) completion of order job or fabrication the knitting department or third party knitting vendor/manufacturer issue the knitted fabric to the Grey Fabric store for delivery.

In case of any discrepancy related to job order or problem in production the system back to the knitting department or to the third party. Finally the product delivers to the customer and closed the job successfully.

During the manufacturing and execution, an intelligent system clearly defines the steps for production and also provides the support in an efficient manner which is not possible traditionally. In order to access and to utilize the information, they need a well-planned and mature information management system. The role of information system toward automation and order tracking and monitoring support the organizations for batter management and also to serve their customer efficiently.

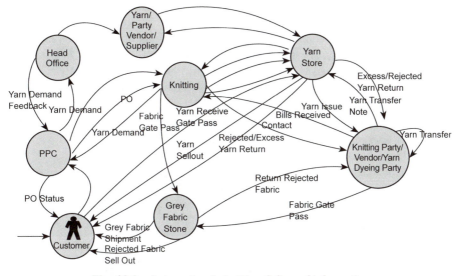

Fig. 16.2 Automation in knitting & flow of information

During manufacturing and execution for manufacturing, intelligent system clearly defines the steps for production, planning and also provides the support in efficient manners, which is not possible traditionally. In order to access and to utilize the information, they need a well-planned and mature information system. Where it serve for automation and monitoring and tracking that support the organizations towards the better management and also to serve their customer efficiently and timely?

Lastly, we offer our regards and blessings to the Management team of Masood textile mills who supported us in any respect during the completion of the project. We are also very thankful to Dr AD Chaudhry (Dean Faculty of Engineering) for his kind support.

References

1. K. Snnivasan. *The Evolving Role of Automation in Intel Microprocessor Development and Manufacfuring.* Intel T echnical Journal, May 2001.
2. JOSEPH A. REINE, JR.t, The Operational Information System and Automation of Sterlington Steam Electric Station, ire transactions on industrial electronics
3. U. Singh and D. Caceres – KEMA Inc, An Integrated Approach for Implementing a Distribution Automation System, 2004 IEEUPES Transmission 8 Distribution Conference & Exposition: Latin America
4. C.M. Nadeem Faisal, Usability Evaluation of Cloud Based Application, Department of Interaction and System design school of engineering Blekinge Institute of T echnology, Sweden, Jan 2009

5. E. L. Wiener and R. E. Curry, "Flight-deck automation: Promises and problems," *Ergonomics,* vol. 23, pp. 995–1011, 1980.

6. R. Parasuraman and V. A. Riley, "Humans and automation: Use, misuse, disuse, abuse," *Human Factors,* vol. 39, pp. 230–253.

7. D. D. Woods, "Decomposing automation: Apparent simplicity, real complexity," in *Automation and Human Performance: Theory and Applications,* R. Parasuraman and M. Mouloua, Eds. Mahwah, NJ: Erlbaum, 1996, pp. 1–16.

8. C. E. Billings, Aviation Automation: *The Search for a Human-Centered Approach. Mahwah,* NJ: Erlbaum, 1997.

9. C. D.Wickens, A. Mavor, R. Parasuraman, and J. McGee, *The Future of Air Traffic Control: Human Operators and Automation.* Washington, DC: National Academy Press, 1998

10. U. Singh and D. Caceres – KEMA Inc, An Integrated Approach for Implementing a Distribution Automation System, 2004 IEEUPES Transmission 8 Distribution Conference & Exposition: Latin America

11. Rowan D.A.; 1989; On-line expert systems in process industries; *AIExpert,* august 1989, pp. 30–38.

12. hitch R.; 1992; Artificial intelligence in control: some myths, some fears but plenty of prospects; *Comp. & Control Eng. J,* July 1992, pp. 153–163.

13. Chaudhry Muhammad Nadeem Faisal, Muhammad Sheraz Arshad Malik "Usability evaluation of Software as Service from Individuals perspective" Vol. II No. 7 (March 2011). ISSN: 1697-9613 (print) – 1887-3022 (online). www.eminds.uniovi.es

14. http://www.wisegeek.com/what-is-an-information-management-system.htm

15. http://prtl.uhcl.edu/portal/page/portal/HR/HANDBOOKS/Automated_Information_Systems

16. http://www.wisegeek.com/what-is-an-information-management-system.htm

☺☺☹

17

ERP in Manufacturing Industry

Arun Madapusi[1]

Over the past nearly two decades, firms have increasingly invested in enterprise resource planning (ERP) systems to manage their information needs. Firms in developed countries account for the bulb of ERP deployments worldwide. In the past few years there has been increasing penetration of ERP in developing countries. The extent of ERP implementations among firms in developed countries is a well researched issue. In contrast, very few studies have examined the extent of ERP deployments in developing countries. In this study, we address the above research gap by presenting a rigorous empirical assessment of ERP implementations in Indian production firms. The implementation status of different ERP modules, performance benefits and the influence of critical success factors (CSFs) are bey issues examined in this study.

KEYWORDS CSFs | Performance | Indian Production Firms | ERP | Organization Size

17.1 INTRODUCTION

Increased globalization has forced firms to invest in information technology (IT) to meet their global information needs. In particular, more and more firms across the world are implementing packaged enterprise resource planning (ERP) systems. ERP systems collect data through a single comprehensive database and make it available to modular applications that support all of a firm's value chain activities across functions, business units, and geographical areas (Davenport, 1998; Klaus et al., 2000). The rise in the popularity of ERP systems worldwide can be gauged from their rapid growth – $1 billion in 1990 (Mabert et al., 2000) to over $400 billion by 2006 (Bonasera, 2000; Gartner, 2003; IDC India, 2003; IDC, 2004; Reilly, 2005; Jacobson et al.,2007). The worldwide ERP market continues to grow at an annual rate of over 10% with revenues reaching $65 billion in 2008, and an estimated $61 billion in 2009, and $65 billion in 2010 (D'Aquila et al., 2009).

[1] Department of Decision Sciences, Bennett S. LeBow College of Business, Drexel University, Philadelphia

Firms in developed countries account for the bulk of ERP deployments worldwide (Mabert et al., 2003; Datamonitor, 2005) and most ERP system research focuses on implementations in the developed markets. It is only in the past few years that there has been an increasing penetration of ERP systems in developing markets and hence there is a paucity of studies that have examined the extent of ERP deployments in developing countries. Researchers attribute the rapid growth of ERP in developed markets in the 1990s due to their having built up a mature stock of ERP-related infrastructure requirements that support economic activity thus leaving room for productive ERP investment (Chandra and Sastry, 1998; 2002; Dewan and Kraemer, 2000; Huang and Palvia, 2001). Further, their studies suggest that the slow growth of ERP in developing markets, such as India, in the 1990s is due to their having to build up their basic ERP and complementary infrastructure before they can implement and begin to realize the benefits of ERP- related investments. In this study, we address the ERP research gaps in a developing market - India - and present a systematic and rigorous empirical assessment of ERP implementations in Indian production firms.

There was very low penetration of ERP systems in India till the mid-1990s with the market valued at about $3 million in 1995-96. The late 1990s witnessed higher growth rates, with the Indian ERP market growing at a compounded annual growth rate of 20 to 30% to reach $54 million in 2001 (De, 2001). Apart from a brief slump in the early 2000s, the Indian ERP market has been on a high growth trajectory clocking compounded annual growth rates of more than 10% to reach $83 million in 2004, $197 million in 2007, $241 million in 2008, and $260 million in 2009 (De, 2008; Chawla, 2009). The Indian ERP market is expected to reach $341 million in 2012 according to industry research analysts International Data Corporation (IDC) and Arc Advisory (Askari, 2007; De, 2007; Boparai, 2008).

Due to the relative newness of the ERP field in India and the rapid advances in ERP technologies, practitioner-oriented articles dominate literature. Descriptive and case studies form the bulk of Indian ERP research and empirical work is limited. Most studies have examined ERP issues - modules implemented, critical success factors (CSFs) emphasized, benefits realized - separately using a piecemeal approach and systematic studies with scientific rigor are by and large absent. Besides the above, the high incidence of problematic and delayed implementations in Indian firms also calls for a pan-Indian study on ERP deployments. De (2004) indicates that the average cost overrun among Indian ERP system implementers is 178 %, the average schedule overrun is 230% percent of original expectations, and the average decline in functional improvements is 59%. His study further indicates that 90% of ERP system deployments in India are problematic implementations.

Most researchers view the evolution of ERP systems from a manufacturing perspective - from materials requirements planning (MRP) to manufacturing resources planning (MRP II) to ERP (Rondeau and Litteral, 2001; Jacobs and Weston, 2007). Hence, most ERP systems are initially implemented in production firms (Mabert et al., 2000; Olhager and Selldin, 2003; Wang et al., 2005). The above suggests that production firms would account for the bulk of ERP system implementations in India. Gartner (2003) estimates the ERP penetration levels in the Indian manufacturing industry to be about 37%, customer relationship management (CRM) about 15%, and supply chain management (SCM) about 10%. Recent studies by Forrester Research indicate that investments in ERP, SCM, and CRM by the manufacturing sector accounts for the majority of enterprise application spending in India (Pasha, The above findings lend support to the identification of production firms as the sample population for this study.

17.2 RESEARCH METHODOLOGY

This research used survey methodology to obtain data from Indian firms across a variety of production environments. An integral part of the research involved the development of a questionnaire to maximize understanding of ERP implementations among academicians and practitioners. Dillman's (2000) tailored design method (TDM) for constructing the questionnaire was followed to the extent possible. The initial questionnaire was developed from a synthesis of ERP as well as other relevant system studies. Inputs from two international focus groups of eight academicians and eight practitioners, a pre-test using a graduate ERP class in India, and a pilot study in an Indian production firm that had implemented ERP were used to develop and validate the questionnaire. Feedback from the focus and respondent groups was incorporated at each step of the questionnaire development process and allowed for an incremental and comprehensive development of the survey instrument. The final questionnaire collected information pertaining to five areas: business unit characteristics, respondent characteristics, implementation status of ERP modules, critical success factors to facilitate the ERP deployment process, and benefits obtained from the ERP implementation.

The 2,937 production firms represented in the Confederation of Indian Industry (CII) member directory and a list of 240 production firms from other media sources served as the target population for this study. The CII is India's apex business association and its member firms can be considered to be leaders in the use of IT systems such as ERP. Dillman's (2000) mixed mode TDM survey methodology was followed to the extent possible. Telephone calls were made to each of the 3,177 firms to ascertain whether the firm had implemented an ERP system, whether the firm was willing to participate in the survey, and who would be the best person in the firm to send the survey instrument to and their contact details. This approach resulted in the selection of the names of 900 firms from the target population. Two mailings of the questionnaire were made. Of the surveys mailed in the two waves, a total of 231 responses were returned for a response rate of 25.67%. The Figure 17. 1 given below shows the research methodology employed.

Literature Review and identification of key study variables

Questionnaire Development (using Dillman's TDM method)
Selection of questionnaire items from literature to measure variables
Questionnaire review by international focus group of academicians (N = 8)
Questionnaire review by international focus group of ERP consultants (N = 8)
Questionnaire review by graduate MBA (ERP) class (N = 29)
Questionnaire review by pilot study firm (N = 72)
Purposive sampling method to extract names of production firms, identified as having implemented ERP. from the Confederation of Indian Industry (CII) member directory and other media sources
Use of Survey Methodology (using Dillman's mixed mode TDM method)
Pre-notice Letter sent to firms that have implemented ERP (N = 900)
Telephone Reminders made to all the second wave respondents two weeks after the second mailing date Second wave response(N = 104)
Total response (N = 231) for a response rate of 25.67% On obtainment of this satisfactory response rate, all additional mailings/contacts discontinued Review of returned questionnaires for accuracy and completeness
Data Analyses
Thank you/Reminder Note sent by postal mail as well as email one week after the first wave mailing date First wave response(N = 127)

Fig. 17.1 Research Methodology

An examination of the 231 completed questionnaires revealed that 12 firms were yet to go live with their ERP systems and their responses were discarded. Three additional questionnaires were discarded because they missed most of the data on key items. Since the focus of this study is on investigating ERP system implementations in production firms, the 216 remaining responses were evaluated based on the firm's level of manufacturing activities. A frequency distribution revealed that firms with 70% or more of their sales coming from production activities was a logical cut-off point to categorize firms as a majority of sales coming from production activities. This approach resulted in the omission of an additional 13 responses that represented primarily service firms. Only firms that realized 70% or more of their sales from production activities were included in the sample and thus the final dataset for analysis comprised of 203 responses.

17.2.1 Survey Results: Enterprise Characteristics

The data pertaining to the characteristics of the sampled firms are summarized in Table 17.1.

Table 17.1 Enterprise Characteristics

Number of Employees	Frequency	Percent
0–99	4	2.0
100–249	25	12.3
250–499	40	19.7
500–999	50	24.6
Over 1000	84	41.4

Sector	Frequency	Percent
Private	167	82.3
Public	32	15.8
Joint	4	2.0

Origin	Frequency	Percent
Multinational	40	19.7
Indian	157	77.3
Joint Venture	6	3.0

Union Status	Frequency Percent	Percent
Unionized	45	22.2
Non-Unionized	47	23.2
Both	111	54.7

Industries	Frequency	Percent
Automotive	44	21.7
Machinery and Equipment	20	9.9
Basic Metal/Coal/Lignite/ Uranium /Thorium/Others	13	6.4
Electronic/Telecommunic ation Equipment	11	5.4
Apparel and Textiles	11	5.4
Food Products & Beverages	11	5.4
Coke/Crude/Petroleum/N atural Gas/Others	9	4.4
Fabricated Metal Products	7	3.4
Rubber/Plastic Products	5	2.5
Paper and Paper Products	5	2.5
Others	67	33.0

The results in Table 17.1 indicate that the sample is a good representation of the Indian production sector comprising of firms of different sizes. The size of the firms was assessed in terms of the number of employees. The number of employees over 1,000 is the category most frequently represented and accounts for 41.4% of the sample. This, together with the number of employees in the 500 to 999 category, represents 66% of the sample. The number of employees in the two categories 0 to 99 and 100 to 249 account for only 14.3% of the sample.

Production Environment	Percent of Products Produced
Make-to-Order	61.8
Make-to-Stock	38.2

Production Flow Type	Percent of Products Produced
Project	20.0
Job Shop	13.9
Batch	22.0
Repetitive	26.4
Flow	17.7

Type of ERP System Implemented	Frequency	Percent
Single Vendor ERP System		
SAP	60	29.6
Oracle/PeopleSo ft	21	10.3
SSA Global/Baan	9	4.4
Microsoft	9	4.4
Ramco	8	3.9
QAD	5	2.5
ESS	5	2.5
Others	15	7.4
Best of Breed ERP System		
SAP & Oracle/PeopleSo ft	2	1.0
SAP & SSA Global/Baan	2	1.0
Others	10	4.9
In-House Developed ERP System		
In-House Developed ERP	57	28.1

More than half the firms in the sample have a mix of both unionized and non-unionized environments and represent 54.7% of the sample. The firms constituting the remaining part of the sample are more or less evenly distributed between unionized (22.2%) and non-unionized (23.2%) environments. Studies indicate that unions could affect the implementation of ERP systems (Rose et al., 2005; Vijayabaskar, 2005); however, the results indicate that unions are not a compounding factor in Indian ERP deployments. Most of the sampled firms belong to the private sector and represent 82.3% of the sample. Thirty two public sector firms responded to the survey and form 15.8% of the sample. Joint sector firms account for 2% of the sample. This is in accordance with past research, which suggests that the private sector drives IT growth in India and accounts for over 70% of the total IT investment in the country (Chandrasekhar, 2005). A majority of firms are of Indian origin and comprise 77.3% of the sample. Multinational firms of foreign origin represent 19.7% of the sample while joint ventures constitute 6% of the sample. A wide variety of industries are represented in the sample. The majority of industries (67%) fall into one of ten major industry groups. Firms in the automotive industry are the most frequently represented group accounting for 21.7% of the sample.

Make-to-order was the primary production system used by firms in the sample. The mean percentage of products produced with a make-to-order (MTO) system was 61.8%; 38.2% of the products were produced with a make-to-stock (MTS) system. The sample data indicates that most firms employed a mix of different production processes; however, many firms also employed only one production process. Firms using the repetitive production process (26.4%) formed the largest mean percentage of the sample. Firms were more or less evenly distributed between the batch process (22.0%) and the project process (20.0%) types. The flow process type had a mean percentage of 17.7% and the job shop type 13.9%.

Table 17.1 also provides the frequency distribution for firms by the type of ERP system implemented. The table indicates that the majority of the firms implemented a single vendor ERP system representing 65% of the sample. SAP is the most dominant ERP system implemented by 29.6% of the sampled firms. This is followed by Oracle/PeopleSoft accounting for 10.3% of the sample, SSA Global/Baan and Microsoft representing 4.4% of the sample each, and Ramco comprising 3.9% of the sample. The other major ERP vendors are QAD and ESS, together representing 5.0% of the sample. A small number of firms have implemented two or more Best-of-Breed (BoB) ERP systems accounting for 6.9% of the sample. In-house developed ERP systems represent the second most dominant ERP system implemented among the sampled firms accounting for 28.1% of the sample. The above distribution, with the exception of in-house developed ERP systems, is similar to that seen in well developed ERP markets. For example, Mabert et al. (2000) indicates that single vendor ERP implementations, with SAP as the dominant ERP system (25%) adopted, account for the bulk of ERP deployments in the US production sector. Their study further indicates that BoB systems account for a small portion (9.8%) of the ERP systems in use.

17.2.2 Respondent Characteristics

The respondents' characteristics are given in Table 17.2. The respondents to the survey provided both their total number of years of work experience as well as years of work experience in the present firm. For ease of presentation, however, as shown in the first two parts of the table, responses were grouped into one of three categories: less than 5 years, 5 to 10 years, and over 10 years. The majority of the respondents possess more than 10 years of work experience accounting for 92.1% of the sample. The most frequently reported category is that of respondents with more than 10 years of work experience at the present firm accounting for 56.7% of the sample. The next highest category is respondents with less than 5 years of experience forming 29.5% of the sample. Twenty eight respondents have been with the same firm between 5 to 10 years and account for 13.8% of the sample.

Table 17.2 Respondent Characteristics

Total Experience	Frequency	Percent
Less than 5 years	6	3.0
5 to 10 years	10	4.9
Over 10 years	187	92.1

Experience with Present Organization	Frequency	Percent
Less than 5 years	60	29.5
5 to 10 years	28	13.8
Over 10 years	115	56.7

Current Position	Frequency	Percent
Top Management	103	50.7
Middle Management	81	39.9
Lower Management	8	3.9
Team Leaders	7	3.4
Others	4	2.0

Current Work Area	Frequency	Percent
Finance	15	7.4
Production	2	1.0
Marketing	4	2.0
Information	7	3.4
Technology/Systems	175	86.2
Others	7	3.4

Level of Education	Frequency	Percent
Bachelor's degree	78	38.4
Master's degree	120	59.1
Doctorate	3	1.5
Others	2	1.0

About half the respondents belong to the top management category and constitute 50.7% of the sample. The next highest category of respondents is middle management and represents 39.9% of the sample. Lower management and team leaders account for 3.9% and 3.4% of the sample respectively. A majority of the respondents work in the information technology/ information systems area and represent 86.2% of the sample. Finance is the next highest work area reported and accounts for 7.4% of the sample. The other two functional areas reported are marketing and production accounting for 2% and 1% of the sample respectively. A majority of the respondents posses a master's degree and account for 59.1% of the sample. Seventy eight respondents have completed their bachelor's degree and represent 38.4% of the sample. Three respondents have reported completion of a doctoral degree and constitute 1.5% of the sample.

17.2.3 ERP Implementation Status

The average time in years since implementation began and the frequencies of implementations varied among the fourteen ERP modules in the sample. The average time in years since implementation began for each of the ERP modules was determined by first assigning values based on the midpoint of the scale ranges and then calculating the means of the assigned values for each of the modules. The means represent a relative measure for average time in years since implementation began for each ERP module or the length of time each ERP module has been in use. Past research on implementations such as Just-InTime (JIT) systems (White et al., 1999; Chong et al., 2001) and quality systems (Berry, 1996) have similarly derived relative measures for average time in years since implementation began for JIT practices and quality practices respectively. Table 17.3 summarizes the respondents' answers to questions pertaining to their ERP implementation status.

The high extent of usage of ERP modules covering the financial and logistics areas of the sampled firms show remarkably similar trends with those in advanced ERP markets (Mabert et al. 2000). The data in Table 17.3 indicates that the module most implemented (197 firms) and with the highest extent of usage (3.66 years) was materials management. The second most frequently implemented module was financials (189 firms) with an average time since implementation began of 3.61 years. A majority of firms have also implemented the sales and distribution module (182 firms) with the extent of usage being 3.40 years. The customer relationship module (CRM) is the most recent module (.38 years) deployed by a small number of firms (40 firms). The second least frequently implemented module (42 firms) was advanced planner optimizer/ advanced planner scheduler (APO/APS) with an average time since implementation began of .42 years. Only 45 firms have implemented the

Table 17.3 ERP Implementation Status

ERP Modules	Average Time in Years Since Implementation*	Number of Organizations with Module Implemented	Percent of Organizations with Module Implemented
Materials Management	3.66	197	97.0
Financials	3.61	189	93.1
Sales & Distribution	3.4C	182	89.7
Production Planning 2.96	163	80.3	
Quality Management	2.24	134	66.0
Controlling	2.23	125	61.6
General Logistics	1.84	100	49.3
Human Resources	1.72	117	57.6
Plant Maintenance	1.55	95	46.8
Supply Chain Management	1.02	62	30.5
Project System	0.92	63	31.0
E-commerce	0.45	34	16.7
Advanced Planner Optimizer/Scheduler	0.42	34	16.7
Customer	0.38	40	19.7
Relationship Management			

Note: N = 203
* Scale: Not implemented, Implementation started within the last year, Implementation started one to three years ago, Implementation started three to five years ago, and Implementation started more than five years ago.

electronic-commerce module (E-Commerce) with the extent of usage being .45 years. The above findings are in tune with past ERP research, which suggests that firms first automate intra-firm activities before implementing modules that cater to inter-firm activities (Mabert et al., 2000; Shields, 2001; Olhager and Selldin, 2003).

17.3 ERP PERFORMANCE BENEFITS

A majority of the respondents (82.3%) indicated that ERP provided an overall net performance benefit for their firm. Only 9.4% reported no overall net performance benefit from deployment of ERP. The remaining 8.3% indicated obtainment of partial performance benefits as it was too early in the implementation process to measure an overall net performance benefit. The changes in performance measures attributable to ERP were recorded on a Likert type scale ranging from 1 (Disagree) to 7 (Agree). Table 17.4

summarizes the mean, median, and mode responses to questions pertaining to the benefits attributable to the firms' ERP implementations.

The data in Table 17.4 indicates that the maximum benefit derived by firms from implementing ERP systems was an increase in information availability. This was closely followed by increases in information quality and then standardization. The performance measure that registered the least improvement was increase in competitive advantage. The above findings are in accordance with past ERP research, which suggests that most firms initially derive informational benefits from their ERP implementations (Mabert et al., 2000; Mabert et al., 2003; Olhager and Selldin, 2003). ERP information is then leveraged to improve operational performance measures such as inventory and on-time delivery. Efficiency in operations in turn leads to financial and organizational benefits (Mabert et al., 2000; Tarafdar and Roy, 2003; Hawking and Stein, 2004).

Table 17.4   ERP Performance Benefits

Performance	Mean*	Median	Mode
Information Availability	6.35	7.0	7.0
Information Quality	6.24	7.0	7.0
Standardization Inventory	6.05	6.0	7.0
Management	5.97	6.0	7.0
On-Time Delivery	5.91	6.0	7.0
User Satisfaction	5.83	6.0	6.0
Profitability	5.43	5.0	5.0
Return on Investment	5.43	6.0	6.0
Customer Satisfaction	5.38	6.0	6.0
Competitive Advantage	5.15	5.0	5.0

Note: * Scale: 1 to 7, "disagree" to "agree"

17.3.1 ERP Critical Success Factors

The influence of CSFs on the ERP implementation were recorded on a Likert type scale ranging from 1 (Disagree) to 7 (Agree). Table 17.5 summarizes the mean, median, and mode responses to questions pertaining to the CSFs influencing the firms' ERP implementations. The role of communication in facilitating the ERP implementation was rated the highest. This was closely followed by data accuracy and then implementation team support. Respondents rated the influence of national culture the least among all the CSFs. The above findings are aligned with past research, which suggests that CSFs that pertain to organizational support and data integrity are crucial for successful deployment of ERP systems (Stratman and Roth, 2002; Kumar et al., 2003; Guido et. al., 2007).

17.3.2 ERP and Organization Size

Mabert et al. (2003) indicates that organization size plays an important role in ERP implementations. Their study suggests that firms of different sizes tend to do different things in their implementations leading to different outcomes and benefits. In this section, we examine the experience of Indian production firms on three key issues—implementation status, CSFs, performance benefits - across organizations of different sizes. In tune with past research (Kimberly, 1976; Yasai-Ardekani, 1989; Swamidas and Kotha, 1998), in this study we use number of employees as a measure of organization size.

Table 17.5   ERP Critical Success Factors

Critical Success Factors	Mean*	Median	Mode
Communication	6.42	6.7	7.0
Data Accuracy	6.18	6.5	7.0
Implementation Team	6.09	6.5	7.0
Project Management	5.85	6.2	7.0
Top Management Support	5.81	6.2	7.0
Alignment	5.80	6.0	7.0
Training	5.64	6.0	7.0
User Support	5.59	5.8	7.0
Planning	5.56	5.3	6.5
Consultants	5.42	5.7	7.0
Organizational Culture	5.20	5.4	6.0
Learning	5.10	5.3	5.5
National Culture	4.94	5.0	5.0

Note: * Scale: 1 to 7, "disagree" to "agree"

The average time in years since implementation began and the frequencies of implementations varied among the fourteen ERP modules across different organization size categories ranging from 1 (smallest) to 5 (largest) (see Table 17.6). Table 17.6 summarizes the ERP implementation status of the sampled firms according to organization categories.

The data in Table 17.6 indicates that the materials management module has the highest extent of usage and is the one most often implemented among firms in categories 2, 3, and 5. The financials module has the highest extent of usage and is the one most implemented among firms in categories 1 and 4. A majority of firms across all size categories have also implemented the sales and distribution module. The CRM, APO/APS, and E-Commerce modules are least often implemented across all organization categories. The results in Table 17.6 indicate that none of the firms in category 1 have deployed the E- Commerce module. The above findings suggest that large firms are early adopters of ERP

Table 17.6 ERP Implementation Status by Organization Size

ERP Modules	Organization Size Category*									
	Category 1		Category 2		Category 3		Category 4		Category 5	
	Average Time in Years^ and Percent Since Implementation									
Materials Management	Time	%	Time	%	Time	%	Time	%	Time	%
	2.13	100.0	3.50	88.0	3.24	92.5	3.50	98.0	4.08	97.6
Financials	2.26	75.0	3.48	84.0	3.00	90.0	3.58	94.0	4.01	94.0
Sales & Distribution	2.50	75.0	3.16	84.0	2.79	85.0	3.23	90.0	3.91	96.4
Production Planning	2.00	75.0	3.02	80.0	2.44	75.0	2.64	72.0	3.44	88.1
Quality Management	2.13	75.0	2.44	68.0	1.29	60.0	2.10	60.0	2.73	71.4
Controlling	2.00	50.0	1.67	56.0	1.08	42.5	2.36	60.0	2.88	73.8
General Logistics	0.13	25.0	1.46	44.0	1.25	45.0	1.42	44.0	2.57	57.1
Human Resources	0.50	25.0	2.08	72.0	1.65	60.0	1.65	50.0	1.74	58.3
Plant Maintenance	0.13	25.0	1.32	48.0	0.99	42.5	1.54	40.0	1.96	53.6
Supply Chain Management	0.50	25.0	1.62	40.0	0.91	25.0	0.70	24.0	1.11	44.5
Project System	0.13	25.0	0.76	28.0	0.50	20.0	0.70	20.0	1.35	44.0
E-commerce	0.0	0.0	0.68	28.0	0.26	12.5	0.29	12.0	0.58	19.0
Advanced Planner Optimizer/Scheduler	0.13	25.0	0.68	28.0	0.11	5.0	0.22	10.0	0.63	22.6
Customer Relationship Management	0.13	25.0	1.08	36.0	0.24	12.5	0.22	14.0	0.34	21.4

Note: * Category 1 = less than 99 employees (n = 4), Category 2 = 100 to 249 employees (n = 25), Category 3 = 250 to 499 employees (n = 40), Category 4 = 500 to 999 employees (n = 50), and Category 5 = greater than 1000 employees (n = 84)
^Scale: Not implemented, Implementation started within the last year, Implementation started one to three years ago, Implementation started three to five years ago, and Implementation started more than five years ago.

systems followed by medium and small firms. The extent of usage of different modules for large firms reveals that firms initially implement modules that cover intra-firm areas such as financials and logistics. They then implement the next wave of modules such as CRM and E-Commerce to extend their ERP system to cover inter-firm areas. The results further indicate a similar usage pattern for medium and small firms.

Respondents from firms in categories 2 to 5 reported the greatest change in the information quality performance measure (see Table 17.7). This was closely followed by changes in the information availability measure. The above suggests that most firms in categories 2 to 5 are yet to leverage their informational benefits to obtain transactional and organizational benefits. Respondents from firms in category 1 reported the greatest changes in the inventory management and on-time delivery performance measures. This suggests that small firms are more flexible than their larger counterparts in leveraging ERP to address their business imperatives. Respondents from firms in categories 2 to 5 reported the least change in the competitive advantage performance measure; whereas respondents from firms in category 1 indicated the least change in the customer satisfaction performance measure. Table 17.7 presents the benefits attributable to ERP implementations among firms of different sizes.

Table 17.7 ERP Performance Benefits by Organization Size

Performance	Organization Size Category*				
	Category 1	Category 2	Category 3	Category 4	Category 5
	Mean^	Mean	Mean	Mean	Mean
Information Avail-ability	6.25	6.16	6.25	6.32	6.48
Information Quality	6.25	6.16	6.12	6.14	6.37
Standardization	6.0	5.92	6.10	6.00	6.10
Inventory Manage-ment	6.50	6.08	5.78	6.00	5.98
On-Time Delivery	6.50	6.04	5.80	6.00	5.85
User Satisfaction	5.75	5.88	5.98	5.58	5.90
Profitability	5.25	5.64	5.48	5.28	5.44
Return on Invest-ment	5.25	5.32	5.48	5.18	5.61
Customer Satis-faction	4.75	5.64	5.40	5.38	5.33
Competitive Advantage	5.00	5.12	5.08	4.96	5.31

Note: * Category 1 = less than 99 employees (n = 4), Category 2 = 100 to 249 employees (n = 25), Category 3 = 250 to 499 employees (n = 40), Category 4 = 500 to 999 employees (n = 50), and Category 5 = greater than 1000 employees (n = 84)
^ Scale: 1 to 7, "disagree" to "agree"

The role of communication and ensuring data accuracy in facilitating the ERP implementation were rated the highest across firms of different sizes. The need for implementation team support was rated higher by larger firms (categories 3 to 5) than smaller firms (categories 1 and 2). Top management support and planning was considered more important by firms in category 1 when compared to firms in all the other categories. This suggests that centralized decision-making processes tend to drive ERP deployments in smaller firms when compared to larger firms. Respondents across firms of different sizes rated the learning and national culture CSFs as least important in facilitating ERP deployments. A majority of firms across all size categories do not accord much importance to organizational culture changes in tandem with their technical implementations. Table

17.8 present the CSFs that facilitate ERP implementations among firms of different sizes.

Table 17.8 ERP Critical Success Factors by Organization Size

Performance	Organization Size Category*				
	Category 1	Category 2	Category 3	Category 4	Category 5
	Mean^	Mean	Mean	Mean	Mean
Communication	6.58	6.12	6.46	6.46	6.45
Data Accuracy	6.56	6.00	6.29	6.20	6.13
Implementation Team	5.75	5.82	6.06	6.01	6.25
Project Management	5.45	5.58	5.68	5.65	6.14
Top Management Support	6.05	5.88	5.46	5.69	6.00
Alignment	5.92	5.93	5.69	5.60	5.93
Training	5.70	5.24	5.51	5.57	5.86
User Support	5.75	5.41	5.51	5.45	5.76
Planning	6.00	5.27	5.62	5.32	5.73
Consultants	5.41	5.14	5.21	5.44	5.60
Organizational Culture	5.60	5.20	5.34	4.95	5.26
Learning	4.81	4.89	5.07	4.88	5.32
National Culture	4.85	5.29	5.08	4.83	4.84

Note: * Category 1 = less than 99 employees (n = 4), Category 2 = 100 to 249 employees (n = 25), Category 3 = 250 to 499 employees (n = 40), Category 4 = 500 to 999 employees (n = 50), and Category 5 = greater than 1000 employees (n = 84)
^ Scale: 1 to 7, "disagree" to "agree"

The purpose of this study was to conduct a systematic and rigorous survey on ERP implementations by Indian production firms. The data collected reveal a number of interesting facts important to academicians and practitioners. The use of ERP systems is pervasive in the Indian production sector. Private sector firms are spearheading the move to ERP. The automotive industry accounts for the bulk of ERP deployments. Most firms using ERP operate in a make-to-order production environment. SAP is the dominant ERP vendor closely followed by in-house developed and deployed ERP. There is a common core of modules being implemented by a majority of firms – materials management, financials, sales and distribution, production planning, quality management, and controlling. Firms are yet to extend their ERP deployments to cover inter-firm activities. The above deployment pattern is noticeable among firms across all organization size categories.

ERP benefits are focused on quickly providing high quality information within the firm. Accordingly, firms place high emphasis on ensuring data accuracy. At the moment, barring small firms (in category 1), respondents indicate that ERP has not resulted in significant improvements in operational performance. This suggests that the benefits of ERP accruing to firms are yet to impact their external stakeholders such as customers. Most firms, however, indicate a net overall benefit from their ERP deployments. This suggests that extreme stories of failed implementations are reported in the popular press and typical beneficial outcomes are ignored. Communication and data integrity are crucial factors in facilitating implementations across firms of all sizes.

In this study, we have identified the common modules implemented, the benefits derived, and the critical success factors that firms emphasize in their ERP deployments. We also examined the above differ with respect to the size of the firm. A perusal of the study results indicates that the Indian ERP market follows remarkably similar trends to the developed ERP markets such as the US of the 1990s and the early 2000s (Mabert et al. 2000; 2001; 2003)—in terms of implementation status, CSFS emphasized, and the performance benefits obtained. The Indian ERP market remains focused on implementation issues – how to effectively meet the challenges of getting the system up and running. Most implementers are yet to focus on management issues – how to extract the maximum business benefits from the system.

This study provides a foundation for carrying out further investigations. For example, the data reveals that firms are yet to attain significant operating cost reductions and overall organizational benefits from their ERP deployments. Why is that the case? Is it a reflection of poor alignment between ERP and business processes? Have firms not instituted organizational culture changes in tandem with the technical ERP deployments? Does the extent of ERP adoption determine the level of benefits obtained? Does throwing more and more ERP modules at business problems result in those problems being solved? What should firms do to move beyond implementation and maintenance issues and focus on operational and strategic usage issues? This study is an initial step to seek answers to such questions that could help firms' leverage their ERP to achieve better business performance.

References

1. Askari, F. (2007). "Microsoft in India." Available at:
   http://www.expresscomputeronline.com/20071224/market01.shtml.
2. Berry, R.W. (1996). *An Investigation of the Relationship between World Class Quality System Components and Performance.* PhD Thesis, University of North Texas.
3. Bonasera, J. (2000). "AMR Research predicts enterprise application market will reach $78 billion by 2004." Available at: *http://www.amrresearch.com/Content/ View.asp?pmillid=1327*

4. Boparai, R. (2008). "All about Enterprise Resource Planning." Available at: *http://www.techtribe.com/viewArticle.html?articleId=03a49a6a-6bda-102b-a627-000flf68a9bf.*

5. Chandra, P. and Sastry, T. (1998). Competitiveness of Indian Manufacturing: Findings of the 1997 Manufacturing Futures Survey. *Vikalpa,* 23(3), 25–36.

6. Chandra, P. and Sastry, T. (2002). "Competitiveness of Indian Manufacturing: Findings of the 2001 Manufacturing Futures Survey." Available at *http://www.iimahd.ernet.in/publications/data/2002-09-04PanhaiChandra.pdj.*

7. Chandrasekhar, C.P. (2005). "The Diffusion of Information Technology and Implications for Development: A Perspective Based on the Indian Experience," in *ICTs and Indian Economic Development Economy, Work, Regulation,* A. Saith and M. Vijayabaskar (eds.), CA: Sage Publications.

8. Chawla, M. (2009). "Business Applications: Just a Patch of Red." Available at: *http://dqindia.ciol.com/content/dqtop2009/IndustryAnalyses/2009/109081303.asp.*

9. Chong, H., White, R.E. and Prybutok, V. (2001). "Relationship among organizational support, JIT implementation and performance." *Industrial Management & Data Systems,* 101(6), 273–280.

10. Datamonitor. (2005). "Manufacturing Applications Model." Available at: *http://www.datamonitor.com/technology.*

11. Davenport, T.H. (1998). "Putting the Enterprise into the Enterprise System." *Harvard Business Review,* 76 (4), 121–131.

12. De, R. (2001). "ERP is back with a bang." Available at: *http://www.expresscomputeronline.com/20011008/indtrend1.htm.*

13. De, R. (2004). "Manufacturing: Back on the Rebound." Available at: *www.dqindia.com/dqtop20/2004/artdisp.asp?artid=60678.*

14. De, R. (2007). "Application: Engines of Growth." Available at: *http://dqindia.ciol.com/content/DQTop2007/ITGaintsQ7/2007/107080304.asp.*

15. De, R. (2008). "Modest and Inconsistent." Available at: *http://dqindia.ciol.com/content/dqtop2008/IndustryOverview/2008/108080132.asp.*

16. Dewan, S. and Kraemer, K.L. (2000). "Information Technology and Productivity Evidence from Country-Level Data." *Management Science,* 46(4), 548–562.

17. Dillman, D.A. (2000). *Mail and Internet Surveys: The Tailored Design Method.* New York: John Wiley and Sons.

18. D'Aquila, M, Shepherd, J. and Friscia, T. (2009). "The Global Enterprise Applications Software Market Forecast Update 2009–2010." *AMR Research.*

19. Gartner. (2003). "Enterprise application software: winning in the Indian marketplace." *Gartner Research.*

20. Guido, C., Lelio, R. and Pierluigi, R. (2007). "A methodological approach to assess the feasibility of ERP implementation strategies." *Journal of Information Technology Management* 10 (4), 35–53.

21. Hawking, P. and Stein, A. (2004). "Revisiting ERP Systems: Benefit Realization." *Proceedings of the 37th. Hawaii International Conference on System Sciences,* 1–8.

22. Huang, Z. and Palvia, P. (2001). "ERP Implementation Issues in Advanced and Developing Countries." *Business Process Management Journal,* 7(3), 276–284.

23. IDC. (2004). "IDC Releases Top 10 Vendors in ERP Applications Market; Market Consolidation Will Continue at Gradual Pace." Available at: *http://www.idc.com.*

24. IDC India. (2003). "Competition Intensifies in the Indian ERP Space – Market Expected to cross 800 crores by 2006." Available at: *http://www.idcinida.com.*

25. Jacobs, F.R. and Weston, Jr., F.C. (2007). "Enterprise Resource Planning (ERP)—A brief history." *Journal of Operations Management,* 25(2), 357–363.

26. Jacobson, S., Shepherd, J., D'Aquila, M. and Carter, K. (2007). "The ERP Market Sizing Report 2006–2011." 2007 Market Sizing Series. *AMR Research.*

27. Kimberly, J.R. (1976). "Organization size and the structuralist perspective: a review, critique, And Proposal." *Administrative Science Quarterly,* 21(4), 571–597.

28. Klaus, H., Rosemann, M. and Gable, G.G. (2000). "What is ERP?" *Information Systems Frontiers,* 2(2), 141–162.

29. Kumar, V., Maheshwari, B. and Kumar, U. (2003). "An Investigation of Critical Management Issues in ERP Implementation: Empirical Evidence from Canadian Organizations." *Technovation,* 23(10), 793–807.

30. Mabert, V.A., Soni, A. and Venkataramanan, M.A. (2000). "Enterprise Resource Planning Survey of US Manufacturing Firms." *Production and Inventory Management Journal* 41(2), 52–58.

31. Mabert, V.A., Soni, A. and Venkataramanan, M.A. (2001). "Enterprise Resource Planning: Measuring Value." *Production and Inventory Management Journal,* 42(3/4), 46–51.

32. Mabert, V.A., Soni, A. and Venkatramanan, M.A. (2003). "The Impact of Organization size in Enterprise Resource Planning (ERP) Implementations in the US Manufacturing Sector." *Omega—The International Journal of Management Science,* 31(3), 235–246.

33. Madapusi, A. and Ortiz, D. An Empirical Assessment of ERP in Indian Production Firms. *South West Decision Sciences Institute Annual Meeting 2010,* Dallas.

34. Olhager, J. and Selldin, E. (2003). "Enterprise Resource Planning Survey of Swedish Manufacturing Firms." *European Journal of Operational Research,* 146(2), 365–373.

35. Pasha, A. (2008). "Bull Run Continues in EAS." Available at: *http://www.expresscomputeronline.com/20080331/anniversaryspeciall0.shtml.*

36. Reilly, K. (2005). "AMR research releases ERP market report showing overall market growth of 14% in 2004." Available at: *http://www.amrresearch.com/ Content/View.asp?pmillid=1835*

37. Rondeau, P.J. and Litteral, L.A. (2001). "Evolution of Manufacturing Planning and Control Systems: From Reorder Point to Enterprise Resource Planning." *Production and Inventory Management Journal,* 42(2), 1–7.

38. Rose, J., Jones, M. and Truex, D. (2005). "Socio-Theoretic Accounts of IS: The Problem of Agency." *Scandinavian Journal of Information Systems,* 17(1), 133–152.

39. Shields, M.G. (2001). *E-business and ERP: Rapid Implementation and Project Planning.* New York: John Wiley & Sons, Inc.

40. Stratman, J.K. and Roth, A.V. (2002). "Enterprise Resource Planning (ERP) Competence Constructs: Two-Stage MultiItem Scale Development and Validation." *Decision Sciences,* 33(4), 601–628.

41. Swamidass, P. and Kotha, S. (1998). "Explaining manufacturing technology use, firm size and performance using a multidimensional view of technology." *Journal of Operations Management* 17(1), 23–35.

42. Tarafdar, M., & Roy, R.K. (2003). "Analyzing the adoption of enterprise resource planning systems in Indian organizations: A process framework." *Journal of Global Information Technology Management,* 6(1), 31–51.

43. Vijaybaskar, M. (2005). "ICTs and Transformation of Traditional Workplaces: The Case of the Automobile Industry in India," in *ICTs and Indian Economic Development: Economy, Work, Regulation,* A. Saith and M. Vijayabaskar (eds.), CA: Sage Publications.

44. Wang, C., Xu, L., Liu, X. and Qin, X. (2005). "ERP research, development and implementation in China: An overview." *International Journal of Production Research,* 43(18), 3915–3932.

45. White, R.E., Pearson, J.N. and Wilson, J.R. (1999). "JIT Manufacturing: A Survey of Implementations in Small and Large US Manufacturers." *Management Science,* 45(1), 1–15.

46. Yasai-Ardekani, M. (1989). "Effects of environmental scarcity and munificence on the relationship context to organizational structure." *Academy of Management Journal,* 32(1), 131–156.

☺☹☹

PART **3**

Cyber, Security and Threat

18

Information Security and Risk Management

Shikha Gupta[1] and Anil K Saini[2]

Information Technology (IT) based information systems have become the backbone of not only success but of survival of organizations in this highly competitive world. Considering that IT is an important asset it must be managed efficiently to minimize the risks associated with it and the systems it supports. The chapter is based on literature review of existing work on information security and risk management. It attempts to describe the theoretical perspective of information system security. It also discusses and analyses the various information security methodologies in practice.

KEYWORDS Information Security Implementation | IT Risk | Information Security Methodologies

18.1 INTRODUCTION

Information Systems (IS) are set of interrelated components that retrieve, process, store and distribute information to support decision making and control in organizations. IS basically consists of data hardware, software, procedures and people which are usually developed to support business function (Godbole, 2009). In the present scenario information systems have become an essential aspect and an integral part of any business have graduated from being just a tool and information provider to facilitator in effective decision making to help in improving efficiency. Growing dependence of most organizations on their information systems has provided problems such as theft of data, attacks using malicious code, denial of service etc. New opportunities for IT related issues coupled with risks have made IT Governance an increasingly critical facet of overall governance. Information security is not just a technology problem, it is a business issue, it was seen as a negative factor creating value through nonoccurrence. Organizations that make extensive use of information technology can be more efficient and productive. However, this ever-growing dependence on IT also leads to a dramatic increase in expensive information security incidents and failures (BSI, 2004).

[1] School of Computer Applications, Ansal University, Gurgaon, India
[2] University School of Management Studies, GGS Indraprasth University, India

As organizations become increasingly dependent on information systems (IS) for strategic advantage and operations, the issue of IS security also becomes increasingly important (Kankanhalli, Teo, Tan, & Wei, 2003). The information must be protected from harm caused due to threats leading to loss, non-availability, alteration and wrongful disclosure. Threats include errors and omissions, fraud, accidents and intentional changes (Saleh, Alfantookh, 2011). The main goal of information security is to protect the interest of stakeholders by ensuring confidentiality (disclosure of information to the righteous persons), availability (information systems are available and usable) and integrity (information is protected against unauthorized changes). Thus, Information Security is a key aspect of information technology governance.

Information security industry in itself encompasses diverse set of products, services, processes and policies ranging from encryption algorithm to human resource management. The success of information security implementation can be determined through technological, operational and managerial controls. The lack of a fully inclusive guideline document to assist the functioning of sufficient Information Security Governance is common in the business environment.

18.2 IMPACT OF IT IMPLEMENTATION ON ORGANIZATIONS

There has been an exponential growth in IT in years which can be exploited by corporation to meet the challenges of rapidly changing economy (Morton, 1991). The relationship between IT and business in recent years has changed from strategic level to supporting operational processes in business (eg. Workflow systems, document management, case management, etc) (Radianti & Gonzalez, 2007). 'Modern societies, organizations & business depend on reliable information system (Hallberg, Hallberg & Hunstad, 2007).

One can not deny the role of IT in success of a business. In fact, IT services have proven to be directly affecting business process performance & organization success (Hosseini, 2005).

As per the companies, IT services have resulted in companies performance enhancement in terms of higher return on sales and even the market share is directly impacted by efficient use of IT (Kempis, & Ringback, 1999) and researchers indicated this linkage of IT to enterprise very strongly. Studies suggest that this linkage can significantly affect the efficiency of the business and hence give it a competitive edge above others (Hosseini, 2005). It majorly improves customer service; integrate supplier and customer operations (Luftman, Lewis, & Oldach, 1993). In a way financial and non-financial, both business functions are impacted by adoption, implementation and expansion of an information system in organizations (Chatzoglou, & Diamantidis, 2009). Researchers even advocated the positive impact of investments in IT on firms' production process (Shao, & tin, 2001). Some are of the view that though IT impact performance, but the improvement in productivity is not as per expectation (Ko, & Bryson, 2002).

18.3 IT IMPLEMENTATION: NOT A RISK FREE AFFAIR

Though several researchers have advocated the positive role of It in improving organization's performance and providing a competitive edge to it (Morton,1991; Radianti & Gonzalez, 2007; Hosseini, 2005; Kempis, & Ringback, 1999; Luftman, Lewis, & Oldach, 1993), the dependence of organizations on IT has made them vulnerable to issues like IT frauds, diverse set of security risks ranging from virus attacks to intentional or unintentional damage to the organization by employees resulting in failures of critical processes, due to problems in infrastructures like servers, data centers (Luftman, Lewis, & Oldach, 1993; Hosseini, 2005). 75% of organizations have confirmed being attacked (Bagchi, & Udo, 2003). Studies have revealed six categories of IT security issues have emerged which are as follows:

- System development
- System operation
- Risk management
- Communication and management of security
- Competence regarding security
- Attainment and preservation of trust (Hosseini, 2005).

Financial and non financial business functions are impacted by IT implementation risks (Chatzoglou, & Diamantidis, 2009). Use of IT encapsulates both systematic and unsystematic risks (Hallikainen, Kivjarvi, & Nurmimaki, 2002). Some studies have revealed that IT risk levels can not be fully eliminated or even lowered by advances in IT (Chatzoglou, & Diamantidis, 2009). As per Netherlands National Bank manual, IT risk is the predictable or possible risk that comes up because of the insufficient processing of existing information system (Chatzoglou, & Diamantidis, 2009). The manual also suggests a descriptive definition of IT risk in terms of following indicators

- Exclusivity—level of inappropriate authorization and unauthorized access
- Integrity—volume of incorrect and irregularly used and processed data
- Controllability—loosely controlled IS procedures
- User operations—inadequate IT support lack of skill and experience applied to IS
- Continuity—non availability of high level data and high volumes of system failures and disruptions
- Manageability—low degree of IS flexibility and maintainability leading to risks (De Nederlandsche Bank, 2001).

This categorization is supported by many researchers (National Institute of Standards and Technology, 2002; O'Donnell, 2005). As per the study 8 types of IT risks impact the performance of an organization which are:

- Operator error-by computer operator
- Hardware malfunctions-errors due to faulty hardware design
- Software errors or bugs-flaw in programs
- Data errors-invalid data
- User's carelessness-leading to accidental disclosure of information
- Protection error-inadequate protection against failure of system components leading to damage to physical infrastructure
- Performance error-failing to meeting the desired expectation
- Liability-system's level of responsibility (Steven, 2002)

Several authors have suggested IT implementation risk to be divided into 5 broad categories

- Application complexity-refers to number of links to other systems
- Application size-refers to number of users needed in development of IS and usage
- Organizational environment-refers to association between users and creators
- Team expertise
- Technology novelty (Hallikainen, Kivjarvi, & Nurmimaki, 2002)

As per the researchers, coordination and partially information ability are the most impacted non-financial factors and IT risk levels can not be fully eliminated or even lowered by just implementing or improving IT (Chatzoglou, & Diamantidis, 2009).

18.4 RISK MANAGEMENT: BASIC PRINCIPLE OF RISK ANALYSIS

Companies Can Estimate Possible Damages if a Threat Event Were to Arise (Godbole, 2008)

There has been tremendous study on handling the information security issue in IT based organizations. Different traditional information security methods have been developed with time. Some researchers have categorized infosec methods into 3 (Baskerville, 1988) generations and some into 5 (Baskerville, 1993) RM among the most commonly used early generation (first or second) infosec method (Siponen, 2005) called traditional method. They are widely used in practice (Baskerville, 1992; Fitzgerald, 1995; Solms, 1996; von Solms, & van de Haar, 2001) these are as follows:

- Checklist-AFIPD, SAFE, Moultan-Moultan, Wood et.al.
- ISS Standards-BS ISO/IEC17999 , GASSP, Sanders et al

- ↵ ISS Maturity Criteria-SSE-CMM, Software Security metrics, The Information Security Maturity Grid
- ↵ Risk Management- The generic RM approach, Hallidat et al. X-ifying RM, LRAM, communication approach
- ↵ Formal methods-Anderson, Barnes (Siponen, 2005)

Most of these methods are not integrated into ISD which results in conflict between normal functionality of Information Systems and Security functionality. These problems range from increased costs, user resistance in implementing the system to malfunctioning of the system which leads to various types of losses.

Of all methods stated above the most common methods are the Infosec management standards which are widely used and advocated. But these standards have limitations that the focus of these standards is on existence of processes rather than its content and effectiveness (Siponen, 2006). The underlying principle of these standards is mere existence of security activities not the extant or quality of their existence and hence they are just guidelines without advising how desired results are to be achieved just the use of a particular security process or activity does not ensure the security of the organization as per the objective. It is the content and quality that really matters (Siponen, 2006).

Studies show that Risk Management is the only traditional method which is useful in practice and the key to success of information security system is the alignment of RM to organizations' business strategies. (Siponen, 2005). Risk analysis is the science of observation, knowledge and evaluation-that is, keen eyesight, anticipation, etc. Risk management is the keystone to an effective performance as well as for targeted, proactive solutions to potential threats and incidents [an incidents is any event that is not a part of the standard operation of a service and that causes, or may cause, an interruption to, or a reduction in, the quality of that service]. Risk management is the ongoing process of identifying risks and implementing plans to address them. Risk evaluation is a process that generates an organization-wide view of information security risks. Risk management is the skill of handling the identified risk in the best possible manner for the interests of the organization.

Asset, threat and vulnerability combined are called triple in risk management domain where asset is defined as a resource, process, product, computing infrastructure etc. that an organization considers important to be protected, threat is the presence of any potential event initiated by humans or natural that could cause an adverse impact on the organization and vulnerability is the absence or weakness of safeguard.

Risk is described by the following mathematical formula.

Risk = threat * vulnerability * asset value.

Some researchers advocate the definition of risk to be changed from 'the chance of something happening that will have an impact on objectives' to 'the effect of uncertainty on objectives' (AS/NZS, 2009)

AS/NZS ISO 31000:2009 risk management-principles and guidelines has earmarked 11 principles for risk management and 5 attributes to enhance risk management (AS/NZS, 2009) Which are as follows:

- Good risk management contributes to the achievement of an agency's objectives through the continuous review of its processes and systems.
- Risk management needs to be integrated with an agency's governance framework and become a part of its planning processes, at both the operational and strategic level.
- The process of risk management assists decision makers to make informed choices, identify priorities and select the most appropriate action.
- By identifying potential risks, agencies can implement controls and treatments to maximize the chance of gain while minimizing the chance of loss.
- The process of risk management should be consistent across an agency to ensure efficiency, consistency and the reliability of results.
- To effectively manage risk it is important to understand and consider all available information relevant to an activity and to be aware that there may be limitations on that information. It is then important to understand how all this information informs the risk management process.
- An agency's risk management framework needs to include its risk profile, as well as take into consideration its internal and external operating environment.
- Risk management needs to recognize the contribution that people and culture have on achieving an agency's objectives.
- Engaging stakeholders, both internal and external,
- Throughout the risk management process recognizes that communication and consultation is key to identifying, analyzing and monitoring risk.
- The process of managing risk needs to be flexible. The challenging environment we operate in requires agencies to consider the context for managing risk as well as continuing to identify new risks that emerge, and make allowances for those risks that no longer exist.

Agencies with a mature risk management culture are those that have invested resources over time and are able to demonstrate the continual achievement of their objectives. (AS/NZS, 2009) Five Attributes to enhance risk management range from organizations accepting the accountability for their risks to develop comprehensive controls and treatment strategies to continuous improvement in risk management through setting and review of performance goals, systems, resources and capability/ skills to ensure continuous improvement, to making individuals accountable for risk management, to inclusion of risk management considerations in decision making and last but not least frequent reporting of the entire risk scenario to all stakeholders (AS/NZS, 2009).

18.5 SECURITY RISK ANALYSIS

There are various approaches for analyzing risk which are as follows

◄ Quantitative risk analysis,

◄ Qualitative risk analysis,

◄ Valuation of IT/ information system assets,

◄ Selection of safeguards (Godbole, 2008)

Quantitative risk analysis deals with assigning independently the objective numeric values in monetary terms to the components of the risk assessment and to the assessment of potential losses. Qualitative risk analysis addresses intangible values, of a data/ information loss and its focus is on other issues, rather than on the pure hard costs.

Risk analysis process is considered fully quantitative when all the elements of the risk analysis (asset value, impact, threat frequency, effectiveness, costs of safeguards/countermeasures, etc.) are measured, rated and values are assigned to them.

Qualitative risk analysis process involves the following steps:

Qualitative risk assessment is based on assessing and ranking the seriousness of threats and the relative sensitivity of the assets, or a qualitative grading is provided to them, by using a scenario approach and creating an exposure rating scale for each scenario (Godbole, 2008).

It has been identified that information system security includes many concepts, facts and techniques. Various researchers and practitioners have defined and formulated the information security and IT risk policies in different ways to accomplish the objectives of securing the information assets in various kinds of organizations. There are a number of methods for information security but risk management should be given the highest priority due to its integration with Information System development. There is a need to address the way risk-based decision making is applied in places that it may not improve the outcomes of the problems being addressed.

References

1. AS/NZS ISO 31000: *2009 Risk Management Principles and Guidelines August 2010.*

2. Bagchi, K. & Udo, G. (2003). An Analysis of the Growth of Computer and Internet Security Breaches. *Communications of the Association for Information Systems, 12,* 684-700.

3. Baskerville, R. L. (1988). *Designing Information Systems Security.* J. Wiley.

4. Baskerville, R. L. (1992). The Developmental Duality of Information Systems Security, *Journal of Management Systems,* 4(1), 1-12. Baskerville, R. (1993). Information systems security design methods: implications for information systems development. *ACM Computing Surveys (CSUR),* 25(4), 375-414. doi=10.1145/162124.162127. Retrieved from http://doi.acm.org/10.1145/162124.162127

5. BSI, (2004). *IT Grundschutz Manual,* http://www.bsi.de/english/gshb/manual/download/index.html

6. Chatzoglou, P. D., & Diamantidis, A. D. (2009). IT/IS implementation risks and their impact on firm performance. *The International Journal of Information Management, 29*(2) 119-128. doi=10.1016/j.ijinfomgt.2008.04.008, Retrieved from http://dx.doi. org/10.1016/j.ijinfomgt.2008.04.008 De Nederlandsche Bank. (2001). fiisk o nalysismanuol (407 11-407 l9). Fitzgerald, K. J. (1995). Information security baselines. *Information Management & Computer Security, 3* (2), 8-12.

7. Godbole, N. (2009). *Information Systems Security.* John Wiley & Sons Hallikainen, P., Kivjarvi, H., & Nurmimaki, K. (2002). Evaluating strategic IT Investment: An assessment of investment alternatives for a Web content management system. *Proceedings of the 35th Hawii International conference on system sciences.*

8. Hallberg, N., Hallberg, J., & Hunstad, A. (2007). Rationale for and Capabilities of IT Security Assessment. *Proceedings of the 2007 IEEE Workshop on Information Assurance United States Military Academy, West Point.*

9. Hosseini, R. (2005). A Practical Approach for Measuring IT-Support of Business Processes. *Proceedings of the 2005, The Fifth International Conference on Computer and Information Technology (CIT'05) IEEE.* Kankanhalli, A., Teo, H. H., Tan, B. C. Y., & Wei, K. K. (2003). An integrative study of information systems security effectiveness. *International Journal of Information Management,* 23(2), 139-154. Kempis, R. D., & Ringback, J. (1999). *Do IT Smart:Seven Rules for Superior Information Technology Performance.* New York: The Free Press, a Division of Simon & Schuster, Inc.

10. Ko. M., & Bryson, K. M. (2002). A regression tree based exploration of the impact of infomation technology investments on the firm level productivity. *ECIS 2002 Proceedings.*

11. Luftman, J. N., Lewis, P. R., & Oldach, S. H. (1993). Transforming the enterprise: The alignment of business and information technology strategies. *IBM Systems Journal,* 32(1), 198-221.

12. Morton, M.S. (1991). *The Corporation of the 1990s: Information Technology and Organizational Transformation.* Oxford University Press.

13. National Institute of Standards and Technology, (2002). *Risk management for information technology systems.* Technology Administration, US Department of Commerce, Special publication 800 30.

14. O'Donnell. E. (2005). Enterprise risk management: A systems-thinking framework for the event identification phase. *International journal of Accounting information Systems, 6,* 177-195.

15. Radianti, J., & Gonzalez, J. J. (2007). Understanding Hidden Information Security Threats: The Vulnerability Black Market. *Proceedings of the 40th Annual Hawaii International Conference on System Sciences (HICSS'07) IEEE.*

16. Saleh, M. S., & Alfantookh, A. (2011).A new comprehensive framework for enterprise information security risk management, *Applied Computing and Informatics,* 9(2), 107-118.

17. Shao, B.B.M., & Lin, W.T. (2001). Measuring the value of information technology in technical efficiency with stochastic production frontiers. *Information and Software Technology, 43*(7) 447-456.

18. Siponen, M. T. (2005). An analysis of the traditional IS security approaches: implications for research and practice. *European Journal of Information Systems, 14(3),* 303-315. doi=10.1057/palgrave. ejis.3000537. Retrieved from http://dx.doi.org/10.1057/palgrave. ejis.3000537

19. Siponen, M. (2006). Information security standards focus on the existence of process, not its content. *Communications of the ACM-Music information retrieval CACM, 49*(8), 97-100. doi = 10.1145/1145287.1145316. Retrived from http://doi. acm. org/10.1145/114287.11453165

20. Siponen M. (2005). Analysis of modern IS security development approaches: towards the next generation of social and adaptable ISS methods. *Information and Organization,* 15(4), 339-375.

21. Solms, R. (1996), Information security management: The second generation, *Computers and Society,* 15(4), 281-288.

22. Steven, A. (2002). *Information Systems: Foundation of E-Business,* (4th ed.). Prentice-Hall lnc.

23. von Solms, R., & van de Haar, H. (2001). Trusted Information Security Controls to a Trusted Information Security Environment. *Sixteenth Annual Working Conference on Information Security,* 29-36, Beijing, China.

☺☺☹

19

Security Threats in e-Business

Narendra Kumar Tyagi[1]

Security is the main considerable part for any and every architectural quality. Critical software must be safe, secure, and dependable. Confidentiality and availability constitute part for measurement of quality consideration along with integrity. Security and most important dependability are particularly the essential part of qualities while dealing with threats in e-business. Architectural tactics, or architectural design decisions, that enhance one aspect of dependability can decrease security and vice versa. The quality attributes are measured on various scales of references. These scales are sometimes not quantitative. This makes it multiscale problem. This chapter proposes a qualitative approach to manage the transactions and exchange among the attributes used to define security threats in e-business.

KEYWORDS	Durability	Interoperability	Soft Goals	Confidentiality	System Quality	Grap3

19.1 INTRODUCTION

To support products security, addressing the functional and nonfunctional requirements of e-business, a well definition of system architecture is required. There is requirement for quality- driven techniques for explicitly considering non-functional quality attributes. Techniques described by **[Kazman1, 2004]** are used to identify the desired quality attributes of a system. Designing the architecture with various quality attributes interacting with each other, is very hard. This is because an architecture decomposition that boosts one attribute may disgrace another. While managing the tradeoffs among qualities, it is hard for several reasons. The quality attributes involved in a particular system are not measured quantitatively, though others are quantitative. For example, security is not measured quantitatively in e-business. Many reasoning frameworks assist the architect in quantitatively analyzing the quality attributes like performance. Few techniques for qualitatively represented attribute reasoning like security are available. This chapter presents a qualitative approach to reasoning about security at the architectural stage.

---

[1] Assistant Professor,DCE,Gurgaon,Haryana, India

19.2 TRADITIONAL AND MODERN APPROACHES

Producing correct software, according to **[Iwasaki,i997]**, needs three approaches process, product and testing. Process approach includes personnel certification with assessments of the software development process. Product approach includes going through the real software product and concerned artifacts by inspections, reviews, tracing, etc. Testing product is reviewed by working the software in its real platform. It is important as inspections and proofs make simple assumptions about the platform. For the correctness **[Kazmanii, 2004]]** provides a good discussion of practical approaches. There are three more approaches: manage complexity, manage change, and manage rationale. Complexity has an inverse relationship to correctness. It is established that up to 90% of project effort goes into maintenance for corrections and enhancements. Heaping changes upon changes creates fragile software. Modifying a legacy system needs attest design rationale. In designing with safety the rationale behind design decisions becomes more important in case security, safety and dependability otherwise it may lead dangerous situations of maintenance of e-business. Zero defect approach is the critical applications **[John D. McGregor, 2007]**, against a reliability growth to eliminate faults in early stages maximization of process and product methods. There is a requirement for the defensive program to guide design of dependable software, abstraction hiding, fault tolerance and integrity. These may require formality and abstraction for creation of right things and recovery from wrong things.

2.1: Dependability is the trust justified on a computer system. It includes the qualities of safety, reliability, integrity, availability, confidentiality with maintainability [Algirdas Avizienis, 2004]. This chapter , on designing dependable systems, identified four interactions among the qualities within dependability involving qualities related to security threats in E-Business, these are:

2.1.1: Safety vs. Confidentiality **[Schneier, B,** 2003]

2.1.2: Safety vs. Integrity **[Schneier, B,** 2003]

2.1.3: Availability vs. Confidentiality **[Warns,** 2005]

2.1.4: Availability vs. Integrity **[Warns,** 2005]

As shown in the Fig:2.1.1

2.2: The tradeoffs, between qualities while designing a dependable system, must be evaluated as qualities are defined in terms of other qualities. These qualities are measured on different scales, some of which are not quantitative, are not readily handled by existing techniques. Security is not measured on a scale, a goal based scale is used to support design reasoning **[John D. McGregor,** 2007].

The goals are called softgoals because there is no precise, objective definition of the goal for satisfying them. A softgoal **[Chung, L.K. Nixon, B. and Yu, E, 2000]** will not capture the level of detail found in performance models but it will provide qualitative "indicators" to guide the architect.

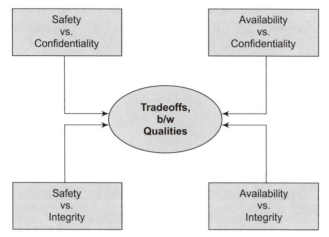

Fig: 2.1 1 Dependability involving qualities related to security threats in e-business

19.3 QUALITATIVE REASONING FOR SECURITY

3.1: Qualitative techniques adopt some type of ordinal scale because Qualitative reasoning **[Iwasaki, 1997]** provides a means of making decisions involving attributes that cannot be expressed quantitatively.

The reasoning rules use -

3.1.1: a current position on an ordinal scale

3.1.2: an indication of whether the attribute is changing its value .

3.2: Security attribute of a software might be rated on an ordinal scale as "very" secure. Qualitative reasoning supports building models to represent these relationships between qualitative values and support inferences about how the values change over time and how they cause other values to change. The model must consider the direction of change for each quality and the inequality relationship that exists among tactics tactic influencing the qualities comprising security. Many strategies are considered to improve confidentiality, integrity, security **[Steel, C. Nagappan, R. and Lai,** 2005] and availability etc. Net effect of these strategies can not be assessed on the degree to which the resulting system is secure since relative magnitudes of the "–"(weak satisfying) effect of replication and the "+" (weak) effect of a validator can not be compared.

4.2: This chapter chooses two strategies the first one implementing security and the second one introducing replication. Figure 4.2 describes influence of above said strategies on confidentiality and integrity in different directions. Any how the confidentiality and integrity of the overall system would have decreased after the application of both the strategies, it is due to an inequality relationship between the strategies (it was determined that "replicated elements %" has a greater impact on confidentiality and integrity than "security %").

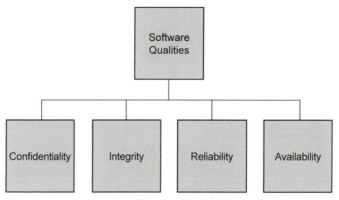

Fig: 4.2 Software Qualities in E-Business

3.3: The complexity in reasoning about these strategies is present partially because these attributes are not quantitative and partially because the measures are on different scales. It can be overwhelming to keep track of how each strategy influences each sub-quality of security threats and how each strategy relates to other strategies. For this reason, we are developing a modeling technique to assist the architect in reasoning about security threats in E-Business.

19.4 SATISFYING SECURITY REQUIREMENTS: AN EXAMPLE

4.1 The qualities that are of most important to web-service are the following:

4.1.1 Confidentiality

4.1.2 Integrity

4.1.3 Reliability

4.1.4 Availability

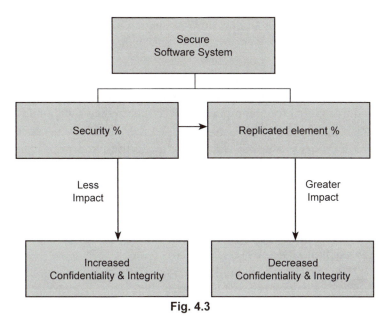

Fig. 4.3

4.3 The software architect is intended to take a decision on the inequality relationships between strategies which change depending on the method of application. Garp3 is a workbench for building, simulating, and inspecting qualitative models. Garp3 is implemented in SWI-Prolog and seamlessly integrates three previously developed software components, including: Garp2 for simulating models, Homer for building models, and VisiGarp for inspecting simulation results. Integrating these tools has led to one new tool that incorporates all of the original functionalities, and thus incorporates the advantages of each tool, but also adds interoperability and an easy to use uniform user interface. Garp3 uses a diagrammatic approach for representing model content, and graphical buttons to communicate the available user options and manipulations. Garp3 can be freely downloaded and used. This chapter uses Garp3 tool for generating all possible cases if no inequality is specified. To facilitate the application of qualitative reasoning to security a qualitative model of security is needed which describes the influences of strategies to the quality standards of the security. It will provide a knowledge base for qualitatively reasoning about security threats in e-business and also contain the necessary data for reasoning about security in a broader context like dependability and availability.

This chapter is the hard work in the direction of establishment that simple models are always superior and supporting in decision making and for prediction purposes. The research **[Hastie, R. and Dawes,** 2001**]** shows that qualitative research methods reasoning for security threats in e-business are not accurate and simple though they appear so in comparison of simple modeling **[simulation model, 2005**]. This research chapter presented the influence of dependability on security architectural strategies and influence of security architectural strategies on dependability. This paper elaborates a reasoning methodology of selecting architectural strategies for the software architect to get quality of system. This is also established that some security strategies register resistances against dependability targets of system. Through this paper it is proved that Garp3 tool incorporates all of the original functionalities, and thus incorporates the advantages of each goal, but also adds interoperability **[Narendra Kumar Tyagi,** 2009] and an easy to use uniform user interface.

References

1. Kazman, R. Klein, M. and Clements, P. *"ATAM: Method for Architecture Evaluation"*. CMU/SEI-2000-TR-2004.
2. Algirdas Avizienis, Jean-Claude Laprie, and Brian Randell. Fundamental Concepts of Dependability.IEEE-CSP-2004
3. Chung, L.K. Nixon, B. and Yu, E. "Non-functional Requirements in Software Engineering", Kluwer Academic Publishers, 2000.
4. Hastie, R. and Dawes, RM. "Rational Choice in an Uncertain World: The Psychology of Judgment and Decision Making", Sage Publications Inc , 2001 Thousand Oaks CA.
5. Iwasaki, Y Real-world applications of qualitative reasoning, Expert, IEEE, 1997, pp. 16—21.
6. John D. McGregor and Tacksoo Im. A Qualitative Approach to Dependability Engineering, Proceedings of Dahstuhl Seminar #07031, January 2007.
7. Schneier, B. Beyond Fear: Thinking Sensibly About Security in an Uncertain World, Copernicus Books, 2003.
8. Warns, Timo Engineering Intrusion-Tolerant Software Systems. In: Dagstuhl Workshop, 22 25 May 2005, Dagstuhl, Germany.
9. Steel, C. Nagappan, R. and Lai, R. Core Security Patterns: Best Practices and Strategies for J2EE(TM), Web Services, and Identity Management, Prentice Hall, 2005.
10. http://metacourses.org/ simulationmodeling/glossary/
11. Narendra Kumar Tyagi, research paper "e-Bus : web services" in International Conference "icsci-2009" held in Hyderabad on 7,8,9,10 Jan 2009.

☺☺☹

20

Digital Signature

Vijaykumar Shrikrushna Chowbe[1]

This article has attempted to understand the nat meaning and scope of 'digital signature'. In turn, article has also focused on the mechanism of affixing 'digital signature' to electronic record. Signature sig authentication, verification and non-repudiation, bu electronic environment this mechanism happens altogether different sense as compare to paper-bc world because paper-based and paper-less world different in its context and contents. The attempt is to understand the effect and impac 'digital signature' in the cyberspace, its techno-le effect and system if issuing, granting and maintaining 'Digital Signature' in India. The limitation of this artic the legal system it focused upon, i.e. Indian Legal syst This article has understand the effect and impact 'digital signature' in general sense, but keeping Information Technology Act, 2000 [Indian piece legislation dealing with Information Technology], 1 context different to that effect.

KEYWORDS   Digital | IT Act | India | Signature | Legal System | IT

20.1 INTRODUCTION

Authentication, repudiation and verification of electronic record is flesh and bone of the electronic transactions. Therefore, unless these objectives have not been achieved, the authentication and secure electronic transaction will merely remain virtual. In order to achieve the authentication and security of electronic record the mechanism of 'digital signature' has been introduced by the Information Technology Act, 2000.

Thus while endeavoring the research on regulatory mechanism of information technology, it is necessitated to focus on the 'digital signature', its functional mechanism, authorities involve and objectives it achieve in electronic environment. The present study title, 'digital signature' has focused its attention on this vary technological aspect which is meant for achieving the goal of authentication, repudiation and verification of electronic record by affixing digital signature.

---

[1] Head, Department of Law, Sant Gadge Baba Amravati University, Amravati, India

20.2 MEANING OF SIGNATURE

Signature signifies the legal identity of the person and requires authenticating the documents. The person affixing signature to the document owes legal responsibility oozing out of it. Thus, a signature is not part of the substance of a transaction, but rather of its representation or form. Signing writings serve the following general purposes: 1

- **Evidence:** A signature authenticates writing by identifying the signer with the signed document. When the signer makes a mark in a distinctive manner, the writing becomes attributable to the singer."

- **Ceremony:** The act of signing a document calls to the singer's attention the legal significance of the signer's act, and thereby helps prevent "inconsiderate engagements.1"

- **Approval:** In certain contexts defined by law or custom, a signature expresses the signer's approval or authorization of the writing, or the signer's intention that it has legal effect.™

- **Efficiency and logistics:** A signature on a written document often imparts a sense of clarity and finality to the transaction and may lessen the subsequent need to inquire beyond the face of a document/ Negotiable instruments, for example, rely upon formal requirements, including a signature, for their ability to change hands with ease, rapidity, and minimal interruption.

20.3 WHAT IS DIGITAL SIGNATURE?

Just the role the 'stamps', 'seal' or 'signature' play in traditional system to create the authentication of paper document, the digital signature plays the role to authenticate the electronic record. It establishes the authenticity of any electronic record which subscriber of digital signature wants to be authenticated the electronic record by affixing his digital signature. Digital signature in facts has two asymmetric pair of private and public key unique to the each subscriber. The private key and public key are corresponds to each other in such a way that the electronic record encrypted with the help of any private key can be decrypted only with the help of corresponding public key. This digital signature creates digital ID for the subscriber holding digital signature certificate. This certificate is issued by Controller of Certifying Authority after due verification and adopting procedure.

This certificate contains basic information about the person holding it. The information such as, the name, public key, place of working, date of issuance, date of expiry of the certificate and name of the Certification Authority. The certificate is also publicly made available through the directories or public folders on WebPages. The law specifically made it clear that Controller will act as a repository for all Digital Signature Certificates issues under the Act and maintain a computerized data base of all public keys in such a manner that such data base and the public keys are available to any member of the public.

This is essential because the public key of subscriber should be known to the interested person and should be readily available these information for them to verify the electronic record encrypted by subscriber of digital signature by affixing his digital signature.

Common features of Digital Signature: As stated above the digital signature play the same role as assigned to seal, stamps and signatures in the traditional system. It performs Signer Authentication, Message authentication and Verification.

- **Signer Authentication**: The digital signature must be capable to identify and link the signer with the electronic record which subscriber of digital signature has created. It is also necessary to ensure that the tampering of documents should not be happened after its creation. The private key belongs to subscriber who signs it and incurs legal responsibility out of it.

- **Message authentication**: The electronic record transformed by algorithm mapping with hash function by affixing private key of digital signature typically identify the matter to be signed, since verification also reveals any tampering with the message.

- **Verification**: The ultimate aim of creation of digitally signed document is capability of its verification at latter moment of its creation. Thus the mechanism must be capable to verify the authenticity and non-repudiation to resolve the disputes between originators and recipient and a third party must be able to verify the signature as independent verifying institution.

20.4 'DIGITAL SIGNATURE'—TECHNO-LEGAL ASPECTS

Due to its varied nature, digital technology has provided faster, easy, accurate and convenient mechanism for creation, storage, transmission and retrieval of data without involving traditional paper- based formalities. This hastens the increasing use of digital technology in everyday life. Distance, transportation, conveyance are withered away between two individuals when they sit in front of their respective terminals sharing common network. They can share information, data, communicate by remaining online without diminishing their efficiency in executing their work. These characteristic features of digital technology have led the world to go online. It has, in turn, increased the techno-dependency. Increasingly the business dealings, communication, official data and commercial transactions are being carried out in Cyberspace. The transformation of world from paper-based to digital based work culture has shifted the attention of world to find out the consequences of this transformation. Despite the speed, convenience and preciseness of the digital technology, some of the weaknesses of this technology has expressly manifested during the course of time. The most debatable issue in forefront is absence of degree of 'privacy' and 'authentication' of transactions, dealings and communication one can enjoy in traditional paper-based culture.

Privacy is an essence of individual liberty. No one wants to enter into the zone where his privacy would be at stake. If one is unable to feel secure about and does not have confidence for the consequences the digital environment put him for, he would hardly chose such medium for his transactions. Therefore, a sense of privacy and assurance of its respect in the medium play vital role for an individual to chose the medium. It is only because of the danger of being prospective violation of privacy, the net is treated is most dangerous zone where the 'privacy' has involved as a basic issue. It should be noted down that the concept of 'privacy' discussed here is not from point of view of any right to privacy, but is should be understood as a part of all transactions, dealing, communication that is used to be carried out by an individual with a feeling to be maintained by the concept of 'privacy'. It can be simply understood by taking an example of 'E-mails' and 'chat rooms'. Nobody assure that how so far these 'E-mails' and 'chatrooms' are safe to safeguard the privacy of an individual.

The 'privacy' is at stake in digital environment in two different ways.

First, because if one remains connected to the network, he loses control over his data. It may possible that the data may be hijacked by someone else, driven out of the computers, or passes from one server to another server without the knowledge of user. Data in digital environment is in the form of bytes which is capable to move, transfer, copy, distribute, disseminate in number of ways sometime, with the knowledge, sometime without the knowledge of user. It is utmost difficult to check the various routes, channels and paths of data in network.

Secondly, because netizens use network for creation, transfer, distribution, storage or dissemination of their data of personal nature. Today, billions of netizens are using Internet and they use the services provided by the Internet Service Providers [ISP]. The netizens use Internet for creating their E-mail account(s), chatting, surfing, gathering information of government offices & companies, to search job opportunities and even put their personal information on matrimonial sites in search of prospective life partner. Once any private information or communicate in digital environment either uploaded or received, transmitted or stored in mail account, everything is stored in the server of the Internet Service Provider. In this case despite the information, which is of private in nature, does not remain in actual possession of the intended recipient, but stored in the server of Internet Service Provider. In most of the cases it is observed that Internet Service Providers treat either the subscriber of their services or the information they generate, as a commodity for their own business promotion or projecting their Internet Services in to Digital Market.

Bigger the number of subscribers availing services of ISPs, more the advertisement revenue generation for Internet Service Provider. This can be more clearly evident by surfing to the matrimonial sites that uses the photographs, liking and disliking, hobbies, what they are looking for, of their subscribers to put on their home page to attract the other. Even in most of the cases, the netizens can view, share, surf and retrieve the data from these matrimonial sites. Therefore, entering into the digital environment is appeared to be risky now a day. Privacy is an essence of individual liberty which remains at stake in digital environment.

Another, serious problem one can pose in digital environment is lack of degree of 'authentication'. 'Authentication' is a soul essential for transactional solidarity. In absence of 'authentication', there would be difficulties in fixing the responsibilities and liabilities arise out of transactions and dealing. If the respective parties do not have the sense of 'authentication' for their counterparts, the documents coming from them, or if it is difficult to scrutinize whether the originator is the same and documents is not tampered in between the transaction, it is always have gap to air the doubt which lead to complex problem of fixing respective responsibility. Therefore, 'authentication' is one of the important ingredients for any transaction and dealing in any medium.

The traditional medium has set a mechanism to safeguards the interest of parties with entering into transaction and dealing with regards to 'privacy' and 'authentication'. Transactions, communication, information are passes in closed enveloped, stored in a locked cabinet, marked as 'confidential' and places has restricted entry for authorized personnel only. Secrete envelopes are marked to be opened by 'only addressee' or even sometime by using secrete codes in cryptographic languages which is able to decrypt by recipient only. The legislation like 'the Official Secrete Act, 1923' is an example to safeguard the information of public offices. The degree of authentication is met out with the help of 'stamps', 'seals', identity cards, 'logos', 'official emblems', 'signatures', 'encrypted messages' and several times by agreements signed by parties and attested by competent witnesses to protect information of 'confidential nature'. Such agreements are generally known as 'Non-disclosure Agreement'. Thus, the mechanism of authentication of information is neither new, nor uncommon to the legal system and there are several ways to generate sufficient degree of 'privacy' and 'authentication'. The need of 'privacy' and 'authenticity' of transactions, information, data, communication is still not diminished at all, which in contrast was lacking in digital environment. Therefore, it was felt necessary to introduce the technological safeguards which would able to provide the same level of authenticity and privacy the traditional system claimed for. 'Digital signature' has been introduced with the purpose to provide a degree of 'authentication' and 'privacy' to digital content. The present mechanism of affixing 'digital signature' is able to provide 'authentication' and to some extend create a degree of 'privacy' in the digital environment.

20.5 GENERAL AND TECHNOLOGICAL ASPECTS

This chapter attempted to understand the 'Digital Signature' in two different parts. The part-I has deal with the general & technological aspects of 'Digital Signature' in which various aspects are touched but from the aspect to understand the nature, scope, working phenomenon and modality of execution of 'Digital Signatures'. The other part will deal with the legal aspects of 'Digital Signatures'.

20.6 DIGITAL SIGNATURE—NECESSITY AND OBJECTIVES

Digital Signature is created by using cryptographic method. For the purpose of under standing the affixing of 'Digital Signature' by way of cryptographic method, it is essential to bear in mind the purpose of affixing 'Digital Signature'. The basic objectives of affixing of 'Digital Signature' are:

20.6.1 Affixing of 'Digital Signature'

- **Create authenticity of the originator**—so that at any moment after the creation of any digital material, the authenticity of the originator can be verified. It will be possible only if the mechanism is capable to create any impossibility of anybody else to represent himself with the digital material which he has not created. At the same time it is also essential that at any latter moment, the originator will not capable to deny the creation of document by him

- **Create authenticity of the document**—so that any recipient will not be in position to modify, change, alter, or tamper with the document created by originator. The mechanism should also ensure to the originator that no one else than him will be capable to modify, change, alter or tamper with the document

- **Non-repudiation**—so that the entire mechanism will ensure that the document and identify mechanism will not play foul and nobody will be in position at any latter moment to deny the responsibility and liability arising out of the document. For originator, that he will not be in position to repudiate what he had created, for recipient, he will not be in position by any means to modify the content created by originator

The 'Digital Signature' has evolved to achieve these objectives. It can be done with the help of 'Public Key Cryptography'. Therefore first it is essential to have fundamental understanding of the concept and meaning of term 'Cryptography'. It can be represented as:

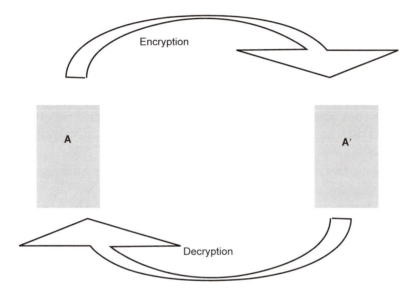

Fig. 20.1 Encryption/Decryption of an electronic record to convert it from one form to another

'Cryptography' is a way of scrambling of electronic record from one form to another form using hash function which leads to create hash result. Encryption stands for the modifying the electronic record in different form and decryption stands for bring it into the original form.

Normally, it is easier to encrypt any electronic record from one form to another and bring it back to its original form by decrypting it. It is important to note here that both encryption and decryption is easy for those who are aware about the methods used in this process. In this process generally a key is used to encrypt the electronic record and by using the same key. This keys act as a secret password and generally know to both the parties i.e. originator and recipient. Therefore, if both the parties are aware about the keys required for encryption and decryption they can assure the authenticity of an electronic record.

20.7 MECHANISM OF DIGITAL SIGNATURES

However, recently, the mechanism has been developed to use two different keys. By one key the encryption can be carried out and decryption used to be carried out by different key. Both the public and private keys are different from each other commonly but correspond to each other in such a way that the public key can decrypt the document encrypted by private key. The main purpose of using two keys is very apparent. The first key of the set is 'private key' which is unique and only know to its holder." It acts as a secrete key of holder and plays very vital role. It helps any holder of this key to encrypt the electronic record. Once the electronic record is encrypted with the help of private key it scrambled the electronic record in such a clever ways so that putting it back to its original form is almost all impossible. Even the holder of private key now cannot put the electronic record into original form. Now only viewing this record is possible with the help of corresponding public key. The mechanism of private key is that it leads every time to the same result for same electronic record. Thus once any electronic record is encrypted with the help of private key the holder of private key cannot deny that it is encrypted with the help of his private key.

The second key in the set is public key which is used to verify electronic record and available and known to the public at large. Anybody who wants to verify the content of the electronic record encrypted with the help of private key, can use corresponding public key to verify the electronic record, however, only verification of electronic record is possible with the help of public key and no alteration, modification, change or tampering is possible furthermore once it is transformed into hash result by applying private key. Both these keys are so related with each other that only the electronic record encrypted by private key can be open by its corresponding public key only. Thus use of this asymmetric pair of keys for encryption and decryption of electronic records serve following purposes:

20.7.1 For Originator

It helps the originator to encrypt the electronic record. Once originator encrypts any electronic record with the help of his private key, nobody [even originator] can modify the content of the electronic record. Thus private wrap the digital content and does not allow modifying, altering, changing or tampering the content of the electronic record. Thus after apply his private keys originator will assure himself that the electronic record cannot be bring to its original format and any change is almost impossible in the electronic record.

Once the electronic record is encrypted it get wrapped, and no further alteration by any means allowed to be made. Therefore originator remains assured that any electronic record he has created is safe. Such electronic record can be decrypted only with the corresponding public key of originator. Thus, if any alteration has been made to electronic record created with the help of originator's private key, the public key of originator will unable to open the electronic record. Therefore, public key of originator will works only in case when the electronic record created by encryption of private key of originator

20.7.2 For Recipient

As the document so created by private key of originator is unique one which can be opened only with the help of public key of originator, recipient can verify and get assured by decrypting the electronic record with public key of originator which is readily available. Once the electronic record is able to decrypt, it is evident that it was encrypted by the private key of originator. If the deception is possible, it is evident that it is not modified after its encryption.

Therefore, if the electronic record is capable to decrypt with the help of public key of originator, the originator cannot deny the authenticity of electronic record. But if electronic record is unable to be verified with the help of public key of originator, it is possible that originator had not created it or it has altered after its creation.

Because technically whenever private keys applies to the electronic record, hash function works upon it to transformed it by algorithm mapping into another electronic record called hash function, this hash function is only able to verify with the help of corresponding public key of the originator. This helps the originator that once he applies his private key to any electronic record, the resulting record [known as hash result] will neither be able to tamper nor any change is possible, and only can be verified with the help of his public key and not otherwise.

20.8 FOR THE PURPOSE OF LEGAL SYSTEM

(*a*) This system also helps to create authenticity and accuracy for electronic record. In case of any doubt and denial of authentication either by originator or recipient, the electronic record can be varied. Because hash function is such algorithm mapping system which generate the same hash result every time with same input.

Therefore, if the electronic record is capable to decrypt with the help of public key of originator, the originator cannot deny the authenticity of electronic record. But if electronic record is unable to be verified with the help of public key of originator, it is possible that originator had not created it or it has altered after its creation.

Verification can be made out in following ways. If the recipient has brought any electronic record in question before the court claiming that it is created by originator, and if originator denies its creation, it can be verified by applying public key of the originator. If the document gets decrypted with the public key of originator, the originator would not be in position to deny that he is a creator of the document. Because there is only one set of corresponding public and private key. It is highly impossible to decrypt the electronic record encrypted by one private key using public key of different originator.

This system in short is called affixing of digital signature. As the originator by using his private key create a electronic record in such a way that his private key act as his signature to the electronic record. The necessity of digital signatures is the essence to create authentic transaction, creating nonrepudiation and integrity. It can be achieved by this process in following manner

Authentication: As discussed above, authentication is achieved in the digital environment because this process ensure that no two sets of public and private key pair match with each other. Again the electronic record encrypted by private key of a pair is only decrypted by public key of the same pair. However, the electronic record once created by applying private key, get tampered, altered, modified or change, the public key will not able to decrypt it anyway.

Therefore, the parties, originator and recipient, can authenticate the genuineness and originality of electronic record. The Information Technology Act, 2000 has created a mechanism for affixing digital signature. The office of Controller of Certifying Authority has entrusted the responsibility for issuing, maintaining and taking all steps for safeguarding the digital signature. It issues the digital signature to subscriber, keep record and provide guidelines for its safeguards. Thus, in case of any dispute office of the Controller of Certifying Authority referred. As the record of the digital signature which constitution a key pair of private and public key is issues and maintained by the Controller of Certifying Authority, the subscriber [holding key pair] is not in position to deny its possession and authenticity.

Non-repudiation: The manner in which digital signature affixed to any electronic record can cerate authenticity of an originator, it also make is disable to repudiate any argument of its non-creation. Thus once the electronic record is created by any private key, the originator cannot deny its creation. He furthermore has to accept all the responsibilities and consequences arise by its creation. His authorship gets fixed to the electronic record and all the right and a liability oozes out automatically lies to the creator. This is important because most of the time, the creator deny the creation of the electronic record to overthrow the legal responsibility. In the eye of law this is called as non-repudiation. It is important to resolve the problems and solve the legal disputes.

Integrity: This is another important objective achieve by the digital signature. By creating a mechanism solidifying authentication and non-repudiation, it develops the sense of integrity of both the parties to the transactions. Once the digital signature are involve, both the parties remain assured, and enter into the transactions, dealing with full sense of assurance that the transactions would capable to fix right and responsibilities oozing out of it. Furthermore, both the parties are having legal alternatives open for them in case of denial or allegations. If the electronic record carries the digital signature, parties are hardly in position to deny creation and participation in the transactions. Again, both parties also remained assured about the so called 'tampering' to the electronic record. If the electronic record gets tampered, it automatically loses its authentication and non-repudiation character and lose it legal genuineness. Thus the digital signature is also capable to achieve the object of 'integrity'.

20.9 TECHNOLOGICAL MECHANISM OF DIGITAL SIGNATURES

It is essential to have brief look at the technological working of a 'digital signature' mechanism. As stated earlier, each user has a pair of private and public key. This can be graphically represented as follows:

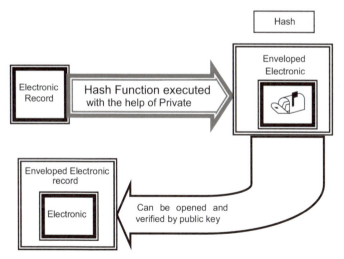

Fig. 20.2 Showing how the "Hash Function" executed by private key to yield "Hash Result". The "Hash Reset is nothing bet the transformed form of' Electronic Record"which get enveloped and only can be viewed but can not bE modified any way after, and it is impossible to get back the original "Electronic Record" from the "Hash Result".

The private key remain secrete with the user and nobody is aware about it, while public key is freely distributed for the public which can be used to decrypt and verify the electronic records encrypted by person. While affixing the digital signature to any electronic record, the originator (subscriber of Digital Signature Certificate) applies his private key. When he applies his private key, an asymmetric crypto system and hash function transform the initial electronic record into another electronic record.

The "hash function" stands for an algorithm mapping or translation of one sequence of bits into another, generally smaller, set known 'as "hash result" such that an electronic record yields the same hash result every time the algorithm is executed with the same electronic record as its input making it computationally infeasible—

- to derive or reconstruct the original electronic record from the hash result produced by the algorithm;
- Those two electronic records can produce the same hash result using the algorithm. And

This mechanism also ensure that the set of private key and the public key are unique to the subscriber and constitute a functioning key pair. The keys (also) have the property that it is computationally not feasible to discover one of the key pairs merely by knowing the elements of the other key"

It can be understood from above that:

- Once the "hash function" works on electronic record, it yield "hash result". This process is such that the hash function yield as hash result each times it works upon.
- "Hash function" is an algorithm which makes it infeasible to derive or reconstruct the original electronic record from the hash result produced by the algorithm.
- The two electronic records cannot produce the same hash result using the algorithm.

Therefore, every mechanism set forth must ensure all these standards. If the algorithm is unable to achieve all or any of the above objectives, the mechanism of digital signature would be futile and unable to ensure authenticity. This criterion is required by S. 3 of the Information Technology Act, 2000 and Controller of Certifying Authority has to ensure that the technological standards are capable to ensure these objectives. However, the different standards can be set forth for government and non-government entity by the Controller of Certifying Authority.

20.10 LEGAL ASPECTS OF DIGITAL SIGNATURES

If the preamble of the Information Technology Act, 2000 has given a close look, it is apparent that the act has enacted to provide 'legal recognition for transactions carried out by means of electronic data interchange and other means of electronic communication.'" The act has attempted to legally recognize the process in sum called 'electronic commerce'. The act is in furtherance of the resolution passed by United Nation on 30th January, 1997 to which India was signatory, where UNCITRAL [United Nation Commission on International Trade Law] has proposed a 'Model Law' and recommend to member states to give favourable consideration while bringing any enactments, amendments, or inceptions in the legislation relating to 'Electronic commerce'. In furtherance to promote the 'Electronic commerce' that is inter alia requires reliability of electronic documents, it is essential to have mechanism that would ensure the trustworthiness of the electronic documents. The concept of 'Digital Signature' has brought into being with the sole purpose to develop mechanism for creating reliability and authenticity of electronic documents.

20.11 LEGAL RECOGNITION OF DIGITAL SIGNATURES

The Act has set forth the objective to provide legal recognition for transactions carried out by means of electronic data interchange. At the same time, the authentication, integration and non-repudiation of electronic record is equally important. But more important than anything else is to provide a provision that would create a sense of responsible and assurance about the mechanism. The genuineness and of medium is equally important than creation of medium, and the information technology in general and digital signature in particular has attempted to bring authentication in this medium.

Therefore, it was important that not only the affixing of 'digital signature' would make important, but it is also necessary to give equal force to the electronic record created by digital signature which in traditional medium has for attested and signed document. S. 5 of the Act fulfill this requirement which runs as under:

Where any law provides that information or any other matter shall be authenticated by affixing the signature or any document shall be signed or bear the signature of any person then, notwithstanding anything contained in such law, such requirement shall be deemed to have been satisfied, if such information or matter is authenticated by means of digital signature affixed in such manner as may be prescribed by the Central Government.

Explanation.—For the purposes of this section, "signed", with its grammatical variations and cognate expressions, shall, with reference to a person, mean affixing of his hand written signature or any mark on any document and the expression "signature" shall be construed accordingly.

Thus the plain reading of S. 5 makes it clear that the electronic record to which the 'digital signature' has been affixed has equal binding force which in traditional system the signed document has. It has also expressly made it clear if any law require that any document must bear signature, the requirement will deem to be satisfied if the electronic record is authenticated by affixing digital signature.

The explanation clause clarifies the meaning of "signed" and "signature". The clause explain that as the word "signed" has the meaning and expression attached to it which is generally done by mean of affixing of his hand written signature or any mark on any document, and signature has its meaning, in the same way, the 'affixing of digital signature should be construed accordingly. One very important differentiation should be beard into mind that in India the Act has adopted "Digital Signature" which is created by hash function and pair of public and private key. In contrast, in most of the nation, it speak about "Electronic Signature". The basic different between "Digital Signature" and "Electronic Signature" is, the digital signature is in digital form contain may be alpha-numerical, where electronic signature may also contain sound, signature by digital pen, watermark, thumb impression, eye scan. Comparatively, 'Electronic Signature' provides more security. The proposed amendment in Sept 2005 which is still pending for want of enactment, which will provide the mechanism for 'Electronic Signature' by replacing 'digital signature', if would take shape of legislation.

20.12 DIGITAL SIGNATURE LEGALITIES

The 'Digital Signature' has been defined by S. 2 (1) (p) of the Information Technology Act, 2000 [the Act] as follows:

2 (1) (p) "digital signature" means authentication of any electronic record by a subscriber by means of an electronic method or procedure in accordance with the provisions of section 3;

Thus, what exactly the 'digital signature' stands for has not been defined by the Act. It simply point out that 'digital signature' means authentication of electronic record by subscriber by and in accordance of the procedure laid down by Chapter II, S. 3 of the Act. For reference it is essential to have a look to Section 3 of the Act which runs as under:

20.13 AUTHENTICATION OF E-RECORDS

- Subject to the provisions of this section any subscriber may authenticate an electronic record by affixing his digital signature.
- The authentication of the electronic record shall be effected by the use of asymmetric crypto system and hash function which envelop and transform the initial electronic record into another electronic record.
- *Explanation.*—For the purposes of this subsection, "hash function" means an algorithm mapping or translation of one sequence of bits into another, generally smaller, set known 'as "hash result" such that an

electronic record yields the same hash result every time the algorithm is executed with the same electronic record as its input making it computationally infeasible—

- to derive or reconstruct the original electronic record from the hash result produced by the algorithm;
- that two electronic records can produce the same hash result using the algorithm.
- Any person by the use of a public key of the subscriber can verify the electronic record.
- The private key and the public key are unique to the subscriber and constitute a functioning key pair.

Ss. 3 (1) of the Act explain the category of person who can authenticate the electronic record. It provides that the 'subscriber' can authentication any electronic record by affixing his digital signature to it. This sub section empowers only to the subscriber, *and not any general person,* the capacity to authenticate the electronic record. The Act also defined 'subscriber' vide S. 2 (1) (zg) as:

"subscriber" means a person in whose name
the Digital Signature Certificate is issued;

Thus the person having Digital Signature Certificate is only empowered to authenticate (any) electronic record by affixing his 'digital signature'. The Act does prescribe that subscriber can authenticate electronic record by affixing his 'digital signature'. Therefore it is not required by the Act that subscriber can authenticate only 'his' electronic record. It is clear from the language of the S. 3 (1) that subscriber can authenticate any of the electronic record whether created by himself or by any other person by affixing his 'digital signature'. It is apparently clear that though only the subscriber can authenticate the electronic record by affixing his 'digital signature', but no limitation has been put on the subscriber to authenticate only his electronic record. He can authenticate the electronic record of other's also, but subject to provision of the Act, and only electronic record bearing valid 'digital signature' is treated reliable and authenticate in the eye of law. The general public using Internet for the purpose of E-mails, Chatting, sharing files, surfing, downloading for educational or any other purpose or even taking information from the WebPages, or government institutions, offices, companies having their Webpage cannot be treated as authenticate electronic record unless the creator of these electronic record has not holding 'digital signature certificate' and even if holding it, he has not authenticated his electronic record by using his 'digital signature'. Therefore, it should be noted down that all those electronic records which exists in digital environment are neither reliable nor authenticated. The authentication process is deliberate attempt by subscriber holding 'digital signature' and an option for him to affix his 'digital signature' to the electronic record. However, once the subscriber opted to authenticate the electronic record, and in this attempt, affix his 'digital signature' to any electronic record, it will be treated authenticate by world at large against the subscriber and subscriber cannot afterward repudiate its authenticity. Anyone can verify the authenticity by applying 'public key' of creator as the mechanism of 'digital signature' is capable to verify the authenticity of electronic record created using 'digital signature' and this mechanism is recognized by means provided by law.

The electronic record bearing 'digital signature' thus presumed to be authenticates and can be relied upon for the purpose of commercial and other transactional business. Subject to other provisions of the Act, the electronic record bearing 'digital signature' carries evidential value and can be used against subscriber if denied or alleged to be non-authenticated.

Ss. 3 (2) prescribe the procedure of affixing of 'digital signature' to the electronic record. It stipulates that the authentication of the electronic record shall be effectuated by use of the asymmetric crypto system and hash function. The Asymmetric Crypto System' is a cryptographic process in which two different asymmetric key pair has been used to secure the record. These two key are private key and public key in which private key is used for creating a digital signature and corresponding public key to verify the digital signature. S. 3 (4) of the Information

Technology Act, 2000 states that the private key and the public key are unique to the subscriber and constitute a functioning key pair. These two keys are related and correspond to each other in such a way that the electronic record created by a private key can only verify by public key related and corresponds to it.

Though traditionally, only one key pair use to encrypt the record and same key pair use to decrypt it. But for securing the record and unable its reversibility, two different key pairs are used in which one key pair modify the record and other key pair can only verify it, but does not able to alter, change its content.

When the private key is used to effectuate the 'digital signature' to the electronic record, hash function which is a kind of algorithm mapping use to envelop and translate one sequence of bits into another work on it to generate "hash result". The hash function is one which whenever works upon the same electronic record yield the same hash result every time.

However, the legal provision prescribe with regard to hash function that -
- The hash function is one which is used to envelop and transform the electronic record into another electronic record which is called hash result

◄◙ The hash function is to yield same hash result every time whenever executed with same electronic record as it input

◄◙ This hash function must bear the feature that deriving or reconstruction of original record from hash result shall not be possible

◄◙ No two electronic records yield same hash result with hash function

These four conditions are mandatory to ensure that nobody able to get the original electronic record back from hash result. The first condition will ensure that hash result shall envelop and transform the electronic record into another electronic record. This process blocks the content and wraps it so that the content of the electronic record get block from any change or modification.

The second condition is to safeguard the interest of subscriber. The quality of hash function to yield same hash result every time whenever executed upon the same input will help the subscriber to verify any latter moment tampering or change into the electronic record. Thus if subscriber is doubtful about the authenticity of the electronic record, he can execute hash function to verify that the result is same or not. If the result remains unchanged each time, he can ensure that the document is one which he had created. But if two hash results differ, he can very well take plea that the input is different. The same methodology can be used by forensic lab to verify that whether the same hash result yield second time or not. They can check it with the alleged electronic record by comparison.

The third condition laid down by the Act is due to the reasons that once the digital signature affixed to the electronic record, it get enveloped and wrapped by the hash function. Now it is only possible that one can only verify it but cannot modify. Once the system ensure this feature, it give a legal presumption that once the electronic record bears digital signature, it is neither modified, changed, altered or tampered by anybody. Even the subscriber cannot able to get original record by any means. Therefore, reliability of electronic record can be ensured.

The last condition ensures that no two results from two different inputs shall yield after execution by hash function. This is because if the two hash result will be identical despite the inputs were different, its authenticity will at stake. Thus for different input, different hash result must be yield and no two hash result shall be identical if the input is different. These conditions can ensure and strengthen the reliability of mechanism and chances of creeping up of loopholes.

20.13.1 Creation and maintenance of Digital Signature

The Information Technology Act, 2000 has also set up the mechanism for creation and maintenance of 'Digital Signatures'. The office of the Controller has been created for the purpose. The Controller grants the licences to the 'Certifying Authority' which further issue 'digital signature' to the subscriber. Thus, Controller does not directly issue 'digital signature', but issues licences to the 'Certifying Authority'. The Certifying Authority issues the 'Digital Signature Certificate' to the subscribers. These can be represented graphically in following manner:

Note : Subscribers are not the constituent part of the office of CCA

The Controller of Certifying Authority [CCA] is appointed by Central Government by notification in Official Gazette in accordance with S. 17 of the Act. by the Central Government. The Controller shall discharge his functions under the Act subject to the general control and directions of the Central Government.'" The functions of the Controller are prescribed by S. 18 of the Act which following major functions:

- exercising supervision over the activities of the Certifying Authorities
- certifying public keys of the Certifying Authorities
- laying down the standards to be maintained by the Certifying Authorities

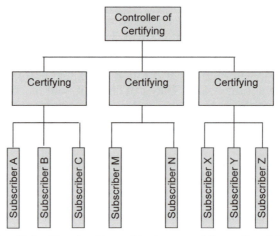

Fig. 20.3 Showing hierarchical set up of Controller of CA

- specifying the qualifications and experience which employees of the Certifying Authorities should possess
- specifying the conditions subject to which the Certifying Authorities shall conduct their business
- specifying the contents of written, printed or visual materials and advertisements that may be distributed or used in respect of a Digital Signature Certificate and the public key
- specifying the form and content of a Digital Signature Certificate and the key,
- specifying the form and manner in which accounts shall be maintained by the Certifying Authorities

- ↵ specifying the terms and conditions subject to which auditors may be appointed and the remuneration to be paid to them
- ↵ facilitating the establishment of any electronic system by a Certifying Authority either solely or jointly with other Certifying Authorities and regulation of such systems
- ↵ specifying the manner in which the Certifying Authorities shall conduct their dealings with the subscribers
- ↵ resolving any conflict of interests between the Certifying Authorities and the subscribers
- ↵ laying down the duties of the Certifying Authorities
- ↵ Maintaining a data base containing the disclosure record of every Certifying Authority containing such particulars as may be specified by regulations, which shall be accessible to public.

If the above functions of the Controller of Certifying Authority are scrutinized closely, it can be averted that Controller enjoys great control over the Certifying Authority. The Controller exercises greater control with regards to the activities of Certifying Authorities as he supervises activities of Certifying Authorities, laying down the standards to be maintained by the Certifying Authorities, specify the qualifications and experience of employees of the Certifying Authorities should employ, specify the conditions of business carried by Certifying Authorities, specify the contents of written, printed or visual materials and advertisements that may be distributed or used in respect of a Digital Signature Certificate and the public key, specify the form and content of a Digital Signature Certificate and the key, specify the form and manner in which accounts shall be maintained by the Certifying Authorities, facilitating the establishment of any electronic system by a Certifying Authority either solely or jointly with other Certifying Authorities and regulation of such systems, specify the manner in which the Certifying Authorities shall conduct their dealings with the subscribers, resolve any conflict of interests between the Certifying Authorities and the subscribers, lay down the duties of the Certifying Authorities and maintain a data base containing the disclosure record of every Certifying Authority containing such particulars as may be specified by regulations, which shall be accessible to public. Therefore, even though Controller does not directly play the role of distribution of 'digital signature' to the subscriber, he enjoy almost all the power in which manner the 'digital signature' shall be issued and maintained by 'Certifying Authorities'. In practices, the Controller of Certifying Authority issue licence to Certifying Authorities who in fact give digital signature to the subscriber.

The Act has also specified the scope for the recognition of foreign Certifying Authorities. For this purpose, the act has prescribed that Controller may with prior approval of Central Government and subject to such conditions and restrictions as may be specified by regulations, and by notification in the Official Gazette, recognise any foreign Certifying Authority as a Certifying Authority for the purposes of the Act. In this case, if the foreign Certifying Authority would given recognition, the 'Digital Signature Certificate' issued by such Certifying Authority either to any citizens having any nationality, any company or institution incorporated in India or any foreign person, company or institution will be treated recognized for the purpose of the Act and will have the same effect and force as if the 'digital signature' is issued by the Certifying Authority having licence by Controller for all purposes laid down by the Act.

Digital Signature—Safeguard and functional mechanism

The Acts prescribe vide various provisions to safeguards and functional mechanism for 'Digital signature'. These safeguards can be put in following ways:

Provisions to safeguard the 'Digital Signature' mechanism

- The Controller acts as the repository of all Digital Signature Certificates and also maintains the computerized data base of all public keys This ensures the availability of public key to any member of public and verification of data is possible

- The Controller has responsibility to ensure from any intrusion and misuse of any hardware, software and procedures to safeguards 'Digital Signature mechanism' and

- Shall observe such other standards as may be prescribed by the Central Government.

- The Controller is empowered to investigate any contravention of any of the provisions of the Act either by himself or through authorized officer.

- S. 30 of the Act provide the procedure which Certifying Authority should follow. This section laid down the responsibility on Certifying Authority with regard to hardware, software and procedures that are secure from intrusion and misuse. It also laid down that Certifying Authority should provide a reasonable level of reliability in its services which are reasonably suited to the performance of intended functions. In addition to it, Certifying Authority should also adhere to security procedures to ensure that the secrecy and privacy of the digital signatures are assured and observe such other standards as may be specified by regulations. This is because to ensure the security measures for 'Digital Signature' and prevents it from any intrusion and misuse.

Provisions with regards to functional aspects of 'Digital Signature'

- The Controller is empowered to issue the licence to issue Digital Signature Certificates any person only after fulfillment of requirement laid down by the Act. The **Terms and conditions of licence to issue Digital Signature Certificate have been provided vide rule 3 of** the Information Technology (Certifying Authority) Regulations, 2001.

- The licence to Certifying Authority is issued only subject to satisfaction of qualification, expertise, manpower, financial resources and infrastructure facilities. This shows that person must comply with the requirement laid down by the Act and corresponding rules from time to time. Therefore, while granting the licence to any Certifying Authority to issue 'Digital Signature' the ability of the Certifying Authority will be tested upon and

- comply with, otherwise Controller will not issue licence to Certifying Authority.

- Though the provision laid down the liberty for Certifying Authorities to set norms and standards for issue 'Digital Signature Certificate' to the subscribers, they must observe the rules and regulation laid down by the Act and instruction given by the Controller from time to time.

- The Certifying Authority may charge the fees for issuing 'Digital Signature' to subscriber not exceeding ₹25000/- [or as may be prescribed by Central Government].

- The licence issued to the Certifying Authority also has expiry date. However the provision for renewal of licence also been prescribed by the Act.

- The Act also prescribed the provision for issuance and suspension of licence for which Controller has been empowered by the Act. The grounds for the suspension of licences are

Providing any Incorrect Information Asked by Any Statement

- Failed to comply with any term and condition on the basis of which the licence has been granted

- Failed to maintain standard or contravened the provision of the Act

- However, Controller will give the Certifying Authority an 'opportunity of being heard' to put his stand before revocation of licence.

Thus, as stated in the beginning of this part of research writing, the mechanism of digital signature functions to achieve authentication, non-repudiation and verification of electronic record. It provides the sense of security in the electronic environment and facilitates the electronic transaction.

20.13.2 Sum Up

The above analysis show that 'digital signature' under the Information Technology Act, 2000, that this is not only essential aspect for creating secure environment for electronic transactions, but it create a sense of authentication and non-repudiation and thus ultimately achieve its objectives of facilitating e-commerce. Thus in its application, digital signature has not only proved an essential techno-legal requirement, but it has made the e- commerce meaningful.

However, looking to the present development across the world, it is essential to reconsider the importation of 'electronic signature' in the legal books as it ensures greater level of safety and security in electronic environment. Beside the same, the need for cross-border recognition of digital/electronic signature is already overdue which cannot be delayed further.

The study of electronic environment from legal point of view would be incomplete without scrutinizing the 'criminality' and its various dimensions. The previous and this chapter of this research writing had focused its attention on legal framework prescribe by law. However, this would be incomplete without having glance to the 'crime' being committed in cyberspace. The study of crime committed in cyberspace will provide a platform to activate the study in proper direction, as the one of the basic role of legal framework is to regulate the 'criminality' and set law and order. Thus this makes it essential to have a glance to 'criminality in cyberspace'. Therefore, next chapter of this investigative writing turn its attention towards this aspect.

References

1. This list is not exhaustive. For e.g. Restatement (Second) of Contracts notes another function, termed the "deterrent function", which seeks to "Discourage transactions of doubtful utility." Restatement (Second) of Contracts 72 Comment c(1981). Professor Perillo notes earmarking of intent, clarification, managerial efficiency, publicity, education, as well as taxation and regulation as functions served by the statute of frauds. Joseph M. Perillo, the Statute of Frauds in the Light of the Functions and Dysfunctions of Form, 43 Fordham L. Rev. 39, 48–64

2. See, Restatement (Second) of Contracts, statutory note preceding S. 110 (1982) (Summarizing purpose of the statute of frauds, which includes a signature requirement): Lon L. Fuller, Consideration and Form, 41 Colum. L. Rev. 799, 800 (1941); 6 Jeremy Bentham, The Works of Jeremy Bentham 508-85 (Bowring Ed. 1962) (1839) (Bentham called forms serving evidentiary functions "preappointed [i.e., made in advance] evidence"). A handwritten signature creates probative evidence in part because of the chemical properties of ink that make it adhere to paper, and because handwriting style is quite unique to the signer. Signed includes any symbol executed or adopted by a party with present intention to authenticate a writing.

3. John Austin, Lectures on jurisprudence 939-44 (44th Ed. 1873); Restatement (Second) of Contracts S. 72 comment c (1982) and statutory note preceding S. 110 (1982) (what is here termed a "Ceremonial" function is termed a "cautionary" function in the Restatement);

4. See, Model law on Electronic Commerce, United National Commission on International Trade Law (UNCITRAL), 29th Session, Art. 7 (1) at 3, Doc., A/CN.9/XXIX.CRP.1/Add. 13 (1996) ("Where a law requires a signature of a person, that requirement is met in relation to a data message if: (a) a method is used to identify that person and to indicate that person's approval of the information contained in the data message...."); Draft Model Law on Legal Aspects of Electronic Data Interchange (EDI) and Related Means of Data Communication, United Nationals Commission on International Trade Law (UNCITRAL), 28th Session, Art. 6, at 44, U.N. Doc. A/CN./9/406 (1994). For example, a signature on a written contract customarily indicates the signer's assent. A signature on the back of a check is customarily taken s an endorsement. See U.C.C. S. 3-204 (1990).

5. Analogizing the form of a legal transaction to minting of coins, which serves to make their metal content and weight apparent without further examination. The notion of clarity and finality provide by a form are largely predicated on the fact that the form provides good evidence. The basic premise of the efficiency and logistical function is that a signed, written document is such a good indicator of what the transaction is, that the transaction should be considered to be as the signed document says. The moment of signing the document thus becomes decision.

6. See, e.g. U.C.C. S. 3-401 (1990) (A Person is not liable on an instrument unless the person signed it); See generally U.C.C. S. 3-104 (1990) (requirements for negotiability).

7. See for details, S 20 of the Information Technology Act, 2000 which runs as under

   S. 20. : **Controller to act as repository.**

   (1) The Controller shall be the repository of all Digital Signature Certificates issued under this Act.

   (2) The Controller shall—

      (*a*) make use of hardware, software and procedures that are secure its {correct after verification} intrusion and misuse;

      (*b*) observe such other standards as may be prescribed by the Central Government, to ensure that the secrecy and security of the digital signatures are assured.

   (3) The Controller shall maintain a computerised data base of all public keys in such a manner that such data base and the public keys are available to any member of the public.

8. Of course, the holder of the private key may choose to divulge it, or may lose control of it (often called 'compromise'), and thereby make forgery possible. The Guidelines seek to address this problem in two ways, (1) by requiring the subscriber, who holds the private key, to use a degree of care in its safekeeping,

and (2) enabling the subscriber to disassociate himself from the key by temporarily suspending or permanently revoking his certificate and publishing these actions in a "certificate revocation list." or "CRL". A verity of methods is available for securing the private key. The safer methods store the private key in a "cryptographic token" (one example is a "smart card") which executes the signature programme within an internal micro processing chip, so that the private key is never divulged outside the token and does not pass into the main memory or processor of the signer's computer. The signer must typically present to the token some authenticating information, such as a password, pass phrase, or personal identification number, for the token to run a process requiring access to the private key. In addition, this token must be physically produced, and biometric authentication such as fingerprints or retinal scan can assure the physical presence of the token's authorized holder. There are also software-based schemes for protecting the security of the private key, generally less secure than hardware schemes, but providing adequate security for many types of applications.

9. See, the information Technology (Certifying Authorities) Rules, 2000
   Schedule V [Glossary] which define key pair as, 'KEY PAIR — In an asymmetric crypto system, means a private key and its mathematically related public key, which are so related that the public key can verify a digital signature created by the private key.

10. See, for detail, S.3 of the Information Technology Act, 2000 (21 of 2000)

11. http://www.state.co.us/gov_dir/gss/cec3/colo_rules.htm visited on 20.10.2006

12. In the first phase of its operation the services being offered are government to government. NIC offers four distinct classes of digital certification services, classes 0-3 for NICNET users within the government. For all its subscribers it issues class 2 digital IDs. These digital IDs are used to identify the subscriber on the net and are legally valid as they are backed by the Information Technology Act, 2000.

13. Preamble of the Information Technology Act, 2000 runs as follows :
    An Act to provide legal recognition for transactions carried out by means of electronic data interchange and other means of electronic communication, commonly referred to as "electronic commerce", which involve the use of alternatives to paper-
    based methods of communication and storage of information, to facilitate electronic filing of documents with the Government agencies and further to amend the Indian Penal Code, the Indian Evidence Act, 1872, the Bankers' Books Evidence Act, 1891 and the Reserve Bank of India Act, 1934 and for matters connected therewith or incidental thereto.
    WHEREAS the General Assembly of the United Nations by resolution A/RES/51/162, dated the 30th January, 1997 has adopted the Model Law on Electronic Commerce adopted by the United Nations Commission on International Trade Law;
    AND WHEREAS the said resolution recommends inter alia that all States give favourable consideration to the said Model Law when they enact or revise their

laws, in view of the need for uniformity of the law applicable to alternatives to paper-cased methods of communication and storage of information;

AND WHEREAS it is considered necessary to give effect to the said resolution and to promote efficient delivery of Government services by means of reliable electronic records.

14. See, State of Punjab and Ors. Vs. Amritsar Beverages Ltd. and Ors. Civil Appeal No. 3419 of 2006 (Arising out of SLP (Civil) Nos. 10371-10374 of 2004) Decided On: 08.08.2006 [para 7] p. 3488. The Supreme Court observed,

We may notice some recent amendments in this behalf Section **464** of the Indian Penal Code deals with the inclusion of the digital signatures. Sections 29, **167**, **172**, **192** and **463** of the Indian Penal Code have been amended to include electronics documents within the definition of Page 3489 'documents'. Section 63 of the Evidence Act has been amended to include admissibility of computer outputs in the media, paper, optical or magnetic form. Section **73A** prescribes procedures for verification of digital signatures. Sections **85A** and **85B** of the Evidence Act raise a presumption as regards electronic contracts, electronic records, digital signature certificates and electronic messages. [para 8]

15. This shall be borne in mind that the amendment brought into effect by the Information Technology Act, 2000 in Evidence Act, 1882 has also create strong presumption in favour of electronic contracts, electronic records, digital signature certificates and electronic messages.

16. Therefore, the term 'verify' has also been defined by the Act which prescribed the meaning and scope as follows :

S. 2 (1) (zh) "verify" in relation to a digital signature, electronic record or public key, with its grammatical variations and cognate expressions means to determine whether—

(a) the initial electronic record was affixed with the digital signature by the use of private key corresponding to the public key of the subscriber;

(b) the initial electronic record is retained intact or has been altered since such electronic record was so affixed with the digital signature.

17. S. 2 (1) (f) of the Information Technology Act, 2000 which define "asymmetric crypto system" as follows:

"asymmetric crypto system" means a system of a secure key pair consisting of a private key for creating a digital signature and a public key to verify the digital signature;

18. S. 3 (4) of the Information Technology Act, 2000. See also, Duggal Pavan, Cyber Law — The Indian Perspective, Saakshar Law Publications New Delhi, 2nd Ed. 2004, pg. 65

19. S. 2 (1) (x) of the Information Technology Act, 2000 which define "Key pair" as follows :

"key pair", in an asymmetric crypto system, means a private key and its mathematically related public key, which are so related that the public key can verify a digital signature created by the private key;

20. See S. 17 of the Information Technology Act, 2000 which runs as under 17. Appointment of Controller and other officers.

    (1) The Central Government may, by notification in the Official Gazette, appoint a Controller of Certifying Authorities for the purposes of this Act and may also by the same or subsequent notification appoint such number of Deputy Controllers and Assistant Controllers as it deems fit.

    (2) The Controller shall discharge his functions under this Act subject to the general control and directions of the Central Government.

    (3) The Deputy Controllers and Assistant Controllers shall perform the functions assigned to them by the Controller under the general superintendence and control of the Controller.

    (4) The qualifications, experience and terms and conditions of service of Controller, Deputy Controllers and Assistant Controllers shall be such as may be prescribed by the Central Government.

    (5) The Head Office and Branch Office of the office of the Controller shall be at such places as the Central Government may specify, and these may be established at such places as the Central Government may think fit.

    (6) There shall be a seal of the Office of the Controller.

21. Id. S. 18

22. For e.g. First digital Contract Note authenticated by digital signature had been issued by Mr. K.N. Gupta, the first Controller of Certifying Authorities, Government of India, has issued the first licence to "Safe Script" to act as a Certifying Authority. Another persons who were in line for the issue of licence were (1) RBI Affiliate, Hyderabad (2) Institution of Development Research and Banking Technology and, (3) National Informatics Centre et. The "Safe Script" had issued a digital signature certificate in the name of "ICICIDIRECT.COM", Mumbai. On March 27, 2002 the subscriber "ICICIDIRECT.COM", became the first firm to issue a Digitally Signed Contract Note (DSCN) to its clients [The Economic Times, Delhi Ed. 29.03.2002 Pg. 5]. The ICICIDIRECT.COM used to issue contract notes for about 22,000 transactions carried out per day. They are physically mailed to the investors. With the introduction of the new system, the investors will investors will instantly receive a legally valid contract note electronically. A report says that the new service is expected to save around Rs. 6 crores which were payable to the brokers.

23. See S. 19 of the Information Technology Act, 2000 which runs as under :

    19. Recognition of foreign Certifying Authorities.

    (1) Subject to such conditions and restrictions as may be specified by regulations, the Controller may with the previous approval of the Central Government, and by notification in the Official Gazette, recognise any foreign Certifying Authority as a Certifying Authority for the purposes of this Act.

    (2) Where any Certifying Authority is recognised under subsection (1), the Digital Signature Certificate issued by such Certifying Authority shall be valid for the purposes of this Act.

(3) The Controller may, if he is satisfied that any Certifying Authority has contravened any of the conditions and restrictions subject to which it was granted recognition under subsection (1) he may, for reasons to be recorded in writing, by notification in the Official Gazette, revoke such recognition.

24. See S. 20 of the Information Technology Act, 2000
25. Ibid.
26. Id. S. 68
27. Id. S. 30
28. Id. S. 21
29. Rule 4 of the Information Technology (Certifying Authority) Regulations, 2001 has prescribed the standards followed by the Certifying Authority for carrying out its functions.
30. See, S. 21 of the Information Technology Act, 2000.
31. Id. S. 23.
32. Id. S. 25.

☺☺☹

21

Emerging Spamming Threats

Laxmi Ahuja[1]

Spam is the abuse of electronic messaging systems (including most broadcast media, digital delivery systems) to send unsolicited bulk messages indiscriminately. While the most widely recognized form of spam is email spam, the term is applied to similar abuses in other media: instant messaging spam, Usenet newsgroup spam, Web search engine spam, spam in blogs, wiki spam, online classified ads spam, mobile phone messaging spam, Internet forum spam, junk fax transmissions, social networking spam, television advertising and file sharing network spam. Spamming remains economically viable because advertisers have no operating costs beyond the management of their mailing lists, and it is difficult to hold senders accountable for their mass mailings. Because the barrier to entry is so low, spammers are numerous, and the volume of unsolicited mail has become very high. The costs, such as lost productivity and fraud, are borne by the public and by Internet service providers, which have been forced to add extra capacity to cope with the deluge. Spamming is universally reviled, and has been the subject of legislation in many jurisdictions. Spamming is now considered to be a serious threat to the Internet and is posing a serious threat to both ISP and users' resource. Service providers are under mounting pressure to prevent, monitor and lessen spam attacks directed toward their customers and their infrastructure. The Internet is part of the serious national infrastructure. Attacks that are seen everyday on the Internet include direct attacks, remote reflective attacks, worms, and viruses. Emerging classes of messaging abuse in the mobile environment have led to neologisms like "SMishing," or SMS phishing. A SMiShing attack could introduce viruses or other malware to the network or add massive charges to corporate cell phone bills.

KEYWORDS   Spam | Virus | Blogs | Internet | Digital

21.1 INTRODUCTION

Attacks of all kinds have become much more complicated and harder to detect. The nature of computer attacks has changed over the past few years. Like

---

[1] Amity Institute of Information Technology, Amity University, Sec 125, Noida, Uttar Pradesh (UP)

early viruses that were often created by hackers whose sole interest was in gaining visibility within the hacker community, the new attacks are much more disturbing and have just the opposite visibility goals; they are usually motivated by the desire for money. The result is often fraud committed on thousands of unsuspecting users, commonly referred to as "crimeware". For example, capturing personal or company information without the knowledge or consent of the owner of the computer system can lead to catastrophic results for individuals, as well as for businesses, government entities, medical/healthcare organizations and educational institutions. Even the innocent act of playing a music CD on a computer can leave it open to attack. Spyware can accompany the music when it is automatically downloaded onto the hard drive, rendering the computer vulnerable to attack.

21.2 TYPES OF ATTACKS

The most common attacks are no longer simple (or even complex) viruses. Many forms of malware and other unwanted software programs are using complex combinations of attacks to spread—not simply relying on one method alone. The following are some of the major areas of vulnerability that could result in attacks.

- Operating system and software application vulnerabilities.
- Accepting downloads from unknown sources when visiting websites.
- Active-X, Java and scripts can either contain malicious code or download malicious code from various websites.
- Email files attachments.

21.2.1 Viruses

A computer virus is a computer program that can copy itself and infect a computer. The term "virus" is also commonly but erroneously used to refer to other types of malware, adware, and spyware programs that do not have the reproductive ability. A true virus can only spread from one computer to another (in some form of executable code) when its host is taken to the target computer; for instance because a user sent it over a network or the Internet, or carried it on a removable medium such as a floppy disk, CD, DVD, or USB drive. Viruses can increase their chances of spreading to other computers by infecting files on a network file system or a file system that is accessed by another computer.

As stated above, the term "computer virus" is sometimes used as a catch-all phrase to include all types of malware, adware, and spyware programs that do not have the reproductive ability. Malware includes computer viruses, worms, trojans, most rootkits, spyware, dishonest adware, crimeware, and other malicious and unwanted software, including true viruses. Viruses are sometimes confused with computer worms and Trojan horses, which are technically different. A worm can exploit security vulnerabilities to spread itself automatically to other computers through networks, while a Trojan is a program that appears harmless but hides malicious functions. Worms and Trojans, like viruses, may harm a computer system's data or performance. Some viruses and other malware have symptoms noticeable to the computer user, but many are surreptitious or simply do nothing to call attention to them. Some viruses do nothing beyond reproducing themselves.

There currently are five recognized types of viruses: File Infector Viruses, Boot Sector Viruses, Master Boot Record Viruses, MultiPartite Viruses and Macro Viruses.

21.2.2 Trojan Horses

Trojan Horses are impostors - files that claim to be something desirable but are, in fact, malicious. A very important distinction between Trojan horse programs and true viruses is that they do not replicate themselves. Trojans contain malicious code that when triggered cause loss, or even theft, of data. For a Trojan horse to spread, you must, "invite" it onto your computers. For example, you could open an email attachment or download and run a file from the Internet.

Trojan horses require interaction with a hacker to fulfill their purpose, though the hacker need not be the individual responsible for distributing the Trojan horse. In fact, it is possible for hackers to scan computers on a network using a port scanner in the hope of finding one with a Trojan horse installed, which the hacker can then use to control the target computer.

A trojan differs from a virus in that only a file specifically designed to carry it can do so.

Due to the growing popularity of botnets among hackers, Trojan horses are becoming more common. According to a survey conducted by BitDefender from January to June 2009, "Trojan-type malware is on the rise, accounting for 83-percent of the global malware detected in the world".

21.2.3 Worms

Worms are programs that replicate themselves from system to system without the use of a host file. This is in contrast to viruses, which require the spreading of an infected host file. Although worms generally exist inside of other files, often Word or Excel documents, there is a difference between how worms and viruses use the host file. Usually the worm will release a document that already has the "worm" macro inside of it. The entire document will travel from computer to computer. In other words, the entire document could be considered the worm. W32.Mydoom.AX@mm is an example of a worm. Worms spread by exploiting vulnerabilities in operating systems. All vendors supply regular security updates, and if these are installed to a machine then the majority of worms are unable to spread to it. If a vendor acknowledges vulnerability, but has yet to release a security update to patch it, a zero day exploit is possible. However, these are relatively rare. Users need to be wary of opening unexpected email, and should not run attached files or programs, or visit web sites that are linked to such emails. However, as with the ILOVEYOUworm, and with the increased growth and efficiency of phishing attacks, it remains possible to trick the end-user into running a malicious code.

21.2.4 Hoax

Virus hoaxes are messages, almost always sent through e-mail, that amount to little more than chain letters. One of my favorite phrases associated with virus hoaxes is, "Forward this warning to everyone you know!" Most hoaxes are sensational in nature and easily identified by the fact that they indicate that the virus will do nearly impossible things, like blow up the recipient's computer and set it on fire, or less sensationally, delete everything on the user's computer. They often include announcements claimed to be from reputable organizations such as Microsoft, IBM, or news sources such as CNN and include emotive language and encouragement to forward the message. These sources are quoted in order to add credibility to the hoax. Virus hoaxes are usually harmless and accomplish nothing more than annoying people who identify it as a hoax and waste the time of people who forward the message. Nevertheless, a number of hoaxes have warned users that vital system files are viruses and encourage the user to delete the file, possibly damaging the system. Examples of this type include thejdbgmgr. exe virus hoax and the SULFNBK.EXE hoax. Some consider virus hoaxes and other chain e-mails to be a computer worm in and of themselves. They replicate by social engineering—exploiting users' concern, ignorance, and disinclination to investigate before acting. Hoaxes are distinct from computer pranks, which are harmless programs that perform unwanted and annoying actions on a computer, such as randomly moving the mouse, turning the screen display upside down, etc.

21.2.5 Spam

Spam is not very different from the junk mail you've been getting at home or in the office for decades. Only now, the junk mail is coming through your e-mail accounts to your computers at home and in the office. Nonetheless, spam is by far worse than junk mail. The only real cost of eliminating junk mail is buying a larger recycling bin. Spam and Phishing, which we will discuss later, can actually cost you and your organizations time, money, and worst of all, the loss of data and confidential information. It can also create legal liability issues because of its content. If you talk to some end users they don't see much difference between Spam and the ordinary junk mail that mail carriers have delivered for years. They may say "all you have to do is hit delete". Obviously these people have never had hundreds of Spam messages hit their inbox in a very short period. Additionally they have never run a network or email gateway. The cost to corporations in bandwidth, delayed email, and employee productivity has become a tremendous problem for anyone who provides email services. Many customers think their Internet Service Provider (ISP) should be able to fix the problem. But Spam is a world-wide problem, and email systems around the world are not setup in a consistent manner.

21.2.6 Real-time Black-hole Lists (RBLs)

RBL's are lists on the Internet that track the IP addresses of machines recently known to be Spamming. Subscribers use these lists to check if a sender is a suspected Spammer and reject email from IP addresses on the list. Unfortunately there are several lists, and they don't all work the same. Some actually charge you to get off the list, and then others may block addresses of innocent users that are in the same IP range as a Spammer. Blacklists prevent millions of innocent e-mails from arriving at their destinations. Don't get me wrong. Blacklists mean well, and have been a helpful tool in helping curb Spam, however too many lists run differently sometimes creates a real problem for email administrators, ISP's, and legitimate users of email. But RBL's have also been very helpful in bringing awareness to the Spam problems, and have played an important part in helping curb issues. Hopefully someday the need for RBL's will be obsolete.

Typically the goal of Spam is to sell some product or service. Of course not all of these services are always good and proper, but then again some are. It would be nice if all Spam advertising could be tracked back to a store front like typical advertising, however Spammer's typically do not operate this way. Why, because if it were easily traced it would be easily stopped. Of course there is always the Spam that comes from "off-shore" where laws do not apply. But the majority of todays Spam comes from compromised end user machines. Think about it, if you could use the computer of some unsuspecting person to send out millions of emails to huge lists of people, your now using the resources of someone else's computer, and some service providers bandwidth to do your "dirty advertising" for free. Then if the recipient of the Spam complains, they are are never really reaching the actual Spam advertiser.

21.2.7 Phishing

Phishing, as the name implies, is when spam is used as a means to "fish" for the credentials necessary to access and manipulate financial accounts. Invariably, the e-mail will ask the recipient for an account number and the related password, explaining that records need updating or a security procedure is being changed that requires confirming an account. Unsuspecting email recipients that supply the information don't know it, but within hours or even minutes, unauthorized transactions will begin to appear their accounts.

By now, most people know that giving this information away on the Internet is a no-no. With Phishing, however, it's almost impossible to tell if the e-mail is a fraud. Like spam, emails from Phishers usually contain spoofed FROM or REPLY TO addresses that make the e-mail look as though it came from a legitimate company.

The RapidShare file sharing site has been targeted by phishing to obtain a premium account, which removes speed caps on downloads, auto-removal of uploads, waits on downloads, and cooldown times between downloads.

21.2.8 Defenses

The daily challenge for IT managers and administrators is to continue the freedom of computer users to access to the information they need, but at the same time, protecting all systems from malicious threats. This has been made more difficult by the growing complexity of threats, especially blended threats that combine Viruses and Spam. These new and emerging combined methods of propagation are, in some cases, taking advantage of the vulnerabilities of Operating Systems.

Wireline-to-wireless threats AND wireless-specific threats These two threat types are considered individually due to technical and economic reasons, which play key roles in how likely they are to proliferate in the wireless environment and what are the appropriate methods to stop them.

21.2.9 Wire line-to-wireless threats

Technology convergence has helped decrease the cost of devices and services that bridge traditional wireline services such as email and Web and wireless services such as SMS and WAP. Economic barriers, such as the relatively high cost of sending SMS from a handset, have kept the wireless space almost clear of the volume of messaging abuse seen by wireline networks. This barrier, however, has been lowered by the increasingly seamless interface between the two technologies. Email to SMS gateways enable any email user to send messages free of charge to mobile subscribers around the world. Since spammers are not penalized for sending SMS/text messages, this potentially opens up the possibility of low- profitability spam, like the "Viagra" spam, being an issue for mobile users. Email to SMS is a popular service that subscribers use to reach friends and page groups of users,so discontinuing or severely restricting this service is not a good option. Therefore, mobile operators need to protect their email to SMS gateways with the same type of filters and content analysis systems that large ISPs use to cover their email infrastructure. As mobile customers demand more features currently available only over the Internet, the economic constraints that restrict mobile messaging abuse will disappear, leaving mobile devices vulnerable to the same forms of messaging abuse as those terminating on laptops and computers. To make matters more complicated, email and other forms of communications are extending to new categories of devices beyond just mobile phones and PDAs. Internet connected devices ranging from television settop boxes to refrigerators are rapidly expanding the footprint of messaging-capable platforms. The latest wave of gaming consoles and portable entertainment devices also have Internet connectivity and messaging capabilities, which raises additional concerns about inappropriate content reaching minors who are the majority of users of these devices. While the incidence of abuse on these platforms is still unknown, the sheer number of these devices together with the affinity of the users makes these platforms compelling targets for spammers

21.2.10 Wireless-specific Threats

Wireless-specific messaging threats will be similar to those pioneered in the wireline domain, but will diverge due to specific economic factors. Asia has consistently led the way in mobile content and usage trends, and events there may be indicative of what's to come in other developed mobile markets such as the U.S. and Europe. In Japan and South Korea, where the cost of sending SMS is around a penny, the rate of mobile spam is almost on par with email spam. On 2 Japan's NTT DoCoMo's network, 9 out of 10 messages are spam. In South Korea, subscribers receive on average one spam per day on their mobile phone. Until the per message cost associated with sending SMS drops in the U.S. and Europe, users there will likely see short codes and narrowly-targeted announcements instead of URL s and large broadcast mailings that are prevalent in wireline networks. For example, a user may receive a spam SMS enticing him to sign up for a text service using a short code that is tied in with the mobile operator's billing system or he may be tricked into calling a premium rate number. The ease in setting up premium rate phone numbers makes this type of fraud particularly appealing to scam artists. These "false pretext" messages have a direct and immediate monetary impact on subscribers, leading to high customer dissatisfaction.

To be concluded we can say that In the past, threats have often been managed using separate threat management components, such as antivirus, anti-spyware, etc. Recent attacks have involved combinations of different kinds of malware, limiting the effectiveness of separate components designed to combat only a single type of attack. A more effective approach is an integrated threat management solution that provides centralized management of all antithreat capabilities. Cloudmark's flexible; content-agnostic solution is uniquely able to combat mobile spam, phishing and viruses that originate from mobile devices or the Internet. Cloudmark can be implemented to stop messaging abuse at the network's edge, thus ensuring that spectrum, network resources and service quality are not impacted. For mobile operators, Cloudmark's comprehensive messaging security leadership translates into lower subscriber churn and support, as well as loyal subscribers who can confidently adopt innovative services.

References

1. http://www.techzoom.net/publications /insecu rity-iceberg/
2. http://ca.com/Files/WhitePapers/ca_t hreat_management_wp.pdf
3. http://www.purewire.com/purewire_w eb_security_service.php
4. http://www.techzoom.net/publications /insecurity-iceberg/
5. http://www.allspammedup.com/anti- spam/knowi ng-the-th reats-of-spam/
6. http://www.cloudmark.com/releasesZd   ocs/wp_taxonomy_of_mobile_threats _2009-05.pdf

☺☹☹

22

Software Quality Assurance

Prashant Gupta[1]

Software Development involves a series of activities which are prone to errors. These errors may occur at an early stage of the development process when user requirements are incorrectly or incompletely defined, and also at later stages when design and programming faults are introduced. To overcome such errors, software development should always be accompanied by Quality Assurance (QA) activities. Requirements inspection and software testing are the two most important quality assurance activities. These activities are often used in different phases of the software development life cycle (SDLC).

KEYWORDS   SQA | Software | QA | SDLC | Quality

22.1 INTRODUCTION

The incorrectness, ambiguity, hidden & missing functionalities and errors in requirement specification documents reflect in multifold as the system development progresses and worst results can be observed when system is fully operational. Thousands of software bugs and failures are reported worldwide due to theses minor or major defects.

Software Development involves a series of activities which are prone to errors. These errors may occur at an early stage of the development process when user requirements are incorrectly or incompletely defined, and also at later stages when design and programming faults are introduced. To overcome such errors, software development should always be accompanied by Quality Assurance (QA) activities. Requirements inspection and software testing are the two most important quality assurance activities. These activities are often used in different phases of the software development life cycle (SDLC).

The formal requirements inspection is carried at an initial stage of SDLC to find defects, problems and see what's missing mostly in specification documents and also help in deciding test plans, test cases etc. It is one of the most cost effective methods to ensure Software Quality. On the other hand,

---

[1] Sr. Programmer, DOEACC Society Chandigarh Centre, Chandigarh, India

testing is usually done at a later stage of SDLC to check for program faults after coding. As the purpose of requirement inspection and testing is different so these are treated as "separate" and "unrelated" tasks by software developers.

One of the most reliable methods of ensuring problems, or failure, in software project is to have properly documented requirements specification document. Requirements are the details describing an application's externally-perceived functionality and properties. Requirements should be clear, complete, detailed, cohesive, attainable, and testable.

It has been now proposed after lots of researches to apply through review and testing techniques to requirements specification at an initial phase of the SDLC. The idea is to uncover requirements defects well before programming starts. Thus, the possibility of inadvertently developing software based on an incorrect specification can be reduced or avoided.

The benefits of such proposals are excellent for small projects as they can fix almost every possible cause of error as well as for large-scale projects where the specifications are complicated and may easily contain many requirements defects, and the costs of repairing these defects at later stages of the SDLC are typically tens or hundreds of times greater than if the defects are corrected early.

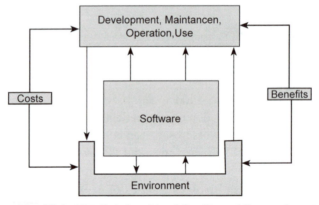

Fig. 22.1 The Relationship of Quality and Economics

Also, it has been observed that a large amount of unexplained variance in the data indicating that other factors must be affecting inspection performance. The nature and extent of these other factors now have to be determined and identified to improve the efficiency of inspections & quality of the software. The hypotheses that the "inputs" into the inspection process (reviewers, authors, and code units) were significant sources of variation **[Adam, 1996]**.

Above discussions underline a direct impact on the Cost, Quality and Reliability and directly affect the time schedule and budget of the overall system. There is clearly a relationship and a need to manage cost, quality and reliability in combination. Moreover, economics should be the basis of any analysis **[Wagner, 2007]**. To support this proposal various concepts are defined in this chapter to apply inspections to requirement specifications, keeping the motive to improve the quality of the specification before software design commences for Quality Assurance.

Let's have an outline of the basic concepts of requirements specification and testing.

22.2 REQUIREMENTS SPECIFICATION

A requirements specification is an important document produced at the initial stage of SDLC. It defines the functionality, scope, and constraints of the software. It also serves as a basis for contracts as well as communication between the software developer and the user. The importance of the specification cannot be over-emphasized. If the development is based on an incomplete and incorrect specification, then even with well written code, the software will still be unsatisfactory and unable to fulfill user requirements. In addition, defects in a vague specification will be propagated to subsequent phases of the SDLC. At best, developers will eventually catch these defects, but at the expense of schedule delays and additional costs. At worst, the defects will remain undetected, resulting in the delivery of a faulty software system to users.

[Fagani, 1986] of IBM is credited with introducing the use of inspections in software development. Although many programmers use informal peer reviews of their code, Fagan made formal inspection an integral part of the development process, for locating defects in code or in other documentation such as requirements specifications and designs. Inspections are team activities; the basic idea is to formally inspect the item by one or more reviewers, typical in a meeting after individual preparations. Other members in the inspection team include the producer of the item to be inspected and a moderator who facilitates the inspection process. Various forms of inspections are now adopted in the software industry. The cost-effectiveness of inspections in revealing defects has been extensively reported. For example, Doolan observed a 30-fold return on investment for every hour spent on inspecting specifications. Russell also reported a similar return of 33 hours of software maintenance saved for every hour of inspection. **[Chen et al, 2006]**

A common practice to do software inspection is to use a checklist, which provides reviewers with a list of items to check. However, well written checklists are not generally available. In addition, most checklists do not help reviewers to focus on particular aspects of a specification, implicitly treating all the information in the specification as equally important. As a result, reviewers are left with an ill-defined responsibility of detecting all defects in the entire specification.

22.3 SOFTWARE TESTING

Testing is commonly regarded as a predominant software quality assurance activity. It is a major means to detect software faults and to prevent them from propagating through to the final production system, where the cost of defect removal is far greater. Unlike inspections, testing can evaluate how well a software system actually performs its function in its intended or simulated environment. Statistics have shown that the cost and time spent on testing in software development projects are significant. There are various forms of testing for discovering different types of faults and effects in software. For instance, testing may be done by the end-user to evaluate the usability or human-interaction issues of the software. Also, performance testing is often done to assess the behavior of software under special usage scenarios such as when the system is under heavy stress of data loading.

Typically, testing consists of a series of tasks, namely: (a) defining testing objectives (b) designing and generating test cases (c) executing the software with the generated test cases and (d) analyzing the result by comparing the actual and the expected outputs. In particular, task (b) will significantly affect the scope of testing and, hence, the chance of detecting software faults.

Two main approaches for test case generation exist: white-box and black-box. The white-box approach generates test cases according to the information derived from the source code of the software under test. Examples are control flow testing and data flow testing. The black-box approach, on the other hand, generates test cases from information derived from the specification, without requiring the knowledge of the internal structure of the software. Nevertheless, neither the white-box nor the black-box approach is sufficient; they complement each other.

The white-box and black-box approaches are general and applicable across all environments, architectures, and applications, but unique guidelines and approaches to testing are sometimes warranted, such as when testing graphical user interfaces (GUIs), client/server architectures, and real-time systems. Also, although our discussions below focus on the techniques for functional correctness testing, other testing techniques may in principle also be applied. Pressman has given more details of techniques for other forms of testing, such as usability and performance testing.

22.4 FAULT DETECTION IN REQUIREMENTS SPECIFICATION

The initial stage of the software development process involves a thorough and careful review of the Requirements specification document. Requirements specification document contains the description of the functionality and performance characteristics of the proposed software product, and it serves as a contractual agreement between user and developer. A complete and accurate Requirements specification document is essential to the success of any project and key for quality assurance. As omissions, inconsistencies, ambiguities, or contradictions not discovered during the initial investigation will propagate through the SDLC and can result in either an improperly functioning system or an expensive and timeconsuming redesign. Detection and correction of faults at early stage in the Requirements specification document is the key to keeping development costs down and to building correct, reliable software. According to **[Boehm, 1987],** and many other researchers,

"Finding and fixing a software problem after delivery is 100 times more expensive than finding and fixing it during the requirements and early design phases." Famous software engineering book author Fairley said that,

"it is 5 times more costly to correct a fault at the design stage than during initial requirements, 10 times more costly to correct it during coding, 20 to 50 times more costly to correct it at acceptance testing and 100 to 200 times more costly to correct that problem during actual operation."

Based on these observations, it is easy to see why it is so important to identify the maximum number of faults in the Requirements specification document. This would definitely reduce the time needed to complete the system and lower the overall cost of the final software.

22.5 TECHNIQUES USED IN INSPECTING REQUIREMENTS

A large number of formal and informal techniques have been developed to aid both the avoidance and detection of requirements faults. These types of error avoidance systems attempt to minimize the faults getting into a requirements document. Irrespective of the techniques opted i.e. formal or informal, faults can still occur, and need to utilize more error detection techniques to locate and remove faults present in the completed requirements specification document. This technique depends on the project, cost factor, team size, client's specifications and many more other factors. Some of these techniques, possible types of errors and factors effecting the inspection are discussed here to support the paper.

22.5.1 Formal Walkthroughs

The most popular technique for validating Requirements specification document remains the relatively simple and straightforward method of formal inspections. Formal inspections, also called Structured Walkthroughs, are a manual review of a requirements document in a group setting using formal review procedures **[Boehm, 1987]**.

This inspection includes:

- ↵ A well-defined team structure with each team member having an assigned role;
- ↵ A checklist specifying what each team member must do to prepare for the inspection process;
- ↵ A formal agenda specifying how the inspection will be carried out; and
- ↵ A procedure for reviewing the results and conclusions reached by the inspection team. Inspections are an easy method to understand and implement; its supporters claim that Inspection is a highly effective method of fault detection. Fagan and many other researchers discussed a lot on the formal inspection & review process. According to **[Boehm, 1987]**,

"The structured walkthrough (software inspection) has been the most cost effective technique to date for eliminating software errors. Walkthroughs catch 60 percent of these errors."

Formal inspection techniques have most commonly been used for design and code reviews; they can also be applied to the validation of user requirements documents.

22.5.2 The N-fold Inspection Method

N-fold inspection method is a revised new approach to the formal inspection of user requirements documents, called N-fold inspection. In this technique, the formal inspection process described in the previous section is replicated in parallel using N independent teams along with a single "moderator" who is responsible for coordinating and merging their efforts **[Michael, 1992]**.

The N-fold inspection method is based on the hypothesis that the N separate inspection teams finds a significant number of Requirements specification faults not located by other teams. If this hypothesis is true, then the total number of faults detected by all N teams will be much higher than the number found by any one team during a single review. Furthermore, a parallel replication of inspections is preferred over sequential replications because of the potentially large time delay caused by carrying out N formal inspections, one after the other **[Michael, 1992]**.

The average number of Requirements specification document's faults found by any one team was about 25-27%, the total number of faults found after 5 parallel replications was about 65%, and after 10 replications it was about 80%— a three fold improvement 27% to over 80%). In fact, the replication of the inspection process with only one additional team (i.e., N=2) raised the fault detection rate from 27% to about 39%. So, it could be worthwhile to invest that much time if the Requirements specification document fault-detection rate increased from 25-30% to 60-80%. [[**Michael, 1992**].

Furthermore, the data gathered thru N-fold Inspection technique could be used to answer additional questions about the requirements analysis phase of the software life cycle: specifically,

—how successful is the traditional single-team inspection at locating Requirements specification document errors?

—how much variability is there between inspection teams in locating Requirements specification document errors?

—are certain types of Requirements specification document faults inherently more difficult to find than others?

Faults commonly occurred have with the following characteristics:

—they reflect fault types that commonly occur in Requirements specification documents;

—they include faults selected from those located during the initial screening process, as well as some which we created to provide a balance of fault types; and

—they are all serious errors, which the reviewers unanimously agreed could, if not corrected, lead to later design and/or implementation problems.

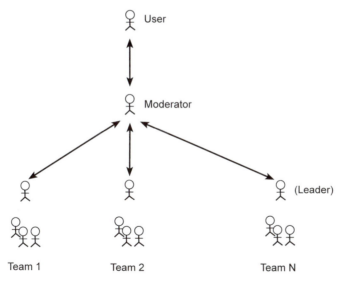

Management structure of the N-fold Inspection Process

The screening operation resulted in a user requirement document containing a known number of faults of specific types to be resolved at later stages of SDLC.

22.6 THE PERSPECTIVE-BASED READING METHOD

Basili **[Shull, 2000]** have developed a technique known as perspective-based reading (PBR), which operates under the premise that different information in a specification has different levels of importance for different uses of the document. More specifically, PBR focuses on the point of view of the people who will make use of the specifications. One reviewer may read from the perspective of the software designer, another from the perspective of the software tester, and yet another from the perspective of the end user of the software. Each of these reviewers then produces a model that can be analyzed to answer questions based on the perspective. For example, Reviewer 1 reading from the designer's perspective would consider questions related to high-level design. Similarly, Reviewer 2 reading from the tester's perspective would consider questions arising from activities related to test case generation, and Reviewer 3 representing the end user would consider questions related to the completeness and correctness of the requirements with regard to system functionality. The premise is that these perspectives together will provide a more comprehensive coverage of the specification. As each reviewer is responsible for a relatively narrowly focused view of the specification, the reading should lead to more in-depth analysis of any potential defects in the specification.

22.7 FAULTS TYPES

There are two types of faults found in the user requirements document:

> Type 1 = Faults: These are caused as necessary and critical information missing in the Requirements specification document. These are called Missing Information faults.
> Type 2 = Faults: These are caused by the inclusion of incorrect, inconsistent, or ambiguous information in the requirements specification document. These are called Wrong Information faults.

These are further classified into six specific subtypes.

Type 1 Faults- Missing Information

- Missing Functionality or Missing Feature (MF): Information describing the desired internal operational behavior of the system has been omitted from the requirements specification document.
- Missing Interface (MI): Information describing how the proposed system will interface and communicate with objects outside the scope of the system has been omitted from the requirements specification document.
- Missing Performance (MP): Information describing the desired performance specifications has either been omitted or described in a way that is unacceptable for acceptance testing.

⌐ Missing Environment (ME): Information describing the required hardware/ software/ database/ personnel environment in which the proposed system will run has been omitted from the requirements specification document.

Type 2 Faults- Wrong Information

⌐ Ambiguous Information (WA): An important term, phrase, or sentence essential to an understanding of system behavior has either been left undefined or defined in a way that can cause confusion and misunderstanding.

⌐ Inconsistent Information (WI): Two sentences contained in the requirements specification document directly contradict each other or express actions that cannot both be correct or cannot both be carried out.

Martin **[Michael, 1992].** explained some examples of fault types in user requirements documents of Centralized Traffic Control (CTC) System of North American Railway.

Case (a)

Text: In the case of two oncoming trains, each of which has access to a siding of adequate length, the slower one is to be routed onto the siding while the faster one continues on the main track.

Error: There is no information about what to do if the two trains are moving at exactly the same speed as measured by the wayside location.

Fault Type: WI, inconsistent information

Case (b)

Text: Each wayside location is to be identified by a unique unsigned three-digit integer. wayside location number 2288 must inform control that . .

Error: This 4 digit number is inconsistent with the earlier statement that wayside locations are identified by unique 3-digit values.

Fault Type: WI, inconsistent information

Case (c)

Text: Each wayside location is periodically asked to report the current status of its devices. A polling timeout failure occurs when a location fails to respond to this status request.

Error: There is no information about how often the polling should be done or how long the central system should wait before it decides that there has been a polling timeout failure.

Case (d)

Text: All CTC device command messages transmit two 8-bit bytes. The meaning of the 16 bits of information received from the wayside computer is as follows: byte 0, bit 0 1 when this track section is occupied 0 otherwise, byte 0, bit 1 ...

> Error: There is no clarification, either via text or picture, whether the bits and bytes of the Control devices command message are numbered from left to right or from right to left.

Fault Type: MP, missing performance information.

The following table summarizes the number of faults from each of these six fault classes that were placed in the completed requirement Specification. [Michael, 1992]

Fault Type	Abbreviation	Number Included
Class 1. Missing Information		
Missing Functionality	MF	34
Missing Interface	MI	11
Missing Performance MP	MP	7
Missing Environmental	ME	9
Total Number of Class 1 Errors		61
Class 2. Wrong Information		
Ambiguous Information	WA	15
Inconsistent Information	WI 23	
Total Number of Class 2 Errors		38
Total Number of Errors Present In Requirement Specification		99

22.7.1 Other Case: e.g. Correlation

According to Law's of Correlation, there are four conditions that must be satisfied before factor A can be said to cause response B:

1. A must occur before B.
2. A and B must be correlated.
3. There is no other factor C that accounts for the correlation between A and B.
4. A mechanism exists that explains how A affects B.

22.8 FACTORS AFFECTING INSPECTIONS

According to Porter, there are several other factors which affect reviewer and author performance and code unit quality that might systematically influence the outcome of the inspection. And for accurate inspections resulting in correct and defined requirements specification documents we must take care of these factors.

22.8.1 Code Unit Factors

Some of the possible variables affecting the number of defects in the code unit include size, author, time period when it was written, and functionality.

Code Size: The size of a code unit is given in terms of non commentary source lines. It is natural to think that as the size of the code increases, the more defects it will contain.

Author: The author of the code may inadvertently inject defects into the code unit. The number of defects could depend on the author's level of understanding and implementation experience.

Development Phase: The performance of the reviewers and the number of defects in the code unit at the time of inspection might well depend also on the state of the project when the inspection was held. There can be a number of defects which may be found over time of system development. A large number of issues are raised at every step but the total number of issues did not. This might indicate that either the reviewers' defect detection performance was weakening in time, or the authors were learning to prevent the true defects but not the other kinds of issues being raised.

Functionality: Functionality refers to the compiler component to which the code unit belongs, e.g., parser, symbol table, code generator, etc. Some functionality may be more straightforward to implement than others and, hence, will have code units with lower number of defects.

Pre-inspection Testing: The code development process employed by the developers allows them to perform some unit testing before the inspection. Performing unit testing before the inspection would remove some of the defects prior to the inspection.

22.8.2 Reviewer Factors

It is a fact that different reviewers affect the number of defects detected. But it is important to look at effect on the number of defects found in preparation, because the effect as a group is different in the collection meeting's setting.

Reviewer: Reviewers differ in their ability to detect defects. Some reviewers find more defects than others. Even for the same code unit, different reviewers may find different numbers of defects. This may be because they were looking for different kinds of issues and their view point may vary.

Preparation Time: The amount of preparation time is a measure of the amount of effort the reviewer put into studying the code unit. Even if preparation time is found to be a significant contributor, it must be noted that preparation time depends not only on the amount of effort the reviewer is planning to put into the preparation, but also on factors related to the code unit itself. In particular, it is influenced by the number of defects existing in the code, i.e., the more defects he finds, the more time he spends in preparation. Hence, high preparation time may be considered a consequence, as well as a cause, of detecting a large number of defects.

22.8.3 Team Factors

Team-specific variables also add to the variance in the number of meeting gains.

Team Composition: Since different reviewers have different abilities and experiences, and possibly interact differently with each other, different teams also differ in combined abilities and experiences. Apparently, this mix tended to form teams with nearly the same performance. Most of the time, the two teams found nearly the same number of defects. This may be due to the mutual interactions among the team members. However, because teams are formed randomly, there are only a few instances where teams composed of the same people were formed more than once, not enough to study the interactions.

Meeting Duration: The meeting duration is the number of hours spent in the meeting. In the meeting, one person is appointed the reader, and he or she reads out the code unit, paraphrasing each chunk of code and centering the meeting. At any time, reviewers may raise issues related to the particular chunk being read, and a discussion may arise. All these contribute toward the pace of the meeting. The meeting duration is positively correlated with the number of meeting gains. As with the case of preparation time, the meeting duration is partly dependent on the number of defects found, as detection of more defects may trigger more discussions, thus lengthening the duration.

Combined Number of Defects Found in Preparation: The number of defects found prior to going into the meeting may also affect the number of defects found at the meeting. Each reviewer gets a chance to raise each issue he or she found in preparation as a point of discussion, possibly resulting in the detection of more defects.

22.9 SOME OTHER FACTORS IN REQUIREMENTS INSPECTION

As discussed, inspection and review should cover the functional and non-functional aspects of software. Most of the aspects are related to the functional aspect of software, it is also proposed to apply through review of requirements specification is also applicable to the non-functional aspect of software, such as performance, security, reliability, and recovery. The evaluation of "non-functional" quality of software is important, because the software must be functionally correct in order for it to serve its designated purpose and be accepted by the acquirer.

Take performance testing as an example. Many software systems have specific performance or efficiency requirements, normally stated in terms of system's response times and throughput rates under certain workload and configuration conditions. A major purpose of performance testing is to assess how the system runs under peak and continuous loads.

Obviously, an important prerequisite for performance testing is to include the relevant software performance or efficiency requirements in the specification in a precise manner. Otherwise, the software tester will have no basis to conclude whether the actual software performance meets user's expectation. Hence, reviewer will naturally ask the following questions when inspecting the specification from the perspective of system performance:

- Are all expected processing times specified?
- Is all data transfer rates specified?
- Is the required level of system performance clearly specified for all different usage scenarios?
- Are all system throughput rates specified?

Now, consider reliability testing, which is another type of non-functional testing. In today's competitive environment, every software system is expected to be reliable. In particular, ultra-high reliability is expected for "safety critical systems" such as those used in nuclear plants, weapon systems, aviation equipment, and medical devices. When software testers inspect the specification from the perspective of reliability testing, they will naturally ask the following questions:

- Is the expected bound for the mean time between failures or a similar metric specified?
- Are the consequences of software failure specified for each requirement?
- How will the system be expected to behave under exceptional or adverse input conditions?
- Does the specification contain enough information to determine how the reliability testing should be performed?
- Is a strategy for error detection specified?
- Is a strategy for error correction specified?

In short, when software testers & reviews inspect the specification from a specific testing perspective, such as functional testing, performance testing, and reliability testing, this inspection approach will automatically provide some clues to the testers as to which types of information in the specification should be focused during the review process. In this way, potential defects in the specification will have a higher chance of being spotted **[Chen Et Al, 2006]**.

The quality of a requirements specification is of vital importance because it critically affects the quality of the resultant software system. In the field of software engineering, requirements inspection and analysis is one of the most important stages of SDLC with regards to developing reliable, robust, and cost- effective software. Faults caught during requirements analysis take the least time and effort to correct, whereas those remains in the requirements specification propagate to downstream phases of the SDLC can have serious consequences for the finished product. Thus, the specification should be inspected for errors at an early stage of the SDLC before it is used for software design so that the development work will not be based on an incorrect specification. The requirement specification inspection is a simple, effective, and least expensive way of detecting and removing defects from requirement documents. The primary fault-detection technique used during requirements analysis has been formal inspection.

This paper discusses the importance of formal inspection and reviews of the requirements specification. Also, various types of errors (faults) and their possible causes and their after affects are briefly explained. Still 20-25 % of the faults present in the specification remain undetected and these faults need to be located during the design, implementation, or testing stages using additional formal reviews & tests. A thorough inspection also helps in deciding the test plans and cases to be used in different software testing at later stages.

The surveys reported in this chapter have shown that formal inspections to requirements specification by a single independent development team is only able to detect about 35% of the faults present while multiple teams can give 60-80% of fault detection. This could have a significant impact on overall software reliability, robustness, and cost & of course the software quality. There are many factors which affects the inspection process, and if these factors are properly administered the result of the inspection may be much higher than our expectations. The overall focus is on to the Quality, Reliability and Cost. These fundamental concepts in software development are closely related. A thorough management of one of these implies the consideration of the other factor. There are several problems in research and practice today that hamper the modeling and evaluation of these relations [Wegner, 2007]. In summary, this paper conveys three important messages to the software community:

- Requirements inspection is important and has to be done as earlier as possible in the SDLC,
- Requirements inspection is more effective when performed with the support of a systematic approach to improve the defect-finding capabilities of inspections, and
- Correct inspection will be very helpful in terms of cost, schedule, reliability and quality with minimum possible efforts.

References

1. Fagan, M.E. *"Advances in Software Inspections"* IEEE Transactions on Software Engineering. Vol. SE-12, no. 7, 1986, pp. 744-751.

2. Boehm, B., "Industrial software metrics: top ten list", IEEE Software, Sept 1987.

3. Michael Schneider, Johnny Martin, W. T. Tsai, "An Experimental Study of Fault Detection In User Requirements Documents", ACM Transactions on Software Engineering and Methodology, Vol 1, No 2, Apr 1992, page 188-204.

4. Shull, F., Rus, I., and Basili, V. "How Perspective-Based Reading Can Improve Requirements Inspections." IEEE Computer. Vol. 33, no. 7, 2000, pp. 73-79.

5. Chen T.Y., Poon P.L., and Tang S.F., Tse T. H., Yu Y. T., "Applying Testing to Requirements Inspection for Software Quality Assurance", To appear in Information Systems Control Journal 6, 2006.

6. Adam Porter , Harvey Siy, Audris Mockus & Lawrence Votta, "Understanding the Sources of Variation in Software Inspections", ACM Transactions on Software Engineering and Methodology, Vol. 7, No. 1, January 1998, Pages 41—79.

7. Stefan Wagner, "Using Economics as Basis for Modeling and Evaluating Software Quality", 29th International Conference on Software Engineering Workshops (ICSEW'07), IEEE 2007.

☺☺☹

Privacy Policies of E-Commerce and BPO

Abha Chandra[1], Vinita Sharma[2], Ponnurangam Kumaraguru[3]
and Subodh Kesharwani[4]

(Privacy preserved e-society consists of three intangible factors firstfy applications, which have data to share with authorized chients; secondly clients who wants data that contains in the applications and finally the privacy control factor which is required to maintain records about the purposes. In a xvorld of virtually countless database capability, security breaches have the possibility to liberate millions of records into the hands of hackers or mischiefs. (People now a day are more concerned about their personal information, which is supposed to be leaded out from the organizations to which they are trading online, dhere are many global and indigenous organizations, which conducts trading xvith Indian group through Internet. 'The significant point to be noted xvith respect to these organizations is to male their personal and financial information totally secure so that no unauthorized person or organization should acquire their data to mistreat over the Internet. Jin empirical study is conducted to evaluate the existence and format of privacy policies of diverse organizations xvith relevance to India in conducting online business through their websites. (The endeavor of this paper is to throw more light on the study, methodology, modus operandi and its results.

KEYWORDS   E-Commerce | BPO | Privacy Policy | World Wide Web | Cookies | Data | B2B | B2C

23.1 INTRODUCTION

Commerce offers the prospect to abridge commerce through supplier rationalization, transaction competence and contract fulfillment. E-Commerce means integration which is a key division of any integration plan involves balancing the natural desire to maximize the use of existing system resources with the need to provide a robust and compelling sales system. An e-commerce system should robust into a company's IT environment.

---

[1] Department of Statistics, Meerut
[2] Department of Computer Science, New Delhi Institute of Management, New Delhi
[3] School of Computer Science, Carnegie Mellon University, Pittsburgh
[4] School of Management Studies, Indira Gandhi National Open University, New Delhi,

Business Process Outsourcing (BPO) can be elucidate as the reassignment of an organizations' entire non-core but critical business process/function to an exterior vendor who uses an IT-based service delivery and facilitates an organization to contemplate on its core competencies, develop efficiency, reduce cost and progress shareholders' value. As much as achievable, it is platform- neutral to sustain the technology our customers use, including .NET and J2EE. The E-commerce also balances the utilization of real-time and batch-mode data transfers from ERP and back-end systems to the e-commerce. ERP is the biggest integration and new-fangled application software, which is a key enabler of business, process transformation and IT automation.

23.2 WHAT IS PRIVACY POLICY

Privacy is defined as a state or condition of limited access to a person. Privacy Policy describes the practices and policies followed by E-Commerce. Privacy Policy represents the way of collecting data, what is the purpose of utilization of data, whether the enterprise provides access to the data, who are the data recipients (beyond the enterprise), how long the data will be retained, and who will be informed in what cases. In simple words, Privacy Policy is the document which is supposed to be attached or linked with the website while collecting the personal or non-personal or both the information of the user of that site at that juncture. The major points that a privacy policy generally has may be listed down as follows:

- Presence of Privacy Seal in the document.
- Type of data that is collected from the user.
- How the data is collected from the user i.e. using sources of the website, the data is collected.
- Use of the data collected.
- Use of cookies.
- Data collected is shared with the third parties or not.
- Use of web beacons or links of third parties on the website.
- Security techniques used to make the user's data secure.
- Children's privacy.
- P3P Reference File and Privacy Policy.

23.3 WHAT WE ARE GOING TO STUDY

In this chapter, we will first study the privacy policies of different Indian B2B, B2C and BPO companies, which are members of NASSCOM (National Association of Software and Services Companies), the Indian chamber of commerce that serves as an interface to the software industry.

23.4 METHODOLOGY

To precede this research work, we collected the list of Indian E-Commerce Organisation's websites from NASSCOM. This long list of websites was then checked whether they included privacy policies or not and what privacy protections were offered to the customers in those privacy policies. After that the present policies were analysed with respect to their format, content and characteristics on the basis of a self-made questionnaire.

23.4.1 Data

A list of 1094 different E-Commerce companies, containing their website addresses (URLs), was collected from NASSCOM.

Out of these organisations, 785 are of B2B type, 43 of B2C type and 53 are of BPO. Also there are 80 companies which provide B2B & B2C services both, 65 companies which provide B2B & BPO services both and 6 companies which provide B2C & BPO services both to the corresponding organisations.

We prepared a Questionnaire which helped us to analyse different Privacy Policies of different domains. There are 36 different questions_related to the following topics-

- ◁ Existence of Privacy Policy in an E-Commerce web site.
- ◁ Type of the web sites.
- ◁ Personal and non-personal information taken from the web sites from the customers.
- ◁ Data sharing and selling to the third party.
- ◁ Options/Choices given by the web sites to the customers related to their personal information.
- ◁ Security
- ◁ Cookies
- ◁ Children under the age of 13 years
- ◁ P3P Reference File, P3P Privacy Policy

23.5 ANALYSIS

In this section, we analyse that how many privacy policies exist among the list of websites of the organisations given by NASSCOM.

Only 94% websites are accessible out of the list of organisations and out of them only 37% have privacy policy. Amongst these organisations -

- ◁ 72% are of B2B type
- ◁ 5% are of BPO
- ◁ 4% are of B2C type
- ◁ 7% organisations provide both B2B and B2C services

  ⮞ 6% organisations provide both B2B and BPO services
  ⮞ 6% organisations provide both BPO and B2C services. (Tables 23.1 and 23.2)

The analysis shows that the organisations providing B2B services have posted maximum number of privacy policies on their websites.

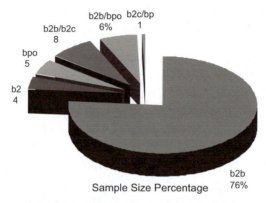

Fig. 23.1 Existence of Privacy Policies

Only about 37% organisations have posted privacy policies on their websites. Table 23.3 provides the information of existence of the privacy policies. Also, 5% websites' URL out of the total list was inaccessible. (Table 23.3).

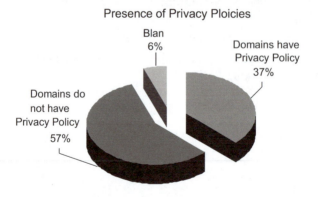

Fig. 23.2 Shortcomings of Privacy Policies posted on websites

Amongst all, we found that 6% organisations (12 pairs) have either same copy of policies or same formats of the policies. (See Table 23.4).

It is observed that in case of about 7% websites of the organisations, there is an inactive link for privacy policy on their home page (See Table 23.5).

Out of all, 4 organisations have very long Privacy Policies (See Table 23.7) whereas 6% privacy policies are exceptionally small and most of them do not include minimum number of points which are required to make a privacy policy (See Table 23.6). eFunds International Private Limited has two different types of privacy policies: Data Privacy and Internet Privacy. (See Table 23.7)

The website of "Sella Synergy India Ltd," has Non-English privacy policy, hence, not understandable by the most of the people. (See Table 23.8)

Privacy Policy of **Hewlett Packard Consumer Support Delivery** (A Div. of Global e-Business Op. P Ltd) seems to be one of the perfect policies which includes moderate number of points and easy to understand. (Table 23.8)

Web site of "Juno Online Services Development Pvt. Ltd." is very lengthy. The statements in the policy should be written in a manner so that the user can grasp the theme quickly. (Table 23.8).

23.5.1 Privacy Statements' Analysis

In this section we analysed different types of statements and points that privacy policies include generally. Some points give positive and some negative feeling to the user towards the safety of their personal information.

First of all we analysed that there is no differentiation of the Personally Identifiable Information (Name, Address, I email id etc) and Non Personal Identifying Information (IP address) in almost all the privacy policies which makes the user confused as many users are not aware of the technical terms like IP address, cookies etc.

The presence of Privacy Seal in privacy policy makes the users more certain for the safety of their personal information but we found that only 5% organisations' policies have privacy seal in it (Table 23.9).

As mentioned earlier, cookies play an important role in loosing the privacy of the user. It is better if the user is told the function of cookies and what personal information can be disclosed through it in the privacy policy posted on the website. We analysed that 67% Privacy Policies declare (only) that the organisations' websites place a cookie to track the users. Most of the privacy policies indicate the presence of cookies to the user, without explaining what specific personal information may be disclosed through them. (Table 23.10).

Almost every business website has "Career" section in it through which it is collecting Resume from the users. Hence, they should also post privacy policy as the resume gives personal and non-personal information of the user.

But we analysed that only 7% such Privacy Policies mention that their website collects Resume and also gives reasons for collection. (Table 23.11).

We also observed this fact that about 19% such organisations collect Personal Information from the users which even do not have privacy policy posted on their website. So, it is much sure that the personal information of the user is unsafe in the database of such organisations (Table 23.12).

Privacy Policies of 66% domains declare that they disclose personal information to the third parties (See Table 23.13). The user is unaware of those third parties in most of the cases and is unable to access their privacy policies which makes him/her feel more unsafe.

Privacy Policies of 22% domains declare that they provide security to the personal data of the users, out of which 7% provide security "During Transmission" (e.g. using SSL) and 97% provide security to the personal data "After

Collection" (See Table 23.14). When the user finds such statements in any privacy policy, he / she may feel relaxed.

One more point of relaxation for the user is that few privacy policies have mentioned that their websites do not collect personal information from the children under 13 years of age without their parent's approval. But only 21% such privacy policies exist which do not register/market/sell products to the children under 13 years of age (Table 23.15).

23.6 DISCUSSION

This paper has shown that only 37% of the organisations have posted their privacy policies on their web sites. However, as privacy policies are becoming increasingly expected on commercial web sites around the world, Indian organisations are beginning to post those Also, the organisations which had privacy policies posted did not express completely the necessary information for the customers.

23.7 SUMMARY

The authentic implementation of e-Commerce these days is moreover dissimilar from its real-life counterpart, and for the most part it's a "Web page" with listing of items and prices. The social facet such as personalization, collaboration, security, interactivity, etc. is lacking. We for that reason argue to come together the solution with a social place, where customers who participate in should get foolproof security. The study shows that 67% websites have cookies which may be one of the main reasons of loosing customer's privacy. Secondly, around 66% websites disclose personal information of the users to Third Parties which may or may not have their own privacy policies and is to be counted as one of the reasons for the same.

This study also finds that no *Universal Standard* format for a Privacy Policy has been designed and declared yet. Some policies are too small whereas some of them are too large and difficult to understand by the customer.

We came to know that few organisations have privacy policies, but the content written in those policies does not prove them as privacy policies.

Actually, it is a document which is not concerned with the personal information of the customers at all. These policies need modifications. There should be an Authority to monitor and control the proper format and points included in the privacy policy so that no such privacy policies will be made by the organisations in future.

There is no general privacy law in India (1998). India does not have any data protection law equivalent to that in the UK and there have been recent cases of information being leaked from call centers to criminals who have then blackmailed the companies involved. The Data Security Council of India (DSCI) is being set up by Indian IT industry group NASSCOM (June 2007).NASSCOM Information Technology Action Plan said that a National Policy on Information Security, Privacy and Data Protection Act for handling of computerised data shall be framed by the Government within six months. However, a recent study tells that more than 40 countries around the world have passed, or are preparing to pass, laws that protect the privacy and integrity of personal consumer data. *India is not however one amongst them.* Some time back, NASSCOM did take some initiatives to push through a drafting exercise but it appears that the exercise has not been pursued further.

23.8 LIMITATIONS

There are few limitations of this research which may be discussed as:

There is no standard format of privacy policy. Some policies are too small whereas some of them are too large and difficult to understand. At least few standard points should be made mandatory in a privacy policy that a website should include.

How will we come to know that the user is more than 13 years of age? Suppose a kid enters his age 18 and registers / buys things himself on the site then how can this procedure be stopped i.e. inserting wrong age?

How can we check that the companies are implementing their privacy policies? If they are not implementing the policies after displaying on the net then how can we make them implement?

23.9 FUTURE WORK

Significance of privacy seal is still an unclear point in general. Further studies can be done to check the awareness and to get suggestions of people from different backgrounds on this topic. Further work may be done to make a standard format of Privacy Policy which should be universal.

References

1. Adkinson F. William And Et Al. Privacy Online: A Report On The Information Practices And Policies Of Commercial Websites.

2. Kumaraguru, P. And Cranor, L. Privacy In India: Attitudes And Awareness. In Proceedings Of The 2005 Workshop On Privacy Enhancing Technologies (Pet 2005), 30 May - 1june 2005, Dubrovnik, Croatia.

3. Kumaraguru, P. Indian Call Center & BPO Organizations: Privacy Policy Analysis.

4. NASSCOM, List of registered companies http://companysearch.nasscom.org/ registered_cos.as p?alpha=A

5. Karjoth and M. Schunter. A Privacy Policy Model for Enterprises. In 15th IEEE Computer Security Foundations Workshop (CSFW) pages 271-281. IEEE Computer Society, 2002.

6. NASSCOM Information Technology Action Plan. http://www.nasscom.in/ upload/38370/action_plan_1.p df.

7. Stephanie; India to Adopt Data Privacy Rules. http://www.cio.com/article/29666/ India_to_Adopt_Dat a_Privacy_Rules.

8. India to set up data privacy watchdog; Tom Young, Computing 08 Jun 2007 http://www.vnunet.com/computing/news/2191739/indi a-gets-privacy-watchdog

9. Data Protection Laws in India; Naavi May 24, 2002. http://www.naavi.org/cl_ editorial/edit_25may_02_1.html

10. Privacy And Human Rights An International Survey of Privacy Laws and Practice http://www.gilc.org/privacy/survey/surveyak.html#India

11. Kesharwani, S. Principles of Management and Information Systems, MCS-052, Block-2 Unit-2 Enterprise Information System pp 46-74, School of Computer and Information Sciences, Indira Gandhi National Open University, India

12. H. Li, D.; Hung, P.C.K. Algorithms for automated negotiations and their applications in information privacy, Proc. IEEE International Conference on e-Commerce Technology, 6-9 July 2004, pp. 255–262.

13. World Internet Secure Key, Privacy Policy, WISeKey S.A, E-Commerce PKI CA Privacy Policy - Version 1.0, 1 July 2001, pp. 1–7.

Appendix

Table 23.1 Percentage of The Type of Domain of the Web sites

	Percentage	Number
b2b	71.755 %	785/1094
b2c	3.930 %	43/1094
bpo	4.844 %	53/1094
b2b & b2c	7.312%	80/1094
b2b&bpo	5.94%	65/1094
b2c&bpo	0.548 %	6/1 094
other / blank	5.667 %	62/1094

Table 23.2 Percentage of Domains that are accessible or not

	Percentage	Number
URL accessible	94.332 %	1032/1094
URL not accessible	04.570 %	50/1094
Blank (URL not in the record)	01.096 %	12/1094

Table 23.3 Percentage of Domains that have Privacy Policy

	Percentage	Number
Domains have Privacy Policy	37.111 %	406/1094
Domains do not have Privacy Policy	57.221 %	626/1094
Blank (not in the record/ not accessible)	5.667 %	62/1094

Table 23.4 Same Policy Holders

Pair No.	Company	URL of website	Remarks
1	Accenture Services Pvt Ltd	www.accenture.com	Policy is same
	A G Technologies Pvt Ltd	www.ag-technologies.com	
2	GE Infrastructure-India Technology Center (A Div of GE India Exports P Ltd)	www.ge.com	Policy is same
	GE Medical Systems (India) Pvt Ltd	www.gehealthcare.com	
3	Hewlett Packard Consumer Support Delivery (A Div. of Global e-Business Op. P Ltd	www.hp.com	Policy is same
	Hewlett-Packard India Sales Pvt Ltd	www.hpindia.com	
4	IBM Daksh Business Process Services Pvt Ltd	www.daksh.com	Policy is same
	IBM India Pvt Ltd	www.ibm.com/in	
5	Keane India Ltd	www.keane.com	Policy is same
	Keane Worldzen India Pvt Ltd	www.keaneworldzen.com	
6	NetEdge Computing Global Services Pvt Ltd	www.netedgecomputing. com	Policy format is same

	Network Programs (India) Ltd	www.networkprograms.com	
7	Philips Electronics India Ltd	www.philips.com	Policy is same
	Philips Software Centre Pvt. Ltd.	www.bangalore.philips.com	
8	Infosys Technologies Ltd.	www.infosys.com	Policy is same
	Progeon Ltd	www.progeon.com	
9	SAP India Pvt. Ltd.	www.sap.com/india	Policy is same
	SAP Labs India Pvt Ltd	www.saplabs.co.in	
10	Siemens Public Communication Networks Pvt Ltd	www.Siemens.com	*url is same for both organisa- tio ns, so*
	Siemens Shared Services India Pvt Ltd	www.Siemens.com	*same policies*
11	Tata Consultancy Services Ltd	www.tcs.com	Policy is same
	Tata Infotech Ltd.	www.tatainfotech.com	
12	UBICS Technologies Pvt Ltd	www.ubics.com	Policy is same
	UBS Service Centre (India) Pvt Ltd	www.ubs.com	

Table 23.5   List of Organisations having Links for Privacy
Policies but do not have any policy

S.No	Company	URL	Remarks
1	Amrut Software Pvt Ltd	www.amruts.com	Inactive link for policy
2	Bebo Technologies Pvt Ltd	www.bebotechnologies.com	Inactive link for policy
3	CG-Smith Software Pvt Ltd	www.cg-smith.com	Inactive link for policy
4	City Info Services Pvt Ltd	www.cityinfoservices.com	Policy under construction
5	CommVault Systems (India) Pvt Ltd	www.commvault.com	Inactive link for policy
6	Compare Infobase Pvt Ltd	www.infobase.co.in	Inactive link for policy
7	Damco Solutions (P) Ltd	www.damcogroup.com	Inactive link for policy
8	Datamatics Ltd.	www.datamatics.com	Inactive link for policy
9	Dewsoft Solution Pvt Ltd	www.dewsoftindia.com	Inactive link for policy
10	eMR Technology Ventures Pvt Ltd	www.emrtechventures.com	Inactive link for policy
11	Exceed Technologies Pvt Ltd	www.exceedintl.com	Inactive link for policy
12	Gurukulonline Learning Solutions (P) Ltd	www.gurukulonline.co.in	Inactive link for policy
13	HCL Technologies BPO Services Ltd	www.infozech.com	Inactive link for policy
15	Integrated Software Solutions (India) Pvt Ltd	www.iss-global.com	

S.No	Company	URL	Remarks
16	Intellicom Contact Centers (A Div. of Jindal Transworld Pvt Ltd)	www.intellicomcenters.com	
17	i-Strat Software Pvt Ltd	www.istrat-india.com	
18	IT Elite Systems Pvt. Ltd.	www.itelitesystems.com	
19	IT Microsystems (India) Ltd	www.itmicrosystems.com	
20	Kanbay Software (India) Pvt Ltd	www.kanbay.com	
21	SEEC Technologies Asia Pvt Ltd	www.seecasia.com	
22	Smart Chip Limited	www.smartchiponli ne.com	
23	smart Data Enterprises (India) Ltd	www.smartdatainc.net	
24	Software Technology Parks Of India	www.stpi.in	
25	Source Quest AP Consulting Pvt Ltd	www.sqapc.com	
26	STAG Software Pvt Ltd	www.stagsoftware.com	
27	Texcity Software Parks Ltd	www.rcsindia.com	
28	TRRS Imaging Ltd	www.indecommglobal.com	

Table 23.6 List of the Organisations having very small Privacy Policies

S.No.	Company	URL
1	Apollo Health Street Pvt Ltd	www.apollohealthstreet.com
2	Bechtel India Pvt. Ltd.	www.bechtel.com
3	Capital One Services (India) Pvt Ltd	www.capitalone.com
4	Career Launcher India Ltd	www.careerlauncher.com
5	Citibank N.A.	www.citibank.co.in
6	Citigroup Information Technology Operations and Solutions Ltd	www.citigroup.com
7	Comat Technologies (P) Ltd.	www.comat.com
8	Contact Singapore	www.contactsingapore.org.sg
9	Corbus (India) Private Limited	www.corbus.com
10	Cordiant Technologies (P) Limited	www.cordiant.com
11	Edurite Technologies Pvt Ltd	www.edurite.com
12	e-Zest Solutions Pvt. Ltd.	www.e-zest.net
13	FCG Software Services (India) Pvt Ltd	www.fcg.co.in
14	Four Soft Limited	www.four-soft.com
15	HCL Technologies Ltd	www.hcl.in

16	Hexaware Technologies Limited	www.hexaware.com
17	Lehman Brothers Services India Pvt Ltd	www.lehman.com
18	Liqwid Krystal India Pvt Ltd	www.liqwidkrystal.com
19	neoIT.Com Pvt Ltd	www.neoIT.com
20	Niteo Technologies (P) Ltd	www.niteo.com
21	S7 Software Solutions Pvt Ltd	www.s7solutions.com
22	Winfoware Technologies Pvt Ltd	www.winfoware.com
23	Zensar Technologies Limited	www.zensar.com

Table 23.7   List of the Organisations having very long Privacy Policies

S.No.	Company	URL
1	eBay India Pvt Ltd	www.eBay.in
2	eFunds International Private Limited	www.efunds.com
3	GE Consumer & Industrial - India Innovation Center (A Div. of GE India Exports)	www.geconsumerandindustrial.com
4	VeriSign India Pvt Ltd	www.verisign.com

Table 23.8   Different Policies than others

S.No.	Company	URL	Remarks
1	First Indian Corporation Pvt Ltd	www.firstindian-corp.com	different from others
2	Ford Business Service Center Private limited	www.ford.com	includes different points
3	Hewlett Packard Consumer Support Delivery (A Div. of Global e-Business Op. P Ltd	www.hp.com	perfect policy
4	Juno Online Services Development Pvt Ltd	www.juno.com	lengthy policy
5	SCA Technologies India Pvt Ltd	www.sca-tech.com	not a privacy policy
6	Sella Synergy India Ltd	www.sella.it	non english policy
7	SNS Technologies Pvt Ltd	www.snstech.com	not a privacy policy
8	TPI Advisory Services India Pvt Ltd	www.tpi.net	not a privacy policy

Table 23.9   Percentage of All Domains that Display a Privacy Sea Privacy

S.No.		Percentage	Number
1	Display a Privacy	5.418%	22.406
2	Sea		

Table 23.10   Percentage of Domains that Post Disclosures about the Domain's Use or Non-Use of Cookies

	Percentage	Number
Domain has Third Party Links	38.916%	158/406
Say that Domain uses Cookies	66.748%	271/406

	Percentage	Number
Say that Domain does not use Cookies	31.773%	129/406
THIRD PARTIES may place cookies/ Web Beacons on the domain	9.359%	38/406

Table 23.11 Percentage of Domains that collect Resume

	Percentage	Number
Domains collect Resumes	40.127%	439/1094
Domains do not collect Resume	27.056%	296/1094
Domains do not have Privacy Policy but collect Resume	28.274%	177/626
Domains have Privacy Policy, which collects Resumes, accepts that website contains Resume and give reasons for collecting Resumes	6.896%	28/406

Table 23.12 Percentage of Domains that collect Personal Information (IPs)

	Percentage	Number
Collect Personal Information	45.703%	500/1094
Collect Personal Identifying Information (only e mail)	35.923%	393/1094
Collect Personal Identifying Information other than e-mail	35.557%	389/1094
Collect Non-Identifying Information	25.045%	274/1094
Does not collect Personal- Identifying Information	21.115%	231/1094
Domains do not have Privacy Policy but collect Personal Information	18.53%	116/626

Table 23.13 Of those Domains with a Privacy Policy, Percentage Privacy disclosure to Third Parties

	Percentage	Number
Domain discloses personal information it collects to the third party	65.517%	266/406
Privacy Policy has option OPT IN	1.47%	6/406
Privacy Policy has option OPT OUT	3.488%	14/406
Privacy Policy has option of CHOICE	22.660%	92/406
Privacy Policy has NO option	38.916%	158/406

Table 23.14 Percentage of those Domains that have Privacy Policy and provide Security

	Percentage	Number
Provide Security	22.120%	242/406
Provide Security during Transmission	07.404%	81/242
Provide Security after collection	96.694%	234/242
Provide Security in both the stages	31.818%	77/242

Table 23.15 Percentage of Privacy Policies that include
something about Children under 13 years of age

	Percentage	Number
Says that domains do not collect information from the children under 13 years without their parent's approval	21.182%	86/406
Says that domains do not register/market/sell products to the children under 13 years of age	17.487%	71/406

24

Virus and Information Security

Arun Bakshi[1], Vikas Dixit[2] and Kaushal Mehta[3]

Computer virus is a program that copy itself to harm the computer without the knowledge of user. A virus can spread from one computer to another through some executable code. The user can sent it over a network or the Internet, or carried it on a removable medium such as a floppy disk, CD, DVD, or USB drive. Its chances of spreading from one computer to other increases by infecting files on a network file system or a file system that is accessed by another computer.

KEYWORDS Virus | Information System | Worm | Unix | Security

24.1 INTRODUCTION

The term "virus" is also commonly but erroneously used to refer to other types of malware, adware, and spyware programs. The correct term that should be used is "Malware". Malware includes computer viruses, worms, Trojan horses, most rootkits, spyware, dishonest adware, crime ware, and other malicious and unwanted software), including true viruses. . A worm can exploit security vulnerabilities to spread itself to other computers without needing to be transferred as part of a host, and a Trojan horse is a program that appears harmless but has a hidden agenda.

Now-a-days, almost all computers are connected to the Internet which increases the chance of spreading malicious code. Viruses may also take advantage of network services such as the World Wide Web, e-mail, Instant Messaging, and file sharing systems to spread.

24.2 HISTORY

Creeper was the first virus detected on ARPANET in early 1970s. It was a self- replicating progam written by Bob Thomas at BBN in 1971. It copied itself to the remote system and displays a message, "I'm the creeper, catch me if you can!" It used ARPANET to infect DEC PDP-10 computers running the TENEX operating system. The Reaper program was created to delete Creeper.

---

[1] Assistant Professor(Sr) (IT), Gitarattan International Business School, Rohini, Delhi
[2] Head Online Division Educosoft International India Pvt. Ltd.
[3] Assistant Professor, Bhai Parmanand Institute of Business Studies, Delhi

"Rother J" was the first computer virus that appears "in the wild" means can spread outside the computer or lab where it was written. It was created by Richard Skrenta in 1981 as a practical joke when he was in high school. This program attached itself to the Apple DOS 3.3 operating system and spread via floppy disk. On its 50th use the Elk Cloner virus would be activated, infecting the computer and displaying a short poem beginning "Elk Cloner: The program with a personality."

A boot sector virus named "Brain" created by Farooq Alvi Brothers in 1986. It was operated out of Lahore, Pakistan, reportedly to detect piracy of the software they had written. A variant of Brain named "Ashar" has predated Brain on the basis of code within the virus.

In early days, users use floppy disks to exchange informat5ion and programs. PCs of the era would attempt to boot first from a floppy. Therefore, most viruses spread using floppy disks and other removable media. Some viruses spread by infecting programs stored on these disks, while others installed themselves into the disk boot sector, ensuring that they would be run when the user booted the computer from the disk, usually inadvertently. Until floppy disks fell out of use, this was the most successful infection strategy and boot sector viruses were the most common in the wild for many years.

Traditional computer viruses emerged in the 1980s, driven by the spread of personal computers and the resultant increase in BBS, modem use, and software sharing. Bulletin board-driven software sharing contributed directly to the spread of Trojan horse programs, and viruses were written to infect popularly traded software. Shareware and bootleg software were equally common vectors for viruses on BBS's. Within the "pirate scene" of hobbyists trading illicit copies of retail software, traders in a hurry to obtain the latest applications were easy targets for viruses.

Macro viruses were introduced in the mid- 1990s. Most of these viruses are written in scripting languages to infect Microsoft programs such as Word and Excel. Since Word and Excel were also available for Mac OS, most could also spread to Macintosh computers. Some old versions of Microsoft Word allow macros to replicate themselves with additional blank lines. If two macro viruses simultaneously infect a document, the combination of the two, if also self-replicating, can appear as a "mating" of the two and would likely be detected as a virus unique from the "parents."

Virus can also be spread though instant message by sending a web address link. If the recipient think that it is from trusted source, he/she will follow the link. The virus hosted at the link can able to infect the computer and continue propagating.

Cross-site scripting viruses emerged recently, and were academically demonstrated in 2005. Since 2005 there have been multiple instances of the cross-site scripting viruses in the wild, exploiting websites such as MySpace and Yahoo.

24.3 INFECTION STRATEGIES

Virus must have permission for execution of code and written to memory to replicate itself. Therefore, viruses attached with executable files and if the user executes the infected file, the virus code will execute simultaneously. Viruses can be divided into two types based on their behavior when they are executed.

24.4 NONRESIDENT VIRUSES

These viruses search for other hosts or applications to spread infection, infect those target hosts and then transfers control to the application they had infected. It can be seen as the combination of the finder module and the replication module. Finder module finds the target hosts which further calls the replication module to infect that file. For each new executable file, finder module is encountered.

24.5 RESIDENT VIRUSES

Rather than searching for new hosts immediately, resident virus loads itself into memory on execution and transfers control to the host program. The virus stays active in the background and infects new hosts as they are accessed.

Resident viruses has replication module similar to the one used by non-resident viruses but does not contain the finder module. As the virus has been executed, it loads the replication module into the memory and called each time a new operation is executed by the operating system.

Resident viruses can be divided into two categories fast infectors and slow infectors.

Fast infectors can infect as many files as possible. For instance, a fast infector can infect every potential host file that is accessed. It might create a problem while using anti-virus software, since the virus scanner will scan all the potential host file while performing system- scan and if the scanner fails to find such virus, the virus can "piggy-back" on the scanner and can infect all the files that are scanned. Infect5ing too much files becomes t5he disadvantage of fast infectors as such infections can detect more easily because of slow performance of computer or any other suspicious action detect by the anti-virus software.

On the other hand, slow infectors infect the hosts infrequently. For instance, slow infectors infect files only when they are copied. Slow infectors are designed to avoid detection by limiting their actions and cannot be easily triggered by the anti-virus software that detects suspicious behavior of the programs. However, this approach does not seem vey successful.

24.6 CROSS-PLATFORM VIRUSES

With the popularity of cross-platform applications, cross-platform viruses are identified in 2007. This was brought to the forefront of malware awareness by the distribution of an Openoffice.org virus called Bad Bunny.

As per the statement of Stuart Smith of Symantec, "What makes this virus worth mentioning is that it illustrates how easily scripting platforms, extensibility, plug-ins, ActiveX, etc, can be abused. All too often, this is forgotten in the pursuit to match features with another vendor. The ability for malware to survive in a cross-platform, cross-application environment has particular relevance as more and more malware is pushed out via Web sites. How long until someone uses something like this to drop a JavaScript infector on a Web server, regardless of platform?"

24.7 ABOUT VECTORS AND HOSTS

Viruses have targeted various types of transmission media or hosts. This list is not exhaustive:

- Binary executable files (such as COM files and EXE files in MS-DOS, Portable Executable files in Microsoft Windows, and ELF files in Linux)
- Volume Boot Records of floppy disks and hard disk partitions
- The master boot record (MBR) of a hard disk
- General-purpose script files (such as batch files in MS- DOS and Microsoft Windows, VBScript files, and shell script files on Unix-like platforms).
- Application-specific script files (such as Telix-scripts)
- System specific autorun script files (such as Autorun.inf file needed to Windows to automatically run software stored on USB Memory Storage Devices).
- Documents that can contain macros (such as Microsoft Word documents, Microsoft Excel spreadsheets, AmiPro documents, and Microsoft Access database files)
- Cross-site scripting vulnerabilities in web applications
- Arbitrary computer files. An exploitable buffer overflow, format string, race condition or other exploitable bug in a program which reads the file could be used to trigger the execution of code hidden within it. Most bugs of this type can be made more difficult to exploit in computer

architectures with protection features such as an execute disable bit and/or address space layout randomization.

Malicious code can be embedded in the PDFs or in HTML code. Operating systems use file extensions to determine program association. These extensions may be hidden from the user by default. For example, an executable may be created named "picture.png.exe", in which the user sees only "picture.png" and therefore assumes that this file is an image and most likely is safe.

An additional method is to generate the virus code from parts of existing operating system files by using the CRC16/CRC32 data. The initial code can be quite small (tens of bytes) and unpack a fairly large virus. This is analogous to a biological "prion" in the way it works but is vulnerable to signature based detection.

24.8 TRICKS OF VIRUS TO AVOID ITS DETECTION

Many approaches are used to avoid detection of virus by users. One oldest approach is, if the file is infected, "last- modified" date of the host file remains same. This approach is especially used in MS-DOS platform. However, this approach does not fool anti-virus software, especially those which maintains date and Cyclic redundancy checks on file changes.

Another approach to avoid detection is: viruses can infect files without increasing their sizes or damaging the files. This can be done by overwriting unused areas of executable files. These are called cavity viruses. For example the CIH virus, or Chernobyl Virus, infects Portable Executable files. As these files have many empty gaps, the virus, which was 1 KB in length, did not add to the size of the file. Some viruses try to avoid detection by killing the tasks associated with antivirus software before it can detect them.

Old hiding techniques need to be replaced or updated as computers and operating systems are growing and becoming complex. File systems may need detailed and explicit permissions of every kind of file access to prevent the computer against viruses.

24.9 AVOIDING BAIT FILES AND OTHER UNDESIRABLE HOSTS

Virus needs to infect the host files to spread further. However, infecting the host files may lead to the detection of virus more easily as much anti-virus software performs an integrity check for their own code. For this reason, some viruses are programmed not to infect programs that are known to be part of anti-virus software.

Another host files that virus needs to avoid are Bait files (or goat files). Bait files are designed by the anti-virus professionals to be infected by virus which helps to detect the virus.

As Bait files are designed to infect themselves by the virus, these files can be used by the anti-virus professionals to find different samples of virus Professionals use these samples to study the behavior of the virus and evaluate detection methods for them. It is more practical to store and exchange a small, infected bait file, than to exchange a large application program that has been infected by the virus. Bait files are especially useful when the virus is polymorphic. In this case, the virus can be made to infect a large number of bait files. The infected files can be used to test whether a virus scanner detects all versions of the virus.

Some Bait files accessed regularly. If any modification finds in these files, the anti-virus software warns the user that virus may be active on the system. Hence, virus needs to avoid such files. This can be done by avoiding the small program files or programs that contain certain patterns of garbage instructions.

Another strategy to avoid Bait files is sparse infection. Sometimes, sparse infectors do not infect a host file that would be a suitable candidate for infection in other circumstances. For instance, virus may decide whether to infect the file or not, or it may infect the host files on a particular day of week.

24.10 STEALTH

STEALTH is a technique used by virus to befool anti-virus software by intercepting the request to the operating system. As anti-virus software requests to read a file, virus intercepts it and receives the request. Thus, the request is passed to the virus rather than to the operating system. The virus will then return the uninfected version of file which seems clean to the anti-virus software. Many techniques are used to avoid stealth but the most reliable technique is to boot from medium which is known to be clean.

24.11 SELF-MODIFICATION

Virus can be easily find using virus signatures while scanning programs through anti-virus software. A signature is a characteristic byte-pattern that is part of a certain virus or family of viruses. If the scanner finds such pattern, it notifies the user that the file is infected. Then it is up to the user whether to delete, clean or heal the file. Some virus makes the detection difficult using signatures as they modify their code at each infection. However, the detection of virus through signatures is not the impossible task.

24.12 ENCRYPTION WITH A VARIABLE KEY

Virus can also be spread using encryption. For this, virus needs decrypted module and the encrypted module. As the virus is encrypted using different keys for each new file which makes the detection of virus difficult. However, the decryption module remains same through which the indirect detection of virus could be possible. Since these would be symmetric keys, stored on the infected host, it is in fact entirely possible to decrypt the final virus, but this is probably not required, since self-modifying code is such a rarity that it may be reason for virus scanners to at least flag the file as suspicious.

An old method used for encryption is XORing each byte of the virus program with a constant and the same XOR operation will repeated for decryption. It is suspicious code that modifies itself, so the code to do the encryption/ decryption may be part of the signature in many virus definitions.

24.13 POLYMORPHIC CODE

Polymorphic code uses the concept of encryption to infect files. However, in encryption, decrypted module remains same whereas in polymorphic code, decryption module is also modified on every new infection. It is a serious threat to virus scanner as there is no identical part between infections which makes the detection of virus too difficult.

Anti-virus software can detect such viruses using an emulator or by statistical pattern analysis of the encrypted virus body. To generate polymorphic code, virus needs to have a polymorphic engine (also called mutating engine or mutation engine) somewhere in its encrypted body

Such slow polymorphic code makes it more difficult for anti-virus professionals to obtain the samples of virus. Polymorphic code makes the detection by virus scanner unreliable and also helps to avoid detection even through Bait files which infect themselves in only one run and contains similar or identical samples of virus.

24.14 METAMORPHIC CODE

Polymorphic code can be detected using emulation. To avoid this detection, metamorphic code is used. Using this technique, virus rewrites themselves completely on the infection of any new executable file. To enable metamorphism, a metamorphic engine is needed. A metamorphic virus is usually very large and complex. For example, W32/Simile consisted of over 14000 lines of Assembly language code, 90% of which is part of the metamorphic engine.

24.15 LINUX VULNERABILITY

Linux supports multi-user environment where users require privileges to access which is implemented using some access control technique. To cause any serious consequence over Linux, malware needs to have the root access to the system.

Shane Coursen, a senior technical consultant with Kaspersky Lab noted, "The growth in Linux malware is simply due to its increasing popularity, particularly as a desktop operating system. The use of an operating system is directly correlated to the interest by the malware writers to develop malware for that OS."

SecurityFocus's Scott Granneman stated, some Linux machines definitely need anti-virus software. For instance, Samba or NFS servers, may store documents in undocumented, vulnerable Microsoft formats, such as Word and Excel which may propagate viruses.

Linux mail servers send mails to other computers which are using different operating systems. Therefore, Linux operating system also needs to run AV software to detect viruses before they show up in the mailboxes of Outlook and Outlook Express users. For example the open source ClamAV "Detects viruses, worms and trojans, including Microsoft Office macro viruses, mobile malware, and other threats." Hence, Linux virus scanners search for all known viruses for all computer platforms.

24.16 VULNERABILITY AND VIRUSES

Just as genetic diversity in a population decreases the chance of a single disease wiping out a population, the diversity of software systems on a network similarly limits the destructive potential of viruses.

This became a particular concern in the 1990s, when Microsoft gained market dominance in desktop operating systems and office suites. The users of Microsoft software (especially networking software such as Microsoft Outlook and Internet Explorer) are especially vulnerable to the spread of viruses.

Microsoft gained market dominance because of its desktop operating system and office suites in 1990s. Hence, the Windows become the most popular OS for virus writers and are often criticized for including many errors and holes for virus writers to exploit. Integrated and non-integrated Microsoft applications (such as Microsoft Office) and applications with scripting languages with access to the file system (for example Visual Basic Script (VBS), and applications with networking features) are also particularly vulnerable.

Windows is the most popular OS among virus writers; however, some viruses also exist for other operating systems. Operating system that allows third-party programs to run over it can affect from virus. Unix-based Operating systems are more secure as they provide the facility to run executable code into its own protected memory space.

Mac OS X (with a Unix-based file system and kernel) is considered better OS than MS-Windows as MAC OS X has relatively few security exploits. One older version of Apple OS named "Mac OS Classic" states that there are only 4 known viruses and independent sources states that t5here are as many as

63 viruses. Virus vulnerability between Macs and Windows is a chief selling point, one that Apple uses in their Get Mac advertising.

As the first virus for Linux named "Bliss" has been released, anti-virus vendors issued a warning that Unix- like systems could fall prey to viruses just like Windows. Bliss needs to run it explicitly and can harm only the files which the users have access permission to modify. Unlike Windows OS, Linux and UNIX blocks normal users access to make changes to the environment and users do not usually log in as an administrator which can save the OS to get infected.

24.17 THE ROLE OF SOFTWARE DEVELOPMENT

Because software is often designed with security features to prevent unauthorized use of system resources, many viruses must exploit software bugs in a system or application to spread. Software development strategies that produce large numbers of bugs will generally also produce potential exploits.

24.18 ANTI-VIRUS SOFTWARE

Anti-virus software's are used to detect and eliminate the known viruses after the computer downloads or runs the executable.

Anti-virus software application uses two common methods to detect viruses. The first common method of virus detection is using a list of virus signature definitions. This can be done by examining the content of the computer's memory (its RAM, and boot sectors) and the files stored on fixed or removable drives (hard drives, floppy drives), and comparing those files against a database of known virus "signatures".

The disadvantage of this detection method is that users are only protected from viruses that pre-date their last virus definition update. The second method is to use a heuristic algorithm to find viruses based on common behaviors. This method has the ability to detect viruses that anti-virus security firms have yet to create a signature for.

Some anti-virus software's uses "on-access scanning" means scanning is performed as and when the file is opened and even while sending and receiving e-mails. Anti-virus software does not change the underlying capability of host software to transmit viruses. Users must update their software regularly to patch security holes.

Anti-virus software also needs to be regularly updated in order to prevent the latest threats.

Damages caused by viruses could be minimized by taking the regular back-ups of data either on devices which kept unconnected to the system (most of the time), read-only or not accessible for other reasons, such as using different file systems. This way, if data is lost through a virus, one can start again using the backup (which should preferably be recent).

Optical media such as CD/DVD stores data in read-only format. Therefore, the data cannot be affected by virus on such devices. Hence, if the OS becomes unusable, an OS on a bootable CD can be used to start the system.

Backups on removable media must be carefully inspected before restoration. The Gammima virus, for example, propagates via removable flash drives.

24.19 RECOVERY METHODS

Once the computer gets infected by virus, it is unsafe to use the infected system without reinstalling the operating system. However, there are number of recovery options available while the actions depend upon the type of virus.

24.20 VIRUS REMOVAL

There is a tool available on Windows Me, Windows XP, and Windows Vista named "System Restore" which restores the registry and critical system files to a previous checkpoint. A virus may hang the system and a subsequent hard reboot corrupt the system restores point on the same day. Restore point from previous days works only if the virus is not designed to corrupt restore files.

Some viruses such as CiaDoor disable system restore and other tools such as Task Manager and Command Prompt. Administrators can disable such tools to access it by other users. However, a virus can block all users to access these tools by modifying the registry. When an infected tool activates it gives message "Task Manager has been disabled by your administrator.", even if the user trying to open the program is the administrator.

24.21 OPERATING SYSTEM REINSTALLATION

Another approach for virus removal is reinstallation of operating system. This is done by formatting the OS partition and install OS using its original media. This approach is faster than using antivirus software and scans the system multiple times. However, it includes the overhead of reinstallation of all other software and drivers

24.22 VIRUSES

Some viruses may threat to Linux systems. Execution of infected binary may infect the system. However, the infection level depends upon the privileges of user which executes the infected binary. Binary file run under root account may infect the entire system. Privilege escalation vulnerabilities may permit malware running under a limited account to infect the entire system.

Virus generators do not require any special malware writing skills. They can simply add a code snippet to any program and as the user downloads that program, it will download through the modified login server. This additional code run anytime, the user logs in. however, special skill may be needed for tricking the user to run the program in the first place.

Threat of installation of malware can be reduced using software repositories. Software repositories are checked by maintainers to ensure that the software is malware-free. For this purpose, md5 checksums are used. Through this, modified versions are identified that may be introduced by different malware attacks. It limits the scope of attacks by only including the original authors, package and release maintainers and possibly others with suitable administrative access, depending on how the keys and checksums are handled. If the user executes the code which is not from trusted user, vulnerability of Trojan horses and viruses may cause. It is also the fault of distributers which do not provide the default checking for authenticity of software downloaded.

24.23 WORMS AND UNIX-LIKE SYSTEMS

UNIX systems have vulnerability in network daemons such as and WWW servers can be used or attacks. Server takes immediate action against vulnerabilities. There is no guarantee on the installation if attack is on targets which are not publicly known. Servers having weak passwords can also be attacked.

24.24 WWW SCRIPTS AND LINUX SERVERS

Rather than attacking the system, Linux servers can also be used by malwares. E.g. WWW content and scripts are restricted as it may be used by malware to attack visitors.

24.25 POTENTIAL THREATS

New malwares are introduced and increasing day by day to cause threat to the system Some of them are given as:

24.26 TROJANS

| Kaiten | Linux.Backdoor.Kaiten trojan horse |
| Rexob | Linux.Backdoor.Rexob trojan |

24.27 VIRUSES

⤹ Alaeda - Virus.Linux.Alaeda

- Bad Bunny - Perl.Badbunny
- Binom - Linux/Binom
- Bliss
- Brundle
- Bukowski
- Diesel - Virus.Linux.Diesel.962
- Kagob a - Virus.Linux.Kagob.a
- Kagob b - Virus.Linux.Kagob.b
- MetaPHOR (also known as Simile)
- Nuxbee - Virus.Linux.Nuxbee.1403
- OSF.8759
- Podloso - Linux.Podloso (The iPod virus)
- Rike - Virus.Linux.Rike.1627
- RST - Virus.Linux.RST.a
- Satyr - Virus.Linux.Satyr.a
- Staog
- Vit - Virus.Linux.Vit.4096
- Winter - Virus.Linux.Winter.341
- Winux (also known as Lindose and PEElf)
- Wit virus
- ZipWorm - Virus.Linux.ZipWorm

24.28 WORMS

- Adm - Net-Worm.Linux.Adm
- Adore
- Cheese - Net-Worm.Linux.Cheese
- Devnull
- Kork
- Linux/Lion
- Mighty - Net-Worm.Linux.Mighty
- Millen - Linux.Millen.Worm
- Ramen worm
- Slapper
- SSH Bruteforce

24.29 SOME ANTI-VIRUS APPLICATIONS

- There is a number of anti-virus applications available are including:

- Avast! (freeware and commercial versions)
- AVG (freeware and commercial versions)
- Avira (freeware and commercial)
- Bitdefender (freeware and commercial versions)
- ClamAV (free open source software)
- Eset (commercial versions)
- F-Secure Linux (commercial)
- Kaspersky Linux Security (commercial)
- McAfee VirusScan Enterprise for Linux (commercial)
- Panda Security for Linux (commercial version)
- Sophos (commercial)
- Symantec AntiVirus for Linux (commercial)
- Trend Micro ServerProtect for Linux (commercial)

As prevention is better than cure, one should take all the preventive measures to safeguard computer against virus threats. Though viruses are dangerous, but there is no need to panic. The name virus itself seems like they can destroy your computer any moment. But it is not the only truth. One can take security measures to protect computer against malicious code using update antivirus and by knowing about the extent of damage and recovery procedures against viruses. The final word of wisdom will be to avoid access of any untrustworthy sources of data whether CD, Pen Drive or online data, and keep your virus scanner updated always.

References

1. http ://www.bartleby.com/61/97/C0539700.html 5-Nov-2009

2. http://www.actlab.utexas.edu/~aviva/compsec/virus/whatis.html 7-Nov-2009

3. "Virus list". http:/ / www.viruslist.com/en/viruses/ encyclopedia?chapter= 153310937. Retrieved on 2008-02-07. 11-Nov-2009

4. Thomas Chen, Jean-Marc Robert (2004). "The Evolution of Viruses and Worms". http://vx.netlux.org/lib/atc01.html. Retrieved on 2009-02-16. 1-Nov-2009

5. See page 86 of Computer Security Basics by Deborah Russell and G. T. Gangemi. O'Reilly, 1991. ISBN 0937175714. 4-Nov-2009

6. Anick Jesdanun. "Prank starts 25 years of security woes". http:// news.yahoo. com/s/ap/20070831/ap_on_hi_te/ computer_virus_an niversary;_ylt=A9G_ R3Ga1NhGH0QBIwZk24cA."The anniversary of a nuisance". http://www.cnn. com/2007/TECH/09/03/computer.virus.ap/. 8-Nov-2009

7. Boot sector virus repair

8. Dr. Solomon's Virus Encyclopedia, 1995, ISBN 1897661002, Abstract at http:// vx.netlux.org/lib/aas10.html 9-Nov-2009

9. Vesselin Bontchev. "Macro Virus Identification Problems". FRISK Software International. http://www.people.fnsk-software.com/~bontchev/ papers/ macidpro.html.

10. Wade Alcorn. "The Cross-site Scripting Virus". http://www.bindshell.net/papers/ xssv/.

11. http://www.pcsecurityalert.com/pcsecurityalert-articles/what-is-a- computer-virus.htm

12. http://www.virusbtn.com/resources/glossary/polymorphic_virus.xml 5- Nov-2009

13. Perriot, Fredrick; Peter Ferrie and Peter Szor (May 2002). "Striking Similarities" (PDF).
    http://securityresponse.symantec.com/avcenter/reference/simile.pdf. Retrieved on September 9, 2007. 6-Nov-2009

14. http://www.virusbtn.com/resources/glossary/metamorphic_virus.xml. 3-Nov-2009

15. Need a computer virus?- download now. 2-Nov-2009

16. http://blog.didierstevens.com/2007/05/07/is-your-pc-virus-free-get-it-infected-here/

17. "Malware Evolution: Mac OS X Vulnerabilities 2005-2006". Kaspersky Lab. 2006-07-24. http:/ /www.viruslist.com/en/analysis?pubid=191968025. Retrieved on August 19, 2006. 4-Nov-2009

18. Apple - Get a Mac. 7-Nov-2009. Retrieved on 2009-02-16. 1-Nov-2009
    See page 86 of *Computer Security Basics* by Deborah Russell and G. T. Gangemi. O'Reilly, 1991. ISBN 0937175714. 4-Nov-2009
    Anick Jesdanun. "Prank starts 25 years of security woes". http:// news.yahoo. com/s/ap/20070831/ap_on_hi_te/ computer_virus_an niversary;_ylt=A9G_ R3Ga1NhGH0QBIwZk24cA."The anniversary of a nuisance". http://www.cnn. com/2007/TECH/09/03/computer.virus.ap/

19. Sutter, John D. (22 April 2009). "Experts: Malicious program targets Macs". CNN.com. http://www.cnn.com/2009/TECH/04/22/first.mac.botn et/index.html. Retrieved on 24 April 2009. 9-Nov-2009

20. McAfee. "McAfee discovers first Linux virus". news article. http:/ / math-www.uni-paderborn.de/~axel/bliss/mcafee_press.html. 3-Nov- 2009

21. Axel Boldt. "Bliss, a Linux "virus"". news article. http://math-www.uni-paderborn.de/~axel/bliss/. 2- Nov-2009

22. "Symantec Security Summary—W32.Gammima.AG." http://www.symantec.com/security_response/writeup.js p?docid=2007-082706-1742-99

23. "Yahoo Tech: Viruses! In! Space!" http://tech.yahoo.com/blogs/ null/103826

24. "Symantec Security Summary—W32.Gammima.AG and removaldetails." http://www.symantec.com/security_response/writeup.js p?docid=2007-082706-1742-99&tabid=3. 2-Nov-2009

☺☺☹

25

Website Monitoring

Raj Bala Simon[1] and Laxmi Ahuja [2]

Website monitoring is the process of testing and verifying that end-users can interact with a website or web application .Website monitoring is often used by business to ensure that their sites are live and responding.

KEYWORDS	Web Monitoring | Test | Verify | URL

25.1 INTRODUCTION

Website monitoring is the process of testing and verifying that end-users can interact with a website or web application .Website monitoring is often used by business to ensure that their sites are live and responding.

The most important online face of your organization is your website. So what damage is caused to your brand and sales when your website is unavailable? It may be that your customers cannot perform online transactions and go to your competitors instead. Or it could be that client email is not received and your helpdesk gets inunded with calls.

Website security monitoring is also used to verify that the domain (and web site) is not only responding properly, but has not been hacked, blacklisted or hijacked. Multiple tools are available to automate site availability checks and security checks.

As a website owner or webmaster, it is your goal to find ways to attract visitors to your site as well as to get them stay longer to use your site services. However, if your website performs poorly and you are not even aware of it, it will be really hard to realize these goals. This is where an efficient web site performance monitoring solution can help.

Various companies like site 24×7 provides the functionality of continually monitors web site's performance on a 24×7 basis and alerts you whenever these is any degradation of performance. A key indicator of the performance

---

[1] AIIT, Amity University, Noida, India
[2] AIIT, Amity University, Noida, India

of any web site is its response time. When a web site is slow or unresponsive, it may drive users away from the site.

According to Gartner 50 % of visitors will abandon a page if it takes more than 15 seconds to load. Therefore, Website owner should never compromise with slow loading Web Pages.

Site 24×7's website performing feature checks for various attributes such as response time, etc. For example, you can add a URL, say//mycompany/estore. jsp, for monitoring. You can set up a threshold for the webpage such that if the page load time of that page is more than 5 seconds, you should be notified through e-mail/SMS/RSS. This helps you in taking quick action before it affects end users.

A perfect monitoring provides daily/weekly performance reports through email to know your site's performance on a daily/weekly basis. Website owner can also view time -based response time reports form 'Reports' tab that give them a fair idea of the performance of their websites over a period of time. If they noticed a constant degradation of performance, then they can take necessary actions to improve it.

The website performance monitors tests your web site URLs as often as every minute from multiple cities around the globe, and generates real-time alerts if page errors or performance problems occur. Also provide detailed reporting and extensive global monitoring to ensure than your site consistently performs at the preferred levels.

Website monitoring has become a full-fledged industry, giving website owners a myriad of choices from monitoring software, to subscription services to live monitoring. There are "inside jobs" and there are global agents. There are do-it-yourself systems and there are experts waiting to serve you. There are web hosting companies that monitor for their clients and there are free agents. What king of website performance monitoring service do you want? It depends on your requirements:

The website performance Monitor captures all performance details for every webpage object, including images, flash, java script, css and more.

25.2 RESPONSE TIME HISTORY

If your business is online, monitoring the performance of your website is must then there is a solution that can help.

The solution is called 'website performance monitor' and includes a choice of the following safety checks on your website:

25.3 AVAILABILITY MONITORING

It is estimated that downtime coasts European businesses 5 billion a year. While every minute of downtime can cost your business in lost revenue, it can also severely damage your brand reputation and bring your business to a halt. With a globally distributed infrastructure of more than 35 monitoring stations, various web hosting companies provides availability monitor continuously checks your websites, servers and applications, to deliver verification that your website is available and functioning properly. Availability monitor conducts checks from an external perspective, to replicate real user's experiences and provide your business with independent information about your website's performance and availability.

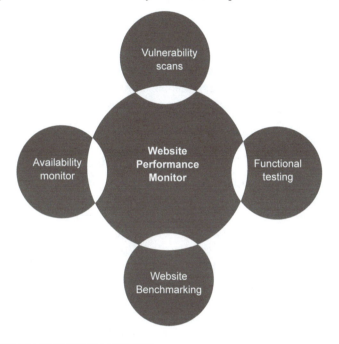

25.4 VULNERABILITY SCANS

With a dramatic rise in malicious attacks it has become critical to scan your websites and servers for security vulnerability. Having the latest firewalls and intrusion detection systems will not protect your organization if they are not kept up-to-date and configured correctly. Vulnerability scan is an affordable way to routinely check company's security risk and provide you with peace-of-mind that software applications cannot be hacked into from those outside of your organization.

25.5 WEBSITE BENCHMARKING

As the internet has become the preferred channel through which many customers obtain information, products and services, can your business afford not to know how your website compares to your competitors? Website Benchmarking measures the performance of your websites from locations across the globe, to provide accurate load time, speed and availability statistics.

These measurements are used to create site performance index (SPI), which represents the users' perceptions of your website. SPI is then ranked, relative to that of your sector and competitors within countries relevant to your business. A website benchmarking report gives you an overview of trends in relative performance and availability across sectors and countries.

25.6 FUNCTIONAL TESTING

Functional testing checks the behavior of your site and identifies where exactly bottle necks or problems occur. It also ensures you know how your customers experience your site when they interact with it from different locations. Functional testing monitoring scripts can be written to identify a wide variety of possible issues, from slow page response times, to monitoring the behavior of forms such as login pages and issues with shopping baskets.

25.7 PRODUCT OPTIONS

Website Performance Monitor is available from various web hosting companies in different cost effective options, allowing you to pick the option that is right for your business.

Receive reliable website monitoring over 25 globally disturbed monitoring stations	Receive independent comprehensive verification of your website's performance	A web based portal for easy viewing of monitors, rules and reports	Respond quickly to website problems, resolving issues before your customers encounter them	Verify internal departments and external suppliers (ISPs/hosting) are meeting their SLAs

25.8 WHAT IS IMPACT

If it's up...	A.K.A... It's down. per year	
90%	n/a	876 hours
95%	n/a 438 hours	
99%	Two 9's	87 hours, 36 minutes
99.9%	Three 9's	8 hours,45 minutes, 36 seconds
99.99%	Four 9's	52 minutes, 33.6 seconds
99.999%	Five 9's	5 minutes, 15.36 seconds
99.9999%	Six 9's	31.68 seconds

There are 2 main types of website monitoring:
- Synthetic monitoring also known as Active monitoring, and
- Passive monitoring also known as Real monitoring.

25.8.1 Synthetic Monitoring

Synthetic monitoring (also known as Active monitoring) is **website monitoring** that is done using a **web browser** emulation or **scripted red web browsers.** Behavioral scripts (or paths) are created to stimulate an action or path that a customer or end user would take on a site. Those paths are then continuously monitored at specified intervals for **availability** and **response time** measures.

Synthetic monitoring is valuable because it enables a webmaster to identify problems and determine if his website or web application is slow or experiencing downtime before that problem affects actual end users or customers. This type of monitoring does not require actual web traffic so it enables companies to test web applications 24x7, or test new applications prior to a live customer facing launch.

Because synthetic monitoring is a simulation of typical user behavior navigation through a website, it is often best used to monitor commonly trafficked paths and critical business processes. Synthetic test must be scripted in advance, so it is not feasible to measure performance to every permutation of a navigational path and an end user might take. This is more suited for passive monitoring. Synthetic testing is useful for measuring availability and response time for critical pages and transaction (how a site performs from all geographies) but doesn't monitor or capture actual end user interactions.

Passive monitoring is also known as real user monitoring and can be used to monitor actual user sessions on web sites to detect and capture errors and performance slowdown. Passive monitoring products are usually based on hardware devices that sit inside the firewall and capture traffics as it enters.

25.9 TYPES OF PROTOCOL USED FOR WEBSITE MONITORING

Website monitoring services can check HTTP pages

- HTTPS
- FTP
- SMTP
- POP3
- IMAP
- DNS
- SSH
- Telnet
- SSL
- TCP
- PING
- Domain Name Expiry

◄ SSL Certificate Expiry

And a range of other ports with great variety of check intervals from every 4 hours to everyone minute. Typically, most website monitoring services test services test your server anywhere between once per hour to once per minute.

Advanced services offer in browser web transaction monitoring based on browser addons such as Selenium or iMacros. These services test a website controlling a large number of web browsers, thus they can also detect websites issues such as Javascripts bugs that are browser specific.

25.9.1 Web Service-SOAP Monitoring

SOAP is a lightweight protocol for the exchange of information in a decentralized, distributed environment. It is an XML based protocol that consists of three parts: an envelope that defines a framework for describing what is in a message and how to process it, a set of encoding rules for expressing instances of application defined data types, and a convention for representing remote procedure calls and responses. The agents can replicate one or more end-client requests and monitor Web Services for availability and proper content.

25.10 MAJOR WEBSITE PERFORMANCE MONITORING TOOLS

25.10.1 Allmon

Description: The main goal of the project is to create a distributed generic system collecting and storing various runtime metrics collections used for continuous system performance, health, quality and availability monitoring purposes. Allmon agents are designed to harvest a range of metrics values coming from many areas of monitored infrastructure (application instrumentation, JMX, HTTP health checks, SNMP). Collected data are base for quantitative and qualitative performance and availability analysis. Allmon collaborates with other analytical tools for OLAP analysis and Data Mining processing.

Requirement: Platform independent Download data: No data feed available.

25.10.2 Apache JMeter

Description: Apache JMeter is a 100% pure Java desktop application designed to load test functional behavior and measure performance. It was originally designed for testing Web Applications but has since expanded to other test functions. Apache JMeter may be used to test performance both on static and dynamic resources (files, Servlets, Perl scripts, Java Objects,

Data Bases and Queries, FTP Servers and more). It can be used to simulate a heavy load on a server, network or object to test its strength or analyze overall performance under different load types. You can use it to make a graphical analysis of performance or to test your server/script/object behavior under heavy concurrent load.

Requirement: Solaris, Linux, Windows (98, NT, 2000). JDK 1.4(or higher).

Download data: No data feed available.

25.10.3 Benerator

Description: Benerator is a framework for creating realistic and valid high-volume test data, used for (unit/integration/load) testing and showcase setup. Metadata constraints are imported from systems and/or configuration files. Data can be imported from and exported to files and systems, anonymized or generated from scratch. Domain packages provide reusable generators for creating domain-specific data as names and addresses internationalizable in language and region. It is strongly customizable with plug-in and configuration options.

Requirement: Platform Independent

25.11 SITE PERFORMANCE

The quality of a website's service depends upon several interrelated factors, such as site architecture, network capacity, and application software. Ebusiness sites may become popular very quickly. Therefore, once the site owners are advised of the stress test results and analysis based on the predicted load, how quickly the site architecture can be scaled up becomes important.

It is important to determine what components of the site should be upgraded- database servers, Web servers, application servers, or the network link bandwidth. Maintaining the quality of services that may be compromised due to enhanced traffic requires careful analysis of the factors involved in order to find the optimum solution.

This is all the more important as many small- or medium-sized companies may not be able to afford frequent hardware upgrades or expansions.

It benefits business of all sizes to know the threshold traffic points above which their website's performance starts to deteriorate. If their predicted E-business traffic is above the threshold, as determined by stimulated load results, then only the remedial action is called for.

The new economy is characterized by an infinite number of purchasing options available right at the moment the customer learns about them. The very impulse to buy is now part of the same process. Through unprecedented levels of information exchange between individuals and organizations, the new economy has changed the way buyers and sellers find each other, compare prices and value added services, optimize business processes, and reduce costs.

Better prepared sites can significantly reduce the amount of volume burst-induced damage to site performance. Although it is difficult to predict erratic patterns of website demand, a site must be prepared for these spikes in traffic. External website load stress testing can play a significant role in providing E-businesses advanced preparations to meet such challenges.

References

1. www.google.co.in
2. www.watchmouse.com
3. www.webmetrics.com
4. www.wikipedia.org
5. www.dotcom-monitor.com

☺☺☹

26

Fingerprint Recognition

Jashwini Narayana[1], Anshu Mala[2] and Rajiv Naidu[3]

Fingerprint identification from a random offline fingerprint image has become a very actively studied field in biometric systems. This paper investigates the possibility to prepare a framework of applying the latent fingerprint obtained from a crime scene to be shared in a central data base. These fingerprints may be extremely useful to reduce the crimes from a country. In this approach each citizen is supposed to put his/ her fingerprint in an organization during entry. This fingerprint will be matched to the central database for checking whether the fingerprint of that citizen matched with any finger print taken from a crime scene. The information system of an organization thus will be able to reveal the suspicious citizens causing to be investigated for further action. The quality of the fingerprint images greatly affects the performance of the minutiae extraction. The photo graph taken from different distances, uneven surface, different finger pressure, dust particles pose problems during recognition process. Improper finger pressure and uneven surface are the major cause to produce breaks in curves in a fingerprint. In order to improve the performance of the system, many researchers have been made efforts on the image enhancement algorithms. Most of the fingerprint recognition algorithms are based on minutia matching features. Therefore, minutiae extraction is one of the important steps in fingerprint verification algorithms. In this chapter we present an algorithm to fill the broken curves on a fingerprint due to low finger pressure and uneven surface. Our proposed approach eliminates false minutiae that connect broken curves in fingerprint.

KEYWORDS   Biometrics | Minutiae | Ridge | Furrows | FRR | FAR

26.1 INTRODUCTION

The term "biometrics" is commonly used today to refer to the authentication of a person by analyzing the physical characteristics (like fingerprints) or behavior

---

[1,2,3] Vidya College of Engineering, Meerut

characteristics. Fingerprint matching is one of the widely used biometric techniques in automatic personal identification or verification, because of its robustness and its justified implementation cost.

When we talk about the performance of biometric systems high FRR (false rejection rate) and low FAR (false acceptance rate) are our major concerns. False Rejection Rate and False Acceptance Rate are complementary in determining how severe a biometric device is in allowing access to individuals. In general, biometric devices commonly include features to allow for sensitivity settings or variable threshold.

26.2 BACKGROUND

The fingerprints obtained from the crime scenes are of very bad quality because these are left unintentionally. Such fingerprints are called latent fingerprints. Poor quality fingerprint images lead to missing and spurious minutiae that degrade the performance of fingerprint matching system. The importance of image processing concepts cannot be ruled out to make a biometric method robust. However, the performance of a minutiae extraction algorithm relies heavily on the quality of the input fingerprint images. Some special treatment is done to reveal such fingerprints. The most obvious structural characteristic of a fingerprint is the pattern of interleaved ridges and branches that often run in parallel. Other important features called minutiae (the end point and branching point) refer to ridge discontinuities. The minutiae are characteristic features of fingerprints that conclude their uniqueness. These are some special points in the fingerprint responsible for identification. In general, they are termed as ridge endings and ridge bifurcation. Most frequently the minutiae types can be separated by terminations, where a ridgeline ends, and bifurcations, where a ridge bifurcates forming a branch. The minutiae can be used in fingerprint matching since they represent unique details of the ridge flow and are considered as a proof of identity. However, shown by intensive researches on fingerprint recognition, their ridges and burrows do not distinguish fingerprints, but by Minutia, which are some abnormal points on the ridges.

26.3 GOOD QUALITY FINGERPRINT IMAGES

Several factors determine the quality of a offline fingerprint image: skin conditions (e.g. dryness, wetness, dirtiness, temporary or permanent cuts and bruises), user cooperation, uneven surface, etc. Some of these factors cannot be avoided and some of them vary along the time.

Practically, the quality of a fingerprint image depends on the clearness of separated ridges by valleys and the uniformity of the separation. Although the change in physical conditions such as temperature and pressure might influence a fingerprint image in different ways, the humidity and oily finger dominate the overall quality of the fingerprint. Dry skin tends to cause inconsistent contact of the finger ridges over the surface at crime scene, causing broken ridges and many white pixels replacing ridge structure (see Figure 26.1 (c)). Opposing to the valleys on the oily skin tend to fill up with moisture, causing them to appear black in the image similar to ridge structure.

Fig. 26.1(a)   Oily Image

Oily Fingerprint Image: Although the separation of ridges and valleys is clear in an oily fingerprint image, but some portion of valleys are filled up causing them to appear dark or neighboring ridges stand close to each other in many regions. The oily fingerprint tends ridges to be very thick.

Fig. 26.1(b)   Neutral Image   **Fig. 26.1(c)**   Dry Image

Neutral Fingerprint Image: Generally, such image has no special properties such as presence of oil and dryness. There is no need of preprocessing steps in case of online image.

Dry Fingerprint Image: The ridges are rough locally and there are many broken curves in the ridges.

26.4 OUR PROPOSED MODEL

In order to reduce crimes, our proposed model collects the latent fingerprints from the crime scenes captured by a high quality camera. The digitized fingerprints are stored in a central database, which are accessed zone wise. When a citizen enters in an organization, he has to put his fingers on scanner connected to an information system shared by a zonal database of fingerprints. If the fingerprints of the citizen are matched to any latent fingerprint stored in existing database then that citizen is suspicious and he/she is supposed to be interrogated by the police. There are maximum chances that such person may be criminal. Our proposed model is Shown by Figure 26.2.

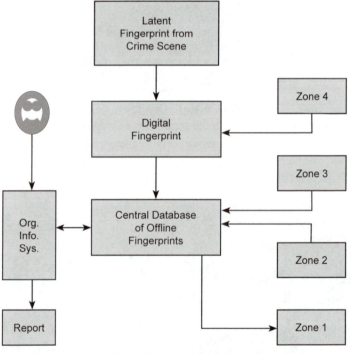

Fig. 26.2 Our proposed model

26.5 MANIPULATIONS WITH FINGERPRINT IMAGE

The performance of a fingerprint image-matching system depends greatly on the quality of the input fingerprint images. Acquisition of good quality images is very important (especially in case of latent fingerprints), but due to some environmental factors or user's body condition, a significant percentage of acquired images are of unacceptable quality for a computerized identification system in practice. The poor quality images produce many spurious minutiae and many genuine minutiae may be ignored. Therefore an image enhancement algorithm is necessary to increase the performance of the minutiae extraction algorithm.

When the feature extraction is performed using the operations binarization and thinning, the triangles, bridges, spurs, opposing minutiae, ladders are some of the structures leading to invalid minutiae detection. Gray level based feature extraction methods such as the ridge base approach are proposed by Maio and Maltoni can eliminate many of the sources of error that are caused by binarization and thinning operations.

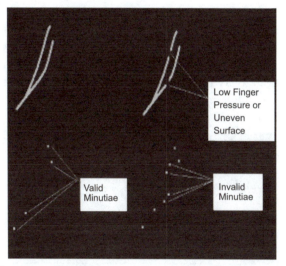

Fig. 26.3   Extraction of invalid minutiae due to presence
of dust particles or cut on finger

26.6 EXTRACTIONS OF VALID AND INVALID MINUTIAE

The basic reason behind false minutiae is the presence of dust particles, oily fingers, dry fingers, and cut on finger. Dry finger may fail to produce a complete line/curve up to the actual end points. As a result the break points create false (invalid) minutiae as seen in Figure 26.4(a). These false minutiae significantly affect the accuracy of matching if they are simply regarded as genuine minutia. Therefore some algorithms of removing false minutia are crucial to keep the fingerprint verification system efficient.

26.7 MANIPULATION TO ELIMINATE INVALID MINUTIAE

Before minutiae marking two operations fingerprint image Binarization and thinning respectively are performed.

ᐊ Fingerprint Image Binarization

Fingerprint image binarization is the process to transform the 8-bit Gray level fingerprint image to a 1-bit (binary) image with 0-value for ridges and 1-value for furrows. After this operation, ridges in the fingerprint are tinted with black color while the furrows are white.

↵ **Thinning**—This turns a binary image to a one pixel wide skeleton image. Thinning operation is must to extract minutiae by determining end points in right way.

↵ **m_connectivity**—This operation is used to refine the skeleton. This is very important manipulation with thinned fingerprint image to achieve high FRR.

↵ **m_margin**—We propose the new manipulation m_margin with m_connected thinned fingerprint image to make matching system more robust. This manipulation increases length of curves by adding white pixel at each end. Although the minutiae marking positions are diverted one pixel far away from the actual position, but as a final result FRR is improved due to elimination of some false (invalid) minutiae as shown in Figure 26.4(b). It filters out all the valid end points.

1	0	0	0	0	0	1	0
0	1	0	0	0	1	0	0
0	0	1	0	1	0	0	0
0	0	0	0	0	0	0	0
1	0	0	0	0	0	0	0
0	1	0	0	0	1	0	0
0	0	1	0	0	0	1	0
0	0	0	1	0	0	0	1

Fig. 26.4(a)   Thinned image with false minutiae (Blue)

1	0	0	0	0	0	1	0
0	1	0	0	0	1	0	0
0	0	1	0	1	0	0	0
0	0	0	1	0	0	0	0
1	0	0	0	1	0	0	0
0	1	0	0	0	1	0	0
0	0	1	0	0	0	1	0
0	0	0	1	0	0	0	1

Fig. 26.4(b)   Thinned image after m_connectivity

26.8 EXPERIMENTS AND RESULTS

We used a database of 1000 fingerprints of 50 different persons at different pressures. At low pressure we got fingerprints with false minutiae due to discontinuation of curves. To eliminate this kind of false minutiae we manipulated the finger print images by increasing the length of each curve having at lest three pixels as shown in Figure 26.4(b). This way the rate of successful matching is increased by 10% we performed.

The fingerprint images obtained at minimum and maximum pressure are shown in Figure 26.5(a) and (b) respectively.

(a)

(b)

Fig. 26.5   Fingerprint image at (a) minimum pressure (b) maximum pressure

During the experiments we have seen that if the finger pressure difference between the images of the same finger was ± 10% we got 98% result for true matching.

With the help of our proposed model, the crimes can be reduced by observing the suspicious persons. For this purpose we will have to use a robust fingerprint matching system, which is shared centrally. The performance of fingerprint identification system relies critically on the image quality. Hence, good quality images make the system performance more robust. However, it is very difficult to obtain good quality fingerprint images from the crime scenes. To overcome this problem, the image enhancement/manipulation steps are applied. But, most of the enhancement algorithms are applied equally to images without considering the image characteristics.

References

1. Stefano Bistarell, Francesco Santini, and Anna Vaccarelli, "An Asymmetric Fingerprint Matching Algorithm for Java Card™"
2. Eun-Kyung Yun, Jin-Hyuk Hong, and Sung-Bae Cho, "Adaptive Enhancing of Fingerprint Image with Image Characteristics Analysis"
3. Sharat Chikkerur, Venu Govindaraju, Sharath Pankanti, Ruud Bolle, Nalini Ratha, "Novel Approaches for Minutiae Verification in Fingerprint Images", Proceedings of the Seventh IEEE Workshop on Applications of Computer Vision (WACV/MOTION'05) 0-7695-2271-8/05
4. D. Maio and D. Maltoni. Direct gray scale minutia detection in fingerprints", *Transactions on PAMI,* 19(1), 1997.
5. J. Fierrez-Aguilar, L.-M. Mu.noz-Serrano, F. Alonso-Fernandez and J. Ortega-Garcia, " On The Effects Of Image Quality Degradation On Minutiae- And Ridge-Based Automatic Fingerprint Recognition"
6. Sharath Pankanti Salil Prabhakary Anil K. Jain, "On the Individuality of Fingerprints", 2002
7. Asker M. Bazen, Martijn van Otterlo, Sabih H. Gerez, Mannes Poel , "A Reinforcement Learning Agent for Minutiae Extraction from Fingerprints", 2004.

☺☺☹

27

Social Break Ups on Facebook

Sarita[1]

The internet has given us the ability to connect with people from around the globe with a few clicks of a button, making it easier than ever to keep in touch with friends and family. Because of that, social networking is the biggest industry of our time, but it wasn't always that way. Now a Days social media is not limited to connecting people. Companies are promoting their products over different social media websites. It has generated the need to find out how customers want to interact with brands over social media and determining the factors leading to social break ups between customer & brands. This paper tries to explore the customer relationship between customers & brands over social media websites in the Indian context based on a questionnaire. The issue of Social Breakups is tackled from the perspective of 'Voice of the Customer'. In this chapter an online survey is administered through questionnaire with a sample of 100 respondents in Delhi & NCR, to examine the customers' satisfaction level involved with the brands promotion over social media websites. An online questionnaire of social breakups was used and response was taken to examine the different aspects associated with customer's satisfaction level.

KEYWORDS   Social | Media | Facebook | Social Networking | People

27.1 INTRODUCTION

Social media industry came into existence about 10 years ago when chat messengers that allowed people to communicate and share content with each other surfaced on the internet. Now, the industry houses Facebook and Twitter under its umbrella. The popularity of these platforms has caused the advertisement industry to focus on strategically placing ads on these platforms, which has changed the media industry.

Nowadays, one can no longer imagine how to catch up with friends and contacts without social networking. Social networking helped us become closer to our friends, even when they are a thousand miles away. Through the World Wide Web, we are able to connect with people from around the world, making it easy to keep in touch with friends and family. Social networking now is a billion dollar industry, but we can barely remember when it didn't exist.

---

[1] Maharaja Agrasen Institute, Delhi, India

Today, social networking is an essential part of life for people from around the world. Social networking is a form of social media, used for either interactive, educational, informational or entertaining purposes. Social media comes in many forms, but all of them are related: blogs, forums, podcasts,

Fig. 27.1 The early years.

photo sharing, social bookmarking, widgets, and video, just to name a few.

Today, social networking websites allow users to make profiles, upload photos and videos, and interact with friends and family. Social networking is a tool to join groups, learn about latest news and events, play games, chat and to share music and video. The top social networking sites of today are: MySpace, Facebook and Twitter.

27.2 HISTORY AND EVOLUTION OF SOCIAL MEDIA INDUSTRY

The History of Social Networking

Social media has become an integral part of modern society. There are general social networks with user bases larger than the population of most countries.

There are niche sites for virtually every special interest out there. There are sites to share photos, videos, status updates, sites for meeting new people and sites to connect with old friends. It seems there are social solutions to just about every need.

27.3 ABOUT THE ORGANIZATION

Facebook (formerly [the facebook]) is an online social networking service headquartered in Menlo Park, California. Its website was launched on February 4, 2004, by Mark Zuckerberg with his college roommates and fellow Harvard University students Eduardo Saverin, Andrew McCollum, Dustin Moskovitz and Chris Hughes. The founders had initially limited the website's membership to Harvard students, but later expanded it to colleges in the Boston area, the Ivy League, and Stanford University. It gradually added support for students at various other universities and later to high-school students. Facebook now allows anyone who claims to be at least 13 years old to become a registered user of the website. Its name comes from a colloquialism for the directory given to it by American universities students.

27.4 SOCIAL BREAK UPS

Social Break Ups is a new term introduced in social media marketing. Basically, it happens between customer or user and brands. There are several reasons for customer's break up with brand but the basic reason is over promotion by brands while hurting customers privacy over social media.

Like any interpersonal relationship, the consumer-brand relationship has a distinct and fascinating life cycle. The relationship begins with the initial "spark"—the decision by the consumer to become a SUBSCRIBER, FAN, or FOLLOWER— followed by a blissful honeymoon period in which the consumer gets to know the company better through communications and social interactions.

As the relationship progresses, the frequency and quality of interactions shapes the consumer's desire to take the relationship to the next level—which may be a purchase, a recommendation, or even brand advocacy. Consumers want to know that companies are committed to the relationship—and that they care. Companies express their commitment to the relationship through engaging communications, delivered at appropriate intervals. But marketers must realize that the definitions of "engaging" and "appropriate" vary by channel. Communication practices that convey warmth and respect for the consumer through one channel can just as easily convey indifference—or desperation— through another.

If the company fails any of these relationship tests, a "social break-up"— i.e., an "unsubscribe," "unfan," "unlike," or "unfol- low"—is all but inevitable. When the consumer is no longer happy in the relationship, they will actively break off contact with the company. ..or just ignore their communications in the hopes the company will get the message that it's over.

27.5 RESEARCH METHODOLOGY

The questionnaire was oriented to the Social Break Ups between Customer and Brand Pages. The design used for the study is descriptive under conclusive design. It is a quantitative design where the reasons for unliking the brand pages were identified on the basis of primary data which is collected with the help of a structured tool called questionnaire.

The study was done with a sample size of 100 respondents. The respondents were selected for the study from the various users of Facebook. A random sampling was taken. The research instrument or tool used for the preparation of this project is Questionnaire. A questionnaire consists of a list of questions printed in a definite order on a form to be asked from respondent.

27.5.1 DATA COLLECTION

The approach used for the data collection is Survey Method. There are two sources of data collection:

27.5.1.1 Primary Data

Data collected for the purpose of this project is through

- Observations
- Survey through Questionnaire

27.5.1.2 Secondary Data

Secondary data collected through

- Websites
- Books

26.6 OBJECTIVES OF THE STUDY

- To study the reasons behind liking the brand pages over Facebook.
- To study the customers satisfaction level with their liked pages over Facebook.
- To know the causes behind breaking up with liked brand over Facebook.
- To check the users perspective about brand pages over Facebook.
- To know about the users expectation towards brand pages over Facebook.
- To know about the breaches to social etiquettes over Facebook.

27.7. ANALYSIS

27.7.1 SERVQUAL Questions

For actual survey several questions were framed to get the correct response from customers which identifies the reasons behind Social Break Ups.

- No. of respondents who liked any pages on Facebook (of any product, brand, service or idea).
- If yes, then how often you like any page on Facebook.

↩ Reasons to like any page on Facebook:

Because it is existing

Because it is in trend

Because I can relate it with me

Because it entertains me (Contests, Activities etc.)

Because it helps me to learn more about the product/ page/ event/ service liked on facebook.

Because I can update myself with new things on the page I liked

↩ Do you unlike the page on facebook after sometimes

↩ If yes then how often do you unlike any page on facebook

↩ I unlike the page on facebook due to following reasons: Because they send their marketing news/ news letters/ promotion details without my permission

Because I don't like bulk emails from them Because content becomes boring & repetitive on the page Because of their anytime mails & notifications kills my personal time on facebook Because of their excessive posting

I unliked the brand after getting what I want

Because my circumstances changed (i.e. moved, married, job etc.)

Almost everyone likes brand pages over Facebook. And people also unlike pages over Facebook due to several reasons. 48 respondents said yes that they unlike pages on Facebook after sometime and rest said no. So, from the responses of the users I can conclude that almost half of the respondents unlike page on Facebook due to several dissatisfying reason also they do it very rarely.

27.8 LIMITATIONS OF THE STUDY

↩ The very first limitation of this study is that Social Break Up is a new term introduced in Social Media Marketing. So, very less amount of information was available about the topic.

↩ The second limitation of this study is that the sample size is confined to Delhi & NCR.

↩ The results of this study cannot be generalized because the samples were heterogeneous in nature and this can be also stated as a limitation for this study.

↩ Another limitation has been the cost, as it involves the collection of primary and secondary data, therefore the cost incurred was much more.

↩ Sometimes user don't share the true information because of ignorance and their busy schedule.

◁ The present study has relied largely on quantitative methodology of data collection (though qualitative methodology was used to a limited extent) and is therefore restrictive.

Another limitation for this study is that study is limited to Facebook only. If this study has been extended to some extent than it would have provided more useful results.

Finally winding up this paper I conclude that every romance or relationship come to an end at some point of time, and— whether conducted through Email, Facebook, or Twitter. Online consumer-brand relationships are not exceptional. Regardless of channel, this research shows that one thing consistently drives consumers away is communication that somehow states that the company doesn't care about their user or customer.

Customers arethe most important asset of any organization. The success of anyorganization ultimately depends on how efficient and effectivelyits customer is being satisfied. Therefore the main aim of theorganization must be to satisfy its customers for longer time duration. Most of the times we hear marketers say that providing quality product to customer is the best way to retain customers. However, this study states that caring about the customer conveys the sentiment that brands place the best interests of their customers ahead of their own balance sheets. Marketers are involved in online marketing from a very long time but the idea of showing "care" may be a new one.

Following are the mistakes which a brand does

Failure to Engage

Many a times marketers don't do follow up after sales which shows that they don't care about their customer. On Facebook— creating a profile page, but never updating it is also one of the failure.

Being too Self-promotional

Consumers expect and want brands to promote their products and services, but they want that information beneficial for them. Hard sell tactics can work in person, but they fail online because you lack the personal interaction to counter the hard-sell message. No matter how personal they are, Email, Facebook, and Twitter don't allow you to replicate a face-to-face conversation.

Unclear Message

Consumers want to learn as much as possible about a product or service before they buy it. If product information is unclear, incomplete, or difficult to find, the brand may be seen as careless, irresponsible, or untrustworthy.

Breaches of Social Etiquette

Every channel has its own rules, and consumers expect companies to know the rules and follow them. Failure to respect the social etiquette in each channel is a clear signal that your brand doesn't care.

Email

Consumers want brands to send them relevant content that is tailored to their personal interests. They expect marketers to honor permissions, and show restraint when it comes to email frequency. They measure your emails not against the best in your industry, but against the best senders in their inbox.

Facebook

Consumers view Facebook as a great way to engage with brands they already know and trust. They expect marketers to keep their Facebook pages fresh and interesting, and to limit their posts to avoid drowning out social interactions.

Acknowledgement

I would like to thank Ms. Nitika Sharma, Assistant Professor, Department of Management for her constant enthusiastic encouragement and valuable suggestions without which this paper would not been successfully completed.

I would also like to thank our classmates who were ready with positive comments all the time, whether it was an off-hand comment to encourage us or a constructive piece of criticism and a special thanks to the faculty of Maharaja Agrasen Institute of Technology who arranged a good environment for us.

References

1. Kumar R. Research Methodology. 2nd ed. Pearson Education; 2009.
2. Kotler P, Keller KL, Koshy A, Jha M. Marketing Management. 2009.
3. Etzel M, Walker B, Stanton W, Pandit A. Marketing Management. Tata McGrawHill; New   Delhi: 2009.
4. Available from http://www.facebook.com
5. Available from http://www.exacttarget.com
6. Available from http://www.convinceandconvert.com

☺☻☹